PUNISHMENT AND FORGIVENESS
IN ISRAEL'S MIGRATORY CAMPAIGN

Punishment and Forgiveness in Israel's Migratory Campaign

WON W. LEE

WILLIAM B. EERDMANS PUBLISHING COMPANY
GRAND RAPIDS, MICHIGAN / CAMBRIDGE, U.K.

© 2003 Wm. B. Eerdmans Publishing Co.

Wm. B. Eerdmans Publishing Co.
255 Jefferson Ave. S.E., Grand Rapids, Michigan 49503 /
P.O. Box 163, Cambridge CB3 9PU U.K.

Printed in the United States of America

08 07 06 05 04 03   7 6 5 4 3 2 1

Library of Congress Cataloging-in-Publication Data

Lee, Won W.
    Punishment and forgiveness in Israel's migratory campaign / Won W. Lee.
       p.   cm.
    Includes bibliographical references (p.   ) and index.
    ISBN 0-8028-0992-8 (pbk.: alk. paper)
      1. Bible. O.T. Numbers — Criticism, interpretation, etc.   I. Title.

    BS1265.52.L44   2003
    222'.1406 — dc22

                              2003060820

www.eerdmans.com

Contents

Preface

In this book I wrestled with an exegetical question: how to articulate the interrelationships among the many units of Numbers 10:11–36:13 with an empirically verifiable procedure. The pursuit of such interrelationships may be viewed by some as our imposition of a modern idea of system on the ancient texts. It has been argued that since the Bible is an amalgamation of ancient people's theological reflections, stemming from different historical and cultural milieus and created by numerous writers and editors, exegetes should seek out the identifiable theologies within a given text and be content with a juxtaposition of the findings at the end of their interpretation. This exegetical practice prevents us from insisting on "the" meaning, or the unifying "center" of a text, and at the same time allows us to celebrate the multivalency and diversity of a text.

Despite the laudable accomplishments that this practice yields, it, however, is susceptible to the trap of relativity and compartmentalization in that every interpretation of the text, whether or not it accounts for the totality of the text, is sustainable and of equal value. To do justice to a biblical text, we should resist the temptation of molding the variety of perspectives operative in the text into a unified whole, and also be cautious not to ignore any conceptual dissonance and conflict evident within the text. Instead, we must reconstruct the interrelationships among multifold units, while neither sacrificing the uniqueness of each individual unit nor harmonizing them. In fact, the disparate materials of Numbers 10:11–36:13 themselves raise the question of interrelationship. To answer this question I first established the text as a self-contained unit marked by a clear beginning and ending within the book of Numbers; second, I identified numerous smaller units with their own distinctive perspectives on various matters; and, third, I reconstructed the structural unity of the text which signals its conceptual coherence. The structural unity reveals the overarching conceptuality, that is, divine punishment and forgiveness in Israel's migratory campaign, to which the individual units within the text owe their existence and their placement and relationship relative to each other in their extant order. In so doing, I was able to implement an exegetical axiom, namely, to interpret the biblical text on its own terms.

Many people have helped me in completing this book. I am profoundly grateful to my teacher, Rolf P. Knierim, whose books and articles have been crucial for my understanding of the Pentateuch as a whole and the book of Numbers in particular. His methodological focus on conceptual aspects of texts is apparent on every page of my book. I must also thank James A. Sanders and Tammi J. Schneider for their instruction at the Claremont Graduate University and continual encouragement and support thereafter. Simon J. DeVries and Thomas B. Dozeman read an earlier draft of this book and offered valuable suggestions. I especially thank Dennis T. Olson, whose thorough analysis and lengthy constructive criticism of my thesis have helped me retune some aspects of my arguments. To Marvin A. Sweeney, who not only offered valuable remarks but also watched over every step of the revision and publication of the book as if it were his own, I am deeply indebted. I thank him for his personal interest in my professional growth.

This book has also benefited from the spiritual, moral, and tangible support of many. I must thank Calvin College for granting me an interim leave to rewrite the second chapter and my colleagues, particularly Richard Whitekettle and David Crump, in the Religion Department at Calvin for their encouragement. I owe special thanks to Rev. Molly Dykstra for her first-rate proofreading and unchanging friendship without which this book would not exist in its present form; to Lee Sytsma for preparing the indexes; and to Mr. William Eerdmans and the staff at Eerdmans Publishing Company for their support in printing the book in a timely fashion.

My heartfelt and deepest gratitude is extended to my family who has carried me through a long process; to my parents and mother-in-law, Rev. Dr. Jong K. and Sook J. Lee and Jung S. Shin, whose bountiful love and devotion to me have been displayed so enormously. As for my children, John and Daniel, who keep saying that I work too much, I am anxious to play with them as long as they want me to. To my wife, Eun Kyung, whose sacrifice and support are evident on each page of this work, I am immensely thankful. With unfailing trust in my study, graceful forgiveness for my shortcomings, and undying love for me, she has stood by my side and shared the ups and downs of publishing this book. To her I dedicate this book as a token of my love.

Abbreviations

ABD	*Anchor Bible Dictionary*
BASOR	*Bulletin of the American Schools of Oriental Research*
BDB	F. Brown, S. R. Driver, and C. A. Briggs, *Hebrew and English Lexicon of the Old Testament*
Bib	*Biblica*
BZ	*Biblische Zeitschrift*
BZAW	Beihefte zur Zeitschrift für die alttestamentliche Wissenschaft
CBQ	*Catholic Biblical Quarterly*
EvT	*Evangelische Theologie*
FOTL	Forms of the Old Testament Literature
HAR	*Hebrew Annual Review*
HBT	*Horizons in Biblical Theology*
ICC	International Critical Commentary
IDB	*Interpreter's Dictionary of the Bible*
IDBSup	*Interpreter's Dictionary of the Bible Supplementary Volume*
Int	*Interpretation*
JBL	*Journal of Biblical Literature*
JETS	*Journal of the Evangelical Theological Society*
JJS	*Journal of Jewish Studies*
JNES	*Journal of Near Eastern Studies*
JQR	*Jewish Quarterly Review*
JSOTSup	Journal for the Study of the Old Testament Supplement Series
KB	L. Koehler and W. Baumgartner, *Hebräisches und Aramäisches Lexikon zum Alten Testament*
NRSV	New Revised Standard Version
OBO	Orbis Biblicus et Orientalis
OTL	Old Testament Library
SBLSP	*Society of Biblical Literature Seminar Papers*

TDOT	*Theological Dictionary of the Old Testament*, ed. G. J. Botterweck, H. Ringgren, and H.-J. Fabry
TRu	*Theologische Rundschau*
TynBul	*Tyndale Bulletin*
VT	*Vetus Testamentum*
ZAW	*Zeitschrift für die alttestamentliche Wissenschaft*
ZDPV	*Zeitschrift des deutschen Palästina-Vereins*

Introduction

Contemporary pentateuchal studies have raised questions concerning the organization of the Pentateuch as it now stands. Until the mid-twentieth century, pentateuchal scholarship predominantly focused on the formation of parts of the Pentateuch rather than the entire work. Instead of explaining the extant form, scholarship was interested in genetic questions regarding pentateuchal materials, such as their authors and origins, the historical circumstances of their composition, the history of their literary growth, and the intentions of their authors and of the redactors who combined them. The history of pentateuchal scholarship is analogous to that of historical-critical method in biblical criticism.[1]

Until the Protestant Reformation, early Jewish and Christian tradition claimed that Moses wrote the entire Pentateuch including the narrative in Genesis. This traditional understanding of Mosaic authorship yielded its dogmatic position to "mosaic" authorship, however, with the rise of historical criticism in the nineteenth century. The issue became not so much whether or not an individual, let alone Moses himself, or a plurality of authors wrote the Pentateuch, but how to understand the varied materials found in the Pentateuch. A number of literary features can be explained by treating the Pentateuch as a composite text in which multiple units were brought together by many editors over several stages. One paradigm, the so-called Newer Documentary Hypothesis, established itself as the point of departure for subsequent discussions on the formation of the Pentateuch.

Today, on the one hand, the Newer Documentary Hypothesis, the

---

1. H. J. Kraus, *Geschichte der historisch-kritischen Erforschung des Alten Testaments von der Reformation bis zur Gegenwart,* 3rd ed. (Neukirchen-Vluyn: Neukirchener, 1982). O. Eissfeldt, *The Old Testament: An Introduction,* trans. P. R. Ackroyd (New York and London: Harper & Row, 1965), pp. 158-241.

model that dominated much of critical biblical scholarship from the late nineteenth century to the mid-twentieth century, has lost ground. Historical scholars no longer accept *a priori* its basic description that the Pentateuch was composed of four independent sources or documents (known as J, E, D, and P) added chronologically by a succession of editors over a period of half a millennium, from the ninth or tenth century to the fifth or early fourth century before the Common Era.[2] Although many still work within the larger framework, they disagree with each other on almost every aspect of this classic hypothesis. They debate about the nature of the sources (whether E and P were independent sources or redactional layers or supplements to J), the scope of the content (whether J extended to the book of Joshua or even tò the end of II Kings; whether the deuteronomist and post-deuteronomist had influence in the Tetrateuch), the character of the material (whether these sources themselves were a compilation of previous written or oral material), the assumed chronological sequence (whether P was prior to J), and its relative dating (whether J was a product of the postexilic period; whether P came from the preexilic milieu). These diverse theories challenge the hypothesis significantly enough not only to undercut the privilege that it has enjoyed, but also to contribute to the methodological confusion of current biblical studies in general, and even to cast doubt that one can say anything reliable about the formation of the Pentateuch.

On the other hand, numerous new approaches (rhetorical criticism, structural criticism, reader-response criticism, etc.), influenced by literary theory outside of biblical studies, have emerged after the mid-twentieth century.[3] In contrast to adherents of the Documentary Hypothesis who, despite their differences, share the common ground of focusing on the sources behind the final form of the Pentateuch, these newer approaches treat its extant form as an equally important historical datum to the layers predating the latest formation. These approaches presuppose that the Pentateuch as it now stands is far more unified than previously assumed, and they explore its artis-

2. For a succinct overview of the history of the field, see J. Blenkinsopp, *The Pentateuch: An Introduction to the First Five Books of the Bible* (New York: Doubleday; London: SCM, 1992), pp. 1-30; D. M. Carr, "Controversy and Convergence in Recent Studies of the Formation of the Pentateuch," *Religious Studies Review* 23 (January 1997): 22-31; E. W. Nicholson, *The Pentateuch in the Twentieth Century: The Legacy of Julius Wellhausen* (Oxford: Clarendon, 1998); A. Rofé, *Introduction to the Composition of the Pentateuch* (Sheffield: Sheffield Academic Press, 1999).

3. For a helpful introduction to a representative sample of these approaches (and also of the traditional ones), see S. L. McKenzie and S. R. Haynes, eds., *To Each Its Own Meaning: An Introduction to Biblical Criticisms and Their Application,* rev. ed. (Louisville: Westminster John Knox Press, 1999).

tic quality and seek to reconstruct its literary organization rather than its historical formation. In spite of their calling for a paradigm shift, these "synchronic" readings of the text themselves (as against the "diachronic" reading of the traditional historical-critical approach) have tended to be divergent due to a variety of exegetical objectives or goals, different theories of the nature of texts, and distinctive hermeneutical implications.[4] They have not yet earned a wide enough acceptance within the academic guild to displace the Newer Documentary Hypothesis completely. Hence, any type of approach providing a definitive explanation for the literary features of the Pentateuch is not yet in sight.

That being said, it is important to note that studies interested in the final form of the text have made substantive advances in understanding the Bible during the last two decades. Undoubtedly, they will continue to contribute in the future. The success of these synchronic approaches depends on whether they establish themselves as empirically controlled methods whose objectives and results are to be tested by the literary phenomenon of the biblical texts and by the way in which they are related to the diachronic methods. Pentateuchal studies may well be the battleground for their success, as they have been in the past. However, synchronic literary studies of the Pentateuch have tended to take on smaller sections within the pentateuchal books or a book, rather than the Pentateuch as a whole.[5]

In view of these limited discussions on the synchronic reading of the Pentateuch as a whole, the present study attempts to contribute to the ongoing debate regarding its composition by discussing the organization of the

---

4. See parts two ("Expanding the Tradition") and three ("Overturning the Tradition") of McKenzie and Haynes, *To Each Its Own Meaning*. J. Barton, *Reading the Old Testament: Method in Biblical Study* (Louisville: Westminster John Knox, 1996), pp. 77-272. J. S. Croatto, *Biblical Hermeneutics: Toward a Theory of Reading as the Production of Meaning*, trans. R. R. Barr (Maryknoll, NY: Orbis, 1987).

5. For example, for synchronic study on Exodus 32–34, see M. Fishbane, *Text and Texture: Close Readings of Selected Biblical Texts* (New York: Schocken, 1979); R. W. L. Moberly, *At the Mountain of God: Story and Theology in Exodus 32–34*, JSOTSup 22 (Sheffield: Sheffield Academic Press, 1983), respectively. See also R. Alter, *The Art of Biblical Narrative* (New York: Basic, 1981). For the book of Genesis, see G. A. Rendsburg, *The Redaction of Genesis* (Winona Lake, IN: Eisenbrauns, 1986); for the book of Numbers, D. T. Olson, *The Death of the Old and the Birth of the New: The Framework of the Book of Numbers and the Pentateuch*, Brown Judaic Studies 71 (Chico, CA: Scholars Press, 1985); for the book of Deuteronomy, R. Polzin, *Moses and the Deuteronomist* (New York: Seabury, 1980). For treating the Pentateuch as a whole, the only notable exceptions are Clines's monograph and Knierim's article, which will be fully analyzed later: D. J. A. Clines, *The Theme of the Pentateuch*, JSOTSup 10 (Sheffield: Sheffield Academic Press, 1978); R. P. Knierim, "The Composition of the Pentateuch," in his book *The Task of Old Testament Theology: Substance, Method, and Cases* (Grand Rapids: Eerdmans, 1995), pp. 351-79.

book of Numbers, especially Numbers 10:11–36:13. The text is chosen because it contains more generically diverse materials than any other pentateuchal book,[6] and it has often been regarded as incoherent, illogical, and secondary to the rest of the Pentateuch.[7] The common acknowledgment that Numbers is a part of the Pentateuch and is located between the books of Leviticus and Deuteronomy has not led interpreters to agree on the composition and structure of Numbers either as a whole or as related to the Pentateuch. The structural problem is all the more acute for Numbers 10:11–36:13 than for 1:1–10:10 because the latter is considered organically connected with the preceding Sinai pericope (Exod 19:1–Num 10:10). Most interpreters easily take the latter to be a coherent literary unit, although some differ on which verse closes the unit. With recognition that the division of Numbers at a macrostructural level is a major structural issue, the present study seeks to reconstruct this division in Numbers 10:11–36:13. The study will discuss the division of Numbers at this highest structural level as it establishes the boundary of this block as a distinct unit. Reconstructing the macrostructure of 10:11–36:13 will make a contribution to the structural inquiry of Numbers in its entirety and to the location of Numbers within the Pentateuch as well.

The structural problem of Numbers 10:11–36:13 originates from the disparate materials found within it and from the uncertainty of the conceptual relationships of those materials. The text begins with a report of the departure of the Israelites from the wilderness of Sinai, where they had been encamped for almost eleven months, and it ends with a statement indicating their remaining "in the plains of Moab by the Jordan at Jericho" and not having entered the promised land. The chapters in between contain numerous generically diverse materials, such as narratives, legislation, poetry, victory songs, and census lists. The narratives report the movement of the Israelites' camp through various places. The Israelites quarrel, and are punished as a consequence; they are denied peaceful passage through Edom's and Sihon's territories; and they conquer several territories through battle. Legal materials and similar yet different laws from those of Exodus and Leviticus are presented; poetry appears mainly in chapters 22–24. At the outset no readily ap-

---

6. J. Milgrom states that "the generic variety that characterizes Numbers surpasses that of any other book of the Bible." As examples, he lists fourteen distinct genres found in Numbers (Milgrom, *Numbers,* JPS Torah Commentary [Philadelphia: Jewish Publication Society, 1990], p. xiii). B. A. Levine also states that "in its textual makeup, Numbers is the most diverse of all Torah books" (Levine, *Numbers 1–20: A New Translation with Introduction and Commentary,* The Anchor Bible [New York: Doubleday, 1993], p. 48).

7. G. B. Gray, *A Critical and Exegetical Commentary on Numbers,* ICC (Edinburgh: T. & T. Clark, 1903), p. xxiv.

parent order of the arrangement of these diverse materials appears. It is conceivable that these heterogeneous pieces have no detectable literary pattern or order in 10:11–36:13. They might have been accumulated in random fashion and, therefore, might be regarded as a collection reflecting the traditions of the Israelites' wilderness experience rather than as a literary entity that presupposes a structural unity with a particular intention. This, however, would be a conclusion that could be reached only by disproving every attempt to show that these chapters are a conceptually structured literary work. Otherwise, the simple characterization of this part of the book of Numbers, and of the whole, as having no unity is exegetically unwarranted. Nevertheless, it is the unity of this material which is the problem and which must be demonstrated.

The pursuit of the present study rests on those publications which claim that the diverse material in 10:11–36:13 has a conceptually coherent structure. This study investigates to what extent and by what criterion the diverse materials in this text are composed into that structure. This goal implies that the text indeed yields a unity among distinctive text units and presents an identifiable concept responsible for their location and arrangement on the surface of the text. Such an implication poses the following questions: How is the identifiable structural unity in 10:11–36:13 evident in the surface composition of the text? How can it be achieved with an empirically controlled investigation that in turn verifies its legitimacy? What does it signal regarding the intention of the text? What does it reveal about the place of the text within the whole of the Pentateuch? These are the questions with which this study will wrestle.

CHAPTER ONE

Organization of the Book of Numbers

A. Preliminary Remarks

The solution to properly understanding Numbers 10:11–36:13 lies in the accurate reconstruction of its structure. The structure, the systematic configuration of conceptualities which reveals the coherence of the text,[1] governs the composition on the surface of the text, creating meaning. Thus, reconstructing the structure of a text is imperative for interpreting the text as a whole. However, except for D. T. Olson's book, which will be thoroughly analyzed later, no critical discussion has yet been conducted on the matter of Numbers's structure. The wide variety of material contained in 10:11–36:13 and in the entire book of Numbers has led many exegetes to claim that there is no readily identifiable unity or structure in it.[2] Even attempting any structural

---

1. This definition of "structure" will be discussed in chapter two.

2. R. N. Whybray, *Introduction to the Pentateuch* (Grand Rapids: Eerdmans, 1995), p. 78; R. Rendtorff, *The Old Testament: An Introduction*, trans. J. Bowden (Philadelphia: Fortress, 1986), p. 147; W. Riggans, *Numbers*, Daily Study Bible (Philadelphia: Westminster, 1983), p. 2; A. Noordtzij, *Numbers*, Bible Student's Commentary (Grand Rapids: Zondervan, 1983), p. 4; R. J. Burns, *Exodus, Leviticus, Numbers: With Excursus on Feasts/Ritual and Typology*, Old Testament Message, vol. 3 (Wilmington: Michael Glazier, 1983), p. 213; B. S. Childs, *Introduction to the Old Testament as Scripture* (Philadelphia: Fortress, 1979), pp. 192, 195; B. A. Levine, "Numbers, book of," in *Interpreter's Dictionary of the Bible Supplementary Volume*, ed. K. Crim (Nashville: Abingdon, 1976), p. 634; J. Sturdy, *Numbers*, Cambridge Bible Commentary on the New English Bible (Cambridge: Cambridge University Press, 1976), p. 1; F. L. Moriarty, "Numbers," in *Jerome Bible Commentary* (Englewood Cliffs: Prentice-Hall, 1968), p. 86; M. Noth, *Numbers: A Commentary*, trans. J. D. Martin, OTL (Philadelphia: Westminster, 1968), pp. 1-2, 4; R. C. Dentan, "Numbers, book of," in *The Interpreter's Dictionary of the Bible*, ed. G. A. Buttrick, vol. 3 (Nashville: Abingdon, 1962), p. 567; L. E. Binns, *The Book of Numbers*, Westminster Commentaries (London: Methuen, 1927), p. xiv; Gray, *A Critical and Exegetical Commentary on Numbers*, p. xxiv.

inquiry on Numbers is questioned: "since the book has no real unity and was not composed in accordance with any logical, predetermined plan, whatever outline may be imposed upon it will have to be recognized as largely subjective and arbitrary."[3] This pessimistic outlook by R. C. Dentan has been balanced by others who hold the possibility that there is indeed a literary unity in the book's arrangement.[4] Regardless of their opinions on the unity of Numbers, most exegetes present an outline of the book.[5] This is true even for some who view the very attempt to outline the book as an arbitrary imposi-

---

3. Dentan, "Numbers," p. 567.

4. R. D. Cole, *Numbers*, The New American Commentary (Nashville: Broadman & Holman, 2000), pp. 36-43; D. T. Olson, *Numbers*, Interpretation: A Biblical Commentary for Teaching and Preaching (Louisville: John Knox, 1996), pp. 3-7; idem, *The Death of the Old and the Birth of the New*; K. D. Sakenfeld, *Numbers: Journeying with God*, International Theological Commentary (Grand Rapids: Eerdmans, 1995), pp. 4-11; E. W. Davies, *Numbers*, The New Century Bible Commentary (Grand Rapids: Eerdmans, 1995), pp. li-lvii; R. P. Knierim, "The Book of Numbers," p. 380; T. R. Ashley, *The Book of Numbers* (Grand Rapids: Eerdmans, 1993), pp. 2-3; R. K. Harrison, *Numbers: An Exegetical Commentary* (Grand Rapids: Baker Book House, 1992), pp. 14-21; Milgrom, *Numbers*, p. xii; T. W. Mann, *The Book of the Torah: The Narrative Integrity of the Pentateuch* (Atlanta: John Knox, 1988), pp. 125-27; P. J. Budd, *Numbers*, Word Biblical Commentary, vol. 5 (Waco: Word, 1984), p. xx; G. J. Wenham, *Numbers: An Introduction and Commentary*, Tyndale Old Testament Commentaries (Downers Grove: InterVarsity, 1981), pp. 13-17; I. Caine, "Numbers, Book of," in *Encyclopaedia Judaica*, vol. 12 (New York: Macmillan, 1971), p. 1250.

5. Not all commentators provide an outline due to their special interests or preunderstandings of Numbers. For example, Gressmann is interested in the form-critical analysis of Numbers, and thus he disassembles Numbers into smaller form-critical units and investigates them separately from its whole. His disinterest in the structure of Numbers in its entirety, however, should not be critically overstated since he follows the form-critical approach consistently in his exposition (see H. Gressmann, *Moses und seine Zeit* [Göttingen: Vandenhoeck & Ruprecht, 1913]). For another example, Artus discusses the links between the narratives and the laws of Num 13:1–20:13 through both a synchronic and a diachronic approach. As the title of his book shows, he does not deal with the extant text of the entire book of Numbers (O. Artus, *Etudes sur le livre des Nombres Récit, Histoire et Loi en Nb 13,1–20,13*, OBO 157 [Fribourg: Fribourg University Press, 1997]). However, recently J. B. Coffman (*Commentary on Leviticus and Numbers: The Third and Fourth Books of Moses* [Abilene: Abilene Christian University Press, 1987], p. 270) states that "it is therefore laughable that scholars tackle the problems of re-locating or combining chapters! How foolish! Numbers is just not that kind of book." This unfavorable word comes from his characterization of Numbers as "a diary, or day by day record." He proposes, then, the best plan for study as "merely that of taking the chapters and verses as they come!" without any outline (p. 270). But in contrast to his strong words, he himself combines chapters: "verse 11 [of ch. 10], therefore, is the beginning of a second major division of Numbers" (p. 343); "these two chapters [chs. 28–29] are being treated together because they actually constitute a summary of the offering Israel was commanded to make throughout the whole year" (p. 513). For other similar statements, see pp. 348, 405, 439, 449, etc.

tion of modern literary principles on the ancient text. The issue, then, is not so much the necessity for subjectively discerning the structure in Numbers, but the method for discovering it through concrete and verifiable processes.

It is undoubtedly evident by the various outlines proposed for Numbers over the past 130 years that its structure has not yet been detected by an empirically controlled method. As noted before, the structural problem of 10:11–36:13 is more eminent than that of 1:1–10:10. According to Olson, who surveys forty-six commentaries on Numbers from the year 1861 to 1984, twenty-four substantially different outlines of Numbers have been proposed.[6] However, one thing stands out from these diverse proposals: of the forty-six, thirty-seven present 1:1–10:10 as a single unit. Therefore, although they may disagree on the number of sections from 10:11 to the end of the book, these thirty-seven commentaries agree that 10:11 is the beginning of a new unit of Numbers at its highest level.

A survey of twenty-eight publications, including thirteen new commentaries published from 1984 to the present, demonstrates a conclusion similar to Olson's.[7] Twenty out of twenty-eight propose 1:1–10:10 as both an uninterrupted unit and the first major part of the book.[8] Two com-

6. Olson, *The Death of the Old and the Birth of the New*, pp. 31-37.

7. In addition to these twenty-eight publications, there are numerous studies on the Pentateuch and introductory matters regarding the Old Testament that mention the nature of Numbers. These studies do not discuss the structure of Numbers due to their primary interests, which are different from structural questions. For example, Whybray, *Introduction to the Pentateuch*; Blenkinsopp, *The Pentateuch*; N. K. Gottwald, *The Hebrew Bible: A Socio-literary Introduction* (Philadelphia: Fortress, 1985), pp. 179-227; and others.

8. Cole, *Numbers*, p. 40; T. B. Dozeman, "The Book of Numbers," in *The New Interpreter's Bible*, ed. L. E. Keck, vol. 2 (Nashville: Abingdon, 1998), p. 23; Sakenfeld, *Numbers*, pp. 9-10; Knierim, "The Book of Numbers," pp. 380-85; J. G. Partain, "Numbers," in *Mercer Commentary on the Bible*, ed. W. E. Mills and R. F. Wilson (Macon: Mercer University Press, 1995), p. 177; Davies, *Numbers*, pp. lxx-lxxiv; B. L. Bandstra, *Reading the Old Testament: An Introduction to the Hebrew Bible* (Belmont: Wadsworth, 1995), p. 156; Ashley, *The Book of Numbers*, pp. 15-17; H. Seebass, *Numeri* (Neukirchen-Vluyn: Neukirchener Verlag des Erziehungsvereins, 1993), p. 1; J. Scharbert, *Numeri* (Würzburg: Echter, 1992), p. 5; Milgrom, *Numbers*, pp. xi, xiii, xviii; idem, "Numbers, Book of," in *ABD*, ed. D. N. Freedman, vol. 4 (New York: Doubleday, 1992), pp. 1146-47; J. L. Crenshaw, *Old Testament: Story and Faith: A Literary and Theological Introduction* (Peabody: Hendrickson, 1992), p. 80; C. E. L'Heureux, "Numbers," in *The New Jerome Biblical Commentary*, ed. R. E. Brown, J. A. Fitzmyer, and R. E. Murphy (Englewood Cliffs: Prentice-Hall, 1990), p. 82; G. Maier, *Das vierte Buch Mose* (Wuppertal: Brockhaus, 1989), pp. 5-8; L. M. Deming, *Numbers and Deuteronomy* (Nashville: Graded, 1988), p. 4; Coffman, *Commentary on Leviticus and Numbers*, pp. 343, 348; J. Philip, *Numbers* (Waco: Word, 1987), p. 25; R. L. Cate, *An Introduction to the Old Testament and Its Study* (Nashville: Broadman, 1987), p. 175; H. K. Mainelli, *Numbers* (Collegeville: Liturgical, 1985), p. 9; Rendtorff, *The Old Testament*, p. 147.

These twenty publications agree that Num 10:11 marks the break in the book for the ma-

mentaries treat this text as one of many parts of Numbers and do not discuss any relationships among the parts.[9] Six publications show different divisions within the book in which 10:11 does not indicate the beginning of any division whatsoever. The divisions that these six publications propose differ not only among themselves but also from the majority of the others and seem to be based on thematic criteria, such as generational transition,[10] divine presence,[11] a spiritual journey,[12] and a trust motif,[13] except for M. Douglas, whose division is based on a literary feature, the alternation of story and law.[14] This empirical survey shows that publications after 1984 surely pay attention to the structural aspect of Numbers and tend to present diverse opinions in their understanding of it. Proportionately, the number of publications after 1984 which propose 1:1–10:10 as a coherent unit and a major division at the highest level has been reduced. Nevertheless, the point can still be made that the majority of the publications designate the text as a coherent literary block and thus 10:11 as the beginning of a new major section in Numbers.

---

jor block at the highest level, except three commentaries (Milgrom, Sakenfeld, and Cole). The latter three agree on 1:1–10:10 as an uninterrupted literary unit, yet they disagree on seeing it as the highest division of Numbers. For them, Numbers has two parts following Olson's bipartite structure for it, and 1:1–10:10 is a subsection of the first part, which runs through 25:18.

9. Harrison (*Numbers*, pp. v-vi) divides Numbers into seven parts whose first two make up 1:1–10:10. Maarsingh divides Numbers into ninety-five small parts, and 1:1–10:10 consists of twenty-three of them (B. Maarsingh, *Numbers: A Practical Commentary* [Grand Rapids: Eerdmans, 1987], pp. iii-v). For Harrison and Maarsingh, their many-fold divisions belong together on the same structural level.

10. Olson, *Numbers*, pp. 5-6. Levine, *Numbers 1–20*, pp. 57-62. Although Olson and Levine share the same theme (the generational succession of the Israelites during the wilderness period) as the criterion for the structure of Numbers, they differ as to when the transition from the old to the new generation occurred. Olson argues that it happened at Numbers 26, based on two census reports, whereas Levine cites Numbers 21, based on a source-critical analysis choosing the Priestly chronology over against the Yahwistic-Elohistic chronology.

11. P. W. Kuske, *Numbers* (Milwaukee: Northwestern Publishing House, 1990), pp. 3-5. Although Kuske claims that the divisions of Numbers are based on the four major geographical areas in which the Israelites were encamped, he actually divides the book according to the theme, "The Lord is with us." As a result, he harmonizes these two criteria without explanation.

12. Mann, *The Book of the Torah*, p. 127.

13. J. H. Sailhamer, *The Pentateuch as Narrative* (Grand Rapids: Zondervan, 1992), p. 370. Sailhamer lists sixteen major sections in his table of contents; 10:11 does not function as the breaking point of any of these sections. Yet, in his explanation of the structure of Numbers, he asserts that Numbers has two main parts with 14:45 as the primary breaking point. For him, these two parts (chs. 1–14 and 15–36) fall on either side of the narrative of Israel's failure to believe in Yahweh.

14. M. Douglas, *In the Wilderness: The Doctrine of Defilement in the Book of Numbers*, JSOTSup 158 (Sheffield: Sheffield Academic Press, 1993), p. 103.

More pointedly, the proposed number of major sections in 10:11–36:13 varies enormously among scholars. This point can be demonstrated by two facts: (1) the suggested number of individual units within 10:11–36:13 and (2) the division of individual units into macro-units. Eight commentaries have been selected and surveyed.[15] First, G. B. Gray has 30 units altogether; M. Noth lists 27; P. J. Budd has 38; G. Maier presents 39 units with 72 subunits; J. Milgrom lists 18 units which are subdivided into 87 smaller units; T. R.

---

15. The eight commentaries are those of Gray, Noth, Budd, Maier, Milgrom, Ashley, Davies, and Olson. They have been selected because they treat Numbers thoroughly and extensively relative to other commentaries and represent the history of the interpretation of Numbers from 1903 (Gray) to 1996 (Olson). They also show diverse approaches to the text of Numbers in that Gray depends on literary-critical distinctions; Noth and Budd are based on tradition-historical criticism interested in the history of the literary growth of the text; others deal with the text in its present or final form. This point will be clearly shown in the following section on the history of research. For a synopsis of their outlines, see the appendix.

The three recent commentaries, Cole (2000), Dozeman (1998), and Levine (1993 for chs. 1–20 and 2000 for chs. 21–36 [*Numbers 21–36: A New Translation with Introduction and Commentary,* The Anchor Bible (New York: Doubleday, 2000)]) were intentionally not chosen. In Levine's commentary, no distinct structural feature is found since it interprets the book almost chapter by chapter (except 10:29–12:16; chs. 13–14, 16–17, 22–24, and 28–29). In the case of Dozeman, he presents two different outlines based on two titles of the book. With the title "Numbers," he adapts Olson's bipartite structure, "chapters 1–25, The Old Generation of Rebellion; chapters 26–36, the New Generation of Hope" ("The Book of Numbers," p. 3); with "in the wilderness," he divides the book into three parts, "1:1–10:10, Forming Community Around a Holy God; 10:11–21:35, The Wilderness Journey; 22:1–36:13, Preparing for Canaan on the Plains of Moab" (p. 4). Without an explanation he chooses the latter as representing his view as to the outline of the book (p. 23). The latter outline is similar to Davies' outline, though there are some differences in subdivisions. Lastly, Cole also presents two different outlines; one is based on Olson's thesis, another on seven cycles of material (1:1–6:27; 7:1–10:10; 10:11–15:41; 16:1–19:22; 20:1–25:19; 26:1–30:16; 31:1–36:13) in three movements (1:1–10:10; 10:11–25:18; 26:1–36:13). The three movements reflect "the three stages of faithfulness (2 cycles), rebellion (3 cycles), and resolution (2 cycles)" in the life of the Israelites in the wilderness (*Numbers,* p. 43). Instead of choosing one, he attempts to harmonize the two outlines with "the central and unifying theme" of the book, "the faithfulness of God to fulfill his promise to his people" (*Numbers,* p. 42). This harmonization, however, indicates a compilation of various structural factors (grammatical indicators, geographical movements, rhetorical devices, and thematic developments) without considering how they are interrelated; hence, his outline is incoherent.

Moreover, there are three commentaries published after 2001: W. H. Bellinger Jr., *Leviticus and Numbers,* New International Biblical Commentary (Peabody, MA: Hendrickson Publishers, 2001); G. S. Martin, *Exodus, Leviticus, Numbers,* Holman Old Testament Commentary (Nashville: Broadman & Holman Publishers, 2002); and S. K. Sherwood, *Leviticus, Numbers, Deuteronomy,* Berit Olam: Studies in Hebrew Narrative and Poetry (Collegeville, MN, 2002). Since these commentaries take little interest in dealing with the issue of the structure of the book of Numbers, they are not included in the present study.

Ashley identifies 42; E. W. Davies ends up having 41; and D. T. Olson presents 26 units. All must have legitimate reasons to divide the text in such ways, but their results show that they do not agree on how the text should be divided. Second, as the synopses of their proposed outlines indicate, the level of groupings is remarkably different. Gray and Noth simply list the units one after another as if they were compositionally equal, whereas Maier, Milgrom, Ashley, Davies, and Olson list the units in great detail; however, the latter also show their understanding of how these units are grouped into hierarchical levels. Budd posits himself in between these two camps: he simply lists all the units in his table of contents, but he interprets his second section, 9:15–25:18, with a thematic outline in his exegesis. Moreover, the eight commentators above show no agreement in their divisions of macro-units of 10:11–36:13. For example, of the eight commentators above, only five of them (Gray, Milgrom, Maier, Ashley, and Davies) consider 10:11 the beginning of the unit as a whole. The remaining three also differ from each other: Noth and Olson take 11:1 as its beginning, but for different reasons, and Budd begins with 9:15. Also, the eight commentators, except Budd, consider 36:13 as an appropriate final verse of the book. Only Budd sees the end of the unit at 35:34, viewing chapter 36 as an appendix. As for the major divisions within the unit, six of them have two parts while Milgrom has three (although their structural levels are not equal) and Ashley has four which share structurally equal levels.[16] The six who divide the unit into two parts cannot even agree on the conclusion of the first division: Gray (21:19), Noth (20:13), Budd (25:18), Maier (20:13), Davies (22:1), and Olson (25:18). These differences are loaded with implications related to their understanding of the macrostructure of the 10:11–36:13.

In short, an empirical survey of the previous scholarship on the organization of Numbers 10:11–36:13 reveals two things. First, there is general consensus in regarding 1:1–10:10 as a coherent literary unit, but no agreement is reached in viewing 10:11–36:13 as a distinct unit sharing equal structural levels with 1:1–10:10. Second, there is no consensus on how to divide 10:11–36:13, not even on the number of its individual units and the boundary of its major parts. These findings are the causes for the problems with which the present study begins.

16. Milgrom has three parts: 10:11–22:1; 22:2–25:19; and 26:1–36:13. The first two parts belong together under the larger unit, 1:1–25:19, and thus they do not share the same structural level with the third part (or the second part in his macrostructure of Numbers). Ashley has four parts: 10:11–12:16; 13:1–19:22; 20:1–22:1; and 22:2–36:13.

B. Major Proposals

The empirical observation above will now be substantiated by a critical review of the previous scholarship on Numbers. This history of research will investigate the question of composition and structure in Numbers 10:11–36:13 as presented in several major commentaries and other works.[17] No serious systematic discussion has been done on this matter except in Olson's book, which will be thoroughly discussed in B.4.[18] Since discovering the structure

---

17. Dozeman's commentary on the book of Numbers, published in 1998, will not be discussed separately because its treatment on the structure is neither distinct from nor as extensive as those of the selected commentaries above. His proposal, however, deserves comment. While suggesting four stages of composition of the book of Numbers, "(1) individual poetry, stories, records, and law; (2) the pre-priestly history; (3) the priestly history; and (4) the canonical book of Numbers" ("The Book of Numbers," p. 8), he stresses the third stage as formative for its essence. His interest in "priestly religion" dominates in explicating its theological themes and is imprinted in its tripartite division. However, his three parts seem to be juxtaposed without any intrinsic connection, moving from "forming community around a holy God at Sinai" to "the wilderness journey of the first generation," and then to "preparing for Canaan on the Plains of Moab" (of the second generation). What is the dominant theme that brings these parts together? Compared to each part of the outline which reflects an organization around a theme, the outline in its entity is compartmentalized. For instance, his assertion of "holiness" as the central theme for the first part (1:1–10:10) is derived from the theme of "Yahweh's descent from heaven to the tabernacle" in Exod 19:1–Num 10:10 (p. 25). This means that the first part of Numbers is understood in relation to Exodus 19–Leviticus 26, rather than to Numbers itself. The part is meaningful because of its association to the Sinai pericope (which is similar to Gary's conclusion). However, Dozeman struggles to find a constitutive criterion for 10:11–36:13 as a whole. Several competing factors are involved: a change of setting from the wilderness to the plains of Moab, a change of character from the first generation to the second generation, and a change of theme from conflicts in the wandering wilderness to final preparation for Canaan. He chooses 22:1 as the demarcation between the second and the third part. But why 22:1? Contrary to his claim, 22:1 reflects only a change of setting because neither thematic nor generational transitions have occurred at this juncture. Israel's unfaithfulness or conflicts continue until chapter 25, though the nature of the conflicts may have been changed "from internal to external" (p. 170). The generational transition may well have happened before 22:1, as Dozeman himself speculates (p. 158). If this is the case, his division of 10:11–36:13 into two parts at 22:1 cannot escape the criticism applied to Gray (see the present study, pp. 8-14). In short, Dozeman departs from Gray's employment of the documentary hypothesis, hence displaying a different understanding of the nature of both the pre-Priestly and the Priestly literature; but he chooses similar themes to Gray for the outline of the book (though his division differs from Gray's).

For a recent discussion on the arrangements of the book of Numbers, see G. J. Wenham, *Numbers* (Sheffield: Sheffield Academic Press, 1997), pp. 14-25. Wenham presents his own outline of the book and analyzes three other proposals (Olson, Douglas, and Milgrom). His analysis is helpful and yet is too brief to represent those proposals adequately.

18. Olson, *The Death of the Old and the Birth of the New*, pp. 9-30. Olson surveys major

of the text is imperative for interpreting the text as a whole, several pertinent questions emerge. Does the scholarship reflect controlled methodologies or simply impressionistic presentations? If there is a controlled methodology, do their methodologies play a role in their exegesis of actual texts? Finally, are their proposals regarding the outline or structure indicative of the theology of Numbers? The present study will not assume any particular structure of Numbers 10:11–36:13 *a priori*. It will begin by critically evaluating scholars' prior attempts to do so and will look at two things: first, their consistency in terminology and methodology and, second, to what extent they consider or neglect other conceptual signals embedded in the text. Although various commentaries and works are considerably different in their presentations of the book of Numbers, a consistent principle to be used later in the exegesis of the biblical text supplies the criterion for a critical review of current scholarship. The history of research begins with a systematic discussion on the commentaries and works as they now stand.

1. George B. Gray

In the history of scholarship on the structure of Numbers 10:11–36:13, Gray's commentary occupies the significant position of a starting point.[19] Although

---

representative commentaries on Numbers from 1861 to 1984 by looking at (1) "their general aim or goal," (2) "their stance on historical-critical issues," and (3) "their views of the theological value of the book of Numbers." This review of the history of scholarship will focus on the question of the composition and structure of Numbers presented by more recent works on the book of Numbers, whereas others have focused on the structure of individual chapters or on a group of chapters rather than on the macrostructure of the entire book of Numbers and of Num 10:11–36:13. The following studies will be reviewed in the discussion of the identification of individual units and their location and arrangement within 10:11–36:13. J. Milgrom, "The Structures of Numbers: Chapters 11–12 and 13–14 and Their Redaction: Preliminary Groupings" in *Judaic Perspectives on Ancient Israel*, ed. Jacob Neusner et al. (Philadelphia: Fortress, 1987), pp. 49-61; T. W. Mann, "Holiness and Death in the Redaction of Numbers 16:1–20:13," in *Love and Death in the Ancient Near East: Essays in Honor of Marvin H. Pope*, ed. J. H. Marks and R. M. Good (Los Angeles: Western Academic Press, 1987), pp. 181-90; C. J. Labuschagne, "Neue Wege und Perspektiven in der Pentateuchforschung," *VT* 36 (1986): 146-62; G. Brin, "Numbers 15:22-23 and the Question of the Composition of the Pentateuch," *VT* 30 (1980): 351-54; D. Jobling, "Structural Analysis of Numbers 11 and 12," *SBLSP* 11 (1977): 171-203.

19. Gray, *A Critical and Exegetical Commentary on Numbers*. By investigating in the area of lexicography and textual and literary criticism and utilizing up-to-date archaeological and anthropological studies, Gray provides one of the most comprehensive yet detailed studies on Numbers available up to that time. Its contribution is still valuable. Gray lays out the blueprint for the commentary in his "Introduction" (pp. xxi-lii).

he characterized the contents as "very miscellaneous," he insists that the book of Numbers has been organized according to a "geographical or chronological skeleton." In the introduction to his commentary, Gray presents two outlines of Numbers. First, he divides the text according to the scenes of the encampments of the Israelites and their marches between these encampments:[20] the wilderness of Sinai (1:1–10:11, 29-32), the wilderness of Paran (12:16b–20:21), and the steppes of Moab at the northeast end of the Dead Sea (22:1–36:13), with two sections based on the connecting marches between the first and second (10:12-28; 10:33–12:16a) and the second and third (20:22–21:32 [35]).[21] Second, he divides Numbers into three parts: Sinai (1:1–10:11), north of Sinai and west of the 'Arabah (10:12–21:9), and east of the 'Arabah (21:10–36:13).[22] These two outlines are juxtaposed in his introduction without explanation, although the second

20. In his book *The Death of the Old and the Birth of the New* (pp. 34-35, n. 13 [207]), Olson claims that geographical markers are used in determining the outline of Numbers in thirty-three out of the forty-six commentaries surveyed, and he provides three basic outlines based on geographical signals: first, I. In the wilderness of Sinai (1:1–10:10), II. From Sinai to Kadesh (10:11–22:1), III. On the plains of Moab (22:2–36:13); second, I. In the wilderness of Sinai (1:1–10:10), II. From Sinai to Kadesh (10:11–20:13), III. From Kadesh to the plains of Moab (20:14–36:13); and third, I. The wilderness of Sinai (1:1–10:10), II. North of Sinai, west of the 'Arabah (10:11–21:19), and III. East of the 'Arabah (21:10–36:13). Although some scholars further subdivide one or more of these divisions and some diverge from it, all pay attention to geographical markers for their outlining of Numbers. Olson, however, regards these divisions as arbitrary because there is no consensus among the thirty-three commentaries. He states his displeasure with this criterion but does not explain why.

Moreover, Olson's titles of the first two outlines refer to the mixture of the place of the Israelites' camp and their movement from one place to another. This mixture indicates that these two outlines have been organized by a criterion different from the geographical one as Olson uncritically assumed. Only the titles of the third, which is the same in essence with Gray, refer to the place of the Israelites' camp consistently. Cf. J. S. Ackerman, "Numbers," in *The Literary Guide to the Bible*, ed. R. Alter and F. Kermode (Cambridge, MA: Harvard University Press, 1987), p. 78; J. de Vaulx, *Les Nombres*, Sources Bibliques (Paris: J. Gabalda et Cie, 1972), pp. 12-13; B. Wilkinson and K. Boa, *Talk thru the Old Testament*, Talk thru the Bible, vol. 1 (Nashville: Thomas Nelson, 1983), pp. 31-35; Bandstra, *Reading the Old Testament*, p. 156.

21. Gray, *A Critical and Exegetical Commentary on Numbers*, pp. xxii-xxiii. In his commentary on Numbers (*Numbers*, pp. 14-21), Wenham adopts Rendtorff's proposal on the literary composition of Genesis (i.e., Genesis was composed by linking back-to-back the larger blocks of originally separate material, such as the primeval history, the Abraham stories, the Jacob stories, and the Joseph stories) and outlines Numbers accordingly. Numbers was composed of three blocks of traditions ([1] the preparation to enter the promised land, the conclusion of the Sinai cycle: 1:1–10:10, [2] the Kadesh cycle: 13:1–19:22, and [3] the plains of Moab cycle: 22:2–36:13) connected by two short travelogues ([1] from Sinai to Kadesh: 10:11–12:16 and [2] from Kadesh to the plains of Moab: 20:1–22:1).

22. Gray, *A Critical and Exegetical Commentary on Numbers*, pp. xxvi-xxix.

one is used in the body of his commentary. His second outline shows that he places all these five sections of the first outline together as both encampment and migration stories and then redivides the text into three geographical areas. The first section, Sinai (1:1–10:11, 29-32), is internally consistent in his treatment. However, this is not true of the second section, which includes not only the marches northward from Sinai to Paran and accompanying events (10:12-28; 10:33–12:16a) but also the marches and events downward from the boundary of Edom to the Gulf of 'Arabah (20:22–21:9). Consequently, the third section has been reduced to the activities reported only east of the 'Arabah (21:10–36:13).

Moreover, Gray's redivision from the first outline to the second one is exegetically warranted unless the criterion for the division is other than a geographical reason. His own titles for these sections provide at least two clues as to how he went about dividing the text. First, he formulates the titles for his sections partially for the second and entirely for the third section as west and east of 'Arabah. These formulations use a particular place-name, the 'Arabah, as constitutive for dividing the territory through which the Israelites wandered after departing the wilderness of Sinai and before entering the promised land. The Brook of the 'Arabah can be considered at best to be a topographical but not a geographical designation, and it is inappropriate in comparison to the geographical title of the first section, the wilderness of Sinai.[23] Thus, Gray's formulation is a mixture of both topographical and geographical designations without distinction. As a result, it undermines his outline of Numbers based on geographical signals. His titles may serve to classify materials, but they are unable to indicate the constitutive criterion for his threefold subdivision of Numbers.

Second, Gray provides another set of titles in the body of exegesis: "The Northward March from Sinai: The Wandering and Marches West of the 'Arabah" for Numbers 10:11–21:9 and "Marches and Events at East of the 'Arabah and the Jordan" for Numbers 21:10–36:13.[24] These titles do not por-

---

23. Geographical and topographical aspects of the texts should be further differentiated. Geographical texts focus on a large territory like lands, regions, and countries, whereas topographical texts focus on particular places, for example, a city or town within a territory or a tract of the land. The former, such as the wilderness of Sinai, includes the latter, such as Kadesh and lists of specific localities (e.g., Num 33; Josh 21). Whether one supersedes the other as a structuring factor has not been addressed in Gray's usage of these terms. Similar to Gray, Wenham (*Numbers*, p. 21) evaluates Kadesh, a topographical reference, as equal to Sinai and the plains of Moab, geographical references. Olson (*The Death of the Old and the Birth of the New*, p. 35) also does not differentiate these two when he refers to Israel's geographical movement from place to place (Kadesh, Edom, Mount Hor, Moab).

24. Gray, *A Critical and Exegetical Commentary on Numbers*, pp. 90, 279; cf. pp. xxvii-xxviii.

tray where the Israelites were as clearly as the titles in his "Introduction" indicate. Of course, this inconsistency of titling between his introduction and the actual body of exegesis can be regarded as an inadvertent mistake. Yet these titles presuppose issues of a more substantive nature: reports on the Israelites' movements from one place to another and reports on the events both on the way and at encampments. Thus, it is quite certain that something other than geographical criteria is operative in these titles. It is the focus both on the Israelites' marches and events throughout the wilderness that Gray extracts from the content of the materials.

The discrepancy between what Gray claims (geography as the constitutive criterion for three sections) and what he actually did (division of materials as 1:1–10:11, 29-32; 10:12–21:9; and 21:10–36:13) can be explored more substantively. In essence, such an organization of the material could be called conceptual or systematic. Given geographical and chronological indicators in the text, Gray seems to prefer the former for the primary conceptual criterion for this organization. The geographical criterion is superordinate, and chronological data play a secondary, supportive role.[25] Numbers itself, however, reveals more than the three geographical indicators: the wilderness of Sinai (1:1; 3:14; 9:1), the wilderness of Paran (10:12; 12:16; 13:3, 26), the wilderness of Zin (13:21; 20:1; 27:14; 33:36; 34:3, 4), the land of Edom (20:23; 21:4; 33:37; 34:3), the Negeb (21:1),

---

25. Gray's three sections cover nineteen days, almost thirty-eight years, and no more than five months, respectively. Numbers provides a number of chronological markers (which are more than Olson lists in his analysis; *The Death of the Old and the Birth of the New*, p. 34): 1:1; 7:1; 9:1, 15; 10:11; 11:18, 32; 13:20, 25; 14:1, 40; 16:7, 16; 17:6, 23; 20:1; 26:1; 33:3, 38. After investigating various dates in Numbers, Gray concluded that these chronological indicators are "less clear" than those of geography. Except for the dates in the first ten chapters, all the rest of the dates are imprecise or dislocated. Note that the dates in 10:11, "In the second year, in the second month, on the twentieth day of the month," and in 33:38, "in the fortieth year after the Israelites had come out of the land of Egypt, on the first day of the fifth month," are clear and precise. (Nowhere else in the rest of Numbers and not until Deut 1:3 has a precise date accompanied an event.) Therefore, these two dates serve as only approximate parameters for the second and the third period. Accordingly, Numbers can be divided chronologically into three sections:

I.	Nineteen days from the 1st day of the 2nd month of the 2nd year to the 20th day of the 2nd month of the 2nd year	1:1–10:10
II.	Approximately more than thirty-eight years between the 2nd month of the 2nd year and the 5th month of the 40th year	1:11–33:49
III.	Approximately six months after the 5th month of the 40th year (until the 1st day of the 11th month of the 40th year: Deut 1:3)	33:50–36:13

But this chronological structure of Numbers has not been explored by either Gray or Olson. They simply state that chronological markers do not provide a constitutive basis for the structure of Numbers without explanation.

the lands/boundary of Moab (21:11, 13, 20; 22:1; 26:3, 63; 31:12; 33:44, 48, 49, 50; 35:1; 36:13), and the boundary of the Amorites (21:13, 25, 31). This textual evidence has not been seriously considered in Gray's geographical criterion for the organization of the "very miscellaneous" materials in Numbers. For him, Sinai and the 'Arabah (Jordan Valley) are the breaking points for the scenes of the Israelites' activities. His description of three sections of Numbers, particularly the second and third, are clearly designated on the basis of these geographical markers: Sinai, *north of* Sinai and *west of* the 'Arabah, and *east of* the 'Arabah. More specifically, Sinai is used as the decisive criterion when a wide area or territory is concerned. However, the 'Arabah is used to divide the particular space between Sinai and the wilderness in which the Israelites wandered before entering the promised land. What Gray's geographical description suggests is that there are only two dominant territories: the wilderness of Sinai and the territory between Sinai and the promised land.

Furthermore, as the above textual evidence shows, Numbers would be organized into seven sections based on the Israelites' activities in seven territories, whether those activities refer to the Israelites' marches or encampments.[26] However, Gray proposes only three areas which classify the seven as Sinai, east of the 'Arabah (the plains of Moab), and the combined areas in between. On the surface, his layout assumes that these three areas are all at an equal level in the composition of Numbers. Yet whether they are equally significant in the structure of Numbers is another matter. But one thing is sure: Sinai and east of the 'Arabah are more important than each of the five listed areas. Sinai and east of the 'Arabah occupy superordinate positions relative to the other five regions. This point implies that some reason (or reasons) other than geographical indicators is the unifying factor of the five areas combined by Gray. Consequently, the basis for Gray's threefold division is not discernible; clearly it is not based on geographical indicators, despite his claim.

After presenting his threefold subdivision of Numbers, Gray discusses the analysis of the book in the context of the placement of Numbers after Exodus and prior to Deuteronomy.[27] The first section (Num 1:1–10:10) needs to be considered in the larger context of Exodus 19:1–Numbers 10:10 because the

---

26. Knierim, "The Book of Numbers," p. 383. Knierim identifies seven parts, but his division differs from the present study. He has two parts in relation to Moab: those for the plains of Moab and those for the lands of Moab. He excludes the wilderness of Zin. This division shows his assumption that the sojourn in the plains of Moab is structurally equal to the sojourn in the wilderness of Sinai. Knierim's survey of seven geographical indicators seems already to be colored by the concept that he prefers for Numbers as a whole. Despite this difference, the essential point of this paragraph comes from Knierim's insight.

27. Gray, *A Critical and Exegetical Commentary on Numbers*, pp. xxiii-xxvi.

scene of the former is the same as that of the latter and their main subjects are closely related. The second and third sections (Num 10:11–36:13) need to be considered in relation to Deuteronomy, although the connection is far less clear than the connection between Exodus and Numbers 1:1–10:10. Gray's point is well taken. A structural analysis of Numbers 10:11–36:13 can be affected by the structure of the larger corpus within which it is placed. The larger literary context in this case can be seen on several levels, such as the book of Numbers, the Moses story, even the Pentateuch as a whole.[28] Yet the larger contexts are not the sum of the individual parts; both the larger context and the individual parts are interrelated. That the structure of an individual part must be approached from the vantage point of the larger corpus of which it forms a part, however, may suggest a circular argument. How can the structure of the larger corpus be achieved apart from the interpretation of the individual components? In other words, the structure of Numbers 10:11–36:13 inevitably depends on that of the Pentateuch, and at the same time the latter must be affected by the former.[29] As is true with any discussion on the interrelationship between a component part and its larger context, Gray reaches the conclusion that "the Book of Numbers is a section somewhat mechanically cut out of the whole of which it forms a part; the result is that it possesses no unity of subject."[30] This conclusion is impressionistic and originates from a simple survey of the surface level of the text. He does not even raise the question regarding the relationship between his own threefold subdivision of Numbers as a whole and three sections of the larger corpus from Exodus to Deuteronomy.

Following the description of his understanding of Numbers, Gray outlines its contents.[31] The second and third sections, with which the present study is concerned, are subdivided into fifteen subsections each. The outline does not reflect any hierarchical configuration of the fifteen parts, making it appear that all of the fifteen parts are structurally equal. One exception is that only one unit in each larger section deals with various laws: five subunits in chapter 15 called "Various laws and regulations" and six in chapters 33:50–36:13 called "Various laws relating to the conquest and settlement of Canaan."

---

28. Harrison, *Numbers*, p. 1. Harrison argues that the intrinsic connection of Numbers to the Pentateuch and Mosaic authorship for overall pentateuchal material are the reasons for using the Pentateuch as the starting point of inquiry for Numbers. These reasons, however, have not been derived from the actual exegesis of the Pentateuch itself but from the traditional designation and the antiquity of the five-volume collection known as the Pentateuch.

29. Despite this exegetical circle, the starting point has to be chosen depending upon the nature and scope of the material under study.

30. Gray, *A Critical and Exegetical Commentary on Numbers*, p. xxiv.

31. Gray, *A Critical and Exegetical Commentary on Numbers*, pp. xxvi-xxix.

Moreover, each subsection has a title that summarizes the contents of the subsection rather than giving any conceptual aspects responsible for their order and the extant arrangement. Inconsistency, however, exists between this outline and actual exegesis. For example, various subsections have been put together under new titles. In the second section, 11:1-3, 11:4-35, and 12:1-16 have been put under "Incidents between Sinai and Kadesh"; 20:1-13 and 20:14-21 have also been placed under "Events at Kadesh"; and in the third section, 21:10-20, 21:21-32, 21:33-35, and 22:1 have been combined under "Marches and Conquests East of the Dead Sea and Jordan Valley."[32] This kind of inconsistency between his preferred outline in the introduction and the outline in the body of the commentary may be easily avoided, but the new descriptions of the combined units suggest that Gray actually struggles with the relationship among subdivided units, although the scope of his effort has unfortunately been limited to units that are situated side by side.

It could be argued that criticizing Gray's literary structure of Numbers 10:11–36:13 is unfair given his primary concern with source-critical distinctions. In his exegesis of each unit, he immediately distinguishes sources J, E, JE, P, or JEP. Even within the Priestly material, he distinguishes three separate layers: Pg, Ps, and Px.[33] Preoccupation with sources inevitably leads him to break the comprised whole down into its individual parts on the basis of identifiable traces of sources and to explain the presence of the parts historically. This diachronic and analytical procedure prevents him from attempting to discover the compositional unity or even structural conceptuality that owes its existence to the extant text. He succeeds in disassembling the text into numerous parts and yet fails in reassembling them into the present text. This may be due to the influence of the concerns of his era in scholarship, an era preoccupied with the issues of source criticism. Gray does not divide Numbers according to his distinctions of sources, however, as would be expected. For instance, although his acknowledgment that P's itinerary differs from that of JE does come to the surface, he does not rearrange the materials for the sake of producing an intelligent or understandable itinerary.[34] Instead, he clearly states

---

32. Gray, *A Critical and Exegetical Commentary on Numbers*, pp. 97-128, 256-69, and 279-307, respectively.

33. Gray, *A Critical and Exegetical Commentary on Numbers*, pp. xxix-xxxix. Gray spends the largest part (ten pages) of his introduction on the explanation of sources.

34. Some examples indicating the difference between P and JE are: there is a clear difference between P and JE in the report on the spies in chs. 13–14 (Gray, *A Critical and Exegetical Commentary on Numbers*, p. 129); and according to P's itinerary the Israelites marched across the north of Edom (pp. 279-82), while in JE they marched south to the Gulf of ʿAkabah and passed around the southern end of Edom (p. 264).

differences and explains them away as a result of the compilation of sources over a long period of time. The critical point for Gray thus is not his preoccupation with source distinctions but his silence on why and how these different sources came together and are located and arranged in the present way.

2. Martin Noth

Compared to the detailed work of Gray, Martin Noth's commentary on the book of Numbers is relatively short.[35] Its contribution to the study on Numbers, however, does not rest on the number of pages but on the advancement and consistent employment of Noth's methodology. Starting from a survey of the contents of Numbers, Noth is totally unconvinced that a unity or a pattern of organization exists. His skepticism about discovering a conceptually oriented structure is based on four specific reasons: (1) "the confusion and lack of order in its contents"; (2) "the juxtaposition of quite varied styles and methods of presentation"; (3) "the repeated confrontation of factually contradictory concepts in one and the same situation"; and (4) "the relationship of secondary dependence which can sometimes be established between one section and another."[36] In the body of commentary, these reasons are explored only in a sporadic fashion, particularly in concise statements prior to actual exegeses of individual units.

The first three reasons are simply a summary of what Gray has already explained very thoroughly. Noth's contribution to the quest for the structure of Numbers lies in the fourth reason. This fourth reason is structural in nature and concerns the relationship between independent sections. It presupposes the disparity of the materials, characterized as a compilation of often contradictory narrative sequences and unsystematized collections of regulations. Compositionally, Noth could find no organic connections between the narratives and divine ordinances. But he is determined to explain these relationships by asking structural questions as to why a unit should stand at a particular point and on what basis and how these diverse materials were put together. His proposal aims at tracing the history of the growth of the literary work through the various stages, which include not only oral and written transmission but also a process of composition by insertions, editions, and simple additions.[37] Consequently, he considers Numbers to be a part of the

---

35. Noth's commentary on Numbers has 258 pages, whereas Gray's has 521.

36. Noth, *Numbers*, p. 4.

37. Noth treats this proposal systematically in his reconstruction of the history of pentateuchal traditions. M. Noth, *A History of Pentateuchal Traditions*, trans. B. W. Anderson

larger whole of the Pentateuch. This means for Noth that Numbers, if it is to be understood intelligently, must be investigated in the alignment of the continuing pentateuchal sources.

In Numbers, more than three written sources (J, E, and P) have been compiled. Not only does a long oral history of tradition exist before the written sources, but also various substantial secondary additions or insertions, which occurred after the completion and combination of these written sources present in Numbers. Attending to these kinds of secondary activities gives Noth an opportunity to explain the lack of compositional unity in Numbers because its main character, he writes, is simply one individual unit added to another in sequence over time as the various units appeared. For example, numerous individual units in Numbers 5:1–9:14 and 25:1–36:13 are attached to each other without having any connections and relationships among them, or special reasons for their arrangement.

Noth's methodology is easy to engage but very difficult to substantiate in its results. On what ground is an individual unit classified as a secondary addition? And as an addition to what? If secondary materials are characterized as "supplements" or "appendixes," then do these terms not presuppose a coherent concept, or at least a cohesive unity, within the materials referred to as such? Without knowing the definite date and source of a unit, how can it be proven that each distinctive unit was attached to the next in the sequence of their appearances? Considering Noth's rationale for the attachment of Numbers 5:1–9:14 (a necessity for achieving Sinaitic authority for the later ordinances) as well as Numbers 25:1–36:13 (due to the addition of Deuteronomy to Genesis-Numbers corpus), is he not in fact saying that there is a certain relationship or even conceptuality behind these compositions? All these questions, one way or the other, point to Noth's proposal that the reconstructed growth of Numbers is an alternative explanation for the structure of the book.

The criteria for the distinctions among old sources of the Pentateuch, such as J, E, and P, as well as secondary additions are, for Noth, the existence of doublets, repetitions, various divine names, and variants.[38] However, these stylistic markers can be considered literary devices artificially imposed by the compiler(s) upon the contents of Numbers, which, according to Noth, have been accumulated in random fashion. As literary devices of the compilers,

---

(Atlanta: Scholars Press, 1981). His commentary on Numbers seems to be a continued exposition of his own hypothesis.

38. Noth, *Numbers,* pp. 4-11. For the most comprehensive arguments on these criteria, see R. N. Whybray, *The Making of the Pentateuch: A Methodological Study,* JSOTSup 53 (Sheffield: Sheffield Academic Press, 1987); for a concise rebuttal, see Nicholson, *The Pentateuch in the Twentieth Century,* pp. 228-37.

these markers might not necessarily claim compositional cohesiveness beyond the aesthetic, which in itself is much more than what Noth wanted to squeeze out of them. Or even more likely, such markers might be susceptible to control by an undergirding concept. They may be signals illuminating hidden or implicit agenda within and underneath the texts. The point is that their existence does not guarantee Noth's claim that the text may be characterized automatically as a compilation of different sources.[39] Thus, Noth's tendency to refer to certain materials as secondary based only on a strict usage of the criteria above is not entirely convincing. These criteria need to be reinforced by more substantive factors based on both content and forms, and even on consideration of the compilers' intentions.

Concerning the framework of the entire Pentateuch, Noth suggests five themes of the pentateuchal traditions: "Guidance out of Egypt," "Guidance into the Arable Land," "Promise to the Patriarchs," "Guidance in the Wilderness," and "Revelation at Sinai."[40] This view holds that these themes were originally separate oral traditions, gradually filled out and linked together with other narrative materials to form the corpus of Genesis through Numbers. From this vantage point, Noth divides Numbers into three sections: "Further ordinances of God at Sinai: 10:1–10:36," "Further sojourn in the wilderness: 11:1–20:13," and "Preparation for and beginning of the conquest: 20:14–36:13."[41] Noth further divides the first section into six units, the second into eight, and the third into nineteen. Interestingly, he subdivides two units concerning divine ordinances: 5:1–6:27 and 8:1–9:14. Except for these two, the rest of the individual units are listed one after the other as if they were set side by side, having no relationship among themselves. This stance is implemented consistently in his actual exegesis; for example, note his statement on 30:1-16: "Both from the literary point of view and from the point of view of content, this passage stands on its own. Without having any connection with what precedes or with what follows. . . ."[42] As a result, his outline of Numbers

---

39. For example, repetition, which has been used extensively in classical literary criticism as one of the criteria for discerning the different levels in the text, has become increasingly recognized as a constitutive signal for a deliberate literary technique or mark of style in the text. Cf. Alter, *The Art of Biblical Narrative*, pp. 88ff.

40. Noth, *A History of Pentateuchal Traditions*, pp. 46-145.

41. Noth, *Numbers*, pp. vii-viii.

42. Noth, *Numbers*, p. 224. A few more quotations will clearly illustrate this point: "It is not quite clear why this rather unsystematically arranged collection of various cultic-ritual ordinances should have found a place at this particular point in the Pentateuchal narrative" (p. 114); "Originally the compilation that is ch. 18 was certainly an independent unit, not intended from the outset for the present context" (p. 133); "In the present context this chapter [ch. 19] is an addition, having no reference to the surrounding material" (p. 139). See more on pp. 151

coincides with his thesis that Numbers lacks unity. He achieves this consistency by regarding numerous materials that do not fit into his classification of J, E, and P as secondary and late additions.

However, his distinctions of sources are not the foundation for his divisions of Numbers; his hypothesis regarding the "themes" of the pentateuchal traditions is responsible.[43] Since, in Noth's view, the themes have been employed so dominantly and consistently in forming the corpus from Genesis to Numbers, geographical or topographical indicators are not in any way to be regarded as constitutive criteria for Numbers' divisions. Even the distinctions of sources play at best a secondary role. Through using the themes for the division of Numbers, what Noth actually does is not discover the structure of Numbers as it stands but rather attempt to portray the history of literary growth in Numbers in the larger context of the Pentateuch. The question of any structural unity for Numbers that would account for Numbers 10:11–36:13 as a literary unit in its present arrangement is, then, hard to demonstrate.

Moreover, this reconstruction of the literary growth of the Pentateuch is undoubtedly hypothetical in nature. That it is hypothetical is not, however, a problem in any scientific investigation. The problem is whether these themes are being reconstructed with or without any concrete grounding in the text. Speaking of a certain theme presupposes an abstraction from the reality of the contents of the text. Consequently, the abstraction inevitably leads to omitting and ignoring textual evidence that does not fit the preconceived themes. This danger seems to be evident in the frequent tendency of Noth to classify materials as secondary and late additions.

In summary, unlike Gray, Noth contributed to the question of the location and arrangement of individual units by using the concept of secondary additions. But his diachronical approach, that is, focusing on the history of literary growth, prevented him from explaining the structure of Numbers as it stands. More substantively, Noth's themes are not identical with the structural aspects of organization, although they are responsible for his outline of Numbers. In general, a story has a theme (or themes) that is (are) abstracted from the contents. The theme of a literary work is, thus, part of the whole. On

---

and 158. Yet Noth struggles to find an assumed connection, however defined, within neighboring units: "Stylistically and thematically, this latter presentation [i.e., the reproach regarding the Cushite marriage, 12:1] stands in obvious relationship to the insertions in ch. 11 (vv. 14-17, 24b-30)" (p. 93). He also explains the position of the report of the death of Moses (27:12-23) in the context of the Pentateuch as a whole (p. 213).

43. For a clear example, Noth treats 21:10-20 as a late editorial addition that functions to compensate for the lack of connection between the stories set on the edge of the desert and the following accounts of the conquest (*Numbers*, p. 159).

the one hand, the compositional question for a story is how a theme is composed, and, on the other hand, the structural question is what the concept for the theme is to be. These questions go unanswered in mere assertion of a theme. A theme may coincide with the concept if there is clear textual proof. Noth's themes, however, are identified by the explanation of the Pentateuch as a whole. These themes are not extracted from the contents of Numbers. Therefore, the outline based on these themes is by nature an imposition on the contents of Numbers. Much more than this, Noth understood these themes as being originally separate. For Noth, neither intrinsic connectedness nor conceptual relationship is evident among them. In Numbers, the themes are simply arranged topically on the basis of a loose attachment to a geographical location, either Sinai or the steppes of Moab, or to a chronological span of forty years. Topics and themes are often impressionistic and do not closely follow the structure which Numbers defines for itself. Thus, Noth's understanding of themes does not provide an explanation of the structure of Numbers, but only of the literary growth of Numbers.

3. Philip J. Budd

Budd's commentary proposes an alternative approach to the question of the structure of Numbers.[44] At the outset Budd seems to break the circular argument regarding the starting point of investigation. According to this author, an investigation of Numbers must be started with its own contents rather than from the vantage point of the larger context of the Pentateuch. Beginning with Numbers itself is not only a legitimate enterprise but also has logical priority when addressing the book's structure. This priority stems from the independence of Numbers as a literary entity, which Budd argues by rejecting O. Eissfeldt. For Budd, the book of Numbers is not an artificial creation resulting from the five divisions of the Pentateuch, which are, according to Eissfeldt, a practical solution to unmanageability of the long, complex literary material. Instead, Numbers has an individuality and integrity as a distinct unit. Thus, starting with Numbers means for Budd treating it in its present form.

Budd's treatment of Numbers as a self-contained unit is a result of his assessment of sources that make up the contents of Numbers. While he agrees with previous scholars regarding the Priestly author's responsibility for its final

---

44. Budd, *Numbers.* Budd organizes the commentary according to an introduction (pp. xvii-xxxii), text, and commentary, which lists fifty-five individual units without any numerical indicators.

compilation, he differs from them in his characterization of the Priestly and Yahwistic material. Budd views P to be a "midrashic commentary" and so describes P's incorporation of the older material with interpretive comments within P's own distinctive theological framework.[45] In other words, the Priestly author revised the existing Yahwistic material, which in itself carries an overall theological coherence, and incorporated it into his own distinctive theological structure. Numbers contains distinctive features and emphases in this Priestly revision that reveal a certain degree of independent production. Thus, paying attention to the significance of these features demands a treatment of Numbers as a self-contained unit. This is particularly different from Noth's understanding of Numbers as the compilation of secondary additions to an already complete and coherent narrative. Consequently, Budd asserts that Numbers as a whole presents itself in a "well ordered" and coherent fashion, showing "few totally inexplicable connections between the various sections."[46] Though such connections are few in number, they do exist. The validity or identifiability of Budd's proposal is not the main thrust of the present study, but its effect on discovering the structure of Numbers is. The question is how Budd's alternative proposal for understanding sources assists him in extracting a structure from Numbers. What is the concept for the Priestly "midrashic" composition on the existing Yahwistic material? Does Budd's structure of Numbers reveal the conceptualized structure of the Priestly author or reflect the conceptual conflict between the Priestly and the Yahwistic materials? If the conflict between two sources exists, then does Budd's claim that Numbers is well ordered and coherent stand exegetically? Budd fails to answer these questions.

In the section of the introduction called "contents," Budd proposes a threefold structure for Numbers.[47]

I. Constituting the community at Sinai   1:1–9:14
II. The Journey — its setbacks and successes   9:15–25:18
III. Final preparations for settlement   26:1–35:34

At the outset, his proposal is unique for excluding the final chapter. This fact indicates an inconsistency between what he claims, that is, to study Numbers

45. Budd, *Numbers*, pp. xxi-xxv. Budd views the Yahwistic material as "a compendium of materials from a variety of sources" that reflects the historical and ideological settings of the Josianic period. He sees the Priestly revision as a provision of an apologia for the returning Babylonian Jews and some programmatic proposals for the upcoming restoration, which aptly reflects the situation of the latter part of the fifth century.

46. Budd, *Numbers*, pp. xvii, xx.

47. Budd, *Numbers*, pp. xvii-xviii.

as a self-contained unit and in its present form, and what he does. Moreover, his characterization of the final chapter (ch. 36) confuses the reader. He regards it as "an appendix, supplementing the information of 27:1-11," on the one hand, and as "a supplement or appendix to the completed book of Numbers," on the other hand.[48] According to the latter statement, what he actually proposes is two sections: one which is constructed with chapters 1 to 35, and the other only with chapter 36. For the relationship of these two sections, Budd uses "appendix" or "supplement" as if these terms meant the same thing and were interchangeable. According to the former statement, it is not quite clear whether he means Numbers has two sections, chapters 1 to 35 and chapter 36, which is the same result of the latter statement. At least this much is clear: chapter 36 is an appendix in its nature, and its nature is qualified by functioning to supplement some information related to that of 27:1-11.

The kernel of confusion is his usage of "appendix" and "supplement" without further clarifying their definitions.[49] On the one hand, appendix is a compositional term which indicates a particular shape or formation of a text. This term implies both a unity of component parts of the text being designated as such and ultimately a conceptuality behind the text. In other words, when Budd designates chapter 36 as an appendix, he supposes the compositional unity of chapter 36 and the concept that is signaled by the surface of the chapter. Much more pointedly, his understanding of the function of chapter 36 as an appendix to the completed book of Numbers must be substantiated by a demonstration of whether the appendedness of chapter 36 constitutes its governing typicality. Budd seems to fail to meet this demand. On the other hand, supplement is a term oriented to focus on the content of the text rather than its form. This term necessarily indicates neither a unity or a concept of the material designated as such, nor its location and arrangement relative to the rest. The main function that this term supposes is to provide further information on a specific subject. This information can be expected to update, modify, correct, or alter the main body, and yet it is only secondary. Regarding the clarifi-

---

48. Budd, *Numbers*, pp. xvii, 389. Budd seems unaware of this inconsistency even in the explanation of the final chapter. For this, compare his statements: "The section appears to be a supplement to Num 27:1-11" (p. 388); "This section is a supplement or appendix to the property regulation given in Num 27:1-11, and it functions as an appendix to the book as a whole" (p. 390). He considers 36:13 to be the concluding remark of the Priestly author.

49. *Webster's Third New International Dictionary*, ed. P. B. Grove (Springfield: G. & C. Merriam Company, 1969). Webster's dictionary defines these terms as follows: appendix, "matter added to a book but not essential to its completeness" (p. 104); supplement, "a part added to or issued as a continuation of a book or periodical to make good its deficiencies, correct its errors, bring it up to date or provide special features not ordinarily included" (p. 2297).

cation of these terms, Budd should have first designated chapter 36 as a supplement to 27:1-11; second, defined its location and arrangement at the end of Numbers; and third, inquired as to the governing conceptuality responsible for the presentation of chapter 36. In short, his failure to provide clear definitions of terms and his failure to engage in a discussion on structural questions prompted by his usage of terms cause his differentiation of chapter 36 from the rest of Numbers to be exegetically unwarranted.

Considering the proposed threefold structure of Numbers, Budd also differs from the previous scholars in his delimitation of major sections. The second section begins with a discussion of the means of guidance in the journey (9:15–10:10) and ends with a recovery from the "third setback" (25:6-18). As the subtitle, "its setbacks and success[es]," indicates, Budd constructs this section as a series of alternations between the Israelites' sins and God's unchanging commitment to them. The following outline shows Budd's point more clearly.[50]

II. The journey — its setbacks and successes	9:15–25:18
A. Discussion on the means of guidance	9:15–10:10
B. The order of movement and the departure from Sinai	10:11-36
C. Three major setbacks and successes	11:1–25:18
1. A preliminary account: Mosaic leadership and authority	11:1–12:16
2. Three accounts	13:1–25:18
a. First round	13:1–15:41
(1) Sin of the community as a whole	13:1–14:45
(2) God's renewed commitment	15:1-41
b. Second round	16:1–19:22
(1) Sin of the Levites	16:1–17:28
(2) God's renewed commitment to the Levitical order	18:1–19:22
c. Third round	20:1–25:18
(1) Sin of Moses and Aaron	20:1-13, 22-29
(2) God's renewed commitment to the priestly order	20:14-21
	21:1–25:18

50. Budd, *Numbers*, pp. xvii-xviii. Budd is able to find some pattern and purpose for the organization of the first and second section and admits his difficulty in finding a coherence in the third section. For the third section, he simply lists thirteen individual units as if they were not related in any fashion, although he is able to propose various facets of a theme related with the land. Cf. Budd, *Numbers*, p. xx. Moreover, the system used in this configuration comes from the FOTL commentary series, but not from Budd's commentary.

This outline, extricated from Budd's own discussion, indicates his effort to find the structure of the second section, although he does not provide any pattern for the third section (26:1–35:34). Explored in detail in the exegesis, the ever-narrowing progression of responsible parties for sin, from the whole community through the Levites to Moses and Aaron, seems to be a genuine contribution of his outline. However, his exegesis on these parts does not correspond to the outline faithfully. For instance, he sees the function of 15:37-41 as being a conclusion of a major section which begins at 11:1, rather than 13:1 as his outline shows.[51] Then, chapters 11–12 are included as part of the theme of the sin of Israel as a whole. In this change Budd emphasizes in each case one aspect over the other in the description of Numbers 11–12. In the proposed outline he focuses on the function of Numbers 11–12 in relationship to Numbers 13–25 on the subject of the disaffection of the Israelites, that is, as a general introduction; whereas in the actual exegesis he zeroes in on who was responsible for the ongoing disaffection, that is, all the Israelites. In other words, he employs two different criteria for Numbers 11–12 and is undecided or ambiguous concerning the relationship between them. Which one is constitutive to which and why go unanswered. The result of his indecisiveness is the inconsistency in his own outline of Numbers 11–25.

More obviously, Budd, instead of analyzing the present arrangement of the text, outlines the Yahwist's stories of the Israelites' disaffection from Sinai to the Jordan independently.[52] While the validity of the chiastic pattern for the Yahwist's story could be argued, its relationship with the assumed pattern of the Priestly materials should be in question. Budd explains that the Priestly author took the theme of Israel's sin from the Yahwist's material and adapted

---

51. Budd, *Numbers*, p. 178. Budd states: "In the wider context they [15:37-41] function as a fitting conclusion to the section dealing with Israel's sin, specifically the rejection of the land in Num 14, but more generally the whole section of disaffection in Num 11–14." According to this statement, the structure of Numbers 11–14 should be:

    A. Disaffection   11:1–14:45
    B. Divine comfort   15:1-36
A+B. Conclusion   15:37-41

52. Budd, *Numbers*, pp. 162, 281.

Apostasy — The Golden Calf (Exod 32:1-35)
    Discontent — Taberah/Quail (Num 11:1-35)
        Insubordination — Individuals (Num 12:1-16)
            Insubordination — Israel (Num 13:1–14:45)
        Insubordination — Individuals (Num 16:1-35)
    Discontent — Serpents (Num 21:4-9)
Apostasy — Baal-Peor (Num 25:1-5)

it for his own theological framework. Consequently, the chiastic pattern of the Yahwist's material has been modified into a threefold pattern of setbacks and successes. Budd, however, provides little discussion on the process of this modification, as if there were no serious conceptual conflict between the Yahwist and the Priestly materials. For instance, he does not explain the arrangement of chapter 20, where the Yahwist's account of the Israelites' encounter with Edom (20:14-21) is cut in the middle by the Priestly account of the third major sin, namely, the sin of Moses and Aaron (20:1-13, 22-29). His silence on this kind of structural question stems both from his oversimplification of the Yahwist material and from his overemphasis on the assumed historical setting of the Priestly authorship.

The oversimplification of the Yahwist's materials is obvious in Budd's proposed chiastic pattern. Forcing dismantled traditions into a certain pattern tends to ignore or suppress and eventually leave out the tradition that does not fit the scheme. Budd's chiastic pattern leaves out 10:29-36; 21:1-3, 10-20, 21-35; 22:1–24:25, which he generally accepts from previous scholarship as JE traditions.[53] His pattern not only omits traditions but also violates the connectedness of the Yahwist's material with the Priestly material. They have been so interwoven that one cannot be understood without the other.[54] Unless all available data have been considered for a possible pattern, any formal pattern emerging out of fragmented sources should be questioned as to its validity and cannot be regarded as one that reflects the entirety of the sources.

Budd's overemphasis on the assumed historical setting of the Priestly authorship is a pervasive tendency throughout the commentary. In attempting to answer structural questions on Numbers, he refers without exception to the Priestly author (perhaps the author of Numbers), whose historical setting is postexilic. Depending heavily on this authorship inevitably leads Budd to outline Numbers according to theological themes and ultimately causes him to be unable to fulfill his exegetical claim that the present form of Numbers is the beginning point of investigation. Budd even goes on to psychologically analyze the Priestly author when he reconstructs the postexilic societal background. In short, Budd's outline, which covers only chapters 1–35, is theologically predetermined.

---

53. Budd, *Numbers*, pp. 113-14, 229-30, 237-39, 243-46, 256-65, respectively.

54. The whole eighteen verses of 25:1-18 have been designated by Budd as "Apostasy at Shittim." Although vv. 1-5 belong to JE, they have been altered significantly by the rest of the verses, which belong to P. By cutting vv. 1-5 and giving them a corresponding place in the chiastic scheme of the Yahwistic tradition, he distorts the nature of vv. 1-5, which can only be understood in the context of vv. 1-18. Moreover, his separation of 21:4-9 from the other Yahwist traditions, such as 21:1-3 and 21:10-20, cannot do justice to either vv. 4-9 or the whole context of 21:1-20.

4. Dennis T. Olson

Similar in primary observation but differing significantly in detail from Budd, Olson claims that the book of Numbers has a "convincing and meaningful structure."[55] Olson's claim for the superstructure of Numbers is based on the compositional signal formed by the two census reports in chapters 1 and 26. These reports mark a clear transition from the old generation who came out of the land of Egypt to the new generation about to enter the promised land. This compositional signal illuminates the governing concept, theological in nature, underneath the book of Numbers, that is, the death of the old generation in the wilderness for their distrusting Yahweh and the birth of the new generation whose hope to enter the promised land still remains a possibility. Not only his division of Numbers into two parts, chapters 1–25 and chapters 26–36, but also his arguments for this division demand a more thorough and critical evaluation than previous scholarship has given. A systematized discussion of Olson's proposals will be presented in three sections: (a) methodological questions; (b) evidence for the census lists in Numbers 1 and 26 as the macrostructural signal; and (c) an overall assessment of Olson's thesis.

a. Methodological Questions

In detecting the structure of Numbers, Olson takes seriously the present form of Numbers as "a book, a separate literary entity," although he acknowledges its integral relationship to the Pentateuch as a whole.[56] To argue for the literary distinctiveness of Numbers at the outset is for him a methodological judgment that Numbers as it stands is the beginning point for structural inquiry. Note his constant use of these three expressions: the structure of "the final canonical form," "the final form," and "the present form." All connote the same thing. They refer to the Masoretic Text of *Leningradensis* as repre-

---

55. Olson, *The Death of the Old and the Birth of the New*, p. 1.

56. Olson, *The Death of the Old and the Birth of the New*, p. 43. Perceiving Numbers as a literary entity presupposes a conceptual unity. As seen in the previous scholarship, there is ambiguity in the usage of outline and structure. Olson employs these terms interchangeably most of the time, but he seems to perceive more in the term "structure" when he conjoins it with the term "concept," as in "The core of the structural or conceptual framework of the book (p. 34)." What he ultimately does in his book is to provide a conceptual or structural analysis of Numbers, and yet he does not clarify the terms used, and he employs them interchangeably or unconsciously throughout the book.

sented in the *Biblia Hebraica Stuttgartensia* text. This text is the basis of and the starting point for his structural analysis.[57]

This point is obvious in Olson's forceful argument for the present canonical fivefold division of the Pentateuch. Its division, Olson holds, legitimates the literary distinctiveness of Numbers. He substantiates the claim with evidence drawn from outside and inside Numbers.[58] As external evidence, the rabbinical tradition, the Hebrew textual tradition, and the Greek textual tradition all bear "the antiquity and unanimity of the tradition" of the Pentateuch's fivefold division. Logically, the compositional nature of Numbers as one of the five divisions and as a separate literary entity in relation to the other four has been established in antiquity. In other words, "antiquity" has been used as a decisive criterion or even as a concept for Numbers as a literary entity independent from the rest of the Pentateuch. If this line of argument stands, the very thrust of seeing Numbers as a literary unit betrays his methodological procedure. Since the antiquity of the fivefold division of the Pentateuch constitutes the antiquity of Numbers as a separate unit, the structure of Numbers depends on the structure of the Pentateuch. Without identifying the overall structure of the whole, the structure of an individual unit can falsify what the individual unit defines for itself. The Pentateuch as a whole should be the starting point for the structural analysis of any one of its five books. Olson fundamentally undercuts his own thesis that Numbers is the beginning point for the investigation of its structure.[59]

For internal evidence, Olson investigates only the endings and beginnings

---

57. Olson scarcely mentions the MT as the text for his analysis. But his preference for the MT is undoubted because of the absence of any other text established on the basis of textual criticism. For example, there is no discussion of whether his text belongs to one of four distinctly different periods in the textual history of the Old Testament: Urtext, textual fluidity, textual stability, and Masoretic. Cf. J. A. Sanders, "Hermeneutics of Text Criticism," in *Textus: Annual of the Hebrew University Bible Project*, vol. 18 (Jerusalem: Magnes, Hebrew University Press, 1997), pp. 7-10.

58. Olson, *The Death of the Old and the Birth of the New*, pp. 43-53.

59. Olson unknowingly starts from the editorial intention of the Pentateuch as a whole when he argues that the *toledot* formulae are the criterion for the structure of the Pentateuch (*The Death of the Old and the Birth of the New*, pp. 97-118). Moreover, if Olson's line of argument has any validity, it may be implemented further in subdividing the book of Numbers. As the tradition of the five divisions of the Pentateuch is ancient, the tradition of the division into paragraphs and verses is also attested from the early manuscripts, although there is no unanimity in the marking system of these divisions among many of the manuscripts and printed editions. Olson, then, should subdivide Numbers according to the markers represented within the present canonical form, which he does not do in his book. See the detailed explanation of these systems of division at #74-78 in I. Yeivin's book, *Introduction to the Tiberian Masorah*, trans. and ed. E. J. Revell, Masoretic Studies 5 (Chico, CA: Scholars Press, 1980), pp. 40-44.

of each book of the Pentateuch.[60] For the transition from Leviticus to Numbers, Olson highlights both geographical and theological differences. Yahweh spoke "*enduring* legal precepts" at the top of *Mount Sinai* as indicated at the end of Leviticus (27:34), whereas Yahweh now speaks "the *one* time" in the *wilderness of Sinai* as at the beginning of Numbers (1:1). Olson succinctly states that

> [a]*t the beginning of Numbers,* the elevated and stationary site of God's revelation on the mountain has been transferred in a decisive transition to a moveable site of revelation in the midst of the people in the wilderness [emphasis added].[61]

The decisive transition of locality from Mount Sinai to the wilderness of Sinai occurs in Numbers 1:1, according to Olson. Not accounting for possible "successive editings" in these endings and beginnings and depending solely on the occurrence of a particular phrase reflect not only Olson's tendency in treating textual evidence but also his stress on the present canonical shape of the text.

His argument, however, is not entirely convincing.[62] The presupposi-

---

60. These endings and beginnings are for Olson editorial and redactional devices that indicate the separateness of each book in the Pentateuch. Diverse criteria have been used for signaling major transitions from one book to another. The transitions from Genesis to Exodus and Exodus to Leviticus are marked by content analysis, whereas that from Numbers to Deuteronomy, by the distinctive vocabulary and style of Deuteronomy.

61. Olson, *The Death of the Old and the Birth of the New,* p. 49. No distinction between geography and topography is highlighted by Olson. The mountain of Sinai is a topographical reference, whereas the wilderness of Sinai is geographical. The relationship between the two is that the wilderness of Sinai includes Mount Sinai, not vice versa.

62. The wilderness of Sinai occurs in Lev 7:38; Num 1:1, 19; 3:4, 14; 9:1, 5; 10:12; 26:64; 33:15, 16, whereas the Mount of Sinai in Lev 7:38; 25:1; 26:46; 27:34; Num 3:1; 28:6. For a discussion of these occurrences, see pp. 92-94 in the present study. A generic identification of Num 1:1 will enhance the argument.

Introductory statement to a Yahweh speech	Num 1:1
I. Speech report formula	1aα1
II. Specifications	1aα2-b
A. Locally	1aα2-β
1. The wilderness of Sinai	1aα2
2. The tent of meeting	1aβ
B. Temporally	1b
1. Day and month	1bα
a. Day	1bα1
b. Month	1bα2
2. Year with reference to Exodus	1bβ
a. Year	1bβ1
b. Reference to Exodus	1bβ2

tion or implication to which these phrases (Mount Sinai and the wilderness of Sinai) allude must be discussed before making any claim. Numbers 1:1 has two localities: במדבר סיני and באהל מועד. As a functional identification, the former is an explicit redactional signal demonstrating the fact that Yahweh is said to have spoken in the wilderness and not on the mountain. It implies the parameters of the broader pericope that is bracketed on the one end by the entrance of the Israelites into the wilderness of Sinai before Yahweh's settling on the mountain (Exod 19:3) and on the other end by their leaving the wilderness of Sinai (Num 10:11ff.). Regarding the locality, the function of the latter is the same as the former. The latter must then be understood in the same way: Yahweh spoke to Moses in the tent of meeting located in the wilderness of Sinai. Note that the same locative, prepositional prefix ב provides grammatical evidence for this point.

The crucial question is, At what point did Yahweh speak to Moses in the tent of meeting and not on Mount Sinai? Olson's argument would say that it is from Numbers 1:1 on, but this position cannot stand because of the dependence of Numbers 1:1 on Leviticus 1:1, where Yahweh called Moses and spoke to him "from the tent of meeting" (מאהל מועד). Of course, the phrase "the wilderness of Sinai" that Olson looks for is absent from Leviticus 1:1. But the wilderness of Sinai as the location of the tent of meeting in Leviticus 1:1 is not only properly assumed, considering the imaginable hardship of erecting the tabernacle on the top of a mountain, but also substantiated exegetically.[63] After receiving Yahweh's instruction regarding the erection of the tabernacle on Mount Sinai, Moses is in the camp (whose location is "before the mountain" [Exod 19:3]) to execute divine instruction (Exod 34:29–39:43). From that time on there is no occurrence of Moses ascending or descending from Mount Sinai. The book of Exodus ends with reports of the erection of the tent of meeting and its inhabitation by the divine presence (40:1-38). These two factors are presupposed in Leviticus 1:1. Yahweh now called and spoke to Moses from the tent of meeting erected in the midst of camp, not from Mount Sinai as in Exodus 24:16-18 and 25:1. Therefore, the events and laws recorded in Leviticus depend on this topological context.

The transition from Mount Sinai to the tabernacle in the camp assumed in Leviticus 1:1 is, however, in clear conflict with various places in Leviticus, including the ending of the book (27:34). Olson chooses empirical evidence

---

63. R. P. Knierim, *Text and Concept in Leviticus 1:1-9: A Case in Exegetical Method* (Tübingen: J. C. B. Mohr, 1992), pp. 6-7; see also his article "The Composition of the Pentateuch," in *The Task of Old Testament Theology: Substance, Method, and Cases* (Grand Rapids: Eerdmans, 1995), pp. 360-72. Note that both texts use different locatives, propositional prefixes: מאהל מועד (Lev 1:1) and באהל מועד (Num 1:1).

provided in Leviticus 27:34 and Numbers 1:1 because of his emphasis on the final shape of the divisions. Even while he attributes the existing conflict to the long process of formation of the Pentateuch, Olson's empirical reason cannot override the exegetical evidence of Numbers 1:1, Leviticus 1:1, and Exodus 19–40. The concept behind Leviticus 1:1, that is, a new revelatory epoch in the movement of Yahweh from the mountain to the tent of meeting, which Numbers 1:1 clearly depends on, is superordinate to the occurrence of the phrase "Mount Sinai" in Leviticus 27:34.

Subsequently, Olson's methodology regarding the present final form of Numbers as the starting point of structural analysis implies a significant undercutting of his aim to discern the definitive literary and theological structure of Numbers. He states: ". . . the definitive shaping of the book's structure occurred *earlier than the final form* but was carried forward in its essentials and enriched by successive editings until the book reached its present shape [emphasis added]."[64] Accordingly, he searches for the definitive structure of Numbers, which has been formed earlier than the final "shape" of the book of Numbers, on the basis of its final "form." With little hesitation he carries this position consistently. For instance, he asserts that the early stage within the formation of the Priestly tradition is the relative date for the overall definitive structure for Numbers. The structure is signaled by two census lists in Numbers 1 and 26 whose definitive function was retained in the course of later editings.[65] This seeming simplification stems from his inclusion of a traditio-historical perspective. With this inclusion he is fully aware of its presupposition of long and continual editorial activities in the process of forming the book, but he seems unaware of its subsequent implication that an earlier established structure may have been modified or altered in the process. Consequently, it is questionable whether the structure of the final shape of the book coincides with that of the previous stage, however relatively its stages are defined. No guarantee can be claimed for the fact that the structure extricated from the present shape of the book is identical to the structure which the book defines for itself. Which structure in the multi-layered stages of Numbers is Olson's actual aim? His predominantly tendentious reading of textual

---

64. Olson, *The Death of the Old and the Birth of the New*, p. 2. This point is affirmed in his later statement: "We need not assume that it was necessarily the last or final editing of the book which provided this definitive structure" (p. 83).

65. Olson (*The Death of the Old and the Birth of the New*, p. 89) states: ". . . it is quite possible that the writer who was responsible for constructing the census lists and for placing them in their present positions within the narrative (perhaps the early stage of the Priestly tradition) was not the same writer or editor who formulated the geographical or chronological indicators which preceded the census list (perhaps a later stage of the Priestly tradition or other editor)."

evidence, his accounting for "successive editings" only when they support his thesis, and his admitted difficulty in dating "absolutely or relatively" each layer of the Priestly tradition all point to the fact that his actual aim is the structure of the final shape of Numbers, not a structure that has been definitely shaped earlier than the final form, as he claims. In other words, his own statements indicate that he aims for a secondary structure rather than the one which Numbers itself presents. His rigid treatment of Leviticus 27:34 and Numbers 1:1 at face value is the prime example for this point. In so doing, he actually discovers the structure of the final form of Numbers. But this is not the same as the one that has been determinative for the final form of the macrostructure of Numbers and that opens a possibility for a few more insertions but has not been altered by them.

b. Evidence for the Census Lists in Numbers 1 and 26 as the Macrostructural Signal

Olson provides three kinds of evidence for the census lists in Numbers 1 and 26 as the macrostructural signal for the structure of Numbers. Two of them, formal indicators and his analysis of theme and content, stem from the book of Numbers itself, whereas the third, "the signs of intentional editorial" devices, stems from the context of the Priestly tradition of Genesis through Numbers.[66] His discussions, however, possess few serious exegetical merits and are purely superficial readings of the text. In this way, he acquires a theological hermeneutic of Numbers and imposes it on the text. This inevitably leads him to suppress or ignore other textual evidence. For example, he categorizes "after the plagues" in Numbers 26:1 as a chronological signal indicating the theological meaning of "after the death of the rest of the first generation." Because of the assumed structural significance of Numbers 26, this phrase has a special theological meaning, and not the other way around. The same logic applies to "in the plains of Moab by the Jordan at Jericho" in Numbers 26:3. For Olson, this is a geographical notation for the new generation, in contrast with the beginning of the old generation in the wilderness. He does not even mention 22:1, where the text says that the Israelites encamped "in the plains of Moab beyond the Jordan at Jericho." If this locality

---

66. Olson, *The Death of the Old and the Birth of the New,* pp. 83-118. Proportionally, Olson spends thirteen pages (pp. 84-97) on the first two evidences, while the rest of the discussion (pp. 97-118) deals with the overall Priestly editorial intention for the larger context of Genesis to Numbers as a whole.

communicates the meaning he suggests, Numbers 22:1 should be the point of the beginning of the new generation. But Olson's silence on 22:1 indicates that Numbers 26 constitutes the locality of the Israelites, not the other way around.

Moreover, Olson argues that in the two census lists linguistic similarities and the same sequence of censuses (the twelve-tribe census first and the Levite census second) provide a symmetrical pattern for Numbers. Yet symmetry means correspondence in size, shape, and relative positions of parts that are on opposite sides of a dividing line. That the two sides of the division must have evenly distributed materials in the bipartite division of a whole illustrates his incorporation of the term symmetry as inaccurate. He also misuses the term "parallel" when he argues that Numbers has parallels between the two halves of the book demarcated by chapter 26. Having some corresponding materials does not mean that the two halves are parallels. They do not have identical syntactic elements in corresponding positions, nor do they extend in the same direction and at the same distance apart at every point. Misemploying terms naturally enhances Olson's tendency to read the text superficially. No indication of a close reading of the text can be found. Even the cohesiveness within each half of the book, as he claims, is strictly based on an empirical survey of the content of each rather than on the accumulation of exegetical results from studies of component parts of the whole.[67]

For the third type of evidence, Olson argues that the *toledot* formulae and the wilderness itineraries are signs of conscious editorial shaping of not only Numbers but the entire Pentateuch. His argument can be summarized as follows:

1. Functions of the *toledot* formula in Numbers 3:1, extended from those in Genesis, are: first, as superscription introducing significant turning points in the Priestly narrative; second, the continual narrowing circle of people, from the heavens and the earth to Adam and Noah and to Abraham, Isaac, and Jacob, to Aaron and Moses, and at the same time including all people in the important events in the life of the community.

2. The *toledot* formulae provide an overarching redactional structure for the Pentateuch which recounts the death of one generation and the birth of a new generation. The final goal of the *toledot* series of succeeding generations within the Pentateuch, then, is the new generation

---

67. Olson's argument on thematic or content indicators cannot escape from this criticism; thus no further comment is necessary.

which starts in Numbers 26. But no new *toledot* formula is required in Numbers 26 since the focus remains fixed on all the descendants within the *toledot* of Jacob, the twelve tribes of Israel, and that of Aaron and Moses.

3. No conflict with the editorial division of the Pentateuch into five books is assumed. The wilderness itinerary notices play a secondary role in subdividing the sections introduced by the *toledot* formulae and genealogies.[68]

A categorical evaluation of these points is in order. First, contrary to previous scholarship, Olson's contribution lies in his persistent inquiry of the role and function of these indicators in the present form of the text. However, as discussed above, the principle of Numbers as the methodological starting point has been completely ignored. The *toledot* formula in Numbers 3:1 has been understood from the vantage point of the concept of succeeding generations implied in the series of genealogies in Genesis. The ever-narrowing circle of people up to Aaron and Moses is due to the redactional intention of the Priestly writer, according to Olson. Even in Numbers the location of 3:1 between the census reports of the twelve tribes (Num 1–2) and of the Levites (Num 3–4) has special meaning, according to Olson, portrayed by the *toledot* formulae in Genesis, that is, a movement of narrowing and a countermovement of widening. Moreover, relative to the census list in Numbers 1, the census list in Numbers 26 is greatly expanded and further segmented into subclans. This relationship between these two census lists is understood as analogous to the relationship between Genesis 35:22-26 and Genesis 46:8-27, which signal important turning points from one generation to another. In summary, the analyses of the *toledot* formulae in Genesis define the meaning, function, and location of Numbers 3:1 in the book of Numbers. Methodologically, the framework of the larger Priestly narrative based on the series of *toledot* formulae is the criterion for the structure of Numbers in which Numbers 3:1 occupies a focal point.

Second, the interrelationship among the *toledot* formulae, the genealogies, and the tribal lists in Genesis, as well as in Numbers 1–4 and 26, is not en-

---

68. Olson, *The Death of the Old and the Birth of the New*, pp. 97-125. A few points for Num 3:1 are:

a. redactor's inclusion of "Mount Sinai" due to the list of all four sons of Aaron in 3:2, thus not in conflict with "the wilderness of Sinai" in 1:1;

b. the order of Aaron and Moses due to their fraternal relationship in the Priestly forms of Levitical genealogy, and the inclusion of Moses in the present text referring to all events that happened to Israel under the leadership of Aaron and Moses; and

c. this formula stems from those in Genesis.

tirely clear. Which one is determinative for which? All three are for Olson interrelated with a simple empirical instance of the occurrence of similar terms. Structurally, the *toledot* formula in Numbers 3:1 should be the macrostructural signal if it shares meaning and function with those in Genesis. Then, the structure of the Pentateuch would have to be constructed accordingly. Two examples can be extracted from his discussions.[69]

Structure one (based on the *toledot* of Jacob as "the most important one"):

I. Generations up to the *toledot* of Jacob	Gen 1–Exod 1:7
II. Generations after the *toledot* of Jacob	Exod 1:8–Deut 34
A. Events up to the *toledot* of Aaron and Moses	Exod 1:8–Num 2
B. Events after the *toledot* of Aaron and Moses	Num 3:1–Deut 34
1. Old generation	Num 3:1–Num 25
2. New generation	Num 26–Deut 34

Structure two (based on the new generation as "the final goal of the *toledot* series within the Pentateuch"):

I. Preparation: generations up to end of "the Exodus generation"	Gen 1–Num 25
II. Goal: the new generation	Num 26–Deut 34

These two structures are based on the concept of succeeding generations signaled by the series of *toledot* formulae in the Pentateuch. Olson claims that this grand framework of the Priestly tradition is "consistent with the definitive structure of the book of Numbers in its present form."[70] Yet his proposal of a bipartite structure, the end of the old generation (Num 1:1–25:18) and the birth of the new generation (Num 26:1–36:13), is quite different and presupposes the census report, not the *toledot* formula, as its criterion. The clear discrepancy between what he discusses and what he actually proposes as a result of that discussion cannot be ignored.

The continuation of this discrepancy is the third point of evaluation. Olson outlines the Pentateuch not based on his theme, the death of the old and the birth of the new, but on its fivefold division, and claims that it does not destroy but rather complements the generational framework. Two completely different criteria have been used. The fivefold division of the Penta-

---

69. Olson, *The Death of the Old and the Birth of the New*, pp. 98-114.
70. Olson, *The Death of the Old and the Birth of the New*, p. 114.

teuch is superordinate to the *toledot* formulae, creating an intolerable confusion in his argument.

c. An Overall Assessment of Olson's Thesis

Olson's theological hermeneutic, found in the larger context of the Priestly tradition, dominates the execution of his goal to find the literary and theological structure of Numbers. The tasks of finding and evaluating textual evidence serve the assumed theme (the death of the old and the birth of the new). It is clear even from the beginning of the book that he surveys previous scholarship with the intention of finding their contribution to the theology of Numbers. His answers to compositional questions and his proposed conceptuality behind the proposed outline do not stand on their own grounds, but always serve to sustain his theological theme.

Silence on the literary growth of Leviticus 27:34 leads him to designate an inadequate theological context for Leviticus as a whole and for the chronological notation at Numbers 3:1. The expanded genealogy in Numbers 26 has been colored theologically in that it indicates a partial fulfillment of the patriarchal promise of Yahweh. The high numbers of the census express the gracious extent of Yahweh's blessing of Israel. In content analysis, is the death of the old generation a correct characterization of the events in Numbers 1–10, which are described in an entirely positive tone?[71] If the new generation does not appear until chapter 26, the future orientation of the laws (chapters

---

71. The positive tone of Num 1:1–10:10 is well demonstrated in the fact that it contains many divine instructions, followed by an execution formula such as "just as the Lord commanded Moses" (1:19; cf. 1:54; 2:33, 34; 3:16, 42, 51; 4:49; 8:3, 20, 22; 9:5, 18, 20, 23). Olson, however, points out that the text also contains "brief warnings about the possibility of death" (3:4, 10; 4:15, 18, 20; 5:2; 6:6-7; 8:17, 19; 9:1-14) underneath the surface of "all the command and fulfillment assurances" (*Numbers*, p. 58). For him, Numbers 1–10 is "a dialogue of two narrative voices. . . . One dominant voice speaks optimistically of repetitive compliance, calm order, and unquestioning faithfulness. The second narrative voice speaks in muted but foreboding tones of lurking powers, divine dangers, and deathly possibilities" (*Numbers*, p. 59, cf. p. 192). Because of its second voice, which foreshadows the coming rebellions and deaths in Numbers 11–25, he may argue that it is integral to and tied to Numbers 11–25 and fits appropriately under the rubric of the death of the old generation. If this is the case, should the books of Exodus and Leviticus, where the similar warnings appear, be regarded as part of "the death of the old generation"? Are these warnings in Numbers 1–10 supposed to be applicable only to the old generation? Whether the voice of warning exists is one thing, and whether it functions significantly in the quest of structure of Numbers is another. In fact, as Olson himself recognizes, the second voice is subordinated to the "dominant" voice expressing positively the correspondence of divine command and Israel's execution.

15 and 19), the defeat of Kings Sihon and Og (21:21-35), and the defeat of the Canaanites (21:1-3), whom the Israelites were unable to defeat in 14:39-45, all seem hardly to belong to the old generation destined to be exterminated in the wilderness.[72] Moreover, how can both the strategic location of the story of Balaam right after the Israelites' encampment "in the plains of Moab beyond the Jordan at Jericho" (22:1) and its message displaying Yahweh's universal power on behalf of the Israelites be incorporated into Olson's structure? These are only a few examples of that which is more clearly shown in his detailed structural outline of the book of Numbers. His diagram does not reflect the literary function of the *toledot* formula in Numbers 3:1, which plays a key role in connecting the two census lists to genealogies and tribal lists in Genesis. Structurally, the second part is deficient due to the fact that no text corresponds to II.B.[73] Since II.B. is essential for his scheme of the whole, Olson's structure of Numbers ultimately collapses. This defect indicates that the theme of the new generation goes beyond Numbers into Deuteronomy.[74]

---

72. It is conceivable that the hopeful signs of chs. 15 and 19 and the victories of ch. 21 testify to a God who remains faithful to promises and blesses the old generation of Israelites in spite of their rebellions. Of course, the fact that God is faithful to his promises, blesses constantly, and works toward a future even in the face of a rebellious people appears throughout the Old Testament. But the question raised by these texts is not whether God will fulfill the promise he made to Israel's ancestors. Rather, the question is how God is going to fulfill his promise to them. God intends to fulfill his promise through the new generation of Israelites while punishing the old due to their constant and chronic rebellions. Numbers 13–14 narrates that this is the way that God has decided with an oath (14:21, 28).

73.   II. The birth of the new: the second generation of God's people
      out of Egypt as they prepare to enter the promised land   Num 26:1–36:13
    A. The preparation and organization of the new holy people
      of God as they prepare to enter the promised land   Num 26:1–36:13
    B. Will this second generation be faithful and enter the
      promised land (promise) or rebel and fail as the first
      generation did (warning)?   ???????

74. Note that the historical review in Deut 1:6–3:29 indicates essentially the Israelites' failure to trust in Yahweh up until the day when Moses spoke: "In the fortieth year, on the first day of the eleventh month" (1:3). Note also that the speeches of Moses in Deuteronomy show a hermeneutical concern and effort to identify the addressee (i.e., the new generation) with the old generation of Israelites: "The Lord our God made a covenant with us at Horeb. Not with our ancestors . . . but with us, who are all of us here alive today" (Deut 5:2-3). What does this identification imply? Is it a rhetorical device indicating that Moses in Deuteronomy retells the story of a past generation as if the new generation was there? Or, does it mean Deuteronomy understands that the present new generation was included in the past history, which is essentially a failure, and hence that the new generation failed as the first Exodus generation did? Olson understands the former by characterizing the new generation in Numbers 26–36 as an obedient

In short, the fact that Olson pays attention to the differences between generations is commendable. But he seeks to prove this idea with mixed perspectives and criteria, and finally by pressing the evidence according to his preconceived idea. His exegesis does not let the textual evidence support or undercut and even reconceptualize his own idea. Ideas should not be idealized. In the end, his structure of Numbers is a theological imposition on the text which is, as a result, unable to be substantiated and cannot account for the compositional signals that Numbers provides.

5. Jacob Milgrom

In his commentary, Jacob Milgrom presents the possibility of multiple structures existing in the book of Numbers.[75] At a macrostructural level, at least three different structures pose themselves side by side, according to Milgrom. The first structure is based on "topographical and chronological data."

I. The wilderness of Sinai	Num 1:1–10:10
II. The vicinity of Kadesh	Num 10:11–20:13
III. From Kadesh to the steppes of Moab	Num 20:14–36:13

---

one in contrast to the first disobedient generation. His position may be reinforced by the editorial statements in Judg 2:7-10 where the new generation of Numbers is clearly contrasted with a later generation "who did not know the Lord or the work that he had done for Israel." For him, the new generation from Numbers 26 to Judg 2:10 is so obedient and faithful, unlike other generations, that they are completely immune from any sort of rebellions, disobedience, and failures. It implies that they deserve the promised land; hence God's fulfillment of the land promise is now dependent on the characters of generations of Israelites, not on God's own faithfulness. But this trajectory ignores the series of warnings in the deuteronomic laws (e.g., warnings about the temptation of pride, self-sufficiency, and self-righteousness in chs. 8–10), Achan's sin, which caused Israel's defeat at Ai (Josh 7), and the incomplete conquest of the promised land (Josh 13–24; Judg 1:1–2:5). If these texts are taken seriously, Olson's argument of the beginning of the new generation at Number 26 would be severely undermined. On the contrary, Deuteronomy's frequent use of "this day" or "today" and its identification of the present addressee with the old generation should indicate something beyond a simple narrative actualization. It means that the new generation is part of the history of the old generation because they are themselves as rebellious as the old generation.

75. Milgrom, *Numbers*. Milgrom provides a comprehensive discussion on the matter from methodology to theology in his "Introduction" (pp. xi-xlii). See also his article, "Numbers, book of." Other commentaries include two different outlines. See G. Barton and M. Seligsohn, "Numbers, book of," in *The Jewish Encyclopedia,* ed. I. Singer et al. (New York: Funk and Wagnalls, 1905), pp. 343-46 and J. J. Owens, "Numbers," in *Leviticus-Ruth,* The Broadman Bible Commentary, ed. C. J. Allen et al., vol. 2 (Nashville: Abingdon, 1970), pp. 75, 80-83.

Milgrom does not specify the time that the Israelites spent in each section. However, it can be assumed to be, as by Gray, nineteen days, almost thirty-eight years, and no more than five months, respectively, for each section, although the delimitation of the second and third sections differ from that of Gray (10:11–21:9; 21:10–36:13). Instead of the 'Arabah in Gray, Milgrom chooses Kadesh as the topographical indicator dividing Numbers 10:11–36:13.

A few difficulties emerge from this first structure. While Kadesh is correctly designated as topographical in its description, it is inappropriately compared with the wilderness of Sinai and the steppes of Moab, which are geographical descriptions. The wilderness of Paran might have been a better choice for him, since it refers to the northern half of the Sinai Peninsula whose northern boundary is Kadesh-barnea. Moreover, like Gray, Milgrom does not account for other geographical indicators that Numbers provides.[76] This criticism implies that the foremost constitutive criterion for this structure is something other than what Milgrom claims. Note that the parameter of the second section, 10:11–20:13, includes not only the events that happened in the vicinity of Kadesh but also the Israelites' journey from Sinai to Kadesh (10:11–12:16). The same is evident in the third section, which includes their journey from Kadesh to the steppes of Moab (20:14–22:1). These data suggest that each section focuses on what went on in an area rather than where something happened. It is not a record of the geography of the Israelites' wandering from Sinai to the steppes of Moab, but rather a record of what happened during their wandering.

The second structure is based on the two generations that the forty years embrace. Milgrom reiterates major points of Olson's content and thematic analysis without critical evaluation of Olson's thesis as a whole. This structure comes into the foreground in the body of Milgrom's exegesis.

  I. The generation of the Exodus   1:1–25:19
     A. The organization of the wilderness camp   1:1–10:10
     B. The march from Sinai to Transjordan   10:11–25:19
  II. The generation of the conquest   26:1–36:13

There are seven units in I.A., eight in I.B., and nine in II, which have been arrayed in a row without portraying any structural hierarchy among them. Unlike Olson, Milgrom follows the traditional delimitation of the Sinai pericope as ending in 10:10 and presupposes a more specific concept for "the new generation," that is, the generation of the conquest, one of the five major themes

---

76. See p. 10 (n. 23) in the present study.

of the Pentateuch developed by Noth. In this structure, Milgrom borrows the form (the two generation scheme) from Olson yet abandons his conceptuality to embrace the traditional duality of the Israelites' activities after Sinaitic revelation and preparations for entering the promised land.

Milgrom's third structure is twofold: I. Leviticus 1–Numbers 10:10 and II. Numbers 10:11–36:13. He develops his third structure from his theological-literary structure of the Hexateuch, which "takes the form of a grand inversion, ABCDEFG X G'F'E'D'C'B'A'."[77] Whereas section I corresponds to Exodus 19–24 regarding the theme of covenant regulations, section II corresponds to Exodus 15:22–18:27 and its theme of wilderness wandering. These themes are at best general descriptions of the text, but not the governing concept operative underneath the text. Contrary to Exodus 15:22–18:27, which concerns the continual moving of the Israelites, Numbers 10:11–36:13 stresses their stationary activities, which by nature are preparations for entering the land. In his macrostructure of the Hexateuch, Milgrom's section E (covenant regulations: Exod 19–24) contains both cultic and civil laws, whereas Leviticus very much consists of cultic laws alone and Numbers 1–10 of discrete materials that cannot be called covenant regulations.

Moreover, his graphic "grand inversion" pattern for the Hexateuch in itself does not necessarily indicate either the composition or the structure of the Hexateuch. The simple presence of an introverted chiastic pattern has no more than an artistic function for the material to which it refers. This pattern must be qualified by a concept in order to point to its intent. Milgrom provides this concept, that is, the transition from slavery to freedom pivoting on the presence of Yahweh in Exodus 33, although he seems unaware of it. Why is Yahweh's presence in the golden bull incident "crucial"? Why are not other in-

---

77. See Milgrom, *Numbers*, pp. xvii-xviii. At least three major difficulties exist in Milgrom's proposal. First, not accounting for Genesis 1–11 and the book of Deuteronomy as a whole undercuts severely his emphasis on a synchronic reading of the text. Do these parts play any role in the presentation of the Hexateuch? What is the significance of the location of these parts for an understanding of the Hexateuch as a whole? If the theme of the book of Deuteronomy is covenant renewed, as he indicates, why does it not correspond to Exodus 34 (F') whose theme is also covenant renewed? How does his exploration of interdependency of sources in Exodus, Numbers, and Deuteronomy (p. xxi) explain this omission? Second, materials in each section are proportionally unbalanced. Note each of G, X, and G' consists of only one chapter, while, for instance, section A consists of thirty-eight chapters. Third, the themes for each section have been defined by purely empirical reasons. Looking only at the selected phrases or words for each section, which supposedly correspond to other sections in this chiastic pattern, reinforces this point clearly. Do these words or phrases represent the concept of the whole pericope? In summary, Milgrom's proposal is an imposition of a chiastic pattern onto the variety of materials in the Hexateuch.

cidents crucial, such as Yahweh's presence in the so-called burning bush or in the tent of meeting, which indicates a dramatic shift of divine presence with the Israelites? Milgrom's silence on this question suggests that his choice of the concept is at best an abstraction from the reality of the text and cannot be substantiated by textual evidence. Furthermore, granting that Milgrom notices a number of "key concepts, terms, and phrases that mark the symmetrical sections"[78] for his chiastic pattern, there nonetheless remain other features (such as substantive conceptualities) of the structure of Numbers 10:11–36:13 and the Hexateuch as a whole which could override the chiastic impulse. By utilizing chiasm, essentially a stylistic convention, Milgrom at best understands the structure of Numbers by virtue of the substantive and compositional qualities of its correspondences in the chiastic pattern. The question of the structural unity of Numbers still remains unanswered.

Finally, but by far not unimportantly, these three structures are simply set one after the other. Considering the purpose of the JPS Torah Commentary series, Milgrom wants to combine or incorporate both traditional Jewish perspectives and the results of modern scholarship.[79] In so doing, he feels no necessity to present *the* structure of Numbers but provides as many options as possible. This tendency is clearly evident in his exposition of the theology of Numbers as abstracted from the content rather than from the proposed two succeeding generations structure. The first two structures stem from a conceptual system based on the surface text, although the criterion for each structure is different, whereas the third stems from the inverse chiastic pattern of the larger Hexateuch. In short, in his commentary, particularly in the three proposed structures, Milgrom juxtaposes the results of both diachronic approaches (source, form, and tradition criticism) and synchronic approaches (redaction criticism, as particularly demonstrated in Olson) without significant synthesis.

6. Timothy R. Ashley

Among the most recent commentaries on Numbers, Ashley's deserves mention.[80] Ashley analyzes the text of Numbers in great philological, textual, and

---

78. Milgrom, *Numbers*, p. xvii.

79. Note diverse subsections within the "Introduction" that are not necessarily connected with each other, such as an alternation of law and narrative, different modes of the sources, and a variety of structural patterns of the units.

80. After Ashley's commentary, at least five new commentaries on Numbers have been published. These are Levine's *Numbers 21–36* (2000), which completes his two-volume com-

historical detail. With regard to the structure of Numbers, he starts with the final form of the text. Stating that this is "the most reasonable and practical approach," although these materials went through a long, complex history of transmission, Ashley argues that divine inspiration yields a literary consistency among diverse materials.[81] Claiming that "God was at work" in the final form as well as other stages in the composition of the text is one thing, but explaining how and by what principles God works is another, and needs to be examined.

Ashley employs the form-critical hierarchical configuration of the various groupings of the text for his presentation of "Analysis of Content," although he does not claim any influence of form criticism on his commentary.[82] Whether his usage of this system is coincidental or an unconscious adaptation due to its widespread acceptance within the guild of biblical scholarship is hard to judge. But the real questions are: Does he understand the implications or presuppositions underneath the system, or does his exegesis of the text reflect a form-critical approach on both the surface level and the substantive level?

In his "Analysis of Contents," Ashley divides Numbers into the following five sections.[83]

I.	Preparation for departure	1:1–10:10
II.	The journey from Mt. Sinai to Kadesh-barnea	10:11–12:16
III.	In and around Kadesh-barnea	13:1–19:22
IV.	The journey from Kadesh-barnea to the plains of Moab	20:1–22:1
V.	On the plains of Moab	22:2–36:13

There are several things to note about this outline. First, the title, "Analysis of Contents," implies his unawareness of a presupposition behind the system he uses. This presupposition is a complex hierarchical configuration that in itself

mentary on Numbers; Dozeman's "The Book of Numbers" (1998), which combines an exegetical analysis with a detailed exposition growing directly out of the analysis; Olson's *Numbers* (1996), which focuses on its literary and theological structures and movements; Sakenfeld's *Numbers* (1995), which addresses "the points that would be obscure or confusing to general readers, as well as . . . the ongoing importance of the material for aspects of Christian life"; and E. W. Davies's *Numbers* (1995), which presents "a general outline of the views of others" with some of his own conclusions.

81. Ashley, *The Book of Numbers*, p. 7.

82. Ashley, *The Book of Numbers*, p. 15. Ashley uses the system developed and articulated by the editors (Knierim, Tucker, and Sweeney) of the FOTL commentary series: I. A. 1. a. (1). (a). etc.

83. Ashley, *The Book of Numbers*, pp. 15-17.

indicates implicit conceptualities as constitutive for the relationships among the components of the text. What he actually does is not to analyze the *contents* but to analyze *the structure*.

Second, the titles of this macrostructure are inconsistent or at least confusing. While the title of section I indicates the description of the contents of 1:1–10:10, the titles of sections II to V stress the locality of the movement and settlement of the Israelites' camp. As a result, these titles show that two conceptually different criteria have been used. If consistency were demanded, a title such as "In the wilderness of Sinai" would be appropriate for the first section.

Third, even if this demand were met, several conceptual confusions remain to be clarified. Like Gray, Olson, and Milgrom, Ashley does not distinguish topographical from geographical terms. He follows Milgrom in placing Kadesh-barnea, a topographical description, on the same level as the plains of Moab and perhaps the wilderness of Sinai, a geographical description.

Fourth, note that a distinction has been made between the Israelites' activity at the settled places and the Israelites' movement to the settled places. Titles of sections I, III, and V depict what happened when the Israelites settled in and around the wilderness of Sinai, Kadesh-barnea, and the plains of Moab, respectively, whereas those of sections II and IV describe what happened when they journeyed from Mount Sinai to Kadesh-barnea, and from Kadesh-barnea to the plains of Moab. Yet no distinction has been made to indicate whether these two are conceptually equal in their position in the macrostructure of Numbers. Which concept is more important? In other words, is the activity in and around the settled places superordinate to the activity on the way to the settled places or vice versa? Without any explanation Ashley simply juxtaposes them.

On the surface level, migration stories account for four chapters (10:11–12:16 and 20:1–22:1), while the settlement stories are told in thirty-two chapters (1:1–10:10, 13:1–19:22, and 22:2–36:13). This statistical observation, although not conclusive, suggests the different levels of importance accorded to these different sections. The stories in and around the wilderness of Sinai, Kadesh-barnea, and the plains of Moab seem to be more important in Numbers, whereas the travel in between appears to be subordinate.[84]

More substantively, both the migration and settlement stories point to

---

84. Ashley follows Wenham's principle for the arrangement of Numbers: the combination of three important eras of revelation, at Sinai, Kadesh, and in the plains of Moab, which are bridged by two separate travelogues. What Ashley does at this point is a simple addition of verses to Wenham's five major divisions. See Wenham, *Numbers: An Introduction and Commentary*, pp. 17-18.

the common undergirding concept, that is, the itinerary, recognized as the primary organizational device for the Moses story from the book of Exodus to the book of Deuteronomy.[85] In this long itinerary, from Rameses (Exod 12:37; Num 33:3) to the plains of Moab, "beyond the Jordan at Jericho" (Num 22:1; 33:49, 50; 36:13; cf. Deut 1:1-5), two locations have been conceptually prioritized: the wilderness of Sinai and the plains of Moab. They are more important than any other locations during the migration. By the same token, according to Ashley, the three locations have primary importance beyond all others in Numbers. The travel sections (10:11–12:16 and 20:1–22:1), then, "must be considered as pre-stages or presuppositions to their respective goals [events in and around the settled places], and as leading up to and being subservient to these goals."[86]

Even if this argument has any validity, allowing Ashley's structure of Numbers to be upgraded as one with three major sections based on the locations and two subordinate sections representing the transitions,[87] his structure needs further conceptualization. The fact that sections II and III consist of both migrations and events and the first section of only an event without migration suggests that something other than the concept of itinerary is responsible for this division. For the necessary criteria, Ashley supplies a theme, the process of orientation to new orientation via disorientation, depending on the mode of the Israelites' obedience to God. Consequently, he breaks Numbers into three constituent parts: I. Orientation (1:1–10:10), which stresses exact obedience to God; II. Disorientation (10:11–22:1), characterized by the Israelites' constant complaints and disobedience; and III. New Orientation (22:2–36:13), which focuses on the blessing of God in the promised land.[88] Not only does this structure stand alongside the description of the subsections in "Analysis of Contents," but its parts also do not correspond to any of those same descriptions. Ashley presents two totally different structures in his introduction, a theological thematic structure, on the one hand, and an itinerary structure, on the other.

---

85. Knierim, "The Composition of the Pentateuch," pp. 355-59.

86. Knierim, "The Composition of the Pentateuch," p. 356.

87.
I. The wilderness of Sinai	1:1–10:10
II. Kadesh-barnea	10:11–19:22
A. Migration from Mount Sinai to Kadesh-barnea	10:11–12:16
B. Events at Kadesh-barnea	13:1–19:22
III. The plains of Moab	20:1–36:13
A. Migration from Kadesh-barnea to the plains of Moab	20:1–22:1
B. Events in the plains of Moab	22:2–36:13

88. Ashley, *The Book of Numbers,* pp. 8-11.

Fifth, Ashley does not remain faithful to his thematic structure because he includes some pericopes that he characterizes differently than the main theme of the section. For example, the main theme of the second section is the Israelites' disobedience, yet it begins with 10:11-13, which reports that "the people leave the sacred mountain in *exact obedience* to the instructions in chapter 2," and with 10:14-36, which he summarizes: "*this obedience* to Yahweh is the way for Israel to maintain holiness and orientation" [emphases added].[89] Moreover, his uncritical adaptation of Olson's two-generational theme causes further confusion. Did the Exodus generation perish around Kadesh-barnea in chapters 16–19 or at the incident of the Baal of Peor in chapter 25? Or did the new orientation begin at 22:2 as his structure suggests, or at 26:1-51, which reports a new census ("it was now time for a new beginning in earnest . . . a *new* orientation because it is a *new* generation" [emphases original])?[90] Utilizing someone's thesis is one thing, but mixing ideas uncritically is another matter. Not only literary cohesion but also conceptual coherence are at stake here.

In summary, the five points argued above demonstrate clearly that what Ashley presents in his introduction is a compilation of previous scholarship on Numbers, particularly the quest for the structure of Numbers. G. J. Wenham's and Milgrom's influence on his five divisions is apparent, including three locations, two transitional migrations, and his choice of Kadesh as being equal in position to the wilderness of Sinai and the plains of Moab. W. Brueggemann, as Ashley acknowledges, provides his theme, the movement from orientation to new orientation through disorientation based on the concept of obedience. Olson supplies the census report in chapter 26 for Ashley's beginning of a new generation signaling new orientation. Knierim, Tucker, and Sweeney pave the road for the system of organizing his materials. Yet Ashley neither seriously analyzes the wealth of this past scholarship nor coherently conceptualizes his theme, nor sufficiently understands the implications of his usage of the hierarchical system.

---

89. Ashley, *The Book of Numbers*, p. 8. Another example (p. 10) is the incident at the Baal of Peor (25:1-18) being characterized as "the last disorientation narrative in the book" yet included in the middle of the new orientation started from 22:2.

90. Ashley (*The Book of Numbers*, p. 2) states: "So for nearly forty years the people wander around Kadesh-barnea in the wilderness until all that generation dies (chs. 16–19)." Compare this with the other statement (p. 11): "Evidently the plague killed the last of the cursed Exodus generation."

C. Concluding Remarks

The results of this critical evaluation of previous scholarship on the structure of Numbers 10:11–36:13 can be categorized into three issues: (1) the book of Numbers as the starting point of structural investigation; (2) the delimitation of the major component parts of the text; and (3) constitutive criteria for the proposed structure. Regarding the first issue, two positions emerged. All six scholars discussed above acknowledge the wide range of disparate materials in Numbers. However, how they approach these generically diverse contents distinguishes Gray and Noth from Budd, Olson, Milgrom, and Ashley. The former started their investigation from the vantage point of accumulated scholarship on the Pentateuch as a whole, and the latter from Numbers itself. Theoretically, both approaches are valid and legitimate in their own right. It is conceivable that the structure of the whole determines the specific significance of the component parts, while at the same time, the structure cannot be established apart from the analysis of the individuality of each part. A broad survey of the contents and a surface reading of the whole does not guarantee the detection of the infratextual structure that the whole presents. As shown above, a quite opposite result has been reached depending on which starting point in this exegetical circle one chooses. Gray and Noth argue that no apparent structure is detectable, and thus no significant unifying concept is identifiable in the book of Numbers. Contrary to this skepticism, Budd, Olson, Milgrom, and Ashley assert that Numbers is well ordered and alludes to a coherent concept. For example, such concepts include Yahweh's unchanging commitment to the Israelites despite their continual setbacks (in Budd's second section) and the death of the old and the birth of the new (in Olson). Milgrom basically follows Olson's scheme with his exposition of the theology of Numbers, although he does not correlate his reading of Numbers as an extant text to that theology. For Ashley, the theme of movement from obedience to a new stage of obedience via disobedience plays a constitutive role in Numbers. It is true that Gray and Noth also present the religious significance and theological aspects of Numbers and that Budd, Olson, and Milgrom must inevitably have been influenced by the concept of the whole Pentateuch. At this juncture in the discussion, the point is that depending on one's methodological judgment as to the starting point, one finds either a structural unity or lack of coherence underlying Numbers.

Second, there is no agreement on the delimitation of either the major divisions of Numbers as a whole or each of the individual literary units within Numbers 10:11–36:13. On the macrostructural level, 26:1 marks the beginning of a major division for Budd, Olson, and Milgrom, whereas this occurs at 22:1(2) for Gray and Ashley and 20:14 for Noth. Numbers 10:11 is regarded as a major signal by Gray, Olson, Milgrom, and Ashley, although its function for the structure as a whole is different for each author. The variety of opinions regarding the parameters of the text and the number of its component parts demands a thorough analysis prior to reconstructing the structure of the text. A particularly noticeable common feature is that all individual units have been arrayed in a row as if they were all equal in compositional plane. Olson indeed struggles to present a conceptual hierarchical pattern and yet could not go the necessary distance due to his preoccupation with the theological hermeneutic of Numbers. Olson's desire is more evident in Ashley, yet Ashley applies inconsistently the degree of hierarchical sophistication. Ashley's conceptual configuration used for the macrostructure level is quite different from that for the rest of the subsections. The simple assertion that there is no hierarchical configuration among the component parts and/ or the uncritical usage of hierarchical configuration do not satisfy the search for a conceptual structure of Numbers; on the contrary, the assertion must be demonstrated.

Third, two categories have been used as constitutive criteria for the proposed structures. On the one hand, Gray and Budd choose geographical and/ or chronological signals as responsible for Numbers' organization. Both of them, however, ignore other geographical and chronological indicators that are mentioned in Numbers, and are unaware of or misuse the distinction between geography and topography. As a result, they come up with quite different structures. This in itself indicates that their criterion for their structure is something other than what they claim. On the other hand, Noth, Olson, Milgrom, and Ashley choose thematic criteria: for Noth, a combination of Sinai revelation, guidance in the wilderness, and preparation for and beginning of the conquest; for Olson, the death of the old and the birth of the new extended from the concept of succeeding generations found in the series of genealogies in Genesis; for Milgrom, two generations (the generation of the Exodus and the generation of the conquest), a concept that presupposes a harmonization of both Noth and Olson; and for Ashley, the concept of obedience in and through a transitional movement of orientation. All these themes have their correspondences more or less in the contents of Numbers, but their themes have emerged from a surface reading rather than from a "close reading" of the text, and their themes are embellished by sketchy markers rather than by compelling literary evidence.

Moreover, compositional questions as to how these themes are composed in their particular shape, order, and arrangement, and structural questions as to what basis or concept is responsible for this surface presentation go unanswered. Thus, these scholars' structures portray their tendency to start with the assumption of a certain kind of thematic reality that in turn determines the literary analysis of the text and, as a result, to impose their themes on the text without considering the generic and functional individuality of each component unit within a whole. In short, a systematic discussion of the structure of Numbers 10:11–36:13, which accounts for generative inexplicit conceptualities underneath the text, is clearly called for.

CHAPTER TWO

Conceptual Analysis

The task of the present study is to reconstruct the conceptual system of Numbers 10:11–36:13 at its highest level, that is, the macrostructure of the text, in order to understand better both its parts and the whole. The macrostructure reveals the various levels of the text's infrastructure, indicating the locations and arrangements of its individual units. This conceptual system is comprised of the information that the text itself provides, located underneath its surface. This infratextual conceptual system, whose presence is implicit, is responsible for the organization of the extant text in its linguistic-semantic aspects, and without it the extant text in its present content and form would not exist. It determines the relationships of the parts of the text, and thus creates meaning. In other words, by reconstructing the system of underlying concepts, however hypothetical such a reconstruction may be, the exegete does more than restate the explicit surface meaning of the text; he or she also explains *why* the text says what it does on the surface. Thus, the task of reconstructing the conceptual system of the text is ultimately in the service of understanding the text properly.

In order to accomplish this task, an exegetical approach called conceptual analysis is employed. This approach is called such because it includes a methodological focus on the conceptual aspects of texts in exegesis. In brief, this approach views the nature of texts as conceptualized linguistic-semantic entities; it pays attention to the information gained from both the surface of a text and the subsurface textual level; it attempts to reconstruct the infratextual conceptual system operative in the text; and it utilizes a set of terms — concept, integrity, composition, and structure — in a distinct way from other critical methods. In relation to the current exegetical debate, this approach stands alongside text-centered methodologies, such as text linguistics, rhetorical criticism, literary criticism, and structuralism, and it has played a part in recent developments of new understandings and applications of the form-critical method. Thus, this chapter will briefly survey methodological developments in the contemporary period in order to provide a context for the development of the conceptual approach, and it will describe what the approach looks like and how it is related to other text-centered methods, especially in their employment of technical terms.

A. Methodological Development in the Contemporary Period

As indicated earlier in the Introduction to this study, newer exegetical methods emphasizing the text itself rather than its historical aspects began to make their appearance in the mid-twentieth century. This phenomenon has inevitably caused a heated debate on how synchronic and diachronic exegetical approaches relate to one another.[1] Diachronic approaches, such as source, form, and tradition criticism, are interested in delineating the layers of the text and in reconstructing the history of literary development predating the text's final form. They move backward from the extant texts, first recovering the earlier stages in the composition of written documents and then searching for the still earlier stages of oral history of individual stories and even of the traditions supposedly embedded in them. Although they investigate the work of redactors who brought the different sources together, they do not attempt to ask how the text, combined from originally independent sources, is to be read and understood. This deficiency is met by synchronic approaches, such as ca-

---

1. Previous scholarship on the problem of the structure of Numbers 10:11–36:13 points to these two trends. On the one hand, scholars such as Gray and Noth, who begin the scholarly process of addressing the problem from the vantage point of accumulated information on the Pentateuch, use a diachronic approach. On the other hand, scholars such as Budd, Olson, Milgrom, and Ashley, who start their analysis from the book of Numbers itself, use a synchronic approach.

There are many ways to diagnose the contemporary situation in biblical criticism. For example, H. Utzschneider articulates the exegetical crisis in relation to the theory of exegesis (Text-Leser-Autor: Bestandsaufnahme und Prolegomena zu einer Theorie der Exegese," *BZ* 43 [1999]: 224-38); J. Barton explains the interrelationship of critical methods and classifies them into one of following categories: (1) historical events or theological ideas, (2) text, (3) author or authors or community, and (4) reader (*Reading the Old Testament*, pp. 237-46); and R. C. Culley surveys the situation with "the general vs. the specific, the historical vs. the literary, and focus on the text vs. focus on context" ("Exploring New Directions," in *The Hebrew Bible and Its Modern Interpreters*, ed. D. Knight and G. M. Tucker [Chico, CA: Scholars Press, 1985], pp. 167-200). While this study chooses the distinction between diachronic and synchronic borrowed from modern linguistics and stresses the difference of literature from history, it also recognizes the tendency of many interpreters to utilize elements from methods of the "other" camp.

nonical, new literary, rhetorical, genre, stylistic, and structural criticism, which treat the text in its own right. They regard the text in its final form as a completed composition and focus on its linguistic and semantic phenomena.[2] R. Rendtorff recently acknowledges that "taking a synchronic approach to the text in its given shape is a task Old Testament scholarship has neglected too long and too intentionally."[3] His point follows a long history of similar observations that can be traceable to the so-called "new criticism" movement in the early decades of the twentieth century. Though unable to present an adequate alternative to the historicism of nineteenth-century literary criticism, according to M. Sternberg, this movement focuses on the text itself for discovering its inner coherence rather than for reconstructing its historical development.[4] Even G. von Rad, writing in the late 1930s, expressed his complaint about the disregard of the "final form" or "final shape" *(Letztgestalt)* of the Hexateuch: "On almost all sides the final form of the Hexateuch has come to be regarded as a starting-point barely worthy of discussion, from which the debate should move away as rapidly as possible in order to reach the real problems underlying it."[5] Instead of dissecting the Hexateuch into many fragments of sources, he found the hand of the Yahwist who used a creed-like statement (Deut 26:5-9) as the basis for creating salvation history (the Exodus-conquest theme) and further incorporated other traditions (such as the giving of the law at Sinai and the patriarchal traditions) into this framework. Though paying attention to the whole of the Hexateuch, his work concentrated on the origin and development of the traditions that the Yahwist treated. Finally, M. Noth expressed clearly his sentiments regarding the neglect of the final shape of the Pentateuch: the pentateuchal narrative as a whole is "a purely literary work, one that has contributed neither new tradition-material nor new substantive viewpoints to the reworking or interpretation of the materials."[6]

2. Although synchronic approaches share the extant text as the starting point for investigation, they differ widely in their specific focus on the extant text. These foci range from literary-critical elements to sociological and political, or to theological and hermeneutical studies.

3. R. Rendtorff, "The Paradigm is Changing: Hopes and Fears," *Biblical Interpretation* 1 (1993): 52. For the same point, see also idem, "Between Historical Criticism and Holistic Interpretation: New Trends in Old Testament Exegesis," in *Congress Volume,* Supplements to Vetus Testamentum 40 (Leiden: Brill, 1988), pp. 298-303. Rendtorff states that he is "highly distrustful of the traditional Literaturkritik so far as it leads to a production of texts. The subject of any interpretation has to be first and foremost the given text of the Hebrew Bible" (p. 300).

4. M. Sternberg, *The Poetics of Biblical Narrative: Ideological Literature and the Drama of Reading* (Bloomington: Indiana University Press, 1985), pp. 7-8.

5. G. von Rad, *The Problem of the Hexateuch and Other Essays,* trans. E. W. Trueman Dicken (Edinburgh: Oliver & Boyd, 1966), p. 1.

6. Noth, *A History of Pentateuchal Traditions,* p. 248.

Rendtorff's observation that there has been a need for a paradigm shift in Old Testament studies from diachronic to synchronic modes of analysis is unarguable. The question is, What caused this paradigm shift to be necessary or even inevitable. Boorer summarizes concisely the reasons contributing to the emergence of a synchronic reading of the final text.[7] First, focusing on the present text "seeks to redress an imbalance" resulting in excessive attention to relative levels of layers lying behind the text. Second, it insists on "the loosening of the almost exclusive grip of the historical-critical method on biblical studies." Third, it stems from the growing skepticism of "our ability to reconstruct the historical situation(s) out of which the text arose." Fourth, "the very possibility of the hermeneutical leap," namely, interpreters crossing the historical gap in order to determine the original meaning of the text, has been attacked. This fourth reason needs comment. The basic attitude of historical-critical scholarship has been to promise that its method will provide an objective analysis of the text in its original settings. This requires the exegete to stand outside of history in order to analyze the text. Fundamentally, this assumption has proven to be false because all exegetes work with their own presuppositions colored by their historical context and implicit agenda. Both the varied results and lack of common consensus regarding the same text prove this point. Neither value-free nor pure objective analysis of the text is possible. While recognizing these factors, R. P. Knierim goes one step further:

> Indeed, the interpretation of the extant Pentateuch is an urgent necessity, not only because its final composition represents another important historical datum in the Pentateuch's and the Old Testament's tradition history but also because attention to this stratum provides an important starting point and control mechanism for studying the Pentateuch's tradition history itself.[8]

His interest is clearly not so much in the paradigm shift itself but in its consequence, the ambiguous relationship between diachronic and synchronic approaches.

---

7. S. Boorer, "The Importance of a Diachronic Approach: The Case of Genesis-Kings," *CBQ* 51 (1989): 206, and n. 17. Utzschneider ("Text-Leser-Autor," pp. 224-26) gives three reasons for the exegetical crisis: "Konsens-Verlust und Theorievermeidung," "Ungenügende Alternativen und Theorieüberfrachtung," and "Akzeptanz-Verlust." See also Childs, *Introduction to the Old Testament as Scripture*, pp. 69-83.

8. Knierim, "The Composition of the Pentateuch," p. 352. F. Crüsemann is concerned with the "end form" *(Endgestalt)* of the Pentateuch in "Der Pentateuch als Torah: Prolegomena zur Interpretation seiner Endgestalt," *EvT* 49/3 (1989): 250-67. He does not discuss the structure of the Pentateuch, although he argues for the concept of the Pentateuch as Torah.

No one can deny that these approaches do in fact overlap in their search for the meaning of the text. Neither of the two can stand alone without paying proper attention to the other. But how do they relate to each other? What precisely is the nature of their relationship? Are they contradictory, complementary, or simply incompatible? A number of scenarios are conceivable. One is that interpreters tend to use diachronic and synchronic approaches as if they were opposites, applying one method while ignoring the other. This suggests that one approach is enough for the comprehension of the totality of the text. Another scenario is that interpreters choose one of the two approaches and accuse the other of incompatibility based on its lack of verifiability. On the one hand, if a diachronic approach is taken, its reconstruction of different literary layers is attacked as artificial and speculative, and for ultimately bringing about no consensus among its adherents. On the other hand, if a synchronic approach is taken, its stress on the multi-valency of a text is said to be confusing and ambiguous for finding the correct meaning of the text. The question is whether exegetes can find each interpretation of a text to be correct merely because it is extricated from the text or because it is sound and profound. Still another perceivable scenario is that the interpretive task is divided peacefully between the two approaches according to their own set of questions, agendas, and criteria. The same text is investigated independently, starting from one approach and ending with another. The results of each then are stated at the end of the discussion without any consideration of the conceivable substantive and conceptual conflicts. The issue of operational priority would be the only controversial point.

These scenarios undoubtedly portray a clear picture of the present status of Old Testament studies. There have been considerable attempts to illumine the meaning of a text by connecting the synchronic approach with the vast achievement of the diachronic approach. The ongoing and superior importance of diachronic interpretation has generally been maintained, but choosing the synchronic approach as the starting point of interpretation has also been argued. Yet interpreters' preference for a synchronic approach is not self-evident. Their choice is based on complex reasons with which one cannot agree or disagree uncritically.[9] However, the complementarity of these exe-

---

9. Boorer, "The Importance of a Diachronic Approach," pp. 195-208. Boorer demonstrates this point well in her presentation of four different results of the synchronic interpretation of the land promise in Genesis-Kings. See also Campbell's and O'Brien's highlighting of the contribution of the source hypothesis in advancing the understanding of the Pentateuch in A. F. Campbell and M. A. O'Brien, *Sources of the Pentateuch: Texts, Introductions, Annotations* (Minneapolis: Fortress, 1993). For a theoretical discussion of this issue, see E. Talstra, *Solomon's Prayer: Synchrony and Diachrony in the Composition of 1 Kings 8, 14-61*, trans. G. Runia-Deenick (Kampen: Kok Pharos, 1993).

getical methods can be postulated. One would argue that this complementarity is not only possible but necessary in order to understand the totality of a text properly. But the nature of the complementarity is rarely investigated, although it is proposed and applied. On what grounds do synchronic and diachronic approaches complement each other? Does their complementarity have an affect on each of them such that the individuality of each approach might be weakened? In other words, does their complementarity create another mode of interpretation? All these questions share a common presupposition, namely, the diametrical opposition of these two approaches. The point is that the present stalemate in biblical criticism stems from the fact that these approaches are perceived as dichotomous. While scholars recognize the justification of these approaches, they are locked in conflict.

The solution may be found in a recent refinement of the form-critical method, particularly in Knierim's program. Form criticism has played an instrumental role in the interpretation of biblical texts since its inception by H. Gunkel. His interests in identifying and classifying the smallest units of biblical texts and in reconstructing the societal setting out of which these units came launched a new direction in historical criticism.[10] Since the mid-twentieth century his formulation has remained normative for providing the framework of subsequent discussion on form-critical research, though many modify it with different emphases. Some prefer to focus on larger textual units than Gunkel's small, self-contained ones, while others expand the definition and function of setting and pay special attention to the role of genre in the formation of texts.[11] However, the contemporary practices of form criticism indicate such a significant departure from its traditional position that

10. For a historical overview of the traditional-historical methods, see Kraus, *Geschichte der historisch-kritischen Erforschung des Alten Testaments*. Especially, see pp. 309-34 for his treatment of Gunkel.

11. J. Barton expresses succinctly the Gunkelian definition of form criticism: "In the OT, form criticism is a method of study that identifies and classifies the smaller compositional units of biblical texts, and seeks to discover the social settings within which units of these types or literary genres were originally used" (J. Barton, "Form Criticism," in *ABD*, vol. 2, ed. D. N. Freedman et al. [New York: Doubleday, 1992], p. 838). For examples of diverse modifications, see von Rad, *The Problem of the Hexateuch and Other Essays*; S. Mowinckel, *The Psalms in Israel's Worship* (Nashville: Abingdon, 1962); A. Alt, "The Origins of Israelites Law," in *Essays on Old Testament History and Religion* (Garden City: Doubleday, 1967), pp. 101-71; C. Westermann, *Basic Forms of Prophetic Speech* (Philadelphia: Westminster, 1967); and Noth, *A History of Pentateuchal Traditions*. A recent concise summary of the history of form criticism can be found in M. Sweeney, "Form Criticism," in *To Each Its Own Meaning: An Introduction to Biblical Criticisms and Their Application*, rev. ed., ed. S. L. McKenzie and S. R. Haynes (Louisville: Westminster John Knox, 1999), pp. 58-89.

one wonders whether Gunkelian form criticism is still viable today. These practices are part of a larger paradigm shift in biblical studies from diachronic approaches to synchronic approaches. Particularly, form-critical research, interacting with literary analysis and structural-linguistic analysis, begins to focus on the structure of the text, the role of language in the formation and identification of genres, and multiple settings.[12] For example, M. Sweeney reformulates the definition of form criticism as "a method of linguistic textual analysis . . . [which] focuses especially on the patterns of language that appear within the overall linguistic configuration or form of a text and the role that these patterns play in giving shape and expression to the text."[13] This definition is heavily influenced by text-linguistic structuralism and literary-synchronic analysis of biblical texts. After reviewing the history of development of form criticism from Gunkel to Knierim, Sweeney argues for the analysis of forms, genres, settings, and intentions of literature based on the present biblical text first, rather than within the source documents; he considers the extant text as constitutive for the determination of the possibility of earlier forms; and he warns form critics of the multiplicity of these aspects in its literary history. For him, this refinement of form criticism is not only a viable mode of biblical interpretation but an indispensable one that will continue to serve as "a fundamental method" to address "both synchronic and diachronic issues in the interpretation of the biblical text."[14]

Sweeney's claim can be justified with the recent development of Knierim's exegetical program. In a 1973 article, Knierim broadens the ways to identify and classify genres, so that the typicality of certain forms may arise from "underlying matrices which the human mind generates" other than specific socio-linguistic settings; he argues for the structure analysis of the individual texts as a means for identifying their genres; and consequently he opens a door for diverse types of genres and settings as well.[15] In a 1985 article, Knierim further stresses the importance of structure analysis, arguing

---

12. For the recent forms of form-critical works, see the twelve publications in the FOTL commentary series edited by R. P. Knierim, G. M. Tucker, and M. Sweeney. D. Peterson reviews seven volumes in this series in "Hebrew Bible Form Criticism," *Religious Studies Review* 18 (1992): 29-33. He argues that the decisive departure from the traditional definition of form criticism was fueled by two articles: J. Muilenburg, "Form Criticism and Beyond," *JBL* 88 (1969): 1-18, and R. P. Knierim's "Old Testament Form Criticism Reconsidered," *Int* 27 (1973): 435-68. He concludes that these works show movement not only "in diverse directions" but also "beyond the classic Gunkelian approach."

13. Sweeney, "Form Criticism," p. 58.

14. Sweeney, "Form Criticism," pp. 68-69.

15. Knierim, "Old Testament Form Criticism Reconsidered."

that it is an integral part of the form-critical method and should be treated as an initial step of its process. Hence, form criticism, which incorporates such structure analysis into its methodology, provides the basis for a unified exegetical system that conceptualizes the correlation of various methodological steps.[16] He has not yet articulated in these articles, however, how to adjudicate the hierarchical relationships among different structuring features in a text. For this question, his recent works pave a road by focusing on infratextual conceptual aspects of a text.[17] Among various structuring elements, Knierim contends that concepts of a text, which are operative in that text, are more fundamental than the generically typical; thus, they govern the analysis of the structure of the text. He presupposes the nature of texts as a conceptualized linguistic-semantic entity; he observes that the text has explicit statements and implicit concepts and an interaction of these two; he then methodologizes this observation by reconstructing the infratextual conceptual system of the text, that is, the structure responsible for its form and content and its explicit statements; and ultimately he goes beyond paraphrasing the text to explaining it. Since his program focuses on the structure of a text, it can be applied to virtually any written document, whether the document is perceived to be composed of various combinations of sources, or compiled of multiple layers, or a complete, self-contained unit. His choice of the extant text as the beginning point of the investigation is an operational decision based on the assertion that the extant text is the realistic basis for a controlled investigation. A structure analysis must be done not only of the final form of the text but also of any stage of the text in its literary growth. Without having a clear understanding of the text at any stage, both the change of the text's meaning throughout its growth and the meaning of its final form could be easily confused and ambiguous.

---

16. R. P. Knierim, "Criticism of Literary Features, Form, Tradition, and Redaction," in *The Hebrew Bible and Its Modern Interpreters*, ed. D. Knight and G. M. Tucker (Chico, CA: Scholars Press, 1985), pp. 123-65.

17. R. P. Knierim, *Text and Concept in Leviticus 1:1-9*; idem, "Interpretation of the Old Testament," in *The Task of Old Testament Theology: Substance, Method, and Cases* (Grand Rapids: Eerdmans, 1995), pp. 57-138 (especially, pp. 58-71); idem, "Conceptual Aspects in Exodus 25:1-9," in *The Task of Old Testament Theology: Substance, Method, and Cases* (Grand Rapids: Eerdmans, 1995), pp. 389-99.

B. Description

What, then, does the conceptual approach look like? Conceptual analysis[18] is interested in explaining a text, specifically as a conceptualized phenomenon. The phenomenon presupposes the nature of a text as an organic linguistic entity that consists of words, sentences, groups of sentences, and larger blocks of material knit together in an identifiable layout. In other words, a text is "a connotative system" that is comprised of a verbal factor, "constituted by all the linguistic elements proper of the sentences" (such as phonological, morphological, etc.); a syntactic factor that refers to "relationships among textual units" (such as sentences, larger units, etc.); and a semantic factor, "a complex product of the semantic content of the linguistic units."[19] These factors are explicit textual information which appears on the surface of a text, and they demand an analysis of the text's grammar, syntax, stylistic and rhetorical features, genre elements, and themes.

More than recognizing the linguistic nature of texts, conceptual analysis is an approach to texts that understands their nature as conceptual entities. Texts are also comprised of assumptions, presuppositions, or concepts that are directly and indirectly operative in their thought system. Knierim states succinctly on this point that "texts are more than lists of independent words (lexemes) and chains of unrelated sentences (syntagms). They are held to-

18. The explanation of conceptual analysis draws primarily upon Knierim's work. His own comprehensive discussion of conceptual analysis with its theoretical implications is yet to come. However, his writings clearly show a descriptive treatment of his approach to a text. He intends to introduce any methodological considerations in a concrete exegesis of a text, rather than as abstract theory isolated from the reality of a text; better said, his exegesis of a text and conceptualization of the method complement and even enhance each other. The following are only some examples. For specific individual texts, see *Text and Concept in Leviticus 1:1-9;* "II. Exodus 3:7-8 in Light of Biblical Theology," in *The Task of Old Testament Theology: Substance, Method, and Cases* (Grand Rapids: Eerdmans, 1995), pp. 130-33; "On the Theology of Psalm 19," in *The Task of Old Testament Theology: Substance, Method, and Cases* (Grand Rapids: Eerdmans, 1995), pp. 322-50; and "Conceptual Aspects in Exodus 25:1-9." For a group of texts or a larger work, see "The Book of Numbers." For groups of larger works, see "The Composition of the Pentateuch." For a concise survey of the development of Knierim's exegetical methodology over four decades, see D. B. Palmer, "Text and Concept in Exodus 1:1–2:25: A Case Study in Exegetical Method," Ph.D. diss., The Claremont Graduate University, 1998, pp. 87-108; and M. A. Sweeney's preface in *Reading the Hebrew Bible for a New Millennium: Form, Concept, and Theological Perspective,* vol. 2: *Exegetical and Theological Studies,* ed. W. Kim et al., Studies in Antiquity and Christianity (Harrisburg, PA: Trinity Press International, 2000), pp. vii-x.

19. O. Ducrot and T. Todorov, *Encyclopedic Dictionary of the Sciences of Language,* trans. C. Porter (Baltimore: The Johns Hopkins University Press, 1979), pp. 294-95.

gether by supra-syntagmatic factors which constitute their entity."[20] The presuppositions or concepts are inexplicit textual information located foundationally underneath the surface expression of a text. They are infratextual and stand at the subsurface level of a text. They are also not general in the sense that they indicate the text's view of reality; instead, they are specific to an individual text in its individuality. This means that conceptual analysis deals with the infratextual concepts that are specific to a particular text and not abstractions from that text.

Knierim's observation on the dual aspects of a text is not particularly new since most exegetes perceive that a certain system of assumptions lies beneath what the text says and contributes to what the text supposes to say. In the process of interpreting a text, however, most exegetes tend to utilize this information in part intentionally and in part accidentally or unintentionally. Their practice of implicitly or even unconsciously reconstructing the infraconceptual framework results in a methodologically uncontrolled interpretation. This interpretation is potentially controlled by their own presuppositions of what the text ought to say. However, Knierim's observation is a launching pad for an advanced methodological discussion. He argues for the necessity of conscious use of the statements expressed at the surface text and presuppositions standing at the subsurface of a text. For Knierim, using this information is necessary and should be given highest priority in order to grasp the meaning of the text. This knowledge must be methodologized so that exegetes "do more than paraphrase what a text says."[21]

Putting both explicit statements and implicit presuppositions of a text through a rigorous analysis, however, is not the end but the beginning of conceptual analysis. Its next step is to investigate the relationship between the two because it presupposes the nature of a text as a conceptualized linguistic-semantic entity "in which the explicit statements and their presuppositions interact."[22] At issue is their "mutual convertibility" in a text. To investigate the interactions resulting from their influence, Knierim asks how the presuppositions are "implicitly operative" in the text and "generate and control its form and content." Thus, for him, the presuppositions of the text are more impor-

---

20. Knierim, *Text and Concept in Leviticus 1:1-9*, p. 2.

21. Knierim, *Text and Concept in Leviticus 1:1-9*, p. 1. In the process of explicating a text, most interpreters end their exegesis with a description of a text (or only some parts of a text), paying attention only to the statements of the text. But a description of a text does not in and of itself explain the text. This does not mean that a description of a text is unimportant; rather, it means that the description must describe the text as a text that is held together by "supra-syntagmatic factors."

22. Knierim, *Text and Concept in Leviticus 1:1-9*, p. 1.

tant than its statements. In other words, the linguistic and literary features of a text are in service to the composition and the structure of the text. This fact by no means undermines the significance of these explicit textual features in their own right, but it implies that their significance is ultimately dependent upon how and on what basis they are related to the presuppositions of the text. The linguistic, literary, or surface features comprise a unified composition by analyses of compositional categories that determine the relationships among distinctive components of the text.[23] These analyses also determine the location and arrangement of different parts in the literary unit. More precisely, the system of conceptual presuppositions that lie underneath a text is responsible for all specific aspects of content and respective linguistic-semantic phenomena. Knierim argues that this insight must be methodologized by reconstructing the systematic configuration of infratextual conceptualities, that is, the structure of the text.[24] Then, through a conscious reconstruction of the mutually convertible system of the text and of its assumptions, Knierim interprets a text in its own right and on its own terms.

In order better to grasp the theoretical aspect of conceptual analysis, it is necessary to define and explain two technical terms: composition and structure.[25] These two terms are distinctive enough to be explored individu-

---

23. The elements of each category vary greatly, but some examples are noticeable. Linguistic devices include a rare word, a typical phrase, an unusual or customary cluster of words, the syntax of sentences, etc. Stylistic elements are word plays, repetitions (including chiasms, inclusios, parallels, rings, and concentric patterns), irony, and poetic justice. Rhetorical devices can have stylistic elements and include such things as the narrator's point of view, descriptions of the characters, development of the plot, and intentional ambiguity. Formal devices include chronological or topographical/geographical indicators, and formulae, such as a Yahweh speech and compliance or execution reports. Generic devices focus on the typical form of a text, such as itinerary, battle report, prophetic oracles, and rebellion or complaint narrative. Cf. Knierim, "Old Testament Form Criticism Reconsidered," pp. 460-61; S. Bar-Erfat, "Some Observations on the Analysis of Structure in Biblical Narrative," *VT* 30 (1980): 154-73; A. Berlin, *Poetics and Interpretation of Biblical Narrative*, Bible and Literature Series 9 (Sheffield: Almond, 1983); G. W. Coats, *Genesis: With an Introduction to Narrative Literature*, FOTL 1 (Grand Rapids: Eerdmans, 1983), pp. 317-22.

24. With the reconstruction of a text's infratextual system, Knierim does not propose a method of extracting abstract or subjective ideas that are in principle separated from the reality of a text. Rather, his reconstruction must not only be controlled by the signals that the text itself provides but also must serve to explain the text: ". . . this sort of reconstruction of the conceptualities of texts has everything to do with the explanation of the texts themselves and nothing to do with a reconstruction in which texts serve only as irrelevant, dispensable shells through which to traverse to the real thing, the vision of meaning in the abstract idea" (Knierim, "Conceptual Aspects in Exodus 25:1-9," pp. 389-90).

25. In the present study a "concept" is defined as a systematized idea embedded in and stood underneath expressions of the surface of a text, while a "conceptuality" refers to a set of

ally, and yet they are integrally related in that they point descriptively to how one is able to move from the explicit aspects of the surface of the text to the infraconceptual system of the subsurface of the text, and how the two influence each other. With an understanding of these terms, a heuristic process of conceptual analysis can be described.

As mentioned above, a text is a conceptualized linguistic-semantic entity that presents information on both its surface and infratextual level. "Composition" deals with information on the surface of the text. It especially focuses on three things. First, it defines the nature of individual components of a self-contained unit. Second, it determines their location and arrangement, and the order in which they are presented. Third, it also determines the location of each textual unit, triggered not only by a unit's separateness from but also by its connectedness to other units. The first is interested in the linguistic patterns and conceptual patterns/schemas in linguistic expression of the sentences of individual units, while the second and third concern themselves with conceptual arrangements within a unit (i.e., intratextual) and combinations of distinguished units in a larger literary work (i.e., contextual). The composition of a text indicates that every individual unit of the text, let alone every individual components within a unit, is not isolated but related to other units in a particular way. The relationship among these units or components of the text can be discerned by comparing various categories of signals that are present on the surface of the text. These categories include linguistic, stylistic, rhetorical, formal, generic, and thematic elements, as mentioned above. Since they are not mutually exclusive and do not function independently, it is possible that not one but a combination of several elements works together to determine the interrelationship among components within a unit and/or with other units. When composition analysis uncovers the cohesion of all these explicit signals, this cohesion is referred to as "compositional integrity."[26]

---

concepts that are integrally related together in a hierarchical relationship. "Infratextual" refers to textual elements that stand foundationally beneath the surface expression of a text, undergirding and determining that surface expression, whereas "intratextural" refers to textual elements that are within a particular text. Cf. Knierim, *Text and Concept in Leviticus 1:1-9*, pp. 2-3; Palmer, *Text and Concept in Exodus 1:1–2:25*, pp. 172-80.

26. The term "cohesive/cohesion" is used here to describe the integrative aspects of the various linguistic and syntactic elements whose presence is explicit on the surface of the text. H. Utzschneider employs "Kohäsion" (cohesion) as a literary description of the function and result of components in the surface text which join a text unit together (*Das Heiligtum und das Gesetz: Studien zur Bedeutung der Sinaitischen Heiligtumstexte (Ex 25–40; Lev 8–9)*, OBO 77 [Göttingen: Vandenhoeck & Ruprecht, 1988], p. 15).

This cohesion does not necessarily reflect a hierarchical system of the text which endows a signal with lesser or greater significance than others. All signals may be organized at a compositionally equivalent level, or cohesion may reflect a compositional hierarchy such that the significance of individual signals can be specifiable only with reference to the whole. Ascertaining the hierarchical system of the text is a legitimate undertaking, and in this hierarchy the compositional unity can be discerned.

"Structure," however, refers to the systematic configuration of conceptualities that reveals the conceptual coherence of the text.[27] Structure analysis investigates questions such as why a text presents itself in one way and not in another. The analysis is interested not in the question of the description of the text but in the reason the text is as it is. The very existence of the unity of component parts of a text indicates a common conceptuality or an underlying structure. In other words, the compositional integrity of the text triggers the exegete to consider the underlying concepts because these concepts are responsible for the extant text in its actual presentation and govern or control the compositional unity of the text. To uncover and reconstruct these infratextual conceptualities and their relationships is the objective of structure analysis.

To recapitulate, an analysis of the structure of a text is an investigation of the concepts without which the extant text in its present content and form would not exist. Moreover, it is these concepts that give meaning to the expressions of the surface text. Without reconstructing the coherent conceptuality within and underneath the text, the text cannot be properly understood. Structure then includes composition, but it is more than composition. Structure and composition do not contradict but complement each other. Conflict between the two is conceivable, but structural unity overrides compositional unity because the latter owes its existence to the former. Therefore, the goal of conceptual analysis is to reconstruct the generative concept *underneath* the text that is operative *in* the text. Furthermore, it is exegetically flawed to use composition and structure as if they were interchangeable. Inconsistent usage of these terms obscures the meaning of the text in study. Composition and structure, as defined in this study or however they may be defined in a different methodological system, are to be controlled by the presentation of the text itself.

From the vantage point of the discussion above, a heuristic process of conceptual analysis may be described. At the outset, this analysis takes the

---

27. The term "coherent/coherence" is used here to describe the conceptual integrity of a text in its components and as a whole. Cf. Utzschneider, *Das Heiligtum und das Gesetz*, p. 16.

text as it now stands as a realistic starting point for an empirically controlled investigation of any of the attendant problems,[28] since the text provides both explicit information and implicit presuppositions. Thus, (A) exegetes must be aware that they begin with what they have, the text, without imposing any preconceived ideas of how the text is supposed to be interpreted. They should analyze first explicit aspects of the text that are readily accessible on the surface level, such as linguistic, stylistic, rhetorical, formal, generic, and thematic elements. (B) Since these explicit aspects are signals pointing, however directly or indirectly, to something beyond themselves, the underlying concepts that are specific to the particular text, exegetes must postulate the implicit, generative, and governing concepts on which these aspects exist. Furthermore, a conceptual system indicating a coherent relationship among these concepts should be reconstructed. (C) Exegetes should return again to the surface of the text in order to verify, validate, or modify the reconstructed conceptual system. It is the text that governs the entire process of exegesis.

The key to a successful implementation of this process lies more or less in how exegetes go about identifying and determining a text's infratextual concepts, and thus reconstructing a coherent relationship among them. This is the case since conceptual analysis understands the concept governing a text comprehensively:

> A concept governing a text may be, e.g., genre-, style-, or situation-specific; it may be a particular theme, plot, concern, or intention. Its presence beneath the surface of a text may be strictly pericope-immanent, i.e., *intratextual,* but it may also be determined contextually as in larger literary works, or intertextually as in the coherence of separate literary works or documents, or even supratextually as, e.g., by certain worldview concepts. [Emphasis original][29]

Due to the comprehensive nature of a "concept," the reconstructed conceptual system can be regarded as arbitrary and resulting from subjective and circular reasoning. However, this criticism may not be necessary if the process of reconstructing a conceptual system satisfies the following criteria. First, the

---

28. The analytical point of departure is the same as that of the FOTL project: "if the results of form criticism are to be verifiable and generally intelligible, then the determination of typical forms and genres, their settings and functions, has to take place through the analysis of the forms in and of the texts themselves." The quote comes from the "Editor's Foreword" by Knierim, Tucker, and Sweeney on p. xii in the latest commentary of the FOTL series: E. Ben Zvi, *Micah,* FOTL 21B (Grand Rapids: Eerdmans, 2000).

29. Knierim, *Text and Concept in Leviticus 1:1-9,* p. 3.

process should account for all the explicit aspects of the surface text. This point has not been self-evident in exegetical methods. For example, form criticism takes the formal features of the text, including the syntax, linguistic patterns, and so forth, as being the primary indicators of the text, while rhetorical criticism focuses on stylistic devices as such. The question is not which category has been selected but whether or not one particular category has been given a special interest without examining other categories within their hierarchical relationship. The process recognizes the possibility of several categories working together to point to the underlying concepts, some of which may be formal or rhetorical features. Nonetheless, it should treat all the compositional data in the surface text.

Second, the process should weigh and compare all the explicit aspects of the surface text in terms of their contributions on cohesiveness of the text. This much is certain: the nature of the constituent components of a self-contained unit and their roles within it can be determined if all its compositional elements have been analyzed. However, it is possible that the same elements in a unit may play differing roles when they are examined in view of the unit's relation to other units that are distinct in larger corpora of literature. This means that the importance of each category may vary in its contextual as well as intertextual milieu. Thus, the reconstructed conceptual system of a text is at the outset provisional. No individual text is independent from its larger context. It is also true that the process of reconstructing the conceptual system governing the larger literary work is inevitably affected by the systems on which its individual parts are based.

Third, the process should weigh and compare all the explicit aspects of the surface text in terms of their directness in expressing the text's underlying concepts. This comparison is crucial in the process of determining the dominant concept to which others are systematically related, since the same compositional elements of different texts may have differing functions and significance once their interface with the underlying concepts is examined. It means that the significance of each category must be determined in light of whether it explains the reason for what the text says. The reconstructed conceptual system of a text should be specific to a particular text and not an abstraction from that text. While satisfying these three criteria, the process can be exercised in a heuristically flexible way in that it is not limited to any one of the exegetical methods, especially text-immanent ones. At the same time, the process should be executed in a programmatic way in that it begins with and is controlled by the information that the text provides.

Last but not least, a word on how the theoretical understanding of conceptual analysis given above applies to Numbers 10:11–36:13. The reconstruction of the macrostructure of Numbers 10:11–36:13 entails the identification of the text's fundamental literary divisions and an explanation of its criteria, the conceptual presuppositions that account for those subdivisions and their arrangement. These goals suggest two parts of an analytical procedure. (1) Identifying the individual units within 10:11–36:13 is the first and necessary step toward discerning and explaining the operative conceptual factors responsible for the units' connectedness to each other and to the whole. (2) These two analyses (identifying the individual units and discovering their relationships) share the assumption of this study that the identifiable individual units of 10:11–36:13 are united into a cohesive literary composition that in fact signals a conceptual coherence of the text.

From these two points, a systematic interpretive procedure emerges. First, the starting point of this investigation is the text as it now stands without presuming a solution to any of the attendant problems.[30] If the structure of Numbers 10:11–36:13 is to be verified, the text as it now stands is a necessary starting point for an empirically controlled investigation. Second, this investigation seeks to establish 10:11–36:13 as a distinct block within the book of Numbers. The question is whether 10:11 and 36:13 constitute the beginning and the ending of a major division in the highest macrostructural level in Numbers. To establish the text as such demands an analysis of its structure in its own right and on its own terms, even if its structure in itself is relative to that of Numbers as a whole and ultimately that of the Pentateuch. Third, the next step of the investigation is to identify the individual units within the text. The central questions are how many individual units the text has, what the elements that identify the limits of the unit are, and what the factors responsible for the structure of each unit are. Fourth, the investigation analyzes the relationships of the individual units to the whole. This step deals with these questions: What are the major constitutive sections? Are all of the component text units compositionally equivalent or are some text units compositionally subordinate to others or situated on different hierarchical levels within the whole? What are the constitutive criteria for the structure of the whole? In other words, the issues are: how the individual units are grouped together to form a macro-unit, how these established macro-units are related to each other, and what the macrostructure of the text throughout the various levels of its infrastructure is. Fifth, the investigation attempts to clarify the theological claim of

---

30. Thus, this study will use the Hebrew text of Numbers 10:11–36:13, as found in *Leningradensis*'s presentation of the Masoretic Text represented by *Biblia Hebraica Stuttgartensia*, ed. K. Elliger and W. Rudolph (Stuttgart: Deutsche Bibelgesellschaft, 1984).

the text reflected by its macrostructure.[31] This systematic interpretive procedure is reflected in the organization of the present study itself.

C. Relation to Other Exegetical Methods

No interpretive approach emerges from a vacuum. The conceptual approach above grows out of a process of refining traditional form criticism and uses a set of terms differently from that of other critical methods, such as rhetorical criticism, narrative criticism, and structuralism. Hence, a brief explanation of how this approach interacts with other methodologies, especially their employment of technical terms, is necessary.

From the inception of form criticism, its goal has been to explain the biblical texts in their present form. However, the early history of its application to texts demonstrates that most form critics move backward to search for a short, self-contained, and "original" oral element behind the sources. This thrust, as J. Muilenburg argues in his 1968 presidential address to the Society of Biblical Literature, creates an unavoidable deficiency in form criticism, namely, its overemphasis of only typical aspects of a text, "what is common to all the representatives of a genre."[32] To be sure, he neither abandons form criticism as a whole nor ignores the concept of a *Gattung* (genre) in particular. Instead, recognizing limitations of reconstructing "pure" *Gattungen,* he attempts to supplement form criticism by highlighting the individuality of texts as expressed in the stylistic and rhetorical features of those texts. He describes his enterprise as rhetorical criticism, whose tasks are to define the boundaries of a literary unit and to recognize the function of rhetorical devices that contribute to the shape and emphasis of the text. In a nutshell, rhetorical criticism, as Muilenburg envisioned, understands the nature of texts as exhibiting "linguistic patterns, word formations ordered or arranged in particular ways, verbal sequences which move in fixed structures from beginning

31. These procedural steps are similar to what A. F. Campbell ("Structure Analysis and the Art of Exegesis (1 Samuel 16:14–18:30)," in *Problems in Biblical Theology: Essays in Honor of Rolf Knierim,* ed. H. T. C. Sun and K. L. Eades, with J. M. Robinson and G. I. Moller [Grand Rapids: Eerdmans, 1997], p. 81) suggests as the central steps of a structure analysis: (1) establishing the limits of the unit constituting a text; (2) establishing the limits of the major blocks within the text; (3) analyzing the elements and their relationship within each block; (4) analyzing the relationships of the blocks to the whole; and (5) establishing an initial hypothesis as to the meaning of the text.

32. Muilenburg, "Form Criticism and Beyond," pp. 1-18 (5).

to end";[33] it demands an analysis of the individuality of a text as well as its typicality in order to interpret it properly.

Among recent diverse modifications of Muilenburg's description of rhetorical criticism, P. Trible's deserves comment.[34] Following Muilenburg, she proposes a guiding principle: "proper articulation of form-content yields proper articulation of meaning."[35] With this statement, she affirms his position that form and content are organically connected. But she understands the nature of their interrelationship differently. By "form" she means rhetorical form that shows "the patterns of relationships residing in the very words, phrases, sentences, and larger units,"[36] not the generic form or a pure *Gattung* to which Muilenburg refers. In addition, Muilenburg understands "content" as the various stylistic and rhetorical devices that ultimately produce a singular meaning of the author. In contrast, by "content" Trible means "not author's intent, but only the unique configuration of details that an interpreter would impose on a text."[37] With this designation, she opens the door for the possibility of multiple meanings from a given text. In fact, she proposes a range of meanings: "more than a single meaning and fewer than unlimited

33. Muilenburg, "Form Criticism and Beyond," p. 18.

34. P. Trible, *Rhetorical Criticism: Context, Method, and the Book of Jonah,* Guides to Biblical Scholarship (Minneapolis: Fortress, 1994). For the history of recent developments in rhetorical criticism, see R. F. Melugin, "Muilenburg, Form Criticism, and Theological Exegesis," in *Encounter with the Text: Form and History in the Hebrew Bible,* ed. M. J. Buss, SBLSS (Philadelphia: Fortress, 1979), pp. 91-100; D. J. A. Clines, ed., *Art and Meaning: Rhetoric in Biblical Literature,* JSOTSup 19 (Sheffield: JSOT Press, 1982); J. M. Sprinkle, "Literary Approaches to the Old Testament: A Survey of Recent Scholarship," *JETS* 32 (1989): 299-310; D. F. Watson and A. J. Hauser, *Rhetorical Criticism of the Bible: A Comprehensive Bibliography with Notes on History and Method* (Leiden: Brill, 1994); P. K. Tull, "Rhetorical Criticism and Intertextuality," in *To Each Its Own Meaning: An Introduction to Biblical Criticisms and Their Application,* rev. ed., ed. S. L. McKenzie and S. R. Haynes (Louisville: Westminster John Knox, 1999), pp. 156-80.

35. Trible, *Rhetorical Criticism,* p. 91.

36. Trible, *Rhetorical Criticism,* p. 92. As an example of the difference in usage of the term "structure" between form criticism and rhetorical criticism, she characterizes how FOTL uses the term: "[structure] constitutes the topical outline of a passage. It designates not the text itself but a schematic synopsis that paraphrases and abridges the text. A word or phrase summarizes each section." She seems to misunderstand the intention of the FOTL series and its practices. Structures in the FOTL express a systematic interpretation of a text including analyses of its genre and typicality as well as its individuality. In later volumes, structures also reflect the analysis focusing on infratextual conceptual aspects of a text. The FOTL series is a representation of a recent refinement of traditional form criticism in that it interacts with other critical methods, especially structuralism and structural linguistics.

37. T. B. Dozeman, "OT Rhetorical Criticism," in *ABD,* ed. D. N. Freedman, vol. 5 (New York: Doubleday, 1992), p. 714. Dozeman articulates similarities and contrasts among Muilenburg and critics representative of recent rhetorical criticism.

meanings."[38] Trible's articulation on form, content, and meaning leads her to move away from Muilenburg's form-critical presuppositions, though she builds on his recognition of the important role that the rhetorical features of a text play in its interpretation. Hence, for her rhetorical criticism is a text-oriented method requiring an intrinsic and synchronic reading of a text. Then, in a sense, she redirects traditional form critics to the original impetus of form criticism, interpretation of the present form of a text. Yet she does not differentiate a text's surface expression from its subsurface assumptions or presuppositions, or concepts. All of the stylistic and rhetorical features belong to what a text says and how it says what it says. But the "saying" cannot be regarded as a representation of a text in its totality. The totality should include what a text presupposes is operative in that text. Her usage of the term "structure" as something that "presents the *ipsissima verba* of the text" demonstrates this point well. In contrast, the conceptual approach uses "structure" to refer to the systematic configuration of conceptualities operative at an infratextual level.

Muilenburg's proposal for detailed rhetorical treatments to identify the structure of a composition and the configuration of its component parts paves the way for other literary approaches, such as structuralism.[39] At the outset, both structuralism and the conceptual approach focus on a system,[40] which means that both of them share a methodological goal of going below the surface of the text to a deep structural level. With its understanding of the text as discourse, produced in a language, structuralism distinguishes linguistic signs that appear at a syntagmatic level (or narrative level) from the signifieds at the discursive level. The goal of structural exegesis is, then, to

---

38. Trible, *Rhetorical Criticism*, p. 99.

39. D. Patte, "Structural Criticism," in *To Each Its Own Meaning: An Introduction to Biblical Criticisms and Their Application*, rev. ed., ed. S. L. McKenzie and S. R. Haynes (Louisville: Westminster John Knox, 1999), pp. 183-200; idem, *What is Structural Exegesis?* (Philadelphia: Fortress, 1976); R. Polzin, "What is Structuralism?" in his *Biblical Structuralism: Method and Subjectivity in the Study of Ancient Texts* (Philadelphia: Fortress, 1977), pp. 1-43; D. Patte and A. Patte, *Structural Exegesis: From Theory to Practice* (Philadelphia: Fortress, 1978); R. Barthes, et al., *Structure Analysis and Biblical Exegesis*, trans. A. M. Johnson (Pittsburgh: Pickwick, 1974); H. C. White, "Structural Analysis of the Old Testament Narrative," in *Encounter with the Text: Form and History in the Hebrew Bible*, ed. M. J. Buss (Philadelphia: Fortress, 1979), pp. 45-65.

40. Patte ("Structural Criticism," p. 186) states clearly, "what is truly significant in any given instance of communication [is] how its features are interrelated in a system, that is, how various words are interrelated with other words in the language (viewed as a system); how the different features of a text are interrelated to form a coherent whole; how a text is interrelated with its literary, social, religious, and political environment (other kinds of systems); how a text participates with its readers in producing meaning (the system being all the features of the reading process)."

bring to light the interrelationship of values signified by signs. In focusing on a system, structuralism places its stress primarily on the mutual relations among components of the whole, paying little attention to the content of the individual components. Moreover, for structuralism, these mutual relations are governed by certain laws and rules, which determine the interaction among the individual elements. These laws and rules are located in the deep structure and are part of the semantic universe that determines all human communications. Structure analysis in conceptual approach, however, deals with the implicit concepts that are specifically operative in a particular text, not the deep values that are abstracted from the surface of a text. Though structuralism talks about the semantic universe beneath the text, this universe is not necessarily specific to that text. In addition, the conceptual approach focuses not only on the mutual relationships of the components of a text within the boundary that it permits, but also on the individual elements and the whole as well. Whereas in structuralism each component of the whole does not independently exist outside the system, and its relationship is understood only in terms of its function within the system of the whole, the conceptual approach starts with the uniqueness of the individual elements of the whole. For example, R. Jacobson understands the relationship of *parole,* the individual forms of expression on the surface of a text, to *langue,* the semantic rules, as analogous to a chess game.[41] For him, *langue* would represent the set of rules for chess that every player should know and is expected to follow, while *parole* would indicate individual moves or sets of moves that the player makes. Conceptual analysis, however, acknowledges that there is more involved in a chess game than these two elements. It presupposes strategies (or concepts) that are specific to and responsible for the moves of a particular game. These strategies are considered part of a game plan (conceptual system) that not only is necessary but also should be coherent in order to carry out a meaningful or successful game. Ultimately, each move on the board is generated according to this plan and reflects, however fragmentarily, the coherence of the plan without which it is meaningless.

Structuralism in general is a hard methodology to grasp since it combines linguistics, philosophy, and psychology and employs numerous technical terms that are not familiar in biblical studies. Hence, its usefulness for biblical exegesis is rather limited. Unlike structuralism, narrative criticism, a parallel to rhetorical criticism, has flourished recently.[42] Narrative criticism, as D. M. Gunn under-

41. R. Jacobson, "The Structuralists and the Bible," *Int* 28 (1974): 147.
42. D. M. Gunn, "Narrative Criticism," in *To Each Its Own Meaning: An Introduction to Biblical Criticisms and Their Application,* rev. ed., ed. S. L. McKenzie and S. R. Haynes (Louis-

stands it, seeks to explain the meaning of the text "by close reading that identifies formal and conventional structures of the narrative, determines plot, develops characterization, distinguishes point of view, exposes language play, and relates all to some overarching, encapsulating theme."[43] This definition makes two points that indicate an advance of narrative criticism upon rhetorical criticism as related to conceptual analysis. First, narrative criticism includes in its task an analysis of plot, characterization, and point of view. Second, it attempts to bring all literary features of narrative together under identifiable themes.

R. Alter's book *The Art of Biblical Narrative* demonstrates the first point. He argues that the Bible's narrative should be perceived as a creative work that demands special attention to "the artful use of language" and to the narrator's employment of "type-scene."[44] For example, he argues that literary features found in the Pentateuch, such as duplicates, inconsistencies, and even contradictions, can still point to a literary unity in terms of "composite artistry." With this designation, he sees "the editorial combination of different literary sources" as "the final stage in the process of artistic creation which produced biblical narrative."[45] Thus, the final product, though still possessing grammatical, literary, and ideological or theological "bumps," is an integrated whole that artfully combines multiple perspectives with "a purposeful pattern." This composite artistry reveals a purposeful technique that presents not a fusion of many views into a harmonization but a montage of viewpoints. Alter's keen observations on perceivable hermeneutical differences between ancient writers and modern readers and his illuminating imagery are instructive in interpreting the biblical narratives, but they raise a few questions. Were the narratives composed artistically simply for the sake of art? Do particular narrative montages allow divergent perspectives to speak only for themselves or do they also present another entity that surpasses all existing differences? Does a montage exist at the narrative level only or also at the semantic or conceptual level? Is demonstrating cohesiveness in the artistry of the composition the main goal of biblical exegesis? These questions point to the role concept plays in the composition of a narrative, even if understood as a montage. Alter's intention to "illuminate the distinctive principles of the Bible's narrative art" should be supplemented to reconstruct the implicit conceptual system that has generated the narratives' artistic expressions and their cohesiveness.

ville: Westminster John Knox, 1999), pp. 201-29; D. M. Gunn and D. N. Fewell, *Narrative in the Hebrew Bible* (Oxford: Oxford University Press, 1993); P. R. House, ed., *Beyond Form Criticism: Essays in Old Testament Literary Criticism* (Winona Lake, IN: Eisenbrauns, 1992), pp. 164-308.

43. Gunn, "Narrative Criticism," p. 201.

44. Alter, *The Art of Biblical Narrative*, p. 12 and pp. 47-62, respectively.

45. Alter, *The Art of Biblical Narrative*, p. 133.

On the second point, narrative criticism's uniting of all literary features under identifiable themes, D. J. A. Clines's book *The Theme of the Pentateuch* provides ample examples since it deals with the single overarching theme of the Pentateuch. Clines lists various definitions of "theme" and states their implications briefly.[46] He ultimately concludes: the theme applied to a literary work is the literary critic's own conceptualization of its plot that accounts most adequately for the content, structure, and development of the work.[47] With this theoretical understanding, he proposes the theme of the Pentateuch as "the partial fulfillment — which implies also the partial non-fulfillment — of the promise to or blessing of the patriarchs."[48] He sees that the divine promise to the patriarchs provides an impetus to move the story forward, to anticipate goals to be fulfilled in the future, and to trace a progression through the Pentateuch. In substance, this promise has three elements, "posterity, divine-human relationship, and land," which constitute the interrelationship among Genesis 12–50 and four books. The element of posterity is dominant in Genesis 12–50, divine-human relationship in Exodus and Leviticus, land in Numbers and Deuteronomy. He recognizes the presence of all three elements in the pentateuchal books, yet he compares the books in terms of the dominance of a specific element. For instance, the promise of land appears "only in scattered allusions in Exodus and Leviticus, compared with the dominant role it will assume in Numbers and Deuteronomy."[49] Moreover, he argues that Genesis 1–11 is "prefatory" to the divine promise to the patriarchs. This means that the divine promise should be read in conjunction with the theme of primeval history, God's continual commitment to this world despite the chronic sinful nature of humanity. Furthermore, according to Clines, the central theme of the Pentateuch has a historical function in that it addresses itself to the Babylonian exiles who find themselves in a position similar to the Israelites at the end of Deuteronomy, assuring them of the validity of God's promise, especially the promise of land.

Clines's approach is helpful for understanding the Pentateuch as a whole and as a literary unity. His affirmation that the amalgam of disparate

---

46. Clines, *The Themes of the Pentateuch*, pp. 17-21.

47. For Clines, the statement of theme serves as "an orientation to the work," "as a warning or protest against large-scale misunderstanding of a work," "evidence that the work is coherent or systematic," and "an historical-critical purpose." Furthermore, a theme should be distinguished from similar terms like "intention," "motif," and "subject." He also argues that there is ultimately only one theme in a literary work that indicates its unity, and that the theme of the literary critic is not necessarily the same as that of the author.

48. Clines, *The Themes of the Pentateuch*, p. 29.

49. Clines, *The Themes of the Pentateuch*, p. 52.

materials in the Pentateuch could have a unifying theme is a real advance in pentateuchal studies. In addition, his stress on the historical purpose and function of a theme shows that he does not totally abandon the diachronic issues pertinent to the literary work. Moreover, his insight that the theme is the literary critic's own conceptualization, which may not be the same as that of the writer, is noteworthy. Along with conceptual analysis, his stand implies that a text can and does have a value system of its own apart from the value system of the writer and the reader. This assertion, however, does not suggest that a text is ahistorical in its orientation or is separated from the reality of the reader, but that a text has its own thought system, which comes out of a distinct historical situation and does not necessarily represent the entire worldview of the writer; further, it is not automatically connected to the world of the exegete but is in need of being reconceptualized to be properly understood, due to its distance from the present.

Clines's work nevertheless raises a few questions concerning the theoretical definition of a theme and its application to the Pentateuch. First, if a theme were to be a conceptualization of the plot of a literary work, the theme for the Pentateuch seems not to have been much conceptualized. It is most likely a summary of the content of the Pentateuch. Why did God promise anything to the patriarchs in the first place? And why did God promise something to the patriarchs and not to other people? What role does the election of Israel play in the whole pentateuchal narrative? What does one make of the fundamental and conceptual differences in the expressions of the nature of God's relationship to humanity before and after the flood? To be sure, Clines presupposes a possibility of multiple themes in a literary work, particularly in the Pentateuch, and a necessity of comparison to distinguish the levels of themes, yet he does not illustrate this comparison sufficiently. No systematic relationship of the themes has been explored. Thus, the central theme, when it is connected to the theme of Genesis 1–11, seems to be broadened into a type of salvation history so that it becomes God's universal and favorable intentions toward all humanity. Second, his theme does not correspond to his assertion that the Pentateuch must be treated as a single literary work. The "partial" fulfillment of the promise presupposes that the full or complete fulfillment still awaits some future; hence the scheme of promise and fulfillment must go beyond the Pentateuch, perhaps to Joshua. In other words, the very formulation of the theme depends on the relation of the Pentateuch to the rest of the Primary History (books from Joshua to 2 Kings). Thus, he does not actually treat the Pentateuch as an independent work in its own right. Third, his rationale for regarding the Pentateuch as a single literary unit is problematic. He states as his reason that "the Pentateuch has been recognized as a literary entity by Jews, Samaritans, Christians and Muslims for somewhere between twelve hundred and twenty-five hundred years."[50] This means it is the history of the canon or the tradition of these religions that determines the Pentateuch as a single literary work, rather than an analysis of the literary nature and content of the work itself. Unless the internal textual evidence shows it to be a self-contained unity, all other rationale are in essence arbitrary impositions. Further, he takes the canonical unit of the Pentateuch for granted. Why does he differentiate Genesis 1–11 from 12–50 while accepting the divisions of the other four books? Is it not the case that Numbers 1:1–10:10 is much closer to the element of divine-human relations than that of land? Should the book of Deuteronomy as Moses' explanation of the laws to the second generation be treated as part of God's instruction to the Israelites similar to Leviticus? Fourth, what is the role of concepts in dominant/subordinate relationships among themes? Are these relationships to be determined based only on content or literary features on the surface of a text? For instance, what is the difference between the conceptual relationship of the theme of the promised land in Exodus-Leviticus and that of Genesis 12–50 or Numbers-Deuteronomy? Clines justifies the dominant/subordinate relationships among themes in light of their appearance on a narrative level. The conceptual aspects of texts need to be examined fully for the determination of an overarching theme of a literary work.

As part of the recent refinement of traditional form criticism, conceptual analysis has been influenced by structural linguistics, especially by W. Richter.[51] From his very complex arguments, three points are particularly relevant. First, he contends that the aspects of form and content must be differentiated substantively from each other in the interpretation of texts. With the criticism that the traditional literary approach has focused mainly on content at the expense of form, he proposes a treatment of the different levels of language as found in structural linguistics. Interpreters must first engage the text in phonemic, morphemic, and syntactic analysis.[52] The concep-

---

50. Clines, *The Themes of the Pentateuch*, pp. 11-12.

51. W. Richter, *Exegese als Literaturwissenschaft: Entwurf einer alttestamentlichen Literaturtheorie und Methodologie* (Göttingen: Vandenhoeck & Ruprecht, 1971). See also a section on "form critical approach" in O. H. Steck, *Old Testament Exegesis: A Guide to the Methodology*, trans. J. D. Nogalski (Atlanta: Scholars Press, 1998), pp. 95-119; K. Koch, "Linguistik und Formgeschichte," in his *Was ist Formgeschichte? Methoden der Bibelexegese*, 3rd ed. (Neukirchen: Neukirchener, 1974), pp. 289-342.

52. Richter (*Exegese als Literaturwissenschaft*, p. 31) outlines his program in six levels of investigation: "die Literal-, Form-, Gattungs-, Traditions-, Kompositions- und Redaktionsebene und die Inhaltsebene." For him this process cannot be reversed.

tual approach does not neglect the importance of the form of texts in explicating the linguistic utterance. However, Richter's clear separation of the formalized expression of texts from the content is difficult to accept. When a text is formulated, intentions and linguistic shape stand together from the beginning. Its linguistic shape is a means of expression that the language provides, yet it ultimately expresses or communicates something other than the linguistic shape itself. Rather than tearing apart the connection of form and content and consequently investigating them separately and sequentially, exegetical analysis must pay attention to their insoluble connection. Second, he distinguishes the analysis of form *(Formkritik)* from that of genre *(Gattungskritik).*[53] The former begins with an analysis of form (the individual text) and establishes an "outer structural form" and an "inner structural form," while the latter deals with a text-type. He contends that the former must precede the latter in methodological sequence and that this movement of investigation is irreversible. The conceptual approach welcomes the distinction of *Gattungskritik* from *Formkritik,* and yet it has difficulty seeing a nonreversibility of the movement in practice. These two *Kritiken* should be mutually convertible in that they influence each other. Third, Richter places *Literarkritik* at the beginning of his six levels of an exegetical process.[54] In essence *Literarkritik* is concerned both with literary features, such as forms, doublets, and repetitions that create thematic tensions within the text, and with parallels to other texts that provide comparisons of thematic or chronological significance. But these literary features could be signals that indicate the compositional integrity of the text and, further, point to the structural unity that comprises the organic linguistic entity of the text. Thus, unless the structural unity of the text has been determined, it is not clear whether these features belong to previous stages of the extant text. Thus, the structure analysis of the conceptual approach must be done before a literary-critical analysis can be attempted. Moreover, regarding the steps of an exegetical process, structure analysis should be undertaken prior to and apart from the textual criticism and translation of a text. Generally, text criticism has been taken as the first step in most exegetical work, as if the validity of the interpretation of a text depended primarily on establishing a correct or "original" text in the first place. But no text-critical work or translation can be done without assuming certain things about the meaning of

---

53. Richter, *Exegese als Literaturwissenschaft,* pp. 72-125, 125-52. He carefully defines his terms. For him, *Formgeschichte* refers to an investigation of the relation between smaller forms, while *Formengeschichte* concerns chronological relationships between groups of forms.

54. Richter, *Exegese als Literaturwissenschaft,* pp. 50-72. See also G. Fohrer et al., *Exegese des Alten Testaments* (Heidelberg: Quelle & Meyer, 1979), pp. 7 and 57.

the text.[55] Regardless of the stage in the history of the literary growth of the text, a structure analysis of the text clarifies the meaning of the text, which in turn provides a fundamental basis for tracing the changes in its meaning.

In short, the conceptual approach stands alongside other critical methodologies concentrating on a synchronic reading of texts. No doubt these other methodologies raise important questions as to the nature of texts and potentially provide contributions to the art of exegesis. Nevertheless, they do not pay much attention to the conceptual aspects of texts, and they lack a methodological focus even when they apply conceptual aspects in the actual interpreting of texts. In this contemporary situation in biblical criticism, the conceptual approach provides an empirically controlled analysis interested in a methodological focus on the interrelationship between explicit statements found at the surface of a text and the implicit concepts that lie underneath it.

---

55. Sanders recognizes this fact: "We attempted to discern the conceptuality lying back of a variant text or reading in each witness we deemed of value. This sometimes requires doing a structure analysis of the pericope in which a variant apparently lurked" ("Hermeneutics of Text Criticism," p. 11). Campbell also stresses the same point: "no text criticism can take place without some idea of the nature of the text under study, what might make sense in such a text and what can be expected of such a text" ("Structure Analysis and the Art of Exegesis," p. 78).

CHAPTER THREE

The Macrostructure of Numbers 10:11–36:13

A. Numbers 10:11–36:13 as a Distinct Unit

Numbers 10:11–36:13 is not an isolated literary entity apart from the rest of the Bible. It is part of the book of Numbers, of the books of Exodus through Deuteronomy (the narrative regarding the time of Moses from his birth to his death), of the Pentateuch, and of the even larger works of the Old Testament and the entire Bible. Nevertheless, there are sufficient reasons for dealing with this text as a distinct literary block relative to its immediate contexts, Numbers 1:1–10:10 and the book of Deuteronomy, and even the rest of the Pentateuch. The independent status of this text demands an analysis of its structure in its own right and on its own terms, even if its structure is relative to that of Numbers and ultimately to that of the Pentateuch. Thus, the first task in analyzing the macrostructure of Numbers 10:11–36:13 is to establish its outer limits within the book of Numbers. The question is whether or not 10:11 and 36:13 constitute the beginning and the end of a major division at the highest macrostructural level in the book of Numbers.

1. Other Structural Indicators

As seen in the survey of previous scholarship, the conclusion that Numbers 10:11 signals a decisive break in the book of Numbers is pervasive among interpreters. This conclusion is not self-evident, however, and needs substantiation. Many verses in Numbers other than 10:11 have been suggested as the beginning of major sections in the structure of the book. D. T. Olson provides a list of these verses: 1:1; 5:1; 7:1; 9:1; 9:15; 10:11; 10:29; 11:1; 13:1; 15:1; 20:1; 20:14; 21:1; 21:10; 22:1; 22:2; 25:1; 25:19 (Eng. 26:1); 28:1; 31:1; 32:1; and 33:1.[1] In the present

---

1. Olson, *The Death of the Old and the Birth of the New*, pp. 32-33. However, Olson does

section, only a few verses (5:1; 7:1; 9:1; 9:15; 10:29; 11:1) will be analyzed to investigate whether Numbers 1:1–10:10 is a self-contained unit in its entirety and whether 10:11 thus marks a new major block in the book. The remaining verses from Olson's list will be discussed later in conjunction with reconstruction of the macrostructure of 10:11-36 from its individual units.

a. Numbers 5:1

Numbers 5:1 constitutes the beginning of a literary unit concerning the exclusion of uncleanness from the camp (5:1-4). 5:1-4 has a coherent structure and consists of two parts: the report of the divine command (vv. 1-3) and the report of Israel's execution of the command (v. 4). The first part also has two sections: an introductory Yahweh speech formula (v. 1) and the speech proper (vv. 2-3). With this structure, how does the unit relate to what precedes it (chs. 1–4) and what follows it? Chapters 1–4 are well structured according to the generative concept of the organization of the sanctuary camp. However, the units following 5:1-4 are a series of laws and rituals not intrinsically related to one another. M. Noth's characterization of the materials in chapters 5–8, particularly the materials in 5:1–6:27, is a typical one: "several ordinances of very varied scope and very varied contents have been juxtaposed, with no recognizably close relationships, as far as subject-matter is concerned, either with each other or with what precedes and follows."[2] His characterization is applicable to the materials beyond chapter 6 up to 10:10.[3] The concerns of most of the pericopes in 5:1–10:10 do not bear any relation to each other, nor does their arrangement show any cohesive thematic progression. Moreover, it is not clear, from the sequence of their appearance in the book, whether they were gathered as a simple miscellaneous collection or compiled intentionally to supplement chapters 1–4. Nor is it entirely clear whether they were gathered by the same redactor or attached to chapters 1–4 as they appeared chronologically. Since 5:1-4 is part of this series of supplements, as Noth argues, its function relative to chapters 1–4 and 5:5–10:10 is ambiguous.

Unlike Noth, some commentators explore the interrelationships among the materials from 5:1–10:10. T. B. Dozeman briefly discusses the concept of

---

not discuss their relative significance on a compositional plane. Whether or not they signal the various structural layers in the book goes unaddressed in his exegesis on Numbers.

2. Noth, *Numbers*, p. 44.

3. Twelve independent literary units can be identified in 5:1–10:10 that appear to bear little relation to each other: 5:1-4; 5:5-10; 5:11-31; 6:1-21; 6:22-27; 7:1-89; 8:1-4; 8:5-22; 8:23-26; 9:1-14; 9:15-23; 10:1-10.

holiness as a thematic thread that binds these materials together.[4] He contends especially that chapters 5–6 "present legislation to protect the holiness of the camp from impurity" and are arranged two possible ways.[5] First, the units of chapters 5–6 are organized based on their relationship to the tabernacle:

I. Movement toward the tabernacle	5:1–6:21
A. From the outside of the camp	5:1-4
B. To the inside of the camp	5:5–6:21
II. Completion of the movement	6:22-27

Second, the units are outlined according to the scheme of divine command and fulfillment:

I. A law with divine command and fulfillment formulas	5:1-4
II. Laws without fulfillment formula	5:5–6:27
A. Laws proper	5:5–6:21
B. The priestly blessing functioning as the formula of completion	6:22-27

With these two outlines, Dozeman certainly goes beyond other commentators who suggest the thematic common denominator of chapters 5–6 and yet lack discussion on how this theme is unfolded in a specific outline. Nevertheless, his arrangements themselves raise questions. Is the first outline based on a theme comparable to the second based on a literary pattern? If not, which aspect (a theme or a literary pattern) is dominant and thus constitutes the macrostructure of 5:1–6:27? Let us assume that he is correct to assert that chapters 5–6 focus on their units' relationship to the tabernacle, as presented in the first outline, and that 1:1–10:10 is divided into two parts (1:1–6:27; 7:1–

---

4. Dozeman, "The Book of Numbers," pp. 26, 59-60. In fact, Dozeman outlines 1:1–10:10 around the concept of holiness: A. 1:1–6:27, Holiness and the Camp; B. 7:1–10:10, Holiness and the Tabernacle. Other commentators argue similarly. For instance, Milgrom (*Numbers*, p. 33) states that "their common denominator is the prevention and elimination of impurity from the camp of the Israelites lest the Lord abandon His sanctuary and people." Also, E. W. Davies (*Numbers*, p. 43) entertains the theme of "ceremonial purity of the camp" as a possible thread that binds the materials in 5:1–10:10 together. He acknowledges (pp. 89-90) that this concept has been proposed by J. de Vaulx (see also Sturdy, *Numbers*, p. 41; Wenham, *Numbers*, pp. 76-78; and Budd, *Numbers*, p. 54). His interest in finding the inner logic of these materials is, however, not enough to lead him to discuss the arrangement of their many units, and thus he remains skeptical that any appropriate function for 5:1-4 relative to what precedes and follows may be discerned. Davies' assertion of difficulty in discovering this interrelationship among the various units does not do justice to the text.

5. Dozeman, "The Book of Numbers," pp. 59-60.

10:10) based on the distinction of the camp and the tabernacle, as the titles indicate. Then, are not chapters 5–6 more closely connected to 7:1–10:10, which he titles as "Holiness and the Tabernacle," than to 1:1–4:49? The point is that his distinction between the camp and the tabernacle does not run through the entire text of 1:1–10:10, as his concept of holiness does. Even his choice of holiness as the constitutive factor for 1:1–10:10 is questionable. He argues that in particular 1:1–6:27 outlines "the effects of divine holiness on Israel's social organization," and that hermeneutically it "is an idealistic picture of community to which the people of God must strive."[6] Yet he neglects to mention the very purpose of the divine command to take a census of the tribes in 1:2-3, that is, a preparation for campaigns.[7] To be sure, Israel's camp must be arranged in reference to the tabernacle reflecting divine holiness, but the camp is organized for anticipated warfare as Israel departs from the Sinai. The concept of divine holiness is subordinate to the militaristic preparation of the camp. Moreover, the concept of the purity or impurity of the camp does not hold the material from 5:1–10:10 together. It is true that 5:1-4 concentrates on the cleanliness of the camp; as verse 3 indicates, "you shall put out both male and female, putting them outside the camp; they must not defile their camp, where I dwell among them." However, other than this verse, all the other pericopes in 5:5–10:10 do not explicitly reflect upon the purity of the camp.

Instead, the priesthood seems to be the likely thread for the material beginning at 5:5. The priests, specifically the Aaronide priests, handle various affairs of the Israelites in 5:5–6:27, while they are the point of differentiation from other sanctuary personnel in 7:1–10:10. For example, 5:11-31, a report on divine judgment for the woman suspected of adultery, is not related to the tent or the camp. The text says that a man must go to the sanctuary with his wife if he suspects his wife of committing adultery. Against the social background in which the Israelites went to the family or local community to solve such a problem, this text is unique in that a woman suspected of adultery is taken to the priest (v. 15a), and the priest handles the case (vv. 16, 17, 18 [x2], 19, 21, 23, 25, 26, 30). It is obvious that the priest controls the situation. Another example may point to the same conclusion. Similar to 5:11-31, the law regarding the Nazirites (6:1-21) shows that the Nazirites have to bring their of-

6. Dozeman, "The Book of Numbers," p. 26.

7. Dozeman provides two explanations for the purpose of the census mentioned in 1:3. First, the purpose is to fulfill "the divine command from Exod 30:11-16, in which the census is a prerequisite for the people to live in proximity to the sanctuary" ("The Book of Numbers," p. 33). Second, the purpose is "to prepare the community for war and to organize them into a regimented militia" ("The Book of Numbers," p. 34). Despite textual evidence in 1:3, he chooses the first over the second as the constitutive theme for 1:1–2:37.

ferings to the priests and must go to the entrance of the tent of meeting (v. 10). It is known that the Nazirites were already an established sect and were independent from the sanctuary, although loosely associated with it. But as 5:11-31 shows, the Nazirites were to be under the supervision of the priests (vv. 11, 16, 17, 19; cf. 20 [x2]). The priests control the removal of the Nazirites' accidental defilement and the termination of their vows. As these two examples show, the pericopes from 5:5 onward are associated with the priests rather than with the tent, the camp, or the tabernacle. The concept of divine holiness is at best an indirect unifier of these pericopes.

Finally, what is the function of 5:1-4? Is it conceptually closer to the description of the organization of the camp (chs. 1–4) or to the supplementary units centered around the priesthood? The text may function as "a suitable conclusion to the description of the camp order," as Gray asserts, because verse 3 states explicitly the protection of Yahweh's sacred dwelling in the midst of Israel as the purpose for the exclusion of unclean persons from the camp. Or 5:1-4 may function to connect 5:5–10:10 to 1:1–4:49 because it implies the priestly role of sanctifying the people in the sanctuary, distinguishing the priests from the Levites. Despite the uncertainty as to the function of 5:1-4, it is clear that this text plays a role within 1:1–10:10 or 1:1–6:21 in terms of its immediate literary context. The text breaks decisively between 1:1–4:49 and 5:1–10:10, but it does not carry its conceptual significance of the priesthood beyond 10:10. Verse 5:1 constitutes the beginning of the second major block within 1:1–10:10. Therefore, this verse signals a structural break that is not at the highest level in the book of Numbers.

b. Numbers 7:1

Numbers 7:1 is the beginning of the report concerning the cultic offering of the tribal leaders (7:1-89). Because of its chronological indicator, 7:1 cannot be the structural marker for a new major block at the highest level in Numbers. The chronological indicator of 7:1aα1 locates the entire content of chapter 7 in the context of Exodus 40.[8] In Exodus 40:1-15, Yahweh commanded Moses to

---

8. Methodologically, while many factors should be considered for reconstructing the macrostructure of a text, syntax is crucial. 7:1 is a good example. Most commentators translate this verse as a circumstantial clause, "On the day when . . .," which does not indicate the temporal gap between 1aα1 and 1aα2-b. Yet its syntax suggests that 1aα1 is to be set apart from the rest of the verse, and that it signals to the reader that the whole chapter should be read into Exodus 40. The microstructure of v. 1, therefore, has two parts: circumstance (which presupposes the erection of the tabernacle, 1aα1) and a report of Moses' actions (1aα2-b).

set up the tabernacle of the tent of meeting with all its furniture (vv. 1-8) and to anoint and consecrate it and its accoutrements (vv. 9-15). Verses 16 and 33b mention Moses' execution of Yahweh's command: "[Moses] did everything just as the LORD had commanded him . . . so [Moses] finished the work." Note, however, that although it is commanded in an earlier verse in the chapter, no acts of anointing or consecrating the tabernacle are reported in verses 17-33a. These are found in Numbers 7. In light of the omission, a chronological sequence of Exodus 40 and Numbers 7 can be reconstructed in the following way:

1. Yahweh's instructions to Moses: establishing the tabernacle with all of its accoutrements	Exod 40:1-15
2. Moses' compliance	
a. A statement of compliance	Exod 40:16
b. Erection of the tabernacle	Exod 40:17-33a
	Num 7:1aα1
c. Anointing and consecrating the tabernacle and altar	Num 7:1aα2-b
d. A statement of completion	Exod 40:33b
3. Yahweh's tabernacling presence by the cloud and glory	Exod 40:34-38
4. The offering of the tribal leaders	
a. For the tabernacle "on that day"	Num 7:2-9
b. For the altar on twelve subsequent days	Num 7:10-88
5. Moses' entering the tent of meeting	Num 7:89

According to this reconstruction, Moses could not go into the tent of meeting because he had not yet fulfilled the entire instructions of Yahweh (Exod 40:35a). Whether or not the author of Numbers 7:1 was aware of the affirmative statements of Moses' compliance in Exodus 40:16 and 33b, and whether or not he knew the clear reason for Moses' inability to enter the tent of meeting in Exodus 40:35b are open questions. But what he did in Numbers 7 is clear. He provided the statement of Moses' fulfillment of Yahweh's instructions and thus enabled Moses to enter the tent in verse 89. In short, Numbers 7 in its present form functions as a supplement to Exodus 40 and is meant to be read into the context of Exodus 40.

Consequently, the literary context for Numbers 7 reveals that the date presupposed in Numbers 7:1 (cf. Exod 40:17) is actually a month earlier than that mentioned in Numbers 1:1. Thus, the chronological indicator in 7:1aα1 reveals two facts: Exodus 40 is the literary background of 7:1-89; and time shifts from the first day of the *second month* in the second year after the Exodus to the first day of the *first month* in the second year. These facts are sufficient evidence not to consider Numbers 7:1 as the structural signal for a new major block in Numbers.

c. Numbers 9:1

Numbers 9:1 constitutes the beginning of the literary unit (9:1-14) concerning the Passover instruction, a supplement to Exodus 12:1-28. This verse is regarded as a structural signal for a major division because 9:1-14 contains precise dates after Numbers 1:1 and before Numbers 10:11. The dates are "in the first month of the second year after they [the Israelites] had come out of the land of Egypt" (9:1), "on the fourteenth day of this month [the first month]" (9:3, 5), and "in the second month on the fourteenth day" (9:11). It is immediately noticeable that these dates, particularly those mentioned in 9:1, 3, 5, create a chronological problem within the timetable of the rest of Numbers 1:1–10:10. The book of Numbers begins by reporting events that occurred in the *second* month in the second year (1:1). Chapter 7 narrates the prescription of offerings from the tribal leaders with the date "on the day when Moses had finished setting up the tabernacle," which is the first day of the *first month* in the second year after Exodus (Exod 40:17). Chapter 9 reports the Israelites' keeping the Passover "in the *first* month, on the fourteenth day of the month" (vv. 1-5), but then says that they are to keep it in the "*second* month on the fourteenth day" (vv. 9-14). What are the reasons for this alternation from the second month to the first month and back to the second? Is there any significance for these dates being where they are in the extant text? Is this inconsistency the result of scribal error, the writer's unawareness, or the writer's intentional entry even though he is aware of the inconsistency? Or did the writer append part of an already existing text to the previous material and not alter it?

Perhaps, as J. Milgrom asserts, there is no chronological inconsistency in 1:1–10:10.[9] The dates are explainable. First of all, none of the offerings mentioned in 7:2-89 were actually sacrificed on the day they were brought to the tabernacle, because בְּיוֹם in 7:1a can mean an indefinite time, and not a specific date. Second, the prescription of the Passover in 9:1-5 is considered a "flashback" to the original observance in Egypt. Third, this prescription is narrated immediately preceding the march from the wilderness of Sinai as a

---

9. Milgrom, *Numbers*, pp. 362-64, 367. Cf. idem, "The Chieftains' Gifts: Numbers, Chapter 7," *HAR* 9 (1985): 224.

reminder. Thus, for Milgrom, the chronological order of 1:1 to 10:11 is not out of joint. Milgrom's explanation may be more probable than treating the shift of time as one of many results from the mixture of different sources.[10] However, his proposal cannot be concretely substantiated. He seems to display loyalty to the integrity of the text, but it compels him to integrate the discrepancy into the text at the expense of textual evidence.

The precise dates in Numbers 1:1, (7:1), 9:1, 10:11 show their significance on different grounds from those that Milgrom suggests. These grounds point to the conceptual system in which the dates themselves are embedded, that is, the cultic calendar on which the chronological framework of the entire Sinai pericope rests. The calendric statements in Exodus through Deuteronomy are expressed in the system of the Babylonian lunar calendar. Yet, Exodus 12 yields a date for the Exodus event as the fifteenth day of the first month of the first year, not the first day of the first month of the first year, which is expected for an epochal event like the Exodus. This phenomenon implies that the expression of the date for the Exodus event follows the system of the Babylonian lunar calendar, but the date itself is formulated on some other basis. A calendrical system is already presupposed and is not triggered by the Exodus event. It is into this system that the Exodus event was projected. Yet the date of the Exodus event is based on Israel's cultic calendar formed by their religiosity. Since all other dates in Exodus through Deuteronomy are oriented upon the Exodus event, these dates are conceptually bound according to the cultic calendar, not the lunar calendar.

This conceptual system sheds light on the dates in the first ten chapters of Numbers. The passage 1:1 introduces the time of the Yahweh speech as being on "the first day of the second month of the second year." Since Exodus 40:17 specifies the first day of the first month of the second year as the date for the erection of the tabernacle, and Leviticus 1:1 gives no date, Leviticus in its entirety is framed within a one-month period. Moreover, since Numbers 1:1 provides the first precise date since Exodus 40:17, this verse is structurally significant. The date in Numbers 1:1 signals a new period within the total section of Leviticus 1:1–Numbers 10:10, yet Numbers 1:1–10:10 is structurally distinct from Leviticus. Despite sharing the same locality between Leviticus 1:1 and Numbers 1:1, Leviticus and Numbers are distinguished by the chronological indicator in Numbers 1:1. The period from the erection of the tabernacle (Exod 40:17; Lev 1:1) to the departure is to be divided into two parts, resulting in two distinguished periods of revelation from the tent, the periods of Leviticus 1–27 and Numbers 1:1–10:10.

10. Cf. Levine, *Numbers 1–20*, p. 295.

In light of this chronological framework of the Sinai pericope, Numbers 7:1 puts the offering of the tribal leaders back to the time of Moses' erection of the tabernacle. In a similar way, the date in 9:1 presupposes two textual blocks, Leviticus 1–27 and Numbers 1:1–10:10, and it directs the reader to regard the forthcoming account as having occurred in the period of time within Leviticus. In other words, the writer of 9:1-14 intended to show that Israel celebrated the Passover at "the wilderness of Sinai" in the first month of the second year. Since nowhere in Exodus 19–Leviticus 27 is there mention of celebrating Passover at "the appointed time," and since celebrating the Passover is very important based on Exodus 12, it is conceivable that 9:1-14 could be expected before Numbers 1:1 and after Exodus 40:17. The fact that it is reported only after Numbers 1:1 could mean that the Passover celebration, which took place in the first month of the second year, was not previously mentioned due to forgetfulness, and now it is reported in Numbers 9:1-14. If this argument is convincing, the dates in 9:1, 3, 5, 11 should not be considered as structural signals for the structure of the text. Other criteria would be needed to support such a division. If 9:1-14 is a textual addendum, a subdivision would divide the text according to each subsequent addition made to the text. Whether Numbers 9:1-14 is an addendum or not, it does not interfere with the chronology of Numbers 1:1–10:10. Consequently, 9:1 cannot be the structural signal for the major division within Numbers 1:1–10:10, let alone within the entire book of Numbers.

d. Numbers 9:15

Numbers 9:15 begins the narrative (9:15-23) concerning how the cloud regulates the movement of Israel during the journey from Sinai and throughout the wilderness wanderings afterward. Whenever the cloud descended upon the tabernacle, the people set up camp, and whenever the cloud lifted, they broke camp to continue their journey. P. J. Budd argues for this text as "the first of two which are clearly preparatory to the beginning of the march."[11] With the trumpets (10:1-10), the cloud in this text is "the means of guidance," which signals for Budd the second major section, whose title is "The Journey." Designating the cloud as one of "the means of guidance" presents no difficulty. But whether the whole text (9:15-23) functions as the beginning of a major section of the prepared journey is debatable. This unit can be under-

---

11. Budd, *Numbers*, p. 103. See the outline presented above (p. 22 in the present study), which is extricated from Budd's discussion on the second section in his tripartite outline.

stood as anticipatory of the journey, but it does not explicitly narrate the resumption of the journey. Numbers 10:11-12 narrates in its typical terminology the actual resumption of the journey, which presupposes Exodus 19:1-2. Then, Numbers 9:15-23 functions at best as the summary statement concerning Yahweh's guidance for Israel's journey from Exodus 14 onward.

The structure of Numbers 9:15-23 reinforces this conclusion. Compositionally, the text is divided into three component parts based on the tenses of the verbs used: I. Perfect tense (v. 15a), II. Imperfect tense (vv. 15b-23a), and III. Perfect tense (v. 23b). The three components appear to be an enlarged chiasm. They also reveal their own distinctive conceptual factors: Yahweh's presence (v. 15a), Yahweh's mobility (vv. 15b-23a: guiding and leading his people), and Israel's faithful obedience (v. 23b).[12] Comparing these three factors indicates that the first two are related more closely to one another than to the third because the first two focus on Yahweh. Thus, the structure of 9:15-23 should be divided into two parts: I. Report of the divine guidance of Israel through the cloud (vv. 15-23a) and II. Report of Israel's obedience (v. 23b).[13] Proportionally, the text as a whole concerns the mode of

---

12. What makes v. 23b noticeable is the tense of the verb, שׁמרו. The simple past indicates that Israel followed the directions of the fire-cloud throughout the wilderness wanderings. Except in v. 15a (הקים and כסה), שׁמרו in v. 23b is the only perfect tense; other verbs between vv. 15a and 23b are imperfects and should be taken as indicating frequent past acts. The question is why the writer used the perfect tense in the narration of the theological program for the future migration. Note the temporal context of Num 9:15-23: Israel was still in the wilderness of Sinai and was about to depart from Sinai. This then suggests that Num 9:15-23 is a summary of the writer's interpretation of the wilderness period, an experience in the remote past. In other words, the past tense in v. 23b stems from the intention of the writer. He is the reporter of the actual wilderness wanderings, and yet he is also the interpreter who uses the old tradition of Israel's repeated faithlessness to transform it into a positive one for his own readers. With this transformation, he shows that Israel fulfilled the divine instructions of the fire-cloud during the wanderings.

13. The structure of Num 9:15-23 is as follows:

Report of the Theological Program for the Migration	9:15-23
I. Divine guidance through the cloud	9:15-23a
A. Preparatory situation (perfect tense)	9:15a
1. Temporal: when the tabernacle was set up	9:15aα
2. Subject: the cloud	9:15aβ
B. Divine guidance proper (imperfect tense)	9:15b-23a
1. The essence of the divine guidance	9:15b-17
a. Regarding the time: evening	9:15b
b. General description	9:16
(1) Statement	9:16aα
(2) Mode	9:16aβ-b
c. Regarding the tent	9:17

Yahweh's guidance, rather than Israel's obedience. Conceptually, Israel's faithful obedience is subordinate to the content of Israel's obedience. It is impossible that Israel should follow God without knowing what and how to follow. This is the very reason that the writer has spent almost the entire passage explaining the essence of divine guidance and the required obedience.[14]

Part one is divided into a preparatory situation (v. 15a) and divine guidance (vv. 15b-23a). Verse 15a locates the text "on the day that the tabernacle was set up" and presents a specific object, "the cloud." These two, "when" and "what," are related in a temporal sequential perspective. Without the erection of the tabernacle, the cloud could never cover it. Moreover, verse 15a presupposes the conceptual shift in the movement of Yahweh's presence from Mount Sinai to the tabernacle, which is in the midst of Israel (cf. Exod 25:8). Throwing the reader back to the previous account of the erection of the tabernacle and the cloud covering the tabernacle in Exodus 40:34-38 implies also Yahweh's closeness to Israel, his permanent presence in their midst, and his readiness to move along and even to lead them forward through the wilderness. Since Israel has already departed from Sinai at Numbers 10:11, and since Numbers 9:15a recalls Exodus 40:34-38, Numbers 9:15a thus far concludes the narrative concerning the organization of Israel's camp, a migratory military camp centered around the sanctuary (Num 1:1–9:14). Exodus 40:34-38 functions similarly regarding Exodus 25:1–40:33.

(1) Lifted up	9:17a
(a) Cause: lifted up	9:17aα
(b) Result: decamp	9:17aβ
(2) Settled	9:17b
(a) Cause: settled	9:17bα
(b) Result: encamp	9:17bβ
2. Required exact obedience	9:18-23a
a. Departure formula	9:18a
b. Encampment formula	9:18bα
c. Exposition of encampment	9:18bβ-19
d. Encamping formula	9:20a
d'. Departing formula	9:20b
c'. Exposition of departure	9:21-22
b'. Encampment formula	9:23aα
a'. Departure formula	9:23aβ
II. Israel's obedience (perfect tense)	9:23b

14. In v. 23b, the writer reversed the order of ‏ושמרו בני־ישׂראל את־משמרת יהוה‎ in v. 19b to ‏את־משמרת יהוה שׁמרו‎. Putting ‏את־משׁמרת‎ in front of the verse to emphasize the associated connotation indicates the writer's implicit intention that the concept of Yahweh's guidance is dominant.

Furthermore, the radical shift of Yahweh's presence from Mount Sinai to the tabernacle is subordinate to the concept of Yahweh's guidance and leadership in Numbers 9:15b-23a. This shift is the dominant infratextual concept responsible for the surface presentation of Numbers 9:15-23 as a whole. It is symbolized by the cloud.[15] However, the text has been less concerned with the cloud itself than with what it signifies: Yahweh's direct guidance. Unlike Exodus 13:21-22, Numbers 9:15-23 speaks of a simple cloud, not in the form of "a pillar of cloud by day and a pillar of fire by night," and describes the cloud not as moving ahead of Israel to guide them in their ways but merely as indicating when Israel should rest from and proceed on their journey. This restricted function of the cloud corresponds to that of Exodus 40:34-38. Thus, the use of the cloud as the confirmation of Yahweh's presence and mobility with the tabernacle in Numbers 9:15-23 is in keeping with the cloud tradition that begins at Exodus 40.[16] The point is that the visible sign of Yahweh's presence serves now as a visible sign of Yahweh's movement and leadership of the Israelites. Israel's march to their promised land is conducted only at the direction of Yahweh, not of humans, not of Moses, and not even of the sign, the cloud. The cloud is only a "sign" of God's mobility. Seven occurrences of עַל־פִּי יהוה "by the order of Yahweh" (vv. 18 [x2], 20 [x2], 23 [x3]) affirm this conclusion without any further suspicion.

The writer reinforces the concept of Yahweh's direct guidance by adjoining to it the required obedience on the part of Israel. Since inexact obedience of the people is the same as disobedience to the divine command, accounts of the people's exact obedience are necessary. This is expressed by a chiasm that moves from departure to encampment and ends with departure. Beginning with the theme of departure in the chiasm not only is a logical step but also characterizes the text as a whole as one having to do with Yahweh's leadership in the wilderness. Accordingly, Israel responded to Yahweh's instructions with utmost diligence. No matter how long the cloud remained over the tent, whether it was only "from evening until morning" (v. 21), "two days" (v. 22), "a month" (v. 22), or even longer, as soon as the cloud lifted from

15. The nature of the cloud is that fire burned inside the cloud at all times, day and night, except that during the day it was not visible, whereas at night it could be seen in contrast to the enveloping darkness. This fiery appearance at night is in agreement with that of Exod 13:21-22.

16. It was only at Sinai that liberated Israel was organized around the tabernacle as a cultic-theocratic community and prepared for its final settlement. While the Exodus community was on a journey led by the pillars of cloud and fire (Exod 13:21-22; 14:19; 16:10), the Sinai community was on a campaign organized around the tabernacle, the place of the revelation of the glory of God, the place to which the cloud became related (Lev 16:2, 13; Num 9:15-21; 10:11-12; 12:10; 14:14; 16:12).

the tabernacle, Israel departed. Israel's encampment and decampment were totally dependent upon the movement of Yahweh, signaled by the ascending and descending of the cloud from the tabernacle.

As seen above, the dominant concept of Num 9:15-23, Yahweh's mobility and guidance represented by the cloud, indicates that this text is a necessary part of the description of the preparation for the upcoming journey. This text belongs to the section before the resumption of the journey and concludes the organization of the migratory sanctuary campaign (Num 1:1–10:10). It belongs to the entire narrative of the encampment (Exod 19–Num 10:10), but not to the narrative of the journey's resuming at Numbers 10:11. Thus, Numbers 9:15 should not be regarded as a structural signal for the major division of Numbers.

e. Numbers 10:29

Numbers 10:29 begins the passage (10:29-36) concerning the departure from Mount Sinai. It has been regarded as the structural signal for a major block in Numbers because 10:29-36 narrates how the prepared journey was conducted differently from that described in the preceding sections, 9:15-23 and 10:11-28. This assertion is understandable from the vantage point of readily noticeable differences between 10:11-28 and 10:29-36. In contrast to 10:12, 10:29-36 mentions no destination. In verse 12 the Israelites decamped from Sinai and encamped at the wilderness of Paran, but in verses 29-32 they were still at "the mount of Yahweh," and only set out from it in verse 33. In verse 21 the ark is carried in the midst of the Israelites; in verse 33, in contrast, it precedes them. As G. B. Gray points out, linguistic differences also exist.[17] Moreover, conceptually, Yahweh's mobility and his guiding role have been greatly stressed in 9:15-23. Yet it is the possibility of a human guide whom Moses sought from Hobab that has been postulated in 10:29-32, and the guiding role has been attributed to the ark in verses 33-36. Although verse 34 reveals a restricted function of the cloud to the same degree as 9:15-23, verse 33 clearly describes the ark of the covenant as leading the Israelites and seeking their next resting place, and verses 35-36 focus on the military function of the ark as an emblem of the divine warrior, who is invisibly enthroned over the ark, fighting for his people.

These literary and conceptual differences distinguish 10:29-36 from what precedes it (9:15-23 and 10:11-28). The passage 10:29-36 forms a parallel to 10:11-28, but not a strict continuation of it. Structurally, what do these dif-

---

17. Gray, *A Critical and Exegetical Commentary on Numbers*, p. 93.

ferences signify? Commentators generally agree that these differences stem from the literary-critical distinction between the Priestly sources and the Yahwistic-Elohistic sources occurring at Numbers 10:29 and onward.[18] At 10:29 the narrative of the composite old sources, JE, resumes for the first time since its last citation at Exodus 34:28. To argue, then, that 10:29 is a structural signal is ultimately based on literary criticism using the so-called Documentary Hypothesis, which assigns Numbers 1:1–10:28 to the P source and 10:29–12:16 to the JE sources.[19] But literary criticism does not carry significant weight in the present investigation, not because its criterion is illegitimate for the scientific study of a text but because it is based on hypothetical predecessors of the extant text. Methodologically, the text as it now stands, the final form of the text, is a realistic starting point for an empirically controlled investigation, if the reconstructed structure of 10:11–36:13 is to be verified. Moreover, the fact that Numbers 1:1–10:28 consists solely of the P source and 10:29 onward of the combination of the P and the JE sources does not mean that literary criticism is the basis for dividing the narrative. It is virtually impossible to divide the entire book of Numbers based on its literary makeup; and no commentary proposes an outline reflecting source analysis, although many commentaries consciously disassemble Numbers according to that method.

f. Numbers 11:1

Numbers 11:1 is seen by Noth and G. W. Coats as the decisive marker for the beginning of a new major block because the first major block in Numbers ends with 10:36.[20] At the outset, it is important to classify Noth's and Coats's arguments separate from an analysis based on literary criticism. They divide Numbers on the basis of "theme," particularly the wilderness theme. If the source distinction is constitutive for the division of Numbers, then why did Noth not end the first major block at 4:49 since he treats what follows (5:1–

18. Gray, *A Critical and Exegetical Commentary on Numbers*, p. 92; Noth, *Numbers*, p. 77; Budd, *Numbers*, p. 113; Levine, *Numbers 1–20*, p. 311; E. W. Davies, *Numbers*, p. 92. Dozeman ("The Book of Numbers," p. 94) is in line with these commentators, though he designates 10:29-36 as part of the pre-Priestly history.

19. For a comprehensive comparison of pentateuchal sources, see the appendix, Table of Pentateuchal Sources, in W. Harrelson, *Interpreting the Old Testament* (New York: Holt, Rinehart and Winston, 1964), pp. 487-92. For a thorough analysis of different literary sources in Numbers, see Levine, *Numbers* (see also Noth, *Numbers* and Budd, *Numbers*).

20. Noth, *Numbers*, p. vii; Coats, *Genesis*, p. 17.

6:27) as nonsource material,[21] or at 7:89 for the same reason,[22] or at 10:28 since he observes in 10:29-36 the first appearance of the old sources "after having been long set aside"?[23] It is true that Noth heavily utilizes a literary-critical distinction between the P and the JE sources, and thus he views the text of Numbers as a compilation of more than three written sources (J, E, and P) that still has room for various substantial secondary additions or insertions even after the completion and combination of the written sources. Through this literary analysis, he traces the "themes" of the pentateuchal traditions, which are themselves abstracted from the text. What Noth actually did in his commentary on Numbers is to reconstruct the literary growth of Numbers by imposing various themes upon the book. Thus, the abstracted themes are responsible for his division of Numbers. Literary criticism for him is at best an analytical tool for tracing the themes.

Similar to Noth, Coats uses literary criticism extensively, but he characterizes the sources substantively different from Noth. For Coats, the P source is "no longer narrative at all . . . but only a schematized report of events which constitute the narrative tradition for the older sources," and, in contrast, J "preserves the structure of successive sagas . . . [and] the flavor of folk tradition."[24] The P and the J sources are not simply compiled anymore; they are systematized with an identifiable thought line. His characterization of sources serves to establish the literary cohesiveness of each source. This is doubtless a much more advanced understanding of sources than Noth's. Fundamentally, Coats's advancement stems from his clarification of the term "theme." He understands theme as "the formative unifying principle for constructing a lengthy narrative."[25] This def-

---

21. Noth (*Numbers*, p. 44) characterizes 5:1–6:27 as a juxtaposition of various and quite different laws "with no recognizably close relationships, as far as subject-matter is concerned, either with each other or with what precedes and follows." He (pp. 44-45) suggests that these laws are inserted at this point because the narrative is nearing the end of the period at Sinai; and these laws follow "the style of the P-narrative and in their present form they come from a comparatively late period, even if they do contain older traditional material."

22. Noth regards Num 8:1-4 as "an isolated fragment" (*A History of Pentateuchal Traditions*, p. 9, n. 12). He also sees its function as an appendix to Exod 25:31-40. For him, it amplifies Exod 25:37b without adding any new information; v. 4 summarizes Exod 25:31-34 with particular emphasis on the hammered work (*Numbers*, pp. 65-66).

23. Noth, *Numbers*, p. 77.

24. Coats, *Genesis*, pp. 19, 21, respectively.

25. Coats (*Genesis*, p. 18) elaborates further by saying that "theme" is "properly a structure term, characterized by an exposition introducing the key leitmotif and a composition that moves from the introduction to some recognizable conclusion. The composition may include diverse materials such as distinct sagas, tales, and novellas. It may include simply a saga. But the point is that the leitmotif combines the diverse units into a larger body of narration."

inition indicates, as in his characterization of the sources, his attempt to bridge the gap between a content-oriented understanding of a theme and a form- or pattern-oriented understanding of structure. A theme functions not only by making reference to the dominant element of content but also by being itself the key to the structural unity of the larger narrative. In this clarification, Coats's theme is closely related to the term "structure" used in the present study. However, he seems not to go beyond a formalistic connection between content and form in the narrative and to cling to content more than form. Thus, although he claims a theme as "a structure term," he understands it as "the leitmotif," the dominant element of content, which "combines the diverse units into a larger body of narration."

This criticism can be proven by Coats's own formulation of themes of the Pentateuch in general and by his structure of the Hexateuch in particular. First, he presents four themes in the Hexateuch: (1) God's blessings to the world through the patriarchal figures; (2) the Exodus from Egypt expressing God's redemption from the oppression of the sons of Jacob; (3) the wilderness wanderings, indicating God's leadership in the journey from Egypt to Canaan; and (4) the conquest, focusing on God's mighty act of securing the land for the Israelites.[26] Neither the quantity nor the quality of Coats's themes are the same as Noth's. With the inclusion of the theme of conquest, which he found solely in the book of Joshua, Coats goes beyond the pentateuchal traditions on which Noth focuses. Instead of Noth's five themes for the pentateuchal traditions, Coats reduces the number of themes for the hexateuchal traditions to four. He combines Noth's themes of "Guidance into the Arable Land," "Guidance in the Wilderness," and "Revelation at Sinai" into one category, "the wilderness wanderings, indicating God's leadership in the journey from Egypt to Canaan." More than the number and boundaries of the themes, his themes are theologically oriented, not purely literary in nature. Theological overtones of the themes clearly prove Coats's tendency to lean toward content rather than form.

Second, Coats presents his structure of the Hexateuch according to the four themes, and thus he has four major blocks. Each block is subdivided into several sections depending on the number of subthemes. The first major block of Numbers, which ends with 10:36, belongs to the wilderness theme. More specifically, Numbers 1:1–10:36 belongs to the subtheme Sinai, which combines Exodus 19:1–40:38 and Leviticus, whereas the rest of Numbers (Num 11:1–36:13) belongs to the subtheme "God's aid in the wilderness," which also includes Exodus 14:1–17:16. In this case, Coats cannot escape from

---

26. Coats, *Genesis*, pp. 18-19.

the critical remarks that apply to Noth.[27] It is sufficient to say that Coats's divisions are not extricated from the text but are imposed on the text based on abstracted themes. Ending the first major section in Numbers at 10:36 is not based on the theme intrinsic to Numbers itself but on the overarching theological theme that begins at Exodus 19:1. The literary integrity and the final form of Numbers have been dissected for the sake of theme. While he understands theme to function as "the formative unifying principle for constructing a lengthy narrative," he focuses more on the dominant element of content and thus ignores the conceptual coherence of the extant text.

Moreover, Coats's clarification of theme leads him to present the structure of the Priestly source in distinction to the structure of the Yahwistic source. Obviously, for him, each source preserves its own literary unity. He does not discuss, however, the literary unity of the combined sources in the extant text, and so he does not pursue the question of whether the structure of each source (1) retains its integrity, which causes possible conceptual conflicts; (2) simply stands juxtaposed to each of the other sources; or (3) has been integrated with the others, creating another conceptual integrity. He is silent on this structural question of the extant text of Numbers. Therefore, Coats's advancement beyond Noth in terms of both characterization of sources and clarification of theme still does not help him validate Noth's argument for ending the first major block at 10:36, which consequently leads Coats to see 11:1 as the structural signal for the next major block.

In short, what has been discussed thus far can be summarized as follows. First, Numbers 5:1 signals a division of Numbers not at the highest level but only at the level of the major break within Numbers 1:1–10:10. Second and third, chronological indicators in 7:1 and 9:1 do not interfere with the chronological framework of 1:1–10:10. The former compels the reader to read the entire chapter 7 into Exodus 40, whereas the latter leads one to see the first celebration of Passover at the appointed time after Exodus 12 as happening before Numbers 1:1 and after Exodus 40:17. Fourth, 9:15-23 plays the role of summarizing Numbers 1:1–9:14 and/or of concluding the Sinai pericope, and thus the passage belongs to the preparation of the anticipated journey rather than to the beginning of the journey itself. Fifth, the literary-critical distinction between the Priestly and the Yahwistic-Elohistic sources that begins at 10:29 does not constitute a division of Numbers. Sixth, that 11:1 institutes the wilderness theme is debatable due to the same theme's location in Exodus 14:1–17:16, and the use of thematic criterion in this instance disregards the literary

---

27. For a critical evaluation on Noth's thematic approach for reconstructing the structure of Numbers, see pp. 15-19 in the present study.

integrity and conceptual coherence of the extant text, particularly in the case of the book of Numbers. Thus, neither Numbers 5:1; 7:1; 9:1, 15; 10:29; nor 11:1 qualifies as the structural signal for the major block of Numbers at the highest level.

2. Numbers 10:11

As mentioned above, most publications designate Numbers 1:1–10:10 as a coherent literary unit and thus 10:11 as the beginning of a major unit in Numbers at the highest level. Textual evidence provided in Numbers itself affirms this conclusion. Numbers is to be subdivided between 10:10 and 10:11 because of chronological, topographical/geographical, and conceptual aspects signaled in 10:11 and 12, the programmatic statement for Israel's departure from the wilderness of Sinai. For chronological data, verse 11a has "in the second year, in the second month, on the twentieth day of the month," one of a few precise dates that connects what follows to Numbers 1:1 in its immediate literary context, to Exodus 40:17 and 19:1 in its larger context, and to Exodus 12 (cf. Num 33:3) in terms of its cultic origin. For topographical/geographical data, verse 12a mentions the wilderness of Sinai, which refers back to the location of Exodus 19:1. New information contained in verse 12b is Israel's movement from the wilderness of Sinai to another place, the wilderness of Paran. In terms of conceptual aspect, the statement נעלה הענן מעל משכן הידת in verse 11b addresses the activity of migration. Particularly, the verb עלה is used for a migration and points to verse 12, which refers back to the theological program for the migration in 9:15-23. Additionally, the verb in verse 12, נסע, denotes a specific kind of movement, decampment for migration or a campaign. Moreover, two of these three factors, the chronological and topographical/geographical indicators, are extricated from the surface level of the text, while the conceptual factor lies underneath the text. Their locations imply that the relationship among them consists in the former playing a secondary or supportive role to the latter. With these three factors, Numbers 10:11, 12 indicate a clear departure from 1:1–10:10. Since chronological and topographical/geographical data are readily available and point to the conceptual factor, these data must be discussed first.

a. Chronological Factors

Among the many chronological data peppered throughout Numbers,[28] only a few give clear and precise dates (1:1; 10:11; 33:38). The entire series of events reported in 1:1–10:10 has happened within nineteen days starting from "the first day of the second month, in the second year" (1:1) to "the second year, in the second month, on the twentieth day of the month" (10:11). Not only is the duration of the events calculated precisely, but also the dates themselves in these chapters are precise and not out of order.[29] Compared to those in the first ten chapters, all dates in the rest of Numbers are imprecise or dislocated. No longer is there a date that follows the calendric formulae and specifies any event in the twenty-six chapters after chapter 10. For example, Moses sent out the spies at the time of the first ripe grapes (13:17-20); the second census took place "after the plague" (26:1); Miriam died "at the first month" (20:1; no day and year is specified; it is probably the fortieth year). The date of Aaron's death may be the only exception, as it is noted "in the fortieth year after the Israelites had come out of the land of Egypt, on the first day of the fifth month" (33:38). No precise date is recorded after this until Deuteronomy 1:3, where Moses spoke to all Israel "in the fortieth year, on the first day of the eleventh month." Then, the duration from 10:11 to 33:38 can be calculated as approximately more than thirty-eight years, and, in the same way, from 33:39 to the end of Numbers approximately six months have elapsed.

The result is obvious. These dates (1:1; 10:11; 33:38) divide Numbers into two distinct periods of time dependent upon whether or not they are precisely calculable: I. the events that occurred within nineteen days (1:1–10:10) and II. the events that occurred in approximately thirty-nine years (10:11–36:13). It is possible to divide section II further into two subsections: A. more than thirty-eight years between the second month of the second year and the fifth month of the fortieth year (10:11–33:49) and B. about six months after the

28. A comprehensive discussion of the editorial and traditio-critical significances that these data imply is beyond the scope of this study. However, some classifications can be made: a simple designation of the time for the next event by "tomorrow" (11:18; 14:25; 16:7, 16); a date referring to the duration such as "all day and all night and all the next day" (11:32; cf. 6:4, 5, etc.); a date for a particular event such as Passover (9:3, 5, 6, 11) or Sabbath (28:9) and other occasions; a date indicating the event following on the next day after the previous event (14:40; 17:6, 23); and a date making reference to "after" an event (26:1, etc.).

29. See p. 11, n. 25 and pp. 77-179 in the present study for the discussion of the chronology of Num 1:1–10:10, particularly the alternation from the second month (1:1) to the first month (9:1, 5; cf. 7:1) and back to the second month (9:11) within the second year after the Exodus event.

fifth month of the fortieth year (33:50–36:13). In this case, 33:38 serves to delimit sections not at the highest level but within section II. On the other hand, the date in 10:11 marks the decisive break in Numbers at the highest level and functions as the beginning of the imprecise period of almost thirty-nine years of the Israelites' wanderings. In other words, the date in 10:11 signals the radical shift from calculable days followed by the calendric formulae to the approximate years of Israel's wanderings in the wilderness.

b. Topographical and Geographical Factors

Many topographical and geographical indicators appear throughout Numbers. Not Numbers 10:11 but verse 12a contains the first geographical reference: "then the Israelites set out by stages from the wilderness of Sinai." This is a summary statement of what Israel had done from 10:11 onward. It is immediately noticeable that the Israelites are moving away from a particular place, the wilderness of Sinai. The phrase "by stages" primarily connotes the numerous places through which Israel went. For example, there is the list of the sites that the twelve spies visited (13:21-24), of the locations that Israel battled against and took from Sihon and Og (21:24-35), of the places that the two tribes and the half-tribe settled in the Transjordan (32:1-3, 33-42), and of the forty-two stations to which the Israelites journeyed by stages after the Exodus. Note that Numbers 10:11–36:13 contains at least six territories (the wilderness of Paran, the wilderness of Zin, the land of Edom, the Negeb, the boundary of the Amorites, and the land/plain of Moab) that inevitably include many topographical localities. Almost all of these topographical and geographical markers are concentrated in the narrative after 10:11, while the dominant geographical location of Numbers 1:1–10:10 is the wilderness of Sinai (1:1, 19; 3:4, 14; 9:1).[30] Numbers 10:11, then, signals a decisive break between the material framed by one particular location and the material concerning many different locations.

However, that all events prior to 10:11 took place in one and the same location, the wilderness of Sinai, may be disputed by two other data: (1) the oc-

---

30. Geographical markers are the wilderness of Paran (10:12; 13:3, 26), the wilderness of Zin (13:21; 20:1; 27:14 [x2]; 33:36; 34:3, 4), the land of Edom (20:23; 21:4; 33:37; 34:3), the Negeb (13:7, 22, 29; 21:1; 33:40), the boundary of the Amorites (21:13, 31), and the land/plain of Moab (21:11, 13 [x2], 15, 20, 28; 22:1, 36; 26:3, 63; 31:12; 33:44, 48, 49, 50; 35:1; 36:13). Some of the topographical markers are Taberah (11:3), Kibroth-hattaavah (11:34), Hazeroth (11:35; 12:16), Kadesh (13:26; 20:1, 14, 16, 22; 27:14; 32:8 [Kadesh-barnea: 34:4]; 33:36, 37), Meribah (20:13), Mount Hor (20:22, 23; 21:4), etc. Cf. Num 33:3-49.

currences at Mount Sinai both before and after 10:11 (3:1 and 28:6) and at the wilderness of Sinai after 10:11 (26:64; 33:15, 16), and (2) the other topographical markers within 1:1–10:10 regarding the localities in which the camp (5:3, 4) and the tent of meeting are situated (1:1; 2:2; 3:7, 38; 7:89; 8:9, 15, 19; 10:3). Yet these facts are rather easily explained. First, Mount Sinai in 3:1 is associated with the chronological marker, "at the time when the LORD spoke with Moses on Mount Sinai." This verse moves the event back to the time of the Exodus.[31] Similarly, the insertion of העשׂיה בהר סיני in 28:6, which interrupts the sequence of verses 5 and 7, refers עלי ימיד back to Exodus 29:38-42 in order to clothe it with the full authority of Sinaitic legislation.[32] Besides, Mount Sinai is a topographical feature included in a geographic territory, and thus all events that occurred on Mount Sinai are inevitably part of the events that happened in the wilderness of Sinai. Unlike the chronological data of 9:1-5, "Mount Sinai" in 3:1 and 28:6 does not create any inconsistency with the dominant reference to "the wilderness of Sinai" in the rest of the first ten chapters. The same conclusion can be drawn from the references to the wilderness of Sinai after 10:11 because they are simple reflections of the first census narrated in Numbers 1 (26:64) and of the early part of Israel's journey reported in Exodus 17:1 and 19:2 (33:15, 16).

Second, it is clear that the tribes pitched their camps on sites different from where the tent of meeting was located. How are these two localities related to each other topographically? In a line, circularly, in a square, or otherwise?[33] In terms of the arrangement of the camp, Numbers presents two different pictures. On the one hand, while the Israelites are at rest, their camp is arranged "around" the tent of meeting (2:3). On the other hand, when they set out, their camp is organized in a linear fashion (2:17b; 10:14).[34] Despite dif-

---

31. Milgrom (*Numbers*, p. 15) suggests that Num 3:1-13 reports the events that may have occurred "after the episode of the golden calf apostasy" in Exodus 32.

32. Ashley, *The Book of Numbers*, p. 564; Milgrom, *Numbers*, p. 239.

33. Milgrom, *Numbers*, pp. 340-41. Milgrom argues that Israel's camp in the wilderness was arranged in the form of a square, parallel to the Egyptian camp of Rameses II, whereas Israel's war camp in later times was arranged in a circle. However, he neglects to comment on the relationship between the camp and the tent of meeting, although he draws the square formation diagrammatically, which shows the tent of meeting at its center.

34. The term סביב means literally "around, surrounding." This fact, coupled with the clear references in 2:3, 10, 18, 25 to east, south, west, and north, respectively, provides a guideline for the camp's arrangement. Yet, it does not specify the shape of the camp, only its position "surrounding" the tent of meeting. 2:17b suggests that the tribal camps were to march consecutively, which is affirmed by "company by company" in 10:14. In terms of the position of the Levites, they are placed around (סביב) the tent of meeting when they are at rest (1:50b, 53a), but they are positioned between (בתוך) the tent of meeting and the other tribes when they march (2:17a).

ferent formations, these two orders, an encampment order and a marching order, share the same aspect in that both of them take the tent of meeting as their point of reference. The terms מנגד and סביב in 2:2b suggest that Israel set up their camp vis-à-vis the tent of meeting, facing it.[35] This means that the tent of meeting is not located at "the center of the camp," but "its place constitutes the center for the camp."[36] This concept is reinforced by the positions of the individual tribes with respect to the tent of meeting. Numbers 2 assigns three tribes to occupy each side of the tent of meeting, east (vv. 3-9), south (vv. 10-16), west (vv. 18-24), north (vv. 25-31), with the tribe of Levi between it and the tribes, surrounding it (v. 17). Each of the three tribes, presumably, is not located behind the other so that each subsequent tribe lies further from the tent of meeting than the previous one. Rather, each would be located side by side facing the tent of meeting with approximately an equal distance from it and all with a direct visual line to it. No matter what shape the encampment may take or where the camp is, the tent of meeting is the point of reference for the placement of the tribes.

It has been determined that the location of Israel's camp depends on the location of the tent of meeting. The question remains: Where then is the tent of meeting located in Numbers 1:1–10:10? Obviously, it is located in the desert of Sinai from the time of its erection (Exod 40; cf. Lev 1:1) until the Israelites set out from there (Num 10:11, 14). The same locative, ב, in both the phrases "the wilderness of Sinai" and "the tent of meeting" in Numbers 1:1, supports this view. The choice between equally valid options reflects the conceptual and perceptual framework of the writer of the text. Thus, the localities of Israel's camp and of the tent of meeting do not create a conceptual tension with the wilderness of Sinai as the dominant geographical indicator for Numbers 1:1–10:10.

c. Conceptual Factors

A calculable duration (nineteen days) and one particular location (the wilderness of Sinai) point beyond themselves. These chronological and geographical indicators are at best explicit information on the surface level of Numbers 10:11-12. What is the relationship between these chronological and

---

35. The combination of מן and נגד in מנגד suggests this point. The word מן means "from," which implies a distance between a point of reference and its object, while נגד means literally "in front of, opposite to."

36. Knierim, *Text and Concept in Leviticus 1:1-9*, p. 32, n. 23.

topographical/geographical components? Are they capable of conveying in themselves the significance of the events that they accompany? Why is it that the short and precise duration of the Israelites' stay in the wilderness of Sinai is important in comparison with the long and imprecise time period of their wanderings in numerous places? Does the Israelites' stay at Sinai function differently from their stay on the plain of Moab (Num 22–36) or from the other geographical territories in which they stayed prior to their arrival at the plain of Moab? These questions emerge from explicit expressions on the surface level of 10:11-12 and point to the conceptuality underneath the text which controls their ultimate importance for the text.

Numbers 10:12a does not simply show where the Israelites were, but it reports what they were about to do. The text is interested not so much in the location of Israel in the wilderness of Sinai as in the Israelites' departure from there. The following verse (v. 13) strengthens the activity of Israel's movement, particularly with the word בראשנה. This movement is primarily indicated by the verb ויסעו and implied by למסעיהם. The verb נסע, "to pull out, set out, or decamp," denotes a specific aspect of movement, decamping from a location with an intention to march from it. For the other aspect of the movement, חנה "to pitch a camp, or encamp" is used since it denotes encamping at a new location with an intention to stay there. These two verbs together indicate a bipolar focus on decamping and encamping as two parts of one process. Linguistically, decamping and encamping by themselves focus only on signaling the beginning and the ending of the march and thus are inadequate to address the question of what happens after decamping and before encamping. The march itself is expressed in terms like בוא "to go, come, or go in," or הלך "to walk, or go." Yet, semantically, נסע and חנה address the movement in its entirety, its beginning, its ending, and the portion in between. Thus, the decampment-encampment cycle does include all relevant events.

A narrative constituted by נסע and חנה can be categorized as a migration narrative expressed on the basis of an itinerary. To understand what 10:11 and 12 imply semantically, the term itinerary needs to be scrutinized.[37] An itinerary in its pure form is a list of place names of a course of travel, but as an account of a journey it certainly includes more than a simple list of place names. The latter understanding of an itinerary focuses primarily on the marching, a translocation from one place to another. This translocation in-

---

37. The following discussion stems mainly from Knierim's analysis on the term "itinerary" from its literary form to its conceptual aspects. His analysis has been communicated in personal conversations.

volves the pattern of decamping and encamping denoted by verbs such as נסע and חנה.

Numbers 33:3-49 and 21:10-20 are good examples. Since Numbers 33:3-49 contains forty-two stations on Israel's march from Rameses, after the Exodus event, to the plains of Moab, and since it constitutes the march with the two verbs נסע and חנה, it is sometimes called an itinerary. However, if an itinerary is the organizational principle of Numbers, Numbers would be divided into forty-two subsections according to the forty-two place names in 33:3-49. No one, even among those who consider geographical indicators responsible for the organization of Numbers, proposes such an outline. The stations found in this text are not the same as the book as a whole. Thus, the migration narrative in 33:3-49 gives no criterion for the structure of Numbers. This text is not an itinerary but a narrative about a certain type of migration based on an itinerary. Place names in this text are at best an indication of a geographical systematization of the topographical material. In the case of Numbers 21:10-20, it is true that these verses contain an itinerary with a series of decampments and encampments at new places. However, this pattern is broken by expansions in verses 13-18b. Not every station in the series is of equal importance. Nor do the Israelites always decamp and encamp at the same intervals; some of the encampments last longer than others. Thus, the importance of events during the period of encampment is highlighted. The value of each station is based on criteria other than a pattern of decamping and encamping.

These two examples show that an uncritical consideration of the nature of Numbers 10:11–36:13 as an itinerary, simply because its narrative is viewed as one of long movements based on the repeated activity of making a camp and breaking a camp through many places, is obviously not accurate. The word "itinerary" is not specific enough to be the constitutive concept for the structure of this text, or the entire book of Numbers, for that matter. Traditions or theological interests sometimes lead to expansions of the narrative of migration.

Specifically, what role does the ongoing repetition of decamping and encamping, as alluded to by ויסעו and למסעיהם in Numbers 10:12a, play in the question of 10:11 as the structural signal for the macrostructure of Numbers? The cycle of decamping and encamping points to the fact that in Numbers 1:1–10:10 no actual breaking of camp by the Israelites with the intention of moving to another place has been reported, although this text has twenty-two occurrences of נסע in it.[38] However, the repeated cycle of decamping and

---

38. 1:51; 2:9, 16, 17 [x2], 24, 31, 34; 4:5, 15; 9:17, 18, 19, 20, 21 [x2], 22 [x2], 23; 10:5, 6 [x2].

encamping by the Israelites from 10:11 onward is undeniable. The Israelites repeatedly decamped from one place and encamped at another (12:16; 14:25; 20:1, 22; 21:4, 10-13; 22:1; cf. ch. 33). This fact is structurally important. Although various aspects of Israel's migration — the distances they journeyed, the numbers of the stations they passed through, the duration they spent at each settled place — may vary in 10:11–36:13, their activity of decamping/encamping and the marches themselves make a sharp distinction between 10:11–36:13 and 1:1–10:10. The nature of 10:11–36:13 is narrative concerning marches — a mixture of statements of the movements themselves and reports of the events that happened both in between the stations and at the settled locations, whereas the nature of 1:1–10:10 is narrative concerning the encampment at one particular location.[39]

This distinction needs to be further qualified in terms of the character of the two passages. Compared to the static encampment of 1:1–10:10, what does the repeated decamping and encamping and the marches between them of 10:11–36:13 signify? R. P. Knierim convincingly argues that this distinction, triggered by the cycle of decamping and encamping, is generated by the infratextual conceptuality. They represent the two different characteristics of a march, that is, the Israelites' preparatory organization of the march and the march itself.[40] For him, the entire narrative of Numbers is organized on the basis of the preparation and execution of a migration. The encampment at the wilderness of Sinai (1:1–10:10) has as its function the organization of the camp for the impending march from it, whereas 10:11 and following function as an account of the execution of that for which they prepared. Many events in 1:1–10:10, which have been argued as not intrinsically connected to a certain date and place, hang together to narrate the preparatory

---

39. Neither the problems and conflicts in the march and at the settled localities nor delays and circumventions of the march were caused by Yahweh's plan or Moses' leadership, only by Israel's disobedience and lack of trust in God. The text's implied negative evaluation of the march's execution is sharply distinguished from its positive evaluation of the preparation for the march.

40. Knierim, "The Book of Numbers," pp. 380-88. Knierim critically evaluates at least eight possible structural indicators in terms of their ability to provide coherence for the entire book of Numbers. They are (1) Numbers has thirty-six chapters; (2) Numbers is comprised of fifty-five distinguishable literary units; (3) Numbers has references to Moses in fifty-one of the fifty-five units; (4) Numbers consists of sixty-six Yahweh speeches; (5) Numbers is constructed by different literary strata (J and P); (6) Numbers contains four chronological indicators in 1:1; 7:1; 10:11; and 33:38; (7) Numbers shows the ongoing movement of the Israelites punctuated by a list of topographical and geographical indicators; and (8) the ongoing movement rests on the decampment-encampment terminology. He discusses (7) and (8) more extensively, as he weights them more heavily than the rest.

organization of the camp. In the same way, Israel's wanderings in 10:11–36:13, which consist of both the movement of the Israelites' camp and the problems that beset it, should be understood as the implementation of the prepared march.

Moreover, Knierim specifies the type of march that Numbers portrays. His arguments can be summarized briefly in three points. First, Israel's movement is certainly a migration — the movement of a group of people from one place to another. Second, it has a pilgrimage aspect, which indicates the cultic mode of the movement. The tribes of Israel have been organized around the sanctuary in chapter 2; the Levites were separated from the tribes for the service at the sanctuary in chapters 3–4; the sanctuary and Israel should follow the guidance of the cloud for their movement in 9:15-23 (wherever and whenever the cloud lifted from the tabernacle, Israel decamped and set out, and wherever and whenever it settled, Israel encamped); the organization of the camp not only shows the hierarchy of the cultic personnel from the Aaronide priests to the Levites, but also involves many cultic objects, such as the ark, the tent, the tabernacle, the sanctuary, the trumpets, the cloud with fire, and so forth. Third, Israel's movement is intrinsically related to the aspects of a military campaign. The census of the whole congregation of Israelites is for those who are twenty years old and older, who are male, and who are able to go to war (1:2-3); the alternation of the camp formation from "quadrangular for the encampment" to "linear for the march" implies military strategy; Israel frequently has military conflicts with various peoples (14:39-45; 20:14-21; 21:1-3, 21-31, 32-35; 31:1-12). All these three aspects are intrinsic to Israel's movement as portrayed in Numbers.[41] In other words, Israel's movement is "an epiphanic campaign" organized with "the host of Yahweh," the cultic personnel, and "the militia of Israel" and "mobilized around the sanctuary, ready to follow Yahweh's lead in Yahweh's own reconquest of the land."[42] Numbers 1:1–10:10 reports the organization of the migratory sanctuary campaign that has been prepared by Yahweh through Moses, and 10:11 and following narrate the actual execution of this campaign.

This concept of preparation and execution of the sanctuary campaign controls and provides the ultimate meanings for the chronological and topographical/geographical indicators. Whether the Israelites stayed at the wilderness for a calculable period (nineteen days) or at various locations for an unknowable period of time, these intervals must be accounted for according to

---

41. Knierim, "The Book of Numbers," pp. 385-88.

42. Knierim, "The Book of Numbers," p. 388. See also Knierim's article "On the Subject of War in Old Testament and Biblical Theology," *HBT* 16 (1994): 1-19.

their significance to the overarching concept of what happened in those periods. Similarly, the list of topographical localities that they marched through and of geographical territories in which they stayed is generated by an intention to narrate an execution of the sanctuary campaign. All aspects of a migration, such as when it begins, from where it starts, to where it is heading, and how long it takes to get there — even what happens in the entire migration process — all are subordinate to the concept of preparation and execution of a migratory sanctuary campaign. Conceptually Numbers 1:1–10:10 concentrates on the preparation for that campaign, whereas the rest of Numbers narrates the campaign itself. Numbers 10:11 and 12 signal the commencement of the actual campaign.

Furthermore, the twofold aspect of the campaign for the entire book of Numbers indicates the first part (1:1–10:10) as an intrinsic part of the Sinai pericope, which consists of Exodus 19–40, Leviticus, and Numbers 1:1–10:10. The Sinai pericope starts at Exodus 19:1-2, not only reporting the precise date that the Israelites came into the wilderness of Sinai but also providing the topographical reference that they camped "in the front of the mountain." The combination of a calendric and a topographical statement provides the perimeter of the entire Sinai pericope in its final form. From "the third new moon after" the Exodus event (19:1) to the second year in the second month at the twentieth day of the month (Num 10:11), the duration of the Israelites' encampment in the wilderness of Sinai can be easily calculable. It is almost eleven months. Moreover, all events narrated in the Sinai pericope are linked to two dominant localities, the camp and the mountain of Sinai (Exod 19–40) and the tent of meeting (Lev 1:1; Num 1:1).[43] Since these two locations are topographical in nature and are included in the geography, all units that are contained in the Sinai pericope must be understood as related to the same geographical location, the wilderness of Sinai. This locality is the basic background that extends to Numbers 10:10, when the Israelites yet remained

---

43. The present study follows Knierim's analysis of the structural organization of the entire Sinai pericope as discussed in "The Composition of the Pentateuch," pp. 360-69. According to Knierim, the macrostructure of the Sinai pericope has two parts:

I. The revelation from the mountain	Exod 19:3–40:38
II. The revelation from the tent of meeting	Lev 1:1–Num 10:10

This macrostructure shows "a fundamental theological program" that Yahweh's revelation moved from the mountain to the tent of meeting. The mountain, however sacred it may be, belongs to the past. Now God would call on and speak to Moses from the tent of meeting, the sanctuary where the glory of God dwells. Thus, the revelation from the mountain is preparatory and preliminary to the revelation from the tent of meeting in Israel's midst. This conceptuality is signaled by Lev 1:1, the highest level in this structure.

in it. Then, Numbers 10:11 starts a new section relative to the entire Sinai pericope, which indirectly supports Number 10:11 as a decisive break within the book of Numbers.

3. Numbers 36:13

a. Preliminary Remarks

With Knierim's understanding of the macrostructure of Numbers, based on the twofold conceptual aspect of the migratory sanctuary campaign, its preparation and execution, it has been argued that 10:11 and 12 signal the decisive break for the second block of Numbers. Numbers 10:11 narrates the beginning of the actual execution of Israel's campaign, prepared at the wilderness of Sinai. Where, then, does this execution end? Does it include Israel's staying at numerous places during the migration, particularly at the plains of Moab (22:1–36:13)? Is Numbers 36:13 the appropriate ending for the execution of the campaign and consequently for the second part of the bipartite structure of Numbers? Or, if the settlement in the promised land is the ultimate goal of Israel's preparation of the sanctuary campaign, then does its execution further include the narrative on their occupation of the land of Canaan (Josh 12), or the narrative of Joshua's death and burial, which implies that Israel finally settled (Josh 24), or the editorial note that reports the transition of generations from those who knew Yahweh and the work that Yahweh had done for Israel to those who did not know Yahweh (Judg 2:10)? In other words, is it not possible that the task of delimiting the end of the execution goes beyond the book of Numbers until the end of the Pentateuch or even the Hexateuch? Is Knierim's twofold conceptual aspect of the campaign for the structure of Numbers in conflict and/or in tension with other concepts that are responsible for the superstructure of the Pentateuch and/or that of the Primary History?[44]

Knierim himself recognizes this conceptual tension, which is conceivable due to the fact that Numbers is part of the larger context of Israel's ongoing story from Genesis, and, more intrinsically, that it is part of Moses' story from his birth in Exodus to his death in Deuteronomy. Knierim asserts that as far as the relevancy of the structure of Numbers in its own right and on its

---

44. Primary History refers to the story line that begins with the creation of the world in Genesis and ends with the fall of Judah, the southern kingdom, in 2 Kings. For the term, cf. D. N. Freedman, "Deuteronomic History," in *IDBSup*, ed. K. Crim (Nashville: Abingdon, 1976), p. 226.

own terms is concerned, it should be considered "in distinction from and in tension with the superstructure of the Pentateuch."[45] For him, the appropriate ending of the execution of the migration, which in turn determines the ending of the second block in the bipartite structure of Numbers, must be discussed in light of the infraconceptuality operative in the Pentateuch.

Recognizing this conceptual tension leads Knierim to suggest two different macrostructures of the second part of the Pentateuch, the Moses story. The first, which appears to be the "official" macrostructure, is as follows:[46]

I. From Egypt to Sinai	Exod 1–Num 10:10
A. Migration to Sinai	Exod 1–18
B. Events at Sinai	Exod 19–Num 10:10
II. From Sinai to Moab	Num 10:11–Deut 34
A. Migration to Moab	Num 10:11–36:13
B. Moses' Testament	Deut 1–34

This structure is based on the conceptual aspects of the migratory process, the migration to and events of a particular place. Sinai and the plains of Moab have primary importance compared to all other localities during the migration. Moreover, the migrations to Sinai and Moab "must be considered as pre-stages or presuppositions to their respective goals, and as leading up to and being subservient to these goals."[47] This structure as a whole, however, appears not to follow through with the operative concept. The titles of this structure correspond to each other, except that of II.B. Unlike other titles, the title of II.B. points not to all events that occurred in the plains of Moab but to only one specific event among them, Moses' final testament.

This inconsistency is reflected in Knierim's second proposal for the macrostructure of the Moses story. Since Numbers 22–36 speaks about the events in the plains of Moab analogous to the Sinai pericope, he subdivides part II without changing part I:

II. From Sinai to Moab	Num 10:11–Deut 34
A. Migration to Moab	Num 10:11–21:35
B. Events in the plains of Moab	Num 22:1–Deut 34
1. Preliminary events	Num 22:1–36:13
2. Moses' Testament	Deut 1–34

45. Knierim, "The Book of Numbers," p. 381.
46. Knierim, "The Composition of the Pentateuch," p. 356.
47. Knierim, "The Composition of the Pentateuch," p. 356.

This subdivision would follow his own operative concept for the entire structure of the Pentateuch more faithfully than the first official version; it even reveals a symmetric correspondence between parts I and II in their details. Why, then, does Knierim not choose this structure and present it as the official one? Has he not argued that the migration process is "governed by the arrival and events" at Sinai and the plains of Moab? Is there any other concept operative in separating Numbers 10:11–36:13 and Deuteronomy 1–34? If so, how does the other concept override the dominant concept of migration in the Moses story?

The even more pressing question is, What do these two structures of Exodus through Deuteronomy imply for the structure of Numbers, especially in the quest for determining the appropriate ending of the second block of Numbers? On the one hand, according to the "official" structure, Knierim divides Numbers into two parts, as he has done in the analysis of the macrostructure of Numbers itself. In it, Num 10:11 marks a decisive break at the highest level, and 36:13 concludes the second part. On the other hand, according to the structure presented as an alternative, Numbers has been divided into three parts with two conceptual aspects. One aspect is the events that happened at two settled locations: Sinai (Num 1:1–10:10) and Moab (22:1–36:13), and the other is the migration itself (10:11–21:35). Numbers begins with a settled place, ends with another settled place, and has movement in between. This division is reinforced by the geographical indicator in 22:1 and 36:13. In 22:1 the Israelites camped in the plains of Moab, and in 36:13 they are still there. Moreover, the execution of the campaign prepared at Sinai (Num 1:1–10:10) is narrated as far as the end of Deuteronomy, not the end of Numbers. The events in Numbers 22:1–36:13 function as "preliminary" to the main events in Deuteronomy. All three parts of Numbers do not share the same hierarchical position in their relationships.

However, Knierim considers the first structure more appropriate for the macrostructure of the Moses story. He provides a few indications for this preference. First, the narrative about Israel's staying in the plains of Moab (Num 22:1–Deut 34) is a combination of the Yahwistic-Priestly and the deuteronomistic materials. While Numbers 22–36 is attributed to the Priestly redactors who utilized the Yahwistic materials, Deuteronomy 1–34 is part of the deuteronomistic narrative extending until the end of 2 Kings. Knierim simply mentions this traditional source combination since it is well known, but he does not explain how it would affect the structure of the Moses story. It is obvious that he does not give any significant weight to this source division, because he takes the final composition of the story seriously at the outset. Second, Numbers 22–36 and Deuteronomy 1–34 concentrate on substantively different aspects within the Moses story, although both of them narrate events occurring in the same location. Numbers 22–36 functions as "the concluding part of the forty years' migration," whereas Deuteronomy 1–34 "focuses on the decisive condition for the impending conquest of and settlement in the promised land proper after Moses."[48] Numbers 22–36 directs attention backward to the previous events, especially Israel's repeated failure to trust Yahweh's plan after they left Sinai; it narrates the continuum of Israel's disobedience to Yahweh and Yahweh's punishment of and additional guidance to Israel. Deuteronomy 1–34, however, not only reflects the entire period of wandering in the wilderness (1:6–3:29) but also directs attention toward preparation for imminent living in the promised land. Then, Numbers 22–36, as the concluding part of the forty-year migration in the wilderness, paves the road for the unique character of Deuteronomy, its "exhorting and admonishing parenesis."

Knierim's suggestions are correct and point in the right direction for solving the relational problem between Numbers 22–36 and the book of Deuteronomy and ultimately for the conceptual problem between Numbers 10:11–36:13 and Deuteronomy 1–34. It is also true that the suggestions are not sufficient enough to justify the break between Numbers 22–36 and Deuteronomy 1–34. The lack of attention to this problem is understandable since Knierim's main task is the structural analysis of the Pentateuch with a particular interest in the Sinai pericope.

With his tips as a launching pad, a working thesis for the present study can be drawn. Numbers 10:11 begins the narrative of the execution of Israel's prepared sanctuary campaign. Since the objective of the campaign is the conquest of the promised land, the execution of the campaign could not end at the end of the book of Numbers, but it could be completed at Joshua 12, before the actual distribution of the land of Canaan, the promised land, begins. No doubt the execution of the ongoing campaign is the fundamental conceptual aspect for the text from Numbers 10:11 to Joshua 12. However, each of the three texts, Numbers 10:11–36:13, the entire book of Deuteronomy, and Joshua 1–12, addresses a substantively distinguishable aspect of this ongoing campaign. Deuteronomy is about Moses' final testament for the new generation at the edge of the promised land — "the decisive condition for the impending conquest of and settlement in the promised land proper" after his death. Joshua 1–12 focuses on Israel's conquest of the land of Canaan: all the Israelites participated in the conquest; they accomplished it in a short amount of time militarily under the leadership of Joshua; and they

---

48. Knierim, "The Composition of the Pentateuch," p. 356.

conquered the entire land of Canaan. Numbers 10:11–36:13, however, reports Israel's failure to conquer the promised land from the south and their forty years wandering in the wilderness as a punishment. This text reveals the reason for Israel's failure and forty years of wandering in the wilderness by focusing on the events that occurred at its beginning and end. This text also provides the necessary basis for Moses' preparation of the new generation, the emergence of Joshua as the successor to Moses, and the reason for the conquest of the promised land from east of Jordan. *In short, Numbers 10:11–36:13 points not to the entire process of the execution of the ongoing campaign but rather to a specific aspect of that execution, namely, the failure of the conquest from the south and its resultant forty years of wandering before the attempt was made once again to conquer the promised land — not from the south but from the east — by the new generation.*

With this working thesis, Numbers 36:13 is the appropriate ending for the second division of Numbers. This is in contrast to Deuteronomy–Joshua 12. In order to substantiate this claim, two issues will be analyzed: (1) the content of Numbers 36:13 and whether this verse in itself addresses the working thesis for Numbers, and (2) the characteristics of Deuteronomy relative to those of Numbers (or the Tetrateuch), and in particular, how Deuteronomy portrays Israel's experience of wandering in the wilderness (Deut 1:1–3:29). When Numbers 36:13 is identified as the appropriate ending, then, together with Numbers 10:11 as the appropriate starting point, Numbers 10:11–36:13 can be treated as a distinct unit which rightfully demands a study of its internal coherence and intention.

b. Numbers 36:13

On the surface, Numbers 36:13 provides a statement regarding "the commandments and the ordinances" that Yahweh "commanded through Moses to the Israelites." This verse begins with אלה, a demonstrative plural pronoun; is coupled with המצות והמשפטים which is modified by the אשר clause; and ends with the geographical reference, בערבת מואב על ירדן ירחו, "in the plains of Moab by the Jordan at Jericho" (26:3, 63; 33:50; 35:1; cf. 22:1; 31:12).[49] It is also true that this verse is located at the end of the book of

---

49. Num 22:1 has ואל־ערבת מואב מעבר לירדן ירחו, and 31:12 has בערבות מואב אשר על־ירדן ירחו. Although these verses are expressed a little differently than 26:3, 63; 33:50; 35:1; and 36:13, they denote the same meaning. The plains of Moab are "the open, fertile area immediately to the north of the Dead Sea on the eastern side of the Jordan." These are further defined by the phrase "across the Jordan from Jericho," which represents the point of view from inside

Numbers. With its linguistic expression, geographical reference, and location in the extant text of Numbers, verse 13 raises at least two questions: What is the function of verse 13 in its present location, and what is its relationship to the surrounding materials? These are related but distinct questions. The former provides a boundary for the possible answers for the latter, whereas the latter substantiates the claims of the former. Closer analysis of these questions demonstrates that Numbers 36:13 (1) is a subscription, not a transitional statement connecting the materials preceding and following it; (2) concludes the text at least from 15:1 to 36:12, regardless of the geographical reference in verse 13b; and (3) includes the entire text without distinguishing the laws from the narratives. Of these three points, the first and the third are justifiable. In contrast, the second point is arguable, not because it lacks textual evidence to support its claim but because it depends on the structural significance of 36:13, which is to be determined by the operative conceptuality of the macrostructure of 10:11–36:13. The claim that 36:13 covers the material from 15:1–36:12 is provisional at this point, and it will be redefined in consideration of the structural significance of 36:13. Therefore, it could be said tentatively that 36:13 is a subscription that closes the corpus that contains generically diverse materials from 15:1 to 36:12.

Regarding the function of verse 13, is it an editorial summary statement of Yahweh's commandments and ordinances? Or is it a combination of a summary and a concluding statement of divine laws? Or does the verse function not only to conclude the materials that precede it but, at the same time, to make a transition to the materials which follow it? First, 36:13 is a self-contained literary unit in its own right. It is not organically connected to its immediate literary context, 36:1-12.[50] Numbers 36:1-12, as an individual unit

---

the land of Canaan. For the syntax of the words and historical implications, see Gray, *A Critical and Exegetical Commentary on Numbers*, pp. 306-7; Ashley, *The Book of Numbers*, p. 431; E. W. Davies, *Numbers*, p. 235. Cf. G. I. Davies, *The Way of the Wilderness: A Geographical Study of the Wilderness Itineraries in the Old Testament* (Cambridge: Cambridge University Press, 1979); Z. Kallai, *Historical Geography of the Bible: The Tribal Territories of Israel* (Jerusalem and Leiden: The Magnes Press, The Hebrew University, 1986).

50. Most commentators are aware of the difference between vv. 1-12 and v. 13, but only a few state clearly the independence of v. 13 from vv. 1-12. The majority are silent on this issue and yet imply v. 13's connectedness to vv. 1-12 by mentioning the materials that v. 13 covers. For the former, see Noth (*Numbers*, p. 258), Budd (*Numbers*, p. 389), and Maier (*Das vierte Buch Mose*, p. 481); and for the latter, see Gray (*A Critical and Exegetical Commentary on Numbers*, p. 478), Harrison (*Numbers*, p. 428), Milgrom (*Numbers*, p. 299), Ashley (*The Book of Numbers*, p. 659), E. W. Davies (*Numbers*, p. 370), Sakenfeld (*Numbers*, pp. 185, 188), Dozeman ("The Book of Numbers," pp. 266-67), and Levine (*Numbers 21–36*, p. 579). Wenham (*Numbers*, p. 239) does not distinguish between vv. 1-12 and v. 13, and Olson does not even mention v. 13 in his commentary on Numbers.

itself apart from verse 13, addresses a specific matter related to and supplementing 27:1-11 (cf. 26:33-34). The daughters of Zelophehad who are allowed to inherit property must marry within their tribe so that tribal property will be maintained intact. Verse 13, however, addresses the broader matter of God's commandments and ordinances. There is little doubt that the narrative about legislation of the inheritance of heiresses is a Yahweh commandment. This law is commanded (use of צוה in vv. 2 [x2], 5, 6, 10) by Yahweh, handed down through Moses (vv. 1, 5, 10), and promulgated in the plains of Moab by the Jordan at Jericho (35:1). But 36:13 certainly includes much more than just 36:1-12, a commandment with a single topic; it has the plural demonstrative אלה and has a unique combination of המצות and המשפטים. With these two pieces of information, verse 13 should be treated as a self-contained literary unit in and of itself that does not belong to the literary unit of 36:1-12. Rather, verse 13 points to Yahweh's commandments and ordinances beyond 36:1-12, its immediate literary context.

Second, it has been generally assumed that 36:13 functions as a subscription, the conclusion of a document.[51] Despite diverse opinions among commentators concerning what specific material verse 13 concludes (to be discussed in detail later), it is reasonable and logical to hold that this verse functions to close the previous material since it is located at the end of the book. (Its location has also been used as evidence against its closure function.) As a subscription, verse 13 closes only the story of the past. It is argued, however, that it may also function as a transition from past events to future events, and thus it directs the reader toward what happens in Deuteronomy and even beyond.[52] This point is made based on the geographical reference in verse 13b, according to K. D. Sakenfeld. She argues that the reference to "the plains of Moab" looks not only backward to the time of Israel's arrival at the place in 22:1 but also forward to the events in Deuteronomy, including Moses' final testament and his death.[53] Note that Moses' speeches begin and end at the same place, the plains of Moab (1:5; 32:49, respectively). The last chapter of Deuteronomy reports that Moses died and is mourned in the plains of

51. Gray, *A Critical and Exegetical Commentary on Numbers*, p. 478; Ashley, *The Book of Numbers*, p. 659; E. W. Davies, *Numbers*, p. 370; Dozeman, "The Book of Numbers," p. 267. Levine (*Numbers 21-36*, p. 579) refers to v. 13 as a postscript.

52. Ashley (*The Book of Numbers*, p. 659) states that Numbers "ends on a forward-looking and open-ended note. What will happen in the land of Canaan?" He speculates the forward-looking function for v. 13 on the basis of the theological theme of 33:50–36:12, "the matters of property and land within the land of promise." But his statement must be substantiated by other evidence.

53. Sakenfeld, *Numbers*, p. 188.

Moab (34:1, 6, 8). Moreover, with the final words, "by the Jordan at Jericho," 36:13 even further directs the reader to "the crossing of the Jordan River to Jericho" as reported in Joshua 1:1–5:1.

These possibilities are conceivable only if the geographical reference in 36:13b is constitutive for the function of 36:13 as a whole. Note that syntactically, verse 13b is a continuation of the relative clause of אֲשֶׁר, which modifies the main clause starting with אֵלֶּה. Considering the linguistic and conceptual differences between Numbers and Deuteronomy (to be discussed later), Sakenfeld's argument that Moses' speeches and the narrative regarding Israel's crossing the Jordan belong to "these" commandments and ordinances in verse 13a is questionable. Besides, the literary dependence of verse 13 to 36:1-12 (only by the root of צוה), the location of verse 13 at the end of the book, and its summarizing and concluding tone must not be ignored. The geographical reference in verse 13b, therefore, plays a secondary or supportive role to the subject matter in verse 13a. Verse 13 as a whole has its importance and meaning because "these" are Yahweh's commandments and ordinances, not because the laws are promulgated in the plains of Moab. Consequently, the future-oriented role of verse 13 should be subordinate to its concluding or subscribing role. Verse 13 summarizes and closes the materials that precede it.

What specific material, then, does 36:13 conclude? What is the antecedent of "these" in verse 13a? At least it is clear that 36:13 concludes its immediate literary context, 36:1-12. Yet this rather obvious claim does not satisfy most commentators, who thus present various proposals on the basis of either textual evidence (the nature of the divine commandments and ordinances, geographical references, and a combination of these two) or theological interests. Numbers 36:13 may cover the laws concerning the land in 33:50–36:12,[54] a collections of laws alone in 28:1–36:12,[55] the whole block of material from chapter 27,[56] the material contained between 22:1–36:12,[57] or, indeed, the book of

---

54. Wenham, *Numbers*, pp. 239-40. Wenham seems to argue two positions: that 36:13 "marks the end of the section beginning in 33:50," and that 36:1-13 as a whole "does provide a fitting conclusion to the book of Numbers itself." This mixture stems from his preoccupation with a theological theme for Numbers. For him, the entire book of Numbers has been directing Israel's movement "towards the land of promise." Since 33:50–36:12 concentrates on the legislation concerning the land, its distribution, its extent, and its holiness, v. 13 closes this section and at the same time is a part of the conclusion of Numbers. However, his overarching theological theme overrides the literary independence of v. 13 from vv. 1-12.

55. Noordtzij, *Numbers*, p. 304. For Noordtzij, v. 13 covers specifically chs. 28–31 and 33:50–36:12.

56. Sturdy, *Numbers*, p. 245; Mainelli, *Numbers*, p. 135.

57. Gray, *A Critical and Exegetical Commentary on Numbers*, p. 478; Milgrom, *Numbers*, p. 299; Ashley, *The Book of Numbers*, pp. 659-60. Ashley follows Wenham's theological theme,

Numbers as a whole.[58] Noth and R. K. Harrison appear ambiguous, saying that verse 13 closes the final sections or chapters of Numbers.[59] For Noth, "the final section" of Numbers may refer to part IV in his structure, "Preparation for and Beginning of the Conquest," which begins with 20:14. For Harrison, "all the material in the final chapters" of Numbers may refer to section 7 in his outline, "Preparations for Settling in Canaan," which starts from 34:1. Sakenfeld seems to propose at least two possibilities different from the others above.[60] First, similar to Noth and Harrison, she ambiguously states that verse 13 "looks back upon the concluding section of the book." This concluding section may refer to her final section, "Miscellaneous Legislation; Events Prior to Moses' Death," beginning at 27:1 (different from Noth and Harrison). Second, with stress on "commandments and ordinances" in verse 13, she suggests that this verse "calls attention particularly to the section of Numbers after the second census (ch. 26)."

Finally, Olson does not have any specific proposal. He, however, seems to argue that because the verse is located at the end of the book, it can be treated as an "editorial conclusion" to the whole book of Numbers. This argument is based on two pieces of evidence: (1) the fivefold division of the Pentateuch, of which Numbers is one; and (2) the literary characteristics of Deuteronomy, which are distinctive from those of Numbers. Since Olson's first

---

that is, Numbers's movement toward the promised land. Interestingly enough, Levine (*Numbers 21–36*, p. 579) suggests that v. 13 covers the material from ch. 25 to 36.

58. Dozeman, "The Book of Numbers," p. 267. But Dozeman also contends that v. 13 provides a conclusion to the laws in chs. 35–36. See also, Budd, *Numbers*, p. 389; E. W. Davies, *Numbers*, p. 370. Budd and E. W. Davies have basically the same understanding: that Num 36:13 "serves as a fitting conclusion to the [whole] book" (Davies, *Numbers*, p. 370). Yet, Budd differs from Davies in consideration of what includes the whole book of Numbers. Whereas for Davies this verse covers Num 1:1–36:12, for Budd it covers "the material from Num 1:1–35:34," because Budd regards 36:1-13 as "a supplement or appendix to the completed book of Numbers" (Budd, *Numbers*, p. 389; see pp. 20-22 in the present study for a critical evaluation of Budd's designation). Regarding the time of the insertion of Numbers 36:13, Budd and Davies differ from each other and from Gray. Gray (*A Critical and Exegetical Commentary on Numbers*, p. 478) argues that the verse was added "when the Pentateuch was divided into five books," while Budd (*Numbers*, p. 389) argues that it happened after the completion of Numbers, including the addition of 36:1-12, and Davies (*Numbers*, p. 370) postulates that v. 13, along with vv. 1-12, was "formulated at a period prior to Israel's entry into Canaan." This difference comes from their particular interests for understanding the text of Numbers. Gray and Budd are interested in the history of the literary growth of the text, and Davies, in the theological significance and the historicity of the text.

59. Noth, *Numbers*, p. 258; Harrison, *Numbers*, p. 428. Noth asserts that v. 13 does not belong specifically to Numbers 36, and Harrison is not aware of this literary independence. They also differ in terms of what materials v. 13 actually closes.

60. Sakenfeld, *Numbers*, p. 188.

consideration has been critically evaluated above and his second will be considered later,[61] only a few words are necessary here. It is sufficient to say that whether the fivefold division of the Pentateuch has been done intentionally or artificially, and regardless of when and by whom it happened, the existence of the story line is the primary factual evidence that the narrative block is older than the division into five books. The fivefold division does not reflect "the formation of the Pentateuch that is intrinsic to its literary nature." "Indeed," as Knierim continues, "at important points the canonical shape has destroyed the literary structure of the whole."[62]

No consensus has been reached among commentators as to what 36:13 concludes. The materials from 35:1, 33:50, 28:1, 27:1, 22:1, 20:14, or 1:1 to 36:12 have been considered as the antecedent of "these" in 36:13a. Since there are already many opinions, it does not seem harmful to propose one or two more. Note that thus far the following points have been determined. Verse 13 covers not only 36:1-12 but also the text beyond it, and it functions to conclude the previous materials rather than connect past events to future ones. In addition, its geographical reference is at best secondary and supportive to its main clause.

With these points, one is tempted to claim that 36:13 closes the material from 10:11 to 36:12. This claim is argued on the basis of external evidence. Since Numbers 10:11 marks the structural signal at the highest level for the bipartite structure of Numbers, and since 36:13 is located at the end of the book of Numbers, 36:13 as a subscription would conclude the materials from 10:11 onward. Moreover, verse 13a shares the same terms as subscriptions in Leviticus 26:46 and 27:34.[63] The linguistic similarity implies a similar function for Numbers 36:13 relative to that of Leviticus 26:46 and 27:34. If the argument that Leviticus 27:34 covers the materials of the second part of the bipartite structure of Leviticus (Lev 11–27) is convincing,[64] then it is reasonable to argue that Numbers 36:13 also covers the entire second part of Numbers (Num

---

61. See pp. 25-30 and 112 in the present study.

62. Knierim, "The Composition of the Pentateuch," p. 353.

63. Lev 27:34a has אלה המצות אשר צוה יהוה את־משה אל־בני ישראל and Lev 26:46 has אלה . . . והמשפטים . . . ביד־משה.

64. According to H. Sun, the macrostructure of Leviticus has two parts (chs. 1–10 and 11–27) based on the relationship between the report of the Yahweh speeches, which totally dominate the book, and several subscriptions. He argues that the subscription of 27:34 replaces that of 26:46, which concludes 11:1–26:45 as a whole. Thus, for him, 27:34 brings the second part of Leviticus, begun in Lev 11, to a close. See, for details, H. T. C. Sun, "An Investigation into the Compositional Integrity of the So-called Holiness Code (Leviticus 17-26)," Ph.D. diss., The Claremont Graduate School, 1990, pp. 486-96.

10:11–36:13). This external evidence, however, needs to be collaborated with concrete textual evidence extricated from 36:13 itself and from 10:11–36:12.

The needed textual evidence is found in the laws narrated in chapters 15 and 18–19. The noun form, with personal suffix, of צוה in 36:13 (המצות) occurs only five times in Numbers. The other four occurrences appear exclusively in chapter 15 (15:22, 31, 39, 40). Moreover, the phrase (כ)אשר צוה יהוה occurs also in 15:23; 17:26; and 19:2.[65] With this statistical observation, one is also tempted to claim that the antecedents of "these" in 36:13b could be the material from 15:1 to 36:12. The antecedents of 36:13a should not include the laws in chapters 5–6 and 10:1-10 since those laws belong to the first block of Numbers and are promulgated in the wilderness of Sinai. However, the antecedents should include the laws in chapters 15 and 18–19 because those laws belong to the second block of Numbers, although they are commanded outside of the plains of Moab. Nevertheless, this claim is provisional no matter how attractive it may be. The ambiguity of the antecedents of "these" in 36:13 is inherent in itself. The various proposals, including the material from 15:1–36:12, must be evaluated from the vantage point of the structural significance that 36:13 plays in the macrostructure of 10:11–36:13.

Regardless of the ambiguity of the antecedents of "these" in 36:13, it must be clarified whether "the commandments and ordinances" refer only to the laws that Yahweh "commanded" through Moses to the Israelites, or to the entire material, including the narratives, in between the laws. This question stems from the unique combination of המשפטים and המצות in verse 13a.[66] Commentators are divided on this issue, although they lack any explanations to support their positions. A. Noordtzij wants to be clear that 36:13 covers only a collection of laws from Numbers 28, and thus he includes only chapters 28–31 and 33:50–36:12. It is understandable to treat the material in between, that is, 32:1–33:49, as a narrative, but to consider chapter 31 as part of a collection of laws is questionable.[67] Milgrom also differentiates clearly between the

---

65. Other places are 3:42; 8:20, 22; 20:17; 27:22; 30:2; 34:13, 19; 36:6. ביד־משה occurs in 4:37, 45, 49; 9:23; 10:13; 15:23; 17:5; 27:23; 33:1; 36:13. Its combination with (כ)אשר צוה יהוה occurs only once, in 36:13 (cf. Lev 8:36). The phrase (כ)אשר צוה יהוה את־משה . . ., however, occurs many times (1:19, 54; 2:33, 34; 3:51; 4:49; 8:3, 20, 22; 9:5; 15:36; 26:4; 27:11; 30:1, 17; 31:7, 21, 31, 41, 47; 36:10). With these statistics, no conclusive point can be drawn, except that these phrases do appear after 10:11 before 22:1.

66. This combination occurs only here. In other places, המשפטים is combined with החקים (Deut 4:45; 5:28; 6:1, 20; 12:1) and התורת (Lev 26:46).

67. See Douglas, *In the Wilderness*, p. 103; Milgrom, *Numbers*, p. xv. Israel's holy war against Midian in Num 31 must be treated as a narrative. Note that they differ slightly from each other on the classification of the laws and the narratives.

laws and the narratives. For him, 36:13 refers to "all the laws" given to Israel beginning at 22:1. He even lists the law portion of the material from 22:1–36:12. Additionally, this distinction leads him to the alternative proposal that this verse includes the laws contained only in chapters 35–36.

Unlike Noordtzij and Milgrom, Gray is unclear on this distinction. Although he states that 36:13 covers "the laws" between 22:1–36:12,[68] he does not state whether "the laws" refers only to the laws in these chapters or whether it is a collective term for expressing the diverse texture of these chapters. Yet he seems inclined to stress the law portion of these chapters since he explains the inappropriate location of Leviticus 27:34 at the end of Leviticus. According to him, although both Numbers 36:13 and Leviticus 27:34 play a role of subscription, the position of Numbers 36:13 in its current place is suitable, whereas that of Leviticus 27:34 is not because more Sinaitic laws follow that verse.[69] Noth, Budd, Harrison, E. W. Davies, Levine, and Dozeman do not attempt to distinguish between the laws and narratives in the material that verse 13 is supposed to cover.

It is true that the laws are easily distinguishable from other materials in Numbers. Nonetheless, they are framed within the narrative. It must be noted that the speech report formulae have the effect of embedding the laws into an ongoing story line. The speech formulae may begin a literary unit or may simply indicate Yahweh's speech to Moses (and Aaron) within literary units. It is possible that one could change the laws and keep the report formulae and still have the book of Numbers, but the converse is almost impossible and hardly conceivable. Therefore, the laws should be understood within the perimeter of the contents and forms of the entire composite materials.

In short, two things are clear. First, Numbers 36:13 is an editorial summary statement which functions as a subscription, similar to Leviticus 27:34. It concludes the materials preceding it and does not make a transition to the book of Deuteronomy. Second, 36:13 closes the corpus that goes beyond its immediate literary context, 36:1-12, perhaps as far as 15:1, and it contains generically diverse materials and not the laws exclusively.

---

68. Gray, *A Critical and Exegetical Commentary on Numbers*, p. 478.

69. Ashley (*The Book of Numbers*, p. 659) follows Gray's unclearness by stating that 36:13 "ends a section of legal material" and concludes "the whole section" that began at 22:1. Moreover, Ashley, like Noordtzij, provides two additional concluding formulae (Lev 7:37-38; 26:46) and claims that these are similar to Num 36:13. Yet, he does not compare the formulae in Leviticus and discuss their relationship, particularly the relationship of Lev 27:34, to Num 36. Do these subscriptions of Leviticus and Numbers play a similar role? What do their different locations or positions indicate? These questions are necessary for understanding the organization or structure of each book, Leviticus and Numbers, respectively.

c. Deuteronomy 1:1-5

The two points extricated from Numbers 36:13 above are inconclusive regarding the designation of the verse as the appropriate ending of the material from Numbers 10:11 on. The verse in itself does not address Israel's ongoing campaign throughout the wilderness. However, its location at the end of the book of Numbers and its function as a subscription which concerns the matters of the past suggest that it signals some sort of decisive ending. By locating Israel in the plains of Moab, the verse implies the end of Israel's forty-year campaign. This implication is important because the end of a forty-year campaign in the wilderness means the end of Yahweh's punishment of Israel (14:33-35), and thus it stimulates the reader to expect something substantially new to follow. The newness comes from the radical departure of Deuteronomy. In its stylistic, linguistic, and conceptual divergence from the text of Numbers 10:11 on (and/or the Moses story from Exodus to Numbers), the book of Deuteronomy supports the appropriateness of Numbers 36:13 as the conclusion of the text beginning at 10:11.

By stating "Deuteronomy is clearly structured as an independent literary unit with its own distinctive vocabulary and style,"[70] Olson claims that the division between Numbers and Deuteronomy is obvious. Unfortunately he does not provide any examples reflecting this characterization. Instead he lists the ending of Numbers (36:13) and the beginning of Deuteronomy (1:1) and concludes that Deuteronomy follows the end of Numbers with a clearly distinguishable introductory formula. Olson's brief touch on the issue, Numbers 36:13 as a decisive break from Deuteronomy, has merit only in that it points in the right direction. On the surface, it must be demonstrated how Deuteronomy differs from Numbers in literary characteristics and theological themes. Conceptually, an exegesis of Deut 1:1 and its immediate literary context, 1:1-5, is needed.[71]

---

70. Olson, *The Death of the Old and the Birth of the New*, p. 49.

71. At the outset, that stylistic, linguistic, and theological differences are evident between Genesis-Numbers and Deuteronomy is undeniable based on the results of the literary-critical approaches (see M. Weinfeld, *Deuteronomy and the Deuteronomistic School* [Oxford: Oxford University Press, 1972], pp. 320-65; idem, "Deuteronomy, Book of," in *ABD*, ed. D. N. Freedman, vol. 2 [New York: Doubleday, 1992], pp. 160-83). Note two comprehensive surveys of Deuteronomy and its relationship to the Pentateuch and to the Deuteronomistic History in S. Boorer, *The Promise of the Land as Oath: A Key to the Formation of the Pentateuch*, BZAW 205 (Berlin and New York: Walter de Gruyter, 1992), pp. 5-33. Boorer surveys the past interpretations of the recognized place and nature of Deuteronomy, which shows affinities both with the material preceding it in Genesis to Numbers and with that following it in Joshua to Kings. She identifies four paradigms together with those who propose them: (1) a many-layered deuteronomistic (dtr) expansion from Genesis through Joshua (Wellhausen) or through Kings (Holscher), (2) a

Deut 1:1-5 as it stands provides the basic information about the act, place, and time of Moses' speaking. This information is not easily obtained due to its markedly complicated nature.[72] The text has repeated introductory phrases in verses 1a, 3b, and 5b, diverse topographical and geographical indicators in verses 1b-2 and 5a, and different descriptions of the time that Moses spoke in verses 3a and 4. Whether these difficulties are due to the combination of different sources, the interpolation of various layers within the same source, or the work of one editor combining components of diverse origin,[73] the difficulties must be understood to exist in the extant text. The seeming inconsistency and repeated formulations are not necessarily in themselves indicative of multiple sources or different layers of one source; they point only to the complex nature of the material.

Deuteronomy 1:1-5 in its present form reveals its structure as follows.[74]

Report of the introduction to the Moses speeches   1:1-5
I. Introduction to the Moses speeches   1:1-4
    A. Introductory formula   1:1a

---

later combination of an independent dtr History with pentateuchal sources (Noth, Lohfink), (3) the Tetrateuch as a later literary extension of dtr History (Van Seters), and (4) the formation of Genesis to Kings from independent blocks of tradition by a dtr school (Rendtorff). Despite this comprehensive survey, she stresses the diachronic approaches and results of the history of interpretation. For the current state of research on Deuteronomy, which includes diverse approaches, see H. D. Preuss, "Zum deuteronomistischen Geschichtswerk," *TRu* 58 (1993): 229-64 (p. 245), and T. Romer, "The Book of Deuteronomy," in *The History of Israel's Traditions: The Heritage of Martin Noth*, ed. S. L. McKenzie and M. P. Graham, JSOTSup 182 (Sheffield: Sheffield Academic Press, 1994), pp. 178-212. The literary relationship between these two portions of the Pentateuch, however, is not the task of the present study and should not be sufficient proof for determining that Num 10:11–36:13 is distinct from Deuteronomy. Rather, the present study is interested in the analysis of the present form of the Pentateuch.

72. For the most comprehensive summarizing discussions concerning the difficulties of Deut 1:1-5, see S. Mittmann, *Deuteronomium 1:1–6:3*, BZAW 139 (Berlin and New York: Walter de Gruyter, 1975), pp. 8-17; L. Perlitt, *Deuteronomium* (Neukirchen-Vluyn: Neukirchener, 1990), pp. 1-25; and Z. Kallai, "Where Did Moses Speak (Deuteronomy 1:1-5)?" *VT* 45 (1995): 188-97.

73. S. R. Driver, *Deuteronomy*, ICC (Edinburgh: T. & T. Clark, 1902), pp. 1-9; M. Noth, *The Deuteronomistic History*, 2nd ed., JSOTSup 15 (Sheffield: Sheffield Academic Press, 1991), p. 46; G. von Rad, *Deuteronomy: A Commentary*, trans. D. Barton (London: SCM, 1966), pp. 36-39; N. Lohfink, "Der Bundesschluss im Land Moab," *BZ* 6 (1962): 32, n. 2, respectively.

74. Several outlines of Deut 1:1-5 are conceivable. For example, von Rad (*Deuteronomy*, p. 36) divides the text into two parts: I. The heading about the "words" of Moses (vv. 1-4) and II. The heading about an explanation of "this law" (v. 5). Or, for Kallai, I. The opening phrase (v. 1a), II. The events from Horeb until the Plains of Moab (vv. 1b-4), and III. An extended renewed opening sentence (v. 5). However, these outlines do not sufficiently integrate the diverse components within the text.

The first part has two sections that report the act of Moses' speaking (I.A) and list the place names and time specifications (I.B). The question is, What is the relationship between I.A. and I.B.? Verse 1ab mentions "beyond the Jordan" as the general area where Moses' speaking took place, and this area is reiterated and added to by "in the land of Moab" in verse 5a. Since no report on further migration is given, the entire book of Deuteronomy is located in the land of Moab where Israel settled at Numbers 22:1. It is defined further by the mixture of topographical and geographical references related to place names from the wandering narrative, although "Tophel, Laban, Hazeroth, Di-zahab" are without parallel. What do these references reveal by their location in the present form of the text, that is, right after "beyond the Jordan," which refers to a general area in which Moses spoke? Does the list of toponyms in verses 1b-2 suggest a continuation of the circumscription of the one location at which Moses spoke? Or does the list refer to the different places and times at which Moses spoke? If either of these is the case, what Moses actually did is not simply speak but recount or remind the people of what he already said before Israel settled in the plains of Moab beyond the Jordan. These speculations are incompatible with the verb דבר in verses 1a and 3b (cf. באר in v. 5b) and the chronological framework in verses 3-4. It is inconceivable that the antecedent of "these" in verse 1aα1 is only the events which occurred before Numbers 22:1, although these events are included in Moses' speech about the history of Israel's wandering in the wilderness at 1:6–3:29.

However, if, as Z. Kallai argues, "the wilderness" refers to the wilderness of Moab (cf. Num 21:11, 13; Deut 2:8b, 26; Judg 11:18), and if the rest of the place names in verse 1b are "designations in the description of the wandering of the Israelites between Kadesh-barnea and the trek in the vicinity of the land of Edom," then the list of toponyms, with verse 2, indicates the representative stations of Israel's wandering in reverse order back to Horeb.[75] This list functions not as a brief summary of places at which Moses spoke but as an implied object of the Moses speeches which follow after 1:6. The toponyms in verse 1b and the abbreviated narrative form of verse 2 are an integral part of verses 1-5, however diverse they may be.

The chronological indicators in verses 3-4 (I.B.2.) strengthen Kallai's proposal, although he does not expand their relationship to the rest of the text. Verse 3a has a precise date following the cultic calendric form of dates from Exodus-Numbers. This date suggests the time at the end of the wilderness wandering. Verse 3b clarifies the fact that whatever Moses said about the end of the whole wandering period, it is spoken at God's command. Moreover, the date is defined further by the historical events (Num 21:21-35) that happened after Israel departed from Kadesh (Num 20:1-29) and in the Transjordan area on the way to the plains of Moab. Verses 3-4, on the surface, indicate the time that Moses spoke, and yet they implicitly point to the time frame in reverse order from Kadesh to the fortieth year, on the first day of the eleventh month. The phase of Israel's wandering that begins at Kadesh and ends with Moses' death is the content of verses 3-4. The point is that verses 1b-4 cover the entire period of wilderness wandering through representative stations and events, and thus they provide the subject matter of which Moses spoke.

That verses 1b-4 contain the Moses speeches (v. 1aα) is clearly demonstrated by its correspondence with 1:6–3:29, the historical review. Since in 1:6-46, Moses spoke about the events which occurred at Mount Horeb and at Kadesh, in it the implied content of the Moses speeches embedded in the geographical framework of 1:1b-2 is spelled out in detail. Likewise, 2:1–3:29 reports Moses' speeches about the events from Kadesh to Zered and from Moab to Hermon, and it reveals the implied content of his speeches framed by the chronological indicators. From this correspondence, it may be argued that the first part (vv. 1-4) is a suitable introductory statement for 1:6–3:29.[76] But

---

75. Kallai, "Where Did Moses Speak?" pp. 193-94.

76. Von Rad (*Deuteronomy*, p. 39) proposes a similar argument. Unit 1:1-5 has two parts: the first (vv. 1-4) is related to 1:6–4:40 and the second (v. 5) is relevant only after 4:44. But his argument is based on the geographical names of vv. 1-2 and the term "torah" in v. 5. Since he does not consider the time element and he understands torah only as "law" rather than a wider sense of "instruction," his argument is not convincing.

verses 1-4 are intrinsically related to verse 5, which reiterates and specifies the introductory statement of verse 1a.

The second part (v. 5) is conceptually distinctive and yet related to the first. The underlying concept for verses 1-5 as a whole is the announcement of the act of Moses' speaking. This conceptual aspect of Moses' activity is constitutive for the two-part division. To describe Moses' act, part I uses the verb דבר (to speak, vv. 1aα and 3b) and is unified by it, whereas part II uses באר (to explain or clarify, v. 5b). Verses 1-4 focus on the fact that what follow are Moses' speeches, and they imply further that these are addresses that Moses had not previously delivered. In addition, the use of באר in verse 5 suggests that Moses' acts are his recapitulations of earlier teachings or instructions.[77] This verb, however, does not negate the speaking activity of Moses; it qualifies that what Moses delivered was not new speeches but a clarification of the divine teachings for, perhaps, new generations (cf. v. 3b). Despite a conceptual tension between verses 1-4 and verse 5, verses 1-5 as a whole are a unified literary unit on the basis of the speaking activity of Moses.

Moreover, it may be argued that since verse 5 reverts to the introductory form of verse 1a, this verse forms a suitable introductory statement to the historical recapitulation of 1:6–3:29. Otherwise, verse 5 is a transitional statement from the opening summary concerning the place and time of Moses' speeches to Moses' speeches proper in the rest of Deuteronomy, or at least to his first speech (1:6–4:43). This speculation, addressing the structure of Deuteronomy as a whole and the function of verses 1-4(5) in that structure, needs to be further explored, but it is not the interest of the present study. It is sufficient to note that "beyond the Jordan" in verse 5 is a reminder of the same place in verse 1aβ, and the announcement of the act of speaking is the dominant concept, reiterated and expanded throughout the five verses. In short, verses 1-5 as a whole are the introduction to Deuteronomy — the book as a whole or at least the historical review of 1:6–3:29 — and characterize the book as the reports of the speeches of Moses.

The more pointed question is how the exegesis of Deuteronomy 1:1-5 re-

---

77. NRSV translates באר as "expound," which may mean both "to give a detailed statement of or set forth" and "to elucidate, explain, or interpret." The former suggests that the Moses speeches in Deuteronomy are something new and have not been addressed previously. Moreover, since the only other occurrences of this verb (Deut 27:9 and Hab 2:2) mean "to write clearly," it can be suggested that Moses wrote down the torah at this time. However, "explain" is the best choice for the meaning of this verb because (1) biblical Hebrew has a particular verb for the act of writing, כתב, (2) the verb in v. 5 is coupled with לאמר, and (3) this meaning agrees with vv. 1-4. Cf. J. H. Tigay, *Deuteronomy*, JPS Torah Commentary (Philadelphia: The Jewish Publication Society, 1996), pp. 5 and 344, n. 17.

lates to Numbers 10:11–36:13. Does Deuteronomy 1:1-5 mark the decisive break from Numbers 36:13? It is obvious that "beyond of Jordan . . . in the land of Moab" in verses 1aβ and 5a and particularly the precise date in verse 3a integrate Deuteronomy into the geographical and chronological framework of Exodus-Numbers. Deuteronomy itself is tied to the earlier books by the story line of Moses' life and by the numerous references to the events already narrated in them. These geographical and chronological aspects of Deuteronomy suggest that it is not particularly distinctive from Numbers 10:11–36:13, or from Exodus-Numbers for that matter.[78]

The crucial difference comes from the fact that Deuteronomy 1:1-5 is unified by the act of Moses speaking to Israel. Verse 1a states clearly that Moses is speaking to Israel, verses 1b-4 supply the content of his speeches (although it is done through geographical and chronological frameworks), and verse 5 qualifies his speaking as not a new revelation but as an interpretation of God's previous instruction. Moses' speaking is also the dominant conceptuality in the entire book of Deuteronomy. The book is the report of Moses' speeches, not of Yahweh's speeches. No doubt Moses did not speak on his own, but the radical difference between the extant text of Numbers 10:11–36:13 and Deuteronomy is that it is Moses who spoke to Israel in the latter, whereas it is Yahweh who spoke to Moses in the former. The occurrence of speech formulae in both texts shows this point clearly.

Numbers 10:11–36:13 contains frequent reports of Yahweh speeches, fifty-three altogether. These speeches are introduced by two speech formulae: וידבר יהוה אל . . . (לאמר) (twenty-three times) and ויאמר יהוה אל . . . (לאמר) (thirty times). Both forms introduce a direct Yahweh speech, and its addressee is almost always Moses; only occasionally are Moses and Aaron addressed, or Aaron alone, or Moses, Aaron, and Miriam, or Moses and Eleazar, or Moses alone implied by the context.[79] In contrast, Moses'

---

78. Since no other precise dates are provided, Moses' speeches may have taken place on the same day that he died (34:1-8). There are no time gaps between the beginning of Moses' speech (1:6) and the ending of his speeches (31:1), his song (31:30), and finally the report of his death (34:1). Tigay (*Deuteronomy*, p. 5), however, calculates the time of Moses' expositions as thirty-six days.

79. (1) Moses alone: וידבר יהוה אל־משה (. . .) (לאמר) (13:1; 15:1, 17; 16:23; 17:1, 9, 16; 18:25; 20:7; 25:10, 16; 26:52; 28:1; 31:1; 33:50; 34:1, 16; 35:1, 9); ויאמר יהוה אל־משה (לאמר) (11:16, 23; 14:11; 15:36, 37; 17:25; 21:8, 34; 25:4; 27:6, 12, 18; 31:25)

(2) Moses and Aaron (דבר — 14:26; 16:20; 19:1; אמר — 20:12, 23);

(3) Aaron alone (דבר — 18:8; אמר — 18:1, 20);

(4) Moses, Aaron, and Miriam (אמר — 12:4);

(5) Moses and Eleazar (אמר — 26:1);

(6) Moses implied (אמר — 14:20).

speeches predominate throughout Deuteronomy. Of the 959 verses in Deuteronomy only 59 clearly contain no direct speech of Moses.[80] These verses report speeches that form the context for Moses' direct speeches, which in turn make up almost every chapter of Deuteronomy. The remainder of the book is a series of Moses' speeches. Moses speaks alone in this section, except on two occasions when he speaks with the elders of Israel (27:1-8) and with the Levitical priests (27:9-10). Moreover, Deuteronomy has only three occurrences of Yahweh speaking to Moses: ויאמר יהוה אל־משה (33:14, 16) and וידבר יהוה אל־משה לאמר (32:48). But it mentions twelve times that Moses spoke about the fact that Yahweh spoke to him: (לאמר) ויאמר יהוה אלי (1:42; 2:2, 9, 31; 3:2, 26; 5:28; 9:12, 13; 10:11; 18:17) and וידבר יהוה אלי לאמר (2:17). It suggests that even when Moses quotes Yahweh's speeches, he makes the point that Yahweh's words are to be transmitted only through him. All the words of Yahweh that Moses quotes are deliberately spoken away from the people so that they are not heard directly by the people. The only exception is the Decalogue in 5:6-21.

Furthermore, as indicated by באר in verse 5b, Moses not only declares what Yahweh has said, but he also interprets or explains the meaning of Yahweh's words for Israel. For example, Moses rearranges Israel's wandering in the wilderness (1:6–3:29) in such a way as to portray their experience more negatively than in Exodus-Numbers. The reason for Moses' exclusion from Canaan has been altered from his own sin against Yahweh (Num 20:1-13) to Israel's failure to trust Yahweh (Deut 1:37; 3:23-29; 4:21-22). Moses claims that it is he who gives the land to Israel (Deut 3:12-22), which suggests his taking over the role of Yahweh.[81] The point is that regardless of whether or not the writer of this text used special material, or material from Exodus-Numbers, his understanding of Israel's wandering and portrayal of Moses is distinct from that of Exodus-Numbers.

What has been said thus far can be summarized as follows: Numbers 10:11–36:13 points to the specific aspect of the execution of Israel's migratory sanctuary campaign. The concept of the execution of the campaign is operative at the fundamental level throughout the text from Numbers 10:11 to at

---

80. R. Polzin, "Reporting Speech in the Book of Deuteronomy: Toward a Compositional Analysis of the Deuteronomic History," in *Traditions in Transformation: Turning Points in Biblical Faith: F. M. Cross Festschrift,* ed. B. Halpern and J. D. Levenson (Winona Lake: Eisenbrauns, 1981), pp. 204-5. These are 1:1-5; 2:10-12, 20-23; 3:9, 11, 13b-14; 4:41–5:1a; 10:6-7, 9; 27:1a, 9a, 11; 28:69; 29:1a; 31:1, 7a, 9-10a, 14a, 14c-16a, 22-23a, 24-25, 30; 32:44-45, 48; 33:1; 34:1-4a, 5-12.

81. Driver (*Deuteronomy,* p. 99) notes several texts in Deuteronomy that portray Moses as slipping into and out of the Yahweh speech in the first person, that is, speaking as though he were Yahweh (7:4; 11:14, 15; 17:3; 28:20; 29:3).

least Joshua 12. Numbers 10:11–36:13 focuses on Israel's failure to conquer the promised land and their forty years of wandering in the wilderness as their punishment. In terms of this focus, Numbers 10:11 and 36:13 are the division's appropriate beginning and ending. In terms of function, Numbers 36:13 as a subscription closes Yahweh's commandments and ordinances to Moses, whereas Deuteronomy 1:1-5 as an introduction to Deuteronomy opens Moses' speeches to the Israelites. In terms of literary character, Numbers 10:11–36:13 is the narrative which includes frequent reports of Yahweh's speeches, and Deuteronomy is a series of Moses' speeches with the virtual absence of narrative. In Deuteronomy, Yahweh is quoted in only thirteen verses (31:14, 16-21, 23; 32:49-52; 34:4). In terms of concept, Numbers 36:13 directs the reader's attention backward to search for Yahweh's commanding and guiding activities, and Deuteronomy 1:1-5 directs one forward to listen for Moses' speaking, his primary activity. Numbers 10:11–36:13 stresses Yahweh's determination to bring Israel to the promised land, the goal set by Yahweh, despite Israel's distrust of his plan in the sanctuary campaign process; and Deuteronomy focuses on Moses' urgent call for preparation for the impending conquest under Joshua's leadership, which requires absolute obedience to Yahweh's instructions or torah.

B. The Individual Units within Numbers 10:11–36:13

1. Preliminary Remarks

Previous scholarship is nowhere near agreement on the number of individual units within 10:11–36:13. A comparison of nine representative commentaries demonstrates this point clearly. Gray has 30 units altogether; Noth lists 27; Budd has 38; Maier presents 39 units with 72 subunits; Milgrom lists 18 units subdivided into 87 smaller units;[82] Ashley identifies 42; Davies ends up with 41; Olson presents 26 units; and Dozeman shows 13 units with

---

82. In the table of contents, Milgrom gives only titles of his alleged individual units without versification. In his exegesis, however, he supplies the applicable verses and chapters for each unit and further subdivides almost all of them (except 27:12-23; 33:1-49; and 36:1-3). His many subunits may be due to the practice of exegesis. For example, he subdivides sixteen verses of 30:2-17 into seven smaller units (30:2-3, 4-6, 7-9, 10, 11-13, 14-16, 17). Since he titles these subunits separately based on various compositional devices, he practices a more limited or rigid definition of a literary unit than others. Maier's practice may be understood along the same lines as Milgrom's, yet this would require further analysis.

48 subunits.[83] The fact that these scholars divide the text into numbers of units implies that they presuppose the definition of a basic and independent literary unit and the criteria for the identification of a unit. These two presuppositions clearly have diverse opinions, as suggested by the lack of consensus on the numbers of units among them. In their commentaries they simply practice their assumed definition of a unit without spelling it out explicitly.[84] As a consequence, their delineation of the limits of a unit within 10:11–36:13 and the exegesis of each unit, especially the relationship of its component parts, are not methodologically controlled, and their results are less verifiable.

To identify the individual units within 10:11–36:13 properly, therefore, a definition of an individual unit is needed. A working definition for an individual unit is that it consists of its own subject, verb, and verb complement; if it contains any pronouns and pronominal suffixes, their antecedents are to be found within its boundary; it displays an identifiable genre; and it conveys an intention or a theme. The criteria for determining its boundary include not only compositional devices, such as linguistic, stylistic, rhetorical, formal, generic, and thematic signals, but also conceptualities under the text. These categories themselves have their own sets of technical features,[85] and yet they are not mutually exclusive but closely related. It is possible that not one but a mixture of several devices works together to circumscribe the limits of a unit, to mark out the unit from adjacent units, and thus to establish the independence of the unit. Nevertheless, a dominant factor that represents the unit as it is should be sought. It is also possible that a unit breaks down into ever smaller subunits. But the same definition above is applied to these subunits to determine whether or not they actually qualify as independent units.

With this definition and in comparison with the selected commentaries, the present section will consist of two parts: (1) the list of individual units within 10:11–36:13 and (2) an analysis of each unit. The second part provides the macrostructure of each unit, which shows the integrity of the unit as a

---

83. In his outline of Numbers, Dozeman presents five major units in 10:11–36:13, which consist of eight subunits. However, he further divides these eight units into forty-eight smaller units differentiated by a green color in his exegesis.

84. Dozeman's commentary may be a possible exception. He discusses briefly the literary outlines of his five major units (subdivided into eight units) in the section entitled "overview," while he makes no reference to the literary nature of the forty-eight smaller units. This uneven treatment may be a result of the brevity of his commentary due to the fact that it is part of six commentaries in one volume.

85. See the present study, p. 57, n. 23.

unit, and a concise explanation of that macrostructure, which will focus on constitutive factors.[86]

2. Individual Units Proper

a. List of Individual Units

From a structural standpoint, Numbers 10:11–36:13 consists of thirty-six units. The individual units are as follows:

(1) 10:11-36   Report of Israel's departure from the wilderness of Sinai

(2) 11:1-3   Taberah etiology: Israel's rebellion against Yahweh regarding the people's misfortunes

(3) 11:4-34   Kibroth-hattaavah etiology: Israel's rebellion against Yahweh regarding the lack of meat

(4) 11:35–12:16   Rebellion narrative of the event at Hazeroth: Miriam and Aaron challenge Moses' authority

(5) 13:1–14:45   Historical narrative concerning Israel's failure to enter the promised land from the south

---

86. In terms of the structure of each unit, the present section presents its macrostructure, since a thorough analysis of the microstructure of each unit lies outside the purview of the present study. Yet, the structure represents as comprehensive an understanding of the unit as this study permits. Moreover, the structures are at the outset provisional. No individual unit is independent from its larger context. It is also true that an interpretation of the larger context or a literary whole is inevitably affected by the information that its individual parts provide. Because of the reality of this exegetical circle, any structure of an individual unit is subject to alteration based on the consideration of the structure of the larger unit. Furthermore, in explaining the structure of the unit, the present section will concentrate on compositional and structural questions. Numerous exegetically important questions for each unit (e.g., linguistic, literary-critical, tradition-critical, and hermeneutical questions) have been discussed extensively in commentaries and other studies. These discussions will be consulted and included whenever they are relevant to the structural inquiry of the unit. Additionally, a similar limitation will be applied to the investigations of genre, setting, and theological intention pertaining to each unit. The generic descriptions of each unit, however, follow the definitions provided in the glossary section of the FOTL commentary series, especially, Coats, *Genesis*, pp. 1-10, 317-22; B. O. Long, *1 Kings, with an Introduction to Historical Literature*, FOTL 9 (Grand Rapids: Eerdmans, 1984), pp. 1-8, 243-65; B. O. Long, *2 Kings*, FOTL 10 (Grand Rapids: Eerdmans, 1991), pp. 291-324, respectively); and M. A. Sweeney, *Isaiah 1–39 with an Introduction to Prophetic Literature*, FOTL 16 (Grand Rapids: Eerdmans, 1996), pp. 512-47.

(6) 15:1-16   Yahweh speech: instructions about cultic regulations for the accompanying aspects of an offering by fire

(7) 15:17-31   Yahweh speech: instructions about the dedication of the first dough

(8) 15:32-36   Report about the wood gatherer on the Sabbath

(9) 15:37-41   Yahweh speech: instructions about tassels

(10) 16:1–17:15   Report about Korah's rebellions against Moses and Aaron
(Eng. 16:1-50)

(11) 17:16-26   Report about Aaron's budding staff
(Eng. 17:1-11)

(12) 17:27–18:32   Yahweh speech: instructions about the duties of the priests and the Levites
(Eng. 17:12–18:32)

(13) 19:1-22   Yahweh speech: instructions about purification from contamination by a corpse

(14) 20:1-13   Report about Yahweh's denial of Moses' and Aaron's prophetic leadership

(15) 20:14-21   Report of Israel's conflicting encounter with Edom

(16) 20:22-29   Report of the event at Mount Hor: the death of Aaron

(17) 21:1-3   Hormah etiology: Israel's victory over the Canaanites

(18) 21:4-9   Rebellion narrative of the event that happened on the way to Oboth: the serpent scourge

(19) 21:10-20   Itinerary report: from Mount Hor to the valley near Pisgah in Moab

(20) 21:21-31   Report of Israel's campaign to occupy the land of the Amorites

(21) 21:32-35   Report of Israel's campaign to possess the land of Bashan

(22) 22:1–24:25   Story of Balak's failed plan to curse Israel

(23) 25:1-18   Rebellion narrative of the event at Shittim: Israel's apostasy to Baal of Peor because of their sexual behavior

(24) 25:19–26:65   Census report: preparation for the allotment of the land
(Eng. 26:1-65)

(25) 27:1-11   Report about the daughters of Zelophehad: heiresses' right to inherit the land

(26) 27:12-23   Yahweh speech: instructions about the commissioning of Joshua as the successor of Moses

(27) 28:1–30:1   Yahweh speech: instructions about various public
                   offerings
                   (Eng. 28:1–29:40)
(28) 30:2-17   Report about male responsibility for the validity of
                   vows
                   (Eng. 30:1-16)
(29) 31:1-54   Report of Israel's holy war against Midian
(30) 32:1-42   Historical narrative concerning the allotment of land in
                   the Transjordan for the Reubenites, the Gadites, and
                   the half-tribe of Manasseh
(31) 33:1-49   Itinerary report: from Rameses to the plains of Moab
(32) 33:50–34:29   Yahweh speech: instructions about the division of the
                   land of Canaan
(33) 35:1-8   Yahweh speech: instructions about the apportionment
                   of the Levites
(34) 35:9-34   Yahweh speech: instructions about the city of refuge for
                   involuntary homicide
(35) 36:1-12   Report of legislation concerning the inheritance of
                   heiresses
(36) 36:13   Subscription

b. The Units

(1) Report of Israel's Departure from the Wilderness of Sinai (10:11-36)

I. Programmatic statement of Israel's departure	10:11-12
II. Elaboration	10:13-36
A. General description	10:13
B. Specific descriptions	10:14-36
1. The order of the camp	10:14-28
2. Leadership in the wilderness	10:29-34
a. Human leadership	10:29-32
b. Divine leadership	10:33-34
1+2. Poetic summary	10:35-36

This unit is unified by the concept of Israel's departure, which is pervasive throughout the unit. It is demonstrated by the use of the root of נסע (10:12, 13, 14, 17, 18, 21, 22, 25, 28, 29, 33 [x2], 34, 35). This concept is clearly stated and further elaborated on in its six component parts (vv. 11-12, 13, 14-28, 29-32, 33-34, 35-36).[87] However, from these six, most commentators, such as Gray, Budd, and Davies, make two independent units, verses 11-28 and verses 29-36.[88] Such a division is based on the literary-critical observation which follows Gray's proposal, that is, verses 12-28 are designated as the Priestly description of Israel's departure, whereas verses 29-36 as the Yahwistic-Elohistic version of it. This argument, however, has already been dismissed in the present study. Noth and Milgrom, however, propose three parts, although they differ regarding the boundaries of these units.[89] For his division, Noth applies a literary-critical analysis more rigidly than Gray. He accepts Gray's division except verses 13-28, which he considers as not belonging to "the basic form of P" due to the divergence of verses 17 and 21 from 2:17. Regardless of this difference, Noth's basic approach to the unit is the same as Gray's, and thus he does not do justice to the unit in its present form by dividing it. Milgrom's division is based on content analysis. It is demonstrated by his titles "the order of the march" for verses 11-28, "guidance in the wilderness: Hobab" for verses 29-32, and "guidance in the wilderness: the ark" for verses 33-36. How are these parts related? What is constitutive for their relationship? Do the second and the third parts belong together relative to the first by sharing the same part of the title, "guidance in the wilderness"? Content analysis reveals what the unit says on the surface level, but it is to be compared with other factors to determine the structure of the unit.[90]

Milgrom's three divisions can be further grouped based on the conceptual aspect of the programmatic statement and its elaboration. The structure of 10:11-36 has two parts: verses 11-12 are considered to be the programmatic statement of Israel's departure from the wilderness of Sinai, and verses 13-36

---

87. For other important exegetical problems, such as the specific designation for the wilderness of Paran (or the theological significance of Paran); the divergence in the order of the Levites in 10:17 (cf. 2:16-17); the identity of Hobab and his relationship to Moses, and the presence of his descendants in the land (Judg 1:16; 4:11), which implies his acceptance of Moses' proposal; the order of march with the ark as the head of the march (cf. 10:21); and the function of the so-called inverted *nuns* that frame vv. 35-36, see Ashley, *The Book of Numbers*, pp. 193-200; Milgrom, *Numbers*, pp. 76-81, 375-76; E. W. Davies, *Numbers*, pp. 90-98; and Dozeman, "The Book of Numbers," pp. 94-95.

88. Gray, *A Critical and Exegetical Commentary on Numbers*, pp. 90-97; Budd, *Numbers*, pp. 109-16; E. W. Davies, *Numbers*, pp. 92-93.

89. For Noth (*Numbers*, pp. 76-77), the three parts are vv. 11-12, 13-28, and 29-36; for Milgrom (*Numbers*, pp. 76-82), vv. 11-28, 29-32, and 33-36.

90. Since Dozeman divides 10:11-36 based on content analysis, though he has four subunits (vv. 11-12, 13-28, 29-32, 33-36), his outline cannot escape the same criticism that applies to Milgrom's outline.

elaborate on this statement. It can be argued that verse 13 is linked to the preceding verses by the fact that the antecedent of ויסעו obviously refers to the
Israelites in verse 12a. But verse 13 provides new information in that Israel's
departure is described as "for the first time" since their stay in the wilderness
of Sinai (Exod 19:1). Moreover, their departure is an execution of Yahweh's
command to Moses, "at the command of the LORD by Moses." The same
point illustrates what follows (vv. 14-28), that is, the order of the marching
camp corresponds to the layout of the camp which Yahweh had instructed
previously in 2:1-31. The new information of verse 13 links the verse to what
follows more closely than to what precedes, and it overrides the verse's syntactical link with verse 12. Therefore, verse 13 is set apart from verse 12 and is
the beginning of the elaboration of Israel's departure in general terms.

The detailed description of Israel's departure (vv. 14-36) has two main
parts, with a poetic summary of the two parts at the end. The first part (vv. 13-
28) narrates the process of the departure, basically following what Yahweh had
commanded previously in 2:1-31 (cf. 1:5-15; 7:10-83); the second part (vv. 29-34)
reports on the leadership conflicts during the journey in the wilderness. Moses' desire to have the special expertise of Hobab for marching in the wilderness (vv. 29-32) is altered by verses 33-36. The one who will lead Israel on the
journey through the wilderness, find the water and resting places, and so forth,
is Yahweh, not Hobab. There is no mention of Hobab's reply to Moses' proposal. In contrast, there are clear statements of Yahweh's leadership represented by the ark: "Israel set out . . . with the ark of the covenant of the LORD
going before them" (v. 33) and "whenever the ark set out . . . and whenever it
[the ark] came to rest" (vv. 35a, 36a). Besides, divine leadership is already implied in verses 11-12 by describing the function of the cloud as signaling the beginning of Israel's departure, when the cloud lifted off the tabernacle.

For the function of verses 33-36, Ashley provides five options.[91] However, out of the five which is the predominant one? None adequately describes
the unit as a whole, although each one points to an aspect of it. The function
of verses 33-36 must be addressed with consideration for its role within the
unit. The passage functions as the continuation of the elaboration of the programmatic statement of verses 11-12. Particularly the poetic portion (vv. 35-

---

91. Ashley, *The Book of Numbers*, pp. 197-98. Ashley proposes five functions for vv. 33-36:
(1) they complete the narrative that begins at v. 11 (12); (2) they affirm divine leadership by
changing the position of the ark from within the tribes to a position at their head; (3) they
maintain that divine leadership continued during the period between the ark's presence and the
presence of the cloud; (4) they make a drastic contrast between divine leadership and Israel's rebellion, which follows immediately (11:1ff.); and (5) similar to Aaron's blessing in 6:22-27, they
function as a poetic conclusion to vv. 11-36 and to the whole Sinai story (Exod 19–Num 10).

36) summarizes the specific elaboration of the main concept, that is, Israel's departure from the wilderness of Sinai.

(2) Taberah Etiology: Israel's Rebellion against Yahweh regarding the People's Misfortunes (11:1-3)

I. Report of event	11:1-2
A. People's complaining: motivation	11:1a
B. Yahweh's responses: reactions	11:1b
1. Initial responses	11:1bα
2. Result	11:1bβ
C. Expansion of the event: Moses' involvement	11:2
1. People's plea to Moses	11:2a
2. Moses' plea to Yahweh	11:2bα
3. Result	11:2bβ
II. Inference to a name of the place	11:3
A. Naming proper	11:3a
B. Reason	11:3b

This unit is an extended etiological tale explaining the origin of Taberah. In a pattern typical of an etiology, it has two parts. The first part (vv. 1-2) reports the event that causes the naming of the place (v. 3), and the second one (v. 3) names the place and provides the reason for that name.[92] Yet it is in an ex-

---

92. B. O. Long, *The Problem of Etiological Narrative in the Old Testament*, BZAW 108 (Berlin: Töpelmann, 1968), pp. 42-43. The text has no traditional formula for arriving at the specific locale and no specification of the problem that Israel complained about, but it contains a quoted speech, instead of a typical speech form, for the direct motivation for the name (v. 3b). With these ambiguities and the additional fact that the place name itself is not listed as one of the stations on the journey (11:35; 33:16-17), Ashley (*The Book of Numbers*, pp. 200-203) focuses on the content of the unit rather than on its recognizable form. Thus, he regards this unit as "the first, and schematic, example of the disaffection and rebellion of Israel in the wilderness." He is obviously more interested in its literary function in relation to what precedes and follows, than in its own literary nature. Similar to Ashley, Dozeman ("The Book of Numbers," p. 104) suggests that its function is to introduce two themes dominant in chs. 11–19 (the death of the first generation in the wilderness and the leadership of Moses). But his outline (p. 23) does not reflect this insight. Granting that 11:1-3 plays a role in the chapters that follow, nonetheless, questions like what specific roles it plays and how far its influence goes should be discussed fully. The present study argues that the text functions as a general example of Israel's distrust of Yahweh's ability to fulfill Yahweh's promise of land to the Israelites' ancestors (this point will be taken up later in the discussion of the conceptual framework responsible for the macrostructure of Numbers 10:11–36:13). Milgrom (*Numbers*, pp. 82, 376) suggests that Israel's complaint involves either a lack of water or the rigors of the forced march from the wilderness of Sinai. This suggestion, however, must remain speculative due to a lack of hard textual evidence.

tended form because the report of the event includes Moses' involvement, the people's plea to Moses, Moses' intercession on their behalf, and the resulting response of Yahweh to Moses (v. 2). With the inclusion of Moses' involvement, the scheme of the people's complaining and Yahweh's punishment is expanded. Nevertheless, the expansion does not affect the typical pattern of an etymological etiology in verses 1 and 3. The people's complaining in verse 1a, although its cause is expressed in general terms, motivates Yahweh's reaction, which in turn provides the direct explanation for the name. The root from which the place name, Taberah, is derived, בער, with its association to fire, is pervasive throughout all three verses.

(3) Kibroth-hattaavah Etiology: Israel's Rebellion against Yahweh regarding the Lack of Meat (11:4-34)

I. Report of the event	11:4-33
A. Complaining: motivation	11:4-9
1. By the rabble	11:4a
2. By the Israelites	11:4b-9
a. Who: the Israelites	11:4bα
b. Content	11:4bβ-9
B. Transition: reactions	11:10-30
1. Initial responses: by Yahweh and by Moses	11:10
2. Dialogues between Moses and Yahweh	11:11-23
a. First	11:11-20
b. Second	11:21-23
3. Moses' execution	11:24-30
C. Yahweh's response	11:31-33
1. Provision	11:31-32
2. Punishment	11:33
II. Inference to a name of the place	11:34
A. Naming proper	11:34a
B. Reason	11:34b

This unit is an etymological etiology. It begins with the people, who had "a strong craving" (v. 4a), and the Israelites, who cried for "meat to eat" (v. 4b), and ends with the name, Kibroth-hattaavah (graves of craving), and the reason for the name, the burial of "the people who had the craving" (v. 34). This etiological tale is greatly extended by the narrative about Moses' questioning of his leadership and Yahweh's provision for it.

This unit may be composed of "three themes," such as food, leadership, and transition, as Ashley argues. These themes are interwoven in a threefold way (A = food theme, B = leadership theme, T = transition):[93]

A	11:4-13	A	11:18-20	A	11:31-34
T	11:14-15	T	11:21-23	T	11:35
B	11:16-17	B	11:24-30	B	12:1-15

But his outline of the interrelationship of these themes is problematic. First, he treats 11:4-34 as part of 11:1–12:16, which he considers to be a literary unit. In order to satisfy the overarching theme for 11:1–12:16, rebellion and murmuring in the wilderness, he insists that some portion of 11:4-34 fit into the preconceived framework. For example, he cuts verses 14-15 out from Moses' speech (vv. 11-15) and describes their function as transitional from the theme of food to leadership. His cutting is unacceptable because it violates the literary and conceptual integrity of Moses' speech as a whole. The speech formula in verse 11aα1 constitutes the following verses (until v. 15) as a speech. In his speech, Moses cries out to Yahweh about his leadership's heavy responsibilities (vv. 11-12, 14-15) brought about by the specific food problem (v. 13). In terms of the content of verses 14-15, Moses repeats in a narrative form what he said previously in rhetorical form (vv. 11-12). Note the similarities between these two: the root נשׂא (vv. 11, 12, and 14), the phrase את כל־העם הזה (vv. 12 and 14), and מצתי חן בעיניך (vv. 11 and 15). Thus, verses 14-15 are an integral part of Moses' speech and are a re-narration of verses 11-12. Verse 13 unifies these two separated yet corresponding parts. Second, another Moses speech in verses 21-23 is intrinsically related to verses 18-20 and is not a transition from the theme of food to leadership. The content of verses 21-23 clearly mentions the theme of food and shows Moses' desire to affirm Yahweh's ability to provide the wanted meat. Third, 11:35 has a totally different function relative to other transitional verses, and yet it plays a role related to 12:16, which Ashley does not include in his framework. In short, Ashley's form and function do not correspond on a one-to-one basis.

Regardless of the hypothetical interrelationship among the three themes, however, this unit is framed by the craving motif. This motif is clearly expressed at the beginning and the end of the unit. Moreover, it is pervasive throughout the unit as indicated by its associated terms, such as "meat" (vv. 4, 13, 18 [x3], 21, 33) and "eat" (vv. 4, 5, 13, 18 [x3], 19, 21). Furthermore, it is the people's complaining for the meat that causes Moses to cry out concerning his heavy responsibilities as a leader in the first place (vv. 11-15), evoking

93. Ashley, *The Book of Numbers*, pp. 206-7.

Yahweh's provision for him and punishment of the people. The leadership "theme" is at best secondary and subordinate to the craving motif.

The structure of this unit is, therefore, similar to that of 11:1-3 in that it has two parts: the report of the event (vv. 4-33) and the naming of the place (v. 34). The second part has the same element as verse 3. Even the report of the event has three parts, as do verses 1 and 2. Yet the differences between the two structures are substantial. In terms of their content, each section of the second part has been greatly elaborated. In narrating the motivation (vv. 4-9), the complainers are identified as "the rabble" and "the Israelites" rather than "the people," and the subject of the complaining is specified as craving for meat and is intensified by the description of manna. Moses' involvement (vv. 10-30) has a different character; he himself complains about his own responsibility instead of making intercession for the sake of the complainers. As a result, a portion of his spirit is transferred to the seventy elders. Yahweh's response has two sides: the provision of the wanted meat (vv. 31-32), along with a great plague as punishment (v. 33). In terms of structure, Moses' own complaint interrupts Yahweh's response to the complaint of the rabble and the Israelites and delays the response until the end of the unit. The unit can be understood even without including Moses' involvement in verses 10b-30. It makes good sense to read verses 4-10a and 31-34 consecutively. Besides, Moses' involvement took place mainly at the tent of meeting (vv. 16, 24, 26; cf. v. 30), instead of the camp (vv. 10a, 31, 32). The point is that this unit shares the same etiological pattern as the previous unit, yet it differs structurally, not necessarily because of the elaboration of the content but because of the distinctive function of Moses' involvement in the middle of the unit.

(4) Rebellion Narrative of the Event at Hazeroth: Miriam and Aaron Challenge Moses' Authority (11:35–12:16)

I. Migration to Hazeroth	11:35a
II. Event at Hazeroth	11:35b-12:15
A. Setting: topographical designation	11:35b
B. Report of the event	12:1-15
1. Event proper	12:1-9
a. Miriam and Aaron question Moses	12:1-2a
b. Yahweh's response: specification of the question	12:2b-9
(1) Preliminary to speech	12:2b-3
(2) Speech proper	12:4-8
(3) Summary statement	12:9

The outer limits of this unit are determined by two itineraries in 11:35 and 12:16. Without any further explanation, most commentators claim that 11:35 and 12:16 are transitional sentences. Yet, the structural functions of these verses are crucial to defining a literary unit.[94] Both 11:35 and 12:16 report Israel's migration from one place to another. Verse 12:16 shows the typical form of an itinerary, חנה . . . נסע, indicating the pattern of decamping and encamping, whereas 11:35 has היה . . . נסע, a slightly different pattern. Despite the change in half of the formula, 11:35 still points to the movement of the people just as 12:16 does. However, 11:1-3 and 11:4-34 have no report of Israel's arrival, which suggests that the focus of these units is on the events that happened while Israel stayed in specific places, rather than on Israel's movement. This is evidenced by the etiological pattern in these units. In view of the focus of 11:4-34 and the etiological pattern of these units, 11:35 is more closely connected to the following unit. It is true that 11:34 and 11:35 have the same topographical locale, Kibroth-hattaavah, but these verses in their entirety convey a different function for the locale. Whereas the former explains the origin of the name of the place, the latter employs the place as the departing point for Israel's ongoing migration.

Moreover, 11:35, coupled with היה, provides another locale for the Hazeroth event. It is Hazeroth toward which Israel journeyed (11:35); at that very place, an event occurs: Miriam and Aaron challenge Moses' authority which is confirmed by Yahweh (11:35b); in addition, Hazeroth is the place from which Israel set out "after" the event (12:16aβ2). Furthermore, the adverb אחר in 12:16aα makes this verse as a whole relate more closely to the pre-

---

94. It is odd that Ashley, who is interested in the composition of the present form of the text, does not discuss these verses in relation to their immediate literary contexts. For other exegetical issues, see Ashley (*The Book of Numbers*, pp. 220-28) and E. W. Davies (*Numbers*, pp. 113-26).

vious event than to the one following in 13:1ff. Therefore, itineraries in 11:35 and 12:16 and their syntactical links to immediate verses define the boundary of this unit and provide the unifier, Hazeroth, for 11:35, 12:1-15, and 12:16.

The event at Hazeroth (vv. 1-15) is reported in three parts. The first part (vv. 1-9) narrates the event. Miriam and Aaron question Moses' marriage to the Cushite woman and his being the unique recipient of Yahweh's word (vv. 1-2a). This situation shows that both the personal and prophetic aspects of Moses' life were being challenged. However, Miriam's and Aaron's challenge are specified in Yahweh's response to them (vv. 2b-9). Moses' prophetic authority for being the unique leader of Israel is questioned, not his marriage. Yahweh's response proves this point by including an editorial statement about Moses' humbleness (v. 3), his command to Moses, Aaron, and Miriam to come "to the tent of meeting" (vv. 4-5), and his own speech regarding the special status that Moses has in relation to other prophets (vv. 6-8). With this specification of the nature of Miriam and Aaron's challenge, Yahweh's initial response to them was anger and departure from them (v. 9).

The second part (vv. 10-15a) is set apart from the first by the phrase "the cloud went away from over the tent" (v. 10aα), the locale where Yahweh's response took place (vv. 2b-9). After Yahweh left, Miriam was afflicted with leprosy as Yahweh's punishment and was forced to stay outside the camp for seven days. For Miriam's cure, a chain of pleas was offered, first from Aaron to Moses, then from Moses to Yahweh, and finally Yahweh's solution came to Miriam.

The third part (v. 15b) is distinctive from the first two because it reports what happened to the whole of Israel. Thus far the event evolved around Miriam, Aaron, Moses, and Yahweh exclusively. No Israelites were involved. Verse 15b reports the people's action in that they did not set out on the march because of Miriam's staying outside the camp. Since Miriam's leprosy is the immediate cause for the delay, it is conceivable that verse 15b is connected to verse 15a only. But, in the larger context, Israel's delay is the consequence of the whole event that begins when Miriam and Aaron question Moses. Thus, this verse shares an equal level structurally with the event and its result. Israel could not set out from Hazeroth because Miriam and Aaron challenged Moses' prophetic leadership.

(5) Historical Narrative concerning Israel's Failure to Enter the Promised Land from the South (13:1–14:45)

I. Report of the event   13:1–14:35

    A. The reconnaissance   13:1-24

The compositeness of this unit is well recognized and discussed.[95] However, its present form should be analyzed to determine its integrity. On the surface, many component parts of 13:1–14:45 are identifiable: Yahweh's speech to Moses to send the spies (13:1-2); Moses' execution of this order (13:3-20), interrupted by the catalog of names of the spies (13:3b-16); the expedition of the spies (13:21-24); their reports of the results (13:25-33); the response of the people (14:1-4); the reactions of Moses and Aaron to the people's response (14:5); the reactions of Joshua and Caleb to the people's response (14:6-10a); the reaction of Yahweh to the people's response (14:10b-12); Moses' plea to Yahweh (14:13-19); Yahweh's answer to Moses' plea (14:20-25); Yahweh's speech to Moses and Aaron (14:26-35); the death of the spies except Joshua and Caleb (14:36-38); and the reaction of the people (14:39-45). These component parts are interwoven to narrate Israel's initial and disastrous attempt to enter the promised land from the south.

How do these parts relate to each other? What are the factors involved in their arrangement? Milgrom, while fully admitting the composite nature of this unit, presents a chiastic structure for the extant text:[96]

95. E. W. Davies (*Numbers*, pp. 126-32) provides a summary of previous scholarship on this text. Recognizing inconsistencies, redundancies, and duplications within the text has led most commentators to focus on the questions of the origin of the text and on distinguishing the various layers of the text. For the history of traditions of the text, see Budd, *Numbers*, pp. 141-44, 150-55; Milgrom, *Numbers*, pp. 387-92. Cf. Olson, *The Death of the Old and the Birth of the New*, pp. 129-52. Olson stresses this text's relationship to the larger editorial structure of Numbers rather than focusing on the text itself.

96. Milgrom, *Numbers*, pp. 387-90. After analyzing the composite nature of the unit, Milgrom concludes that it is a conflation of two traditions (mostly the Priestly) rather than two sources. He claims that his chiastic structure supports the conclusion that two Priestly traditions have been artfully woven together, except for one doublet in 14:20-25, 26-35. However, Dozeman ("The Book of Numbers," pp. 120-28) sees chs. 13–14 in relation to ch. 15 based on the theme of conflict over the land. Accordingly, he divides chs. 13–15 into four parts (13:1-20, 21-33; 14:1-38; 14:39–15:41). For him, the laws in ch. 15 function to provide a positive commentary on Israel's failed conquest of the promised land (14:39-45) or on the events in the entire chapters (13–14). His suggestion is attractive since it explains the awkward position or the interruption of the narrative flow that ch. 15 creates. It also fits well within the overall organization of 11:1–19:22 that he proposes. Yet, questions emerge. Among the three conflicts he argues (prophetic leadership in 11:1–12:16; the land in 13:1–15:41; priestly leadership in 16:1–17:13), are they all equally important conceptually? What is the ultimate purpose for Moses' leadership (prophetic and/or priestly)? Moses' leadership is meaningful only in reference to the conquest of the promised land; hence his leadership is secondary to or subordinate to the concept of the land. In addition, his choice of Deut 1:19-45 as the "point of departure" for understanding Num 13–15 is questionable, as it violates the literary and theological integrity of Num 13–15. Furthermore, Dozeman's claim that "chapters 13–15 are pivotal in the book of Numbers" (p. 120) is not reflected in the outline of the whole book, let alone in 11:1–19:22, where two themes (death in the wilderness and the leadership of Moses, p. 99) are dominant.

A   The scouts' expedition (13:1-24)
  B   The scouts' report (13:25-33)
    X   The people's response (14:1-10a)
  B'   God's response (14:10b-38)
A'   The people's expedition (14:39-45)

However, a chiastic pattern for this story about Israel's attempt to enter the promised land seems to be artificial and overstructured, narrated as it is according to the succession or progression of the event. For example, except for A and A', Milgrom's other sections do not correspond well to each other. A and A' share the same mode of thought with the opposite result. Both of them narrate about the expedition, yet they differ regarding the initiators and the result. In A, it was Yahweh who commanded Moses to send the spies (v. 2), whereas in A', it was the people who initiated going up "to the heights of the hill country" even without Yahweh's presence and with Moses' warning. The scouts' expedition is successful, whereas the people's expedition is a total failure. Furthermore, the correspondence between A and A' is not evident in B and B'. The nature of B is a report, whereas that of B' is a response. In a similar way, the character of B is the scouts' reporting of their reconnaissance, while that of B' is Yahweh's response, a reaction to the people's response. B is not directly related to B'. In fact, X shares the same title with B', which suggests that it has a closer relationship to B' and thus is not a turning point for the entire story.[97] A chiastic pattern is more readily appreciable in a small pericope than in a lengthy narrative, such as this unit, which totals seventy-seven verses of a noticeably composite nature.

Instead, the structure of 13:1–14:45 has two parts based on the narrating mode of an event: the report of the event (13:1–14:35) and the report of the aftermath (14:36-45). The first part has three sections: the scouts' reconnaissance (13:1-24), their report (13:25-33), and reactions to the report (14:1-35). While the first two sections are mostly narrative, including the list of the spies' names (13:4-16) and the list of topographical and geographical localities in the area being surveyed (vv. 21-24), except Moses' command to the scouts (vv. 17-20),[98] the third section is comprised of alternations between speeches.

97. Milgrom (*Numbers,* p. 388) himself acknowledges this point: "[S]ection X is even more tightly linked to the section that follows [section B'], for it is the people's reaction to the scouts' report that determines the nature and form of their punishment."

98. A. Malamat, "The Danite Migration and the Pan-Israelite Exodus-Conquest: A Biblical Narrative Pattern," *Bib* 51 (1970): 1-16. Malamat observes the similarity between this story and that of the Danites in that the scouts are commanded to obtain not only military but also economic, demographic, and political information.

The scouts' report in 13:25-33 is more closely related to the response narrative due to its active interchanges between the ten scouts and Caleb and Joshua. The character of the report has an objective side in that it tells what the scouts surveyed. However, their objective report is impregnated with positive and negative implications of their findings, which eventually lead them to evaluate their findings subjectively. Even their subjective evaluations are split between positive and negative, and this split causes diverse responses to their evaluations. The third section has two subsections: the people's response to the report (14:1-4) and reactions to the people's response (14:5-35). The former shows the people's unprecedented rebellion against Yahweh and provides a justifiable cause for Yahweh to pronounce their fatal destiny. Yahweh's response to the people's rebellion, despite Moses' lengthy intercession, guarantees the death of the Exodus generation and, at the same time, promises continual guidance for the next generation who will inherit the promised land instead of their parents (14:10b-35). The doublet of verses 20-25 and 26-35, which Milgrom takes as an exception to his structure, fits very well within Yahweh's response to the whole rebellious situation. Verses 20-25 are a direct answer to Moses' intercession, while verses 26-35 are an elaboration of Yahweh's response related specifically to the content of the people's rebellion. The specificity of the content of verses 20-25 and 26-35 demonstrates this point well.

The second part reports the aftermath of the event focusing on the initial actualization of Yahweh's punishment for Israel's failure. For the chosen scouts, Yahweh's punishment is realized immediately and individualized in the matter of life and death (vv. 36-38). For the people, Yahweh's punishment is implemented indirectly by Yahweh's being absent during their expedition (vv. 39-45). They attempted to nullify Yahweh's punishment by taking the initiative to conquer the land, which failed completely. This section corresponds to Yahweh's punishment rather than to the scouts' expedition, as Milgrom argues.

(6) Yahweh Speech: Instructions about Cultic Regulations for the Accompanying Aspects of an Offering by Fire (15:1-16)

This unit shows a clear break from the previous units based on stylistic, generic, topical, and temporal aspects. It begins with the narrative formula, וידבר יהוה אל־משה לאמר ("The LORD spoke to Moses, saying") and ends with verse 16, before another instance of the same formula in verse 17. It is a narrative about a speech of Yahweh to Moses. This narrative formula with variation of the verb (אמר) begins ten literary units, including the present unit, within Numbers 10:11–36:13.[99] It is true that a Yahweh speech formula occurs elsewhere in the previous units (11:16, 23; 12:4, 14; 13:1; 14:11, 20, 26). However, as seen above, these occurrences do not begin a new unit but are integral parts of an already established unit that is defined based on factors other than a speech formula. In terms of generic differences, the previous units thus far consist of a report, etiology, rebellion narrative, and historical narrative, whereas this unit consists of Yahweh's instructions regarding a cultic regulation. The topic is distinctive in that this unit narrates a prescription of the tariff or scale, to be kept by Israel for use in the promised land, for the meal and drink offerings. Note that several key terms appear repeatedly in the unit to address the prescription: "a pleasing odor for the LORD" (vv. 3, 7, 10, 13, 14), "an offering by fire" (vv. 3, 10, 13, 14), "burning offering" (vv. 3, 5, 8), "sacrifice" (vv. 3, 5, 8), "meal offering" (vv. 4, 6, 9), and "drink offering" (vv. 5, 7, 10). Additionally, in terms of the temporal aspect, whereas previous units spoke of living in the promised land in the present tense, this unit shifts to the

    99. 15:1-16, 17-31, 37-31; 17:16-24 (Eng. 17:1-11); 19:1-22; 27:12-23; 28:1–30:1 (Eng. 28:1–29:40); 31:1-54; 35:1-8, 9-34.

future tense: "when you come into the land you are to inhabit" (v. 2). Furthermore, this temporal change is made noticeable by the fact that Israel fails to trust Yahweh's guidance in the present situation and yet is commanded to keep the law in the future.

Structurally, this unit consists of two parts: the narrative introduction in 15:1 and the narrated speech in 15:2-16. Acknowledging the narrative formula, וידבר יהוה אל־משה לאמר, in verse 1 is crucial for the nature of this unit. This unit is not just an instruction but a narrative about a speech of Yahweh to Moses. The narrative framework of this unit provides the necessary authorization for the instruction proper (vv. 2b-16).[100] The instruction concerning cultic regulations for the accompanying aspects of an offering by fire is elevated to a divine command, which implies exact obedience to it.

The narrated Yahweh speech contains the command to Moses to speak to the Israelites in 15:2a and the content of the speech in 15:2b-16.[101] The subject matter (vv. 3-16) is not to be restricted to the present time in the wilderness and includes the future when Israel enters the promised land. The subject matter has two parts distinguishable from each other by the substantive distinction between the main offering (v. 3) and its accompanying aspects (vv. 4-16). Furthermore, the accompanying aspects consist of two sections, each with its own system of organization. The instruction regarding the tariff of grain and drink offerings is dependent upon the value of the animals in the main burnt offering. The tariff must be specified according to the burnt offering of the lamb, ram, and bull. In similar fashion, the offerers are classified individually and as a whole assembly. Even the individual offerer needs to be distinguished as a native Israelite or a nonnative: "an alien who lives with you [native Israelites], or who takes up permanent residence among you" (v. 14).

---

100. Knierim, "Conceptual Aspects in Exodus 25:1-9," pp. 390-96. In the exegesis of Exod 25:1-9, Knierim discusses extensively the presuppositions and implications of treating this text as narrative. Despite differences in the content and the literary context between Exod 25:1-9 and Num 15:1-16, the essential points obtained by characterizing these texts as narratives are relevant for the understanding of the latter because these two begin with the same narrative formula.

101. One of many difficulties of the speech in its present form is the shift in person. The text begins and ends with the second person plural (vv. 2b-3, 12-16) and uses the second person singular (vv. 5-8, 10-11) and the third person singular (vv. 4, 9) in the section in between. There is no satisfactory explanation for this phenomenon. See the discussion in Ashley, *The Book of Numbers*, pp. 276-77. E. W. Davies (*Numbers*, p. 151) observes another difficulty, inconsistencies in the flow of the text, without providing further discussion. He also compares this text with Lev 2 and Ezek 46 in terms of their similarity and dependence on the process of chronological development, and he concludes that these texts "merely reflect the custom that happened to prevail at the time when they were written." The remaining question would be, Is any certain way to determine when these texts were written?

These distinctions are presupposed and crucial for the structure of verses 4-16, yet they are not decisive but subordinate to the distinction of the main offering and its accompanying aspects.

(7) Yahweh Speech: Instructions about the Dedication of the First Dough (15:17-31)

I. Introductory Yahweh speech formula	15:17
II. Speech proper: instructions	15:18-31
A. Command to speak	15:18a
B. Content of speech	15:18b-31
1. Temporal aspects	15:18b
2. Subject matter	15:19-31
a. A donation to Yahweh	15:19-21
(1) When: perpetually	15:19a
(2) What: a donation	15:19b
(3) From what: first batch of dough and the threshing floor	15:20
(1) + (2) + (3) Summary statement	15:21
b. Responses	15:22-31
(1) Inadvertent violation	15:22-29
(a) By the whole congregation	15:22-26
(b) By an individual	15:27-29
(2) Deliberate violation	15:30-31

The introductory phrases in verses 17-18 indicate that they possess the same function as 15:1-2 in that they form a complete unit, although they contain some variations in pattern and choice of terms. The Yahweh speech formula in both units is identical (vv. 1-2a and 17-18a). The temporal aspect of these units, although expressed slightly differently, is the same as well, indicating the future time when Israel will be settled in the promised land. In the larger context, even the frequency of the two offerings is the same. Both offerings in 15:1-16 and 15:17-31 are presented to the LORD perpetually, "throughout your generations" (vv. 15b and 21a, 23b). Thus, the structure of this unit is similar to the previous one, and it consists of the narrative introduction in verse 17 and the narrated speech in verses 18-31.

The critical structural question for this unit is whether verses 17-21 and 22-31 are one unified unit or two independent units simply juxtaposed. Most commentators treat these two texts separately as if there were no organic connection between them. Noth's comment is typical: "Vv. 22-31 have no introductory formula of their own, nevertheless they are not a continuation of the preceding passage, since their contents are quite different and self-contained."[102] One of the reasons contributing to the problem of connectedness is the question of what exactly the antecedents of "all these commandments that the LORD has spoken to Moses" in verse 22aβ-b are. The possible antecedents may include all divine commandments recorded in Exodus. Yet, this much is clear: the antecedents surely include the commandments in 15:1-16 and 15:17-21 since these two have the same Yahweh speech formula indicating that they are instructions Yahweh commanded Moses to speak to the Israelites.

In addition to being the immediate literary context of verse 22, verses 17-21 are closely connected to verses 22-31 by at least three more facts. First, verses 22-31 lack an introductory formula, although this can be used against the argument for connectedness.[103] Second, the subject of verses 17-21 and verses 22-26 is the same in number, the second person plural. Third, phrases such as "the LORD spoke to Moses" (v. 17a) and "throughout your generations" (v. 21a) occur in verses 22b and 23b, respectively. If these reasons are convincing, the conclusion follows that verses 22-31 are connected to verses 17-21 and particularly to verses 19-21, which speak about the dedication of the first dough to Yahweh.

The guidelines for the offerings are twofold, based on either the behavior of the offerer or the category of the offerer. On the one hand, if the category of the offerer is the dominant factor, then the guidelines are divided into verses 22-26 and 27-31. The former narrates the involvement of the whole congregation, whereas the latter accounts for that of the individual. This division is reinforced by the third person singular pronoun for the offerer in verses 27-31, which is in contrast to the whole congregation, as the offerer, in verses 24-26. Note that the previous units also employ the category of the offerer. On the other hand, if the behavior of the offerer is the dominant factor, the guidelines are divided into two parts: verses 22-29, unified by their in-

---

102. Noth, *Numbers*, p. 116. Cf. Gray, *A Critical and Exegetical Commentary on Numbers*, pp. 177-82; Budd, *Numbers*, pp. 172-74; Maier, *Das vierte Buch Mose*, pp. 214-19; Milgrom, *Numbers*, pp. 121-25; Dozeman, "The Book of Numbers," pp. 126-27. For a summary of previous interpretation of this question, see E. W. Davies, *Numbers*, pp. 155-56. For a comparison between 15:22-31 and Lev 4–5, see E. W. Davies, *Numbers*, pp. 156-57 and Ashley, *The Book of Numbers*, p. 285.

103. Ashley (*The Book of Numbers*, p. 281) claims that vv. 17-31 form one complete unit based on the single introductory formula that vv. 17-21 and vv. 22-31 share. Yet he discusses no further how or why they are related or what the assigned function of these two units is. He explains them separately in his exegesis.

advertent violation, and verses 30-31, held together by their deliberate violation. Comparing these two factors, verses 22-31 in their entirety are focused on how the people respond to the commanded offering and what the solutions are in case violations occur, but they do not focus on the person responsible for the offering. The distinction between an inadvertent and intentional violation of the divine command overrides the category of offerer, supported by the syntactical link of the use of the third person singular, and is therefore the dominant factor.

(8) Report about the Wood Gatherer on the Sabbath (15:32-36)

I. The case: the people's activities	15:32-34
A. The case	15:32
1. Temporal setting	15:32a
2. The case itself	15:32b
B. Development	15:33-34
1. Public display	15:33
2. Restricted confinement	15:34
II. Solution: Yahweh's action	15:35-36
A. Yahweh speech	15:35
B. Execution of command by the whole congregation	15:36

This unit sets itself apart from the surrounding materials.[104] Unlike the previous units (15:1-16; 15:17-31) and the following unit (15:37-41), 15:32-36 lacks the introductory speech formula. The temporal aspect has shifted once again in that this unit points to a recollection of the past, "when the Israelites were in the wilderness," and goes back to the time period before chapter 15. Moreover, its specificity makes it distinctive. Note the specific topic (the wood gatherer on the Sabbath day), the informational comments (v. 34; brought outside the camp in v. 36a), and a report of the congregation's execution of Yahweh's command (v. 36b). Furthermore, this text is not a prescription of cultic regulations, but a report of a specific case that is being presented and solved.

Structurally, this unit has two parts based on the actors involved in the development of the case: the people (vv. 32-34) and Yahweh (vv. 35-36). The first part (vv. 32-34) reports what the people did, interrupted by a sudden Yahweh speech in verse 35. This part consists of two sections (vv. 32 and 33-

---

104. For the various interpretations of this text, see E. W. Davies, *Numbers*, pp. 158-60; Sakenfeld, *Numbers*, pp. 95-96.

34). Verse 32 narrates the case: the people of Israel found a man gathering sticks on the Sabbath day. Note that verse 32a indicates where this event happened. But the geographical reference in verse 32a does not affect the structure at all because it is too general and functions primarily to note the time period for the case (unlike Hazeroth in 11:35–12:16). Verses 33-34 narrate the development of the case and what the people did to the man, bringing him to Moses, Aaron, and the whole congregation, and confining him. Although the people's action continues in verse 36, where the whole congregation brings him outside of the camp and stones him to death, their action is interrupted by Yahweh's speech in verse 35 because they had not known what their next action should be (v. 34b). Moses and Aaron take no action. It is possible that Yahweh's speech is viewed as a response to Moses' request for the solution, but the text does not include Moses' request. Thus, the second part (vv. 35-36) is distinctive from the first part and begins with Yahweh providing a basis for the next step that the people should take. Yahweh's speech in verse 35 is the basis for the action of the whole congregation in verse 36 and is ultimately the solution to the case.

(9) Yahweh Speech: Instructions about Tassels (15:37-41)

I. Introductory Yahweh speech formula	15:37
II. Speech proper: instructions	15:38-41
A. Command to speak	15:38aα
B. Subject matter	15:38aβ-41
1. What: tassels	15:38aβ-b
2. Purpose	15:39-40
a. Conditions	15:39aα
b. Purpose proper	15:39aβ-b
(1) Positively expressed: remember	15:39aβ
(2) Negatively expressed: do not follow	15:39b
a+b. Summary	15:40
3. Reason: divine self-revelation	15:41

This unit is complete in itself, as demonstrated by the introductory Yahweh speech formula just as in 15:1-2a and 15:17-18a. Here the text uses אמר instead of דבר in 15:1 and 15:17. It also does not have the temporal aspect of either the present or the future. Yet, it seems to stress the perpetual exercise of the instruction "throughout their generations" (v. 38a), as shown in verses 21a and 23b. The structure of this unit is very similar to the structures of 15:1-16 and 15:17-31. The focus of the unit is not on how to make the tassels since the process itself is not given. Instead, what to do when one sees the tassel is extensively reported (vv. 39-40). It is expressed in negative and positive ways, which are then summarized once again. Moreover, by presenting Yahweh's self-revelation at the end (v. 41), this unit arrives at the climax of instruction on the tassels. Yahweh's self-revelation is set aside from the purpose of having tassels because the revelation is unique and seems not to be connected to the subject matter. It is enveloped by the statement אני יהוה אלהיכם and refers to the Exodus event and its purpose. These two aspects of verse 41 function as the purpose of having tassels and seem to go beyond the boundary of the immediate literary context of verse 41 to provide an appropriate ending for the whole set of instructions contained in chapter 15.

(10) Report about Korah's Rebellions against Moses and Aaron (16:1–17:15 [Eng. 16:1-50])

a. The whole congregation involved   17:6
    (1) Rebellion   17:6a
    (2) Reason   17:6b
b. Reaction of Yahweh   17:7-10
    (1) Preparation   17:7-8
    (2) Yahweh speech   17:9-10
c. Moses' intervention   17:11-15
    (1) Moses' speech to Aaron   17:11
    (2) Aaron's execution of Moses' speech   17:12-15

The beginning of this unit in 16:1 is rather obvious. Compared to the previous units in chapter 15, this unit introduces new and specific characters, resumes the interrupted narrative of chapter 14, and shifts the subject matter from cultic regulations to a rebellion narrative. These differences indicate that 16:1 begins a new unit, and yet the differences raise the question of whether or not they also serve as the criteria for defining the appropriate ending of this new unit. Commentators struggle in that they agree on the beginning of this unit but disagree on where it should end.[105] For example, Noth ends this unit at 17:26 (Eng. 17:11) based on content analysis. He views 17:1-5 (Eng. 16:36-40) and 17:16-26 (Eng. 17:1-11) as belonging together because of their emphasis on Aaron's priestly privileges, and 17:6-15 (Eng. 16:41-50) as a connecting passage between Moses and Aaron. These passages have been added successively to the predominantly priestly material of 16:1-35. Noth's content analysis is influenced by a literary-critical judgment. However, he ignores two elementary facts that point to the appropriate ending for this unit. First, the new characters, such as Korah, Dathan and Abiram, and On, cease to exist after 17:15.[106] Particularly Korah, who is involved in all rebellions, is remembered once again in 17:14. Second, the next verse, 17:16, is an introductory Yahweh speech formula that opens another unit focusing on the encroachment of the rebels

---

105. Gray (*A Critical and Exegetical Commentary on Numbers*, pp. xxviii, 186) and Milgrom (*Numbers*, p. 129) extend this unit to 18:32, while Budd (*Numbers*, pp. 179-91) shortens it to 16:35. Ashley (*The Book of Numbers*, pp. 295-97) and Dozeman ("The Book of Numbers," pp. 134-41) have 17:28 (Eng. 17:13) for the ending of this unit. Interestingly, Noth (*Numbers*, pp. 121-22) has 17:26 (Eng. 17:11) and Maier (*Das vierte Buch Mose*, p. 275) has 17:5 (Eng. 16:40). E. W. Davies (*Numbers*, pp. 162-68) ends this unit at 17:15 (Eng. 16:50), as does Olson (*Numbers*, 101-10; in *The Death of the Old and the Birth of the New* [p. 119] he goes as far as 19:22 without any subdivisions).

106. Korah is mentioned eleven times in 16:1–17:15 (16:1, 5, 6, 8, 16, 19, 24, 27, 32; 17:5, 14), but except for a few other instances (Num 26:9, 10, 11; 27:3) his name otherwise disappears. The same is true for Dathan and Abiram (16:1, 12, 24, 25, 27 [x2], 26:9 [x2]); 16:25-34 reports that the earth opened its mouth and swallowed them up. As for On, the son of Peleth, his name is never mentioned again (cf. Milgrom, *Numbers*, p. 313, n. 4).

upon the sanctuary and the priesthood. The same Yahweh speech formula appears in 16:20, 23; 17:1, 9. No doubt these formulae open Yahweh speeches, but they do so within 16:1–17:15. These verses are subordinate to the unit and play the role of defining one of its many component parts, but they do not delineate its outer boundary. These two aspects by themselves are not sufficient evidence for determining the ending of this unit, but they do at least point in the right direction. The analysis of many components of this unit will enhance the argument that it ends at 17:15, not at 16:35; 17:5; 17:11; 17:28; 18:32; or 19:22.

The complicated history of the development of the traditions contained in this unit and its composite character have been well discussed.[107] On the surface level, five rebellion reports can be identified:

Dathan and Abiram versus Moses (16:12-15, 25-34)
Korah and the leaders versus Aaron (16:16-18)
Korah and the Levites versus Aaron (16:8-11)
Korah and the whole congregation versus Moses and Aaron (16:19-23)
The whole congregation versus Moses and Aaron (17:6-15; Eng. 16:41-50).

Dathan and Abiram challenge Moses' leadership on the migration, while the Levites and the leaders attack Aaron's sole priestly function. The rebellion of Korah and the whole congregation against Moses and Aaron has no apparent cause. All the congregation simply gather together under Korah's leadership (16:19) and cry out to Yahweh so that they can avoid the punishment upon everyone who belongs to Korah (16:31-33). After all identified rebels perish, the whole congregation rebels against Moses and Aaron, accusing them of killing Yahweh's people and thus of not upholding the democracy of holiness, as introduced in the unit's introduction (17:6; cf. 16:3).

The remaining question is how these component parts are organized in the extant text. Several factors are noticeable. First, these rebellion reports share a common introduction (vv. 1-3). The sequence of names in verses 1-2 of the introduction implies a development of the rebellion starting among the Levites, then spreading to the tribal leaders (Reubenites), the leaders of the congregation, and finally to the whole congregation. Second, these rebellions are related one way or another with the character of Korah. Note that Korah's name is associated with Dathan and Abiram in their rebellion (vv. 24a and 27b), in their punishment (v. 32b), and even in the punishment of the

---

107. See E. W. Davies, *Numbers*, pp. 162-68 for a summary of previous scholarship on this unit.

whole congregation (17:14). Korah is the head figure for the Levites (vv. 8-11) and also for the 250 leaders of the congregation (vv. 16-19a). Despite different objects each group wants to challenge, Korah, as the representative conspirator of the Levites and of the leaders and as an associate of Dathan and Abiram, instigates their rebellions against Moses and Aaron. Third, these rebellions are narrated in a basic pattern, that is, a rebellion is stated and responses follow. Although there is no pure form or exact sequence to this pattern in the present text, the pattern is nevertheless implied and is operative.

These three aspects combined are responsible for the structure of 16:1–17:15. Since Korah was associated with all five rebellions, the unit can be titled a story about Korah's rebellions against Moses and Aaron. Structurally, this unit is divided into two parts: rebellions and responses. The first part (vv. 1-3) reports a summary of all rebellions, including the identities of the rebels, identification of Moses and Aaron as the ones against whom they rebel, and the comprehensive detailing of the subject matter of the rebellions. The second part (16:4–17:15) specifies both the content of and punishment for the rebellions. This part consists of the responses of Moses (16:4-19a) and Yahweh (16:19b–17:15). In the beginning, Moses tries to handle the rebellions of Korah and the Levites, Dathan and Abiram, and Korah and the leaders by himself (vv. 4-5, 8, 15, 16). The contents of the rebellions are identified, and Moses' responses are shown inadequate. Until Korah assembles the whole congregation against Moses and Aaron at the entrance of the tent of meeting, Yahweh is silent. From verse 19b on, it is Yahweh who handles all rebellions. Note that there are four quoted Yahweh speeches (16:21, 24; 17:2-3, 10a), followed either by execution reports (16:25-26; 17:4-5) or by descriptions of the people's reaction (16:22) and Moses' and Aaron's reactions (17:10b). The cycle of the Yahweh speech and the reaction to the speech is, however, not responsible for the division of the second section. The content of Yahweh's response constitutes the three sections: Yahweh's initial reaction to the congregation in which Yahweh does not know why the people are rebelling (16:19a), Yahweh's specific reaction to or punishment of those who knowingly and purposely rebel (16:22–17:5), and Yahweh's justification for harsh punishment of the whole congregation (17:6-15).

    (11) Report about Aaron's Budding Staff
          (17:16-26 [Eng. 17:1-11])

I. Test of staffs	17:16-22
A. Yahweh's comprehensive instructions	17:16-20
1. Introductory speech formula	17:16

This unit begins with a set of narratives concerning Yahweh's speech to Moses (vv. 16-20) and Moses' execution of the divine commands (vv. 21-22) and ends with another set (vv. 25 and 26). In between these two is a transitional passage narrating Moses' own actions (vv. 23-24). A pattern of Yahweh's speech and Moses' execution of the commands defines this unit as a complete unit. This unit deals with a single topic, that is, the special status of the Levites among the tribes. This topic is demonstrated in the miraculous growth of Aaron's staff (v. 23). Verses 27-28 do not belong to this unit because they recount the people's fear and despair in response not only to the miracle of Aaron's staff but also to the extremely severe punishments of Yahweh reported in the previous unit.

The structure of this unit reveals the interrelationship among the two sets of Yahweh speeches and Moses' execution reports of Yahweh's speeches and the transitional passage in between. The first set shows that Yahweh instructed Moses in the steps necessary for the test, such as what is involved (twelve staffs), how to choose the staffs, what to do with them, what is going to happen to them, and the purpose for the test. Moses then did according to Yahweh's instructions. While the first set focuses on the test's procedure and purpose, the second set concerns Yahweh's intention for Aaron's staff. The comprehensive instructions regarding the test in the first set divides it from the second set. These two sets are related at different structural levels within the whole unit, although they share the same pattern. The transitional passage that narrates the anticipated result of the test belongs more closely to the second set than to the first set. Its temporal aspect, that is, "the next day" (v. 23a), and its focusing on Moses' own action to find out the result strengthen its relation to the second set. Thus, the structure of the unit has two parts: Yahweh's comprehensive instructions concerning the test (vv. 16-21) and the test's result (vv. 22-26). The second part elaborates the changes to Aaron's staff[108] and stresses the intended purpose for the staff.

(12) Yahweh Speech: Instructions about the Duties of the Priests and the Levites (17:27–18:32 [Eng. 17:12–18:32])

I. Problem	17:27-28
A. Introductory speech formula	17:27a
B. Speech proper	17:27b-28
II. Solution	18:1-32
A. Duties of the priests and the Levites	18:1-7
1. Introductory speech formula	18:1aα
2. Speech	18:1aβ-7
a. Principal duty: protect the sanctuary	18:1aβ-5
(1) Explanation of the duty	18:1aβ-5a
(2) Purpose of the duty	18:5b
b. Priests' relation to the Levites	18:6-7
B. Compensation for the priests and the Levites	18:8-32
1. About the priestly emoluments	18:8-20
a. Emoluments proper	18:8-19
(1) From the most holy sacrifices	18:8-10
(2) From the holy sacrifices	18:11-19
b. Consequence	18:20
2. About the Levites	18:21-32
a. Rewards	18:21-24
b. Donation to the priests: a tenth of the tithe	18:25-32

Numbers 17:27-28 can be seen as the conclusion of the previous unit. However, they are more closely related to the following narrative since they con-

---

108. In Yahweh's instructions, the chosen staff will be known by the sprouts on it (v. 20a). In actuality, however, the staff of Aaron chosen by Yahweh is even more greatly transformed: it not only sprouts but buds, produces blossoms, and bears ripe almonds (v. 23).

tain no particular incident that causes the people's panic. Moreover, they end
with a rhetorical question, which in this case requires an actual answer. The
people's crying out, "everyone who approaches the tabernacle of the LORD
will die" (v. 13a), needs a response; the people need further comfort. Furthermore, nowhere in chapters 16–17 is there explicit mention of the Israelites
having approached the tabernacle of Yahweh. The following instructions by
Yahweh to Aaron (18:1-24) and to Moses (18:25-32) provide the answer to the
people's despair. It is now the responsibility of the Aaronide priests and other
Levites to guard the sanctuary and to take the blame for any encroachment
on it.

Structurally, this unit consists of two parts: people's problem (17:27-28)
and Yahweh's solution (18:1-32). For subdivisions of the second part, two facts
are to be noted. First, the second part is made up entirely of Yahweh's
speeches to Aaron (18:1-7, 8-19, 20-24) and Moses (18:25-32). Second, the narrative formula for Yahweh's speech to Aaron is unusual and rare. It occurs at
no other place in the Pentateuch except in Leviticus 10:28 and Numbers 18:1,
8, 20. With these two facts in mind, it is possible to divide Yahweh's solution
into two parts based on the one to whom Yahweh speaks, that is, Yahweh's
speech to Aaron (18:1-24) and Yahweh's speech to Moses (18:25-32). However,
it is also possible that the unit is constructed according to what Yahweh instructs these two leaders to do. The text chooses the latter in that the content
of Yahweh's speeches is constitutive for the structure of the second part. This
is proven by the fact that Yahweh's last speech in this unit, spoken to Moses,
deals with appropriate rewards for the Levites (18:21-24). The same subject
matter is instructed by Yahweh to Aaron in 18:8-19. These two sections are
unified by the content of Yahweh's speeches, the rewards for or compensation
of the Aaronide priests and the Levites. Thus, the structure of the second part
of the unit is divided into two by content analysis: (1) Yahweh's instruction regarding the duties of the priests and the Levites (18:1-7) and (2) their rewards
(18:8-32). From a chronological standpoint, the priests and the Levites must
have their responsibilities set before them before receiving the rewards for
them. Moreover, a hierarchy among the priests and the Levites is also operative in the structure. The priests have higher statutes and a more critical and
fatal responsibility in relation to protecting the sanctuary than the Levites,
and thus rewards are given accordingly. This hierarchy is demonstrated by the
order of Yahweh's speech to the priests first and then to the Levites. It is also
confirmed by 18:25-32 (cf. 18:6) in which the Levites are supposed to donate a
tenth of the tithe to the priests.

(13) Yahweh Speech: Instructions about Purification from Contamination by a Corpse (19:1-22)

I. Introductory Yahweh speech formula	19:1
II. Speech proper: instructions	19:2-22
A. Superscription	19:2a
B. Prescription of the law	19:2b-22
1. Preparation of the ingredients for the purification water	19:2b-10a
a. Burning the materials	19:2b-6
(1) Main: Heifer	19:2b-5
(2) Ancillary	19:6
b. Cleansing for the involved person	19:7-8
c. Gathering	19:9-10a
2. Use of the purification water	19:10b-20
a. For whom	19:10b-16
(1) Inclusive	19:10b
(2) Unclean by touching a corpse	19:11-16
(a) General rule	19:11-13
(b) Specific cases	19:14-16
b. Procedure	19:17-19
(1) For an unclean person	19:17-19a
(2) For the clean who performs this rite	19:19b
c. Summary statement	19:20
3. Perpetual status of the law	19:21-22

Verse 1 is the introductory Yahweh speech formula that opens a literary unit like those discussed previously in 15:1-16; 15:17-31; 15:37-41; and 17:16-28. Yahweh spoke to Moses and Aaron about the law (torah) for purifying a person defiled by a corpse. Yahweh's speech is abruptly broken off at 20:1, which, in a narrative mode, reports Israel's arrival at the wilderness of Zin. The change of topic and different writing style of 20:1 indicate that Yahweh's speech ends at 19:22, and thus 19:1-22 is a self-contained unit.

Concerning the structural integrity of the unit, several observations have been made.[109] Of these observations, Milgrom's "binary structure" de-

---

109. Milgrom, *Numbers*, p. 437. Milgrom lists seven different subjects within the unit, each mentioned seven times, which has already been noted by the rabbis. The number seven seems to bear special significance for Milgrom because his choice of subjects seems forced to fit the number seven: he uses the same subject twice (e.g., priests). But how does this observation enhance a detection of the structure of the unit? Unfortunately, these issues go unan-

serves notice. He divides the text into two parts that show "the structural symmetry:"[110]

Panel A
"This is the ritual law" (v. 2a)
Preparation of the ashes
Renders impure (vv. 2b-10)
Purification procedure (vv. 11-12)
Penalty for nonpurification (v. 13)

Panel B
"This is the ritual" (v. 14aα)
Touching corpse or its derivatives
Renders impure (vv. 14-16)
Purification procedure (vv. 17-19)
Penalty for nonpurification (v. 20)
"Law for all time" (v. 21a)
[Addition (vv. 21b-22)]

Milgrom notes that these two panels begin and end in the same way with similar phraseology (vv. 13 and 20) and form a reverse chiasm, particularly in the middle section.[111] However, it is obvious that his binary structure is not the structure of the present form of the text. He ignores verse 1 in his structure, as if it were not an integral part of the text. Actually, it is verse 1 that distinguishes 19:1-22 from the adjacent units. Without verse 1 his structure loses not only its literary framework but also divine authentication for the law at hand. The law of purification has its ultimate significance because it is promulgated by Yahweh through Moses and Aaron. Not only verse 1 but verses 21b-22 are

---

swered by Milgrom. Nonetheless, he presents his own binary structure for 19:1-22 and does not incorporate the seven subjects he mentions into the structure. E. W. Davies (*Numbers*, pp. 194-96), however, summarizes the previous discussions and lists two possible divisions for the text. A traditional one is that the text is divided into two sections, the preparation of the ingredients of the water for cleansing (vv. 1-13) and instructions for its use in specific cases (vv. 14-22). The other, quoted by R. de Vaux (*Ancient Israel: Religious Institutions*, vol. 2, trans. J. McHugh [London: Darton, Longman, and Todd; New York: McGraw-Hill, 1961], pp. 461-62), is that the text is composed of three sections, vv. 1-10a, 10b-13, and 14-22, based on different literary genres and authors. For Davies, with de Vaux, vv. 10b-13 is added by a redactor to provide a connecting link with the first part (vv. 1-10a). Since Davies does not present his own structure of this text, what he thinks about its structural integrity cannot be evaluated. Dozeman ("The Book of Numbers," pp. 150-52) follows the three-part structure with some reservations. For a literary-critical analysis of 19:1-10a, cf. S. von Wefing, "Beobachtungen zum Ritual mit der roten Kuh (Num 19:1-10a)," *ZAW* 93 (1981): 341-64. For an interesting interpretation on the paradoxical effect of the purifying water: "they purify the defiled and defile the pure," see J. Milgrom, "The Paradox of the Red Cow," *VT* 31 (1981): 62-72, also reprinted in his commentary (*Numbers*, pp. 438-43).

110. Milgrom, *Numbers*, pp. 437-38.

111. Note the significantly different terms employed between vv. 1-13 and 14-22 (Gray, *A Critical and Exegetical Commentary on Numbers*, p. 254) and a different procedure adopted during the ritual itself (E. W. Davies, *Numbers*, pp. 194-95).

also not included in his structure because Milgrom considered them to be later additions. Regardless of whether or not they were added later by a different redactor, their location and relation to the rest of the verses must be taken into consideration in a proposal of the structure of 19:1-22.

Internally, Milgrom's claim for the two halves (Panel A and B) as disclosing a structural symmetry cannot be sustained. The first lines of these halves are not identical because the second half lacks "the law." Regarding the second lines, they should not be included since they do not have corresponding verses. Even their titles suggest a problem, a solution, and the relation between them different from the relationship that other lines have with their corresponding parts. Based on the content of their verses, the rest of the lines describe something other than their titles. Moreover, the fact that panel B has one more line than panel A breaks the definition of symmetry. Furthermore, the title of the added sixth line, quoted from verse 21a, "law for all time," occurs at verse 10b with the same phraseology. Milgrom does not mention this fact because it would break his symmetrical structure. In short, what he actually does in proposing a binary structure for 19:1-22 is manipulate diverse textual information into a preconceived outline that does not represent the present form of the text.

E. W. Davies and S. von Wefing analyze 19:1-22 in detail and identify many elements comprising the text. It is not necessary to repeat their findings here. Rather, the focus must be on showing how these elements are related to form an integrated whole. Structurally, it is important to note that this unit has four superscriptive or summary statements in verses 2a, 10b, 14a, and 21a. They are not equal on a structural level, although they mark the divisions within the unit. Verse 2a is a superscription for the entire prescription of the law (torah) because it is located right after the introductory speech formula and is attached to a modifying clause, "that the Lord has commanded," which summarizes comprehensively what follows. Verses 10b and 21a focus on the perpetual status of the prescription, and they mark the beginning of the second and third subunits within the prescription (vv. 10b-20 and 21-22). However, they are not at the same level. Verse 21a defines the recipients of the law in general terms, and, in contrast, verse 10b specifies that the law is intended, "for the Israelites and for the alien residing among them." Thus, the real focus of verse 10b is not the perpetual status of the law but the distinction between the recipients of the water for cleansing. This distinction is important enough that the text mentions the others separately from the main recipient, the ones contaminated by a corpse. Finally, verse 14a functions to introduce the law to specific examples of how a person becomes unclean. This verse holds the lowest level among the four superscriptive statements.

The structure of the second part of this unit, the reported Yahweh speech, contains two parts: the superscription and prescription of the law (torah). The chronological sequence is decisive in dividing the prescription. The water of purification must be prepared (vv. 2b-10a) before its use (vv. 10b-20). Verse 9 indicates that the ashes of the heifer are to be gathered and deposited outside the camp so that they may be used later by Israel for the water of purification. With 10b, the second subpart concerns the usage of the water of purification. Within the second subpart, 14a leads to the specific cases of unclean people. Verse 21a begins the third subpart that makes a general statement regarding the perpetual status of the law, with a summary of the law's content.

> (14) Report about Yahweh's Denial of Moses' and Aaron's Prophetic Leadership[112] (20:1-13)

I. Setting: itinerary	20:1a
II. Two events	20:1b-13
A. First event: Miriam's death and burial	20:1b
B. Second event: Israel's quarrel against Moses and Aaron	20:2-13
1. Event proper	20:2-12
a. Problem: People's complaint	20:2-5
(1) General statement	20:2
(2) Specific content	20:3-5
b. Solution	20:6-12
(1) Moses' and Aaron's initial response	20:6a-bα
(2) Yahweh's solution	20:6bβ-12
(a) Solution proper	20:6bβ-8
(b) Moses' and Aaron's execution of the solution	20:9-11
(c) Yahweh's evaluation of their execution of the solution	20:12
2. Summary of event	20:13

On the surface level, this text has at least three distinctive elements. Verse 1 reports two things: Israel's travel itinerary and the event that happened at Kadesh (the death and burial of Miriam). Verses 2-12 shift the topic from

112. For the issue of the exclusion of Moses from the promised land, see my article "The Exclusion of Moses from the Promised Land: A Conceptual Approach," in *The Changing Face of Form Criticism for the Twenty-First Century,* ed. M. A. Sweeney and E. Ben Zvi (Grand Rapids: Eerdmans, 2003), pp. 217-39.

verse 1 to Israel's quarrel with Moses and Aaron because of the lack of water, and these leaders' responses to Israel, which bring about Yahweh's punishment for Moses and Aaron: they will not bring Israel into the promised land. Verse 20:13 ends the event with an extended etiologic statement concerning the place name, Meribah.

Is there structural integrity among these three elements, so that this text can be considered a complete unit? First, it is conceivable that 20:1 is the conclusion of 19:1-22 since the motif of death is present in both. Yet the death motif is also present and implied in the following units (vv. 3-4, 18-20, 22-29). At the same time, it is not entirely clear whether 20:1 is an organic part of what follows. However, if 20:1 is not a literary unit by itself,[113] then it is more closely related to 20:2-12 than to 19:1-22. This verse is generically more similar to 20:2-12, a story concerning the leadership of Moses and Aaron, than to 19:1-22, Yahweh's instruction for the purification water. Second, 20:13 does not portray the entirely pure form of an etiology. It does not have typical patterns, such as ויקרא and כי clauses. It also adds another phrase, "by which he showed his holiness" (v. 13b), that is not directly connected with the name Meribah. But there is no doubt that this verse is connected with what is recounted in verses 2-12. Additionally, this verse provides the key to link verse 1 with verses 2-12. It is the concept of holiness expressed in קדש. This term is the linguistic basis for Kadesh where Israel stayed and where Miriam died and was buried (v. 1), and for Yahweh's reason for punishing Moses and Aaron (v. 12). 20:1-13 as a whole reports that Moses and Aaron failed in their prophetic leadership by not showing the holiness of Yahweh to the people, and that Yahweh sentenced them accordingly, denying their future leadership of the assembly in the promised land rather than simply denying them the privilege of entering the promised land.

The structure of 20:1-13 has two parts: the setting of the time and topographical locale (v. 1a) and the reports of the two events that occurred (vv. 1b-13). The first event is narrated very briefly (v. 1b), whereas the second is elaborated upon greatly so that it becomes the main event of the unit. These two are related to each other in that the characters of the event, that is, Miriam in the first and Moses and Aaron in the second, are the leaders of Israel and representatives of Yahweh for Israel's migration in the wilderness. Yet, these two events differ in their operative concepts. The first event is interested in reporting a personal tragedy, the death of Miriam, but the second one points to

---

113. Dozeman ("The Book of Numbers," p. 159) differentiates 20:1 from 20:2-13 and considers it one of seven units in chs. 20–21. However, he fails to provide the rationale for treating 20:1 as such.

the prophetic leadership of Moses and Aaron, although their deaths are implied as a consequence.

The structure of the second event contains two parts: the event proper (vv. 2-12) and a summary of the event (v. 13). The event is reported by the people's complaint (vv. 2-5), which sets the stage for responses from Moses, Aaron, and Yahweh (vv. 6-11) and Yahweh's evaluation of Moses' and Aaron's execution of their leadership (v. 12). The people's complaint is justifiable due to the lack of needed water. Yahweh appears only to Moses and Aaron and gives clear, step-by-step instructions to them so that the people's thirst might be quenched. However, Moses' and Aaron's responses are described as unsympathetic and unjustifiable in both their words and deeds. These responses cause the people to believe that it is Yahweh who does not want to provide the needed water. This conclusion is inevitable for the people because they do not know exactly what Yahweh has told Moses and Aaron. Thus, by their unjustifiable responses, Moses and Aaron not only misunderstood the people's justifiable need, but also misrepresented and even mischaracterized Yahweh's intention to provide water for the people. This is the reason that Yahweh punished their prophetic leadership, forbidding them to bring the people into the promised land. Conceptually, the sin of Moses and Aaron has two sides. As the leaders of the people, they did not understand the people's justifiable complaint, and as the representatives of Yahweh, they misrepresented Yahweh's intention to the people. Despite the leaders' failure, Yahweh brought forth the needed water for the people.[114]

(15) Report of Israel's Conflicting Encounter with Edom (20:14-21)

I. Israel's two attempts at passage through Edom   20:14-20
   A. First attempt   20:14-18
      1. Request   20:14-17

---

114. The conventional translation in v. 11a must be reconsidered. Instead of being translated "then Moses . . . struck the rock twice with his staff, and the water came out abundantly," it should read "then Moses . . . struck the rock twice with his staff, but the water came out abundantly." Two facts need to be mentioned. First, the present study arrives at the reading of 20:2-13 above independently from Dozeman, though it is similar to his in some aspects. Second, Dozeman's content analysis does not reflect his outline of 20:2-13. For him, while the text "recounts a four-part murmuring story about the lack of water" ("The Book of Numbers," p. 160), its structure suggests that "Israel's legal complaint about water is not an instance of rebellion through murmuring" (p. 161). Whether a generic pattern of murmuring stories or individual and specific content is the constitutive factor for the outline/structure of 20:2-13 must be further analyzed.

a. Introductory statement	20:14a
b. Message: speech	20:14b-17
(1) Identity of the speaker: "your brother Israel"	20:14bα
(2) History of Israel	20:14bβ-16
(3) Request itself	20:17
(a) Petition	20:17aα1
(b) Pledge	20:17aα2-b
2. Refusal	20:18
B. Second attempt	20:19-20
1. Request	20:19
a. Introductory statement	20:19aα1
b. Speech: request itself	20:19aα2-b
(1) Pledge	20:19aα2-β
(2) Petition	20:19b
2. Refusal	20:20
a. Speech	20:20a
b. Action	20:20b
II. Summary statement	20:21
A. For request: refusal	20:21a
B. Consequence: turn away	20:21b

Although verse 14a shares its topographical locale, Kadesh, with the previous unit, it begins the newly reported event of Israel's encounter with Edom. This unit starts with Moses' sending messengers to the king of Edom requesting passage through Edom, and it ends with Edom's refusal of passage, which causes Israel to turn away from Edom. Noth questions the integrity of the unit by mentioning several inconsistencies and doublets within it. Against Noth, E. W. Davies defends its integrity by evaluating Noth's findings as less important for the logic of the unit.[115]

But the clue for the structure of this unit lies at the end, in the summary statement in verse 21. Regardless of whether or not Moses and/or Israel as a whole took the initiative to request the passage and whether it was the king of Edom or the Edomites who refused the request, the ending verse reports that Israel's request was denied by Edom, and as a result Israel turned away from Edom's territory. This basic element of the event divides the unit into two parts: Israel's two attempts to obtain passage through Edom (vv. 14-20) and the summary statement (v. 21). The first part is also divided into two parts with the same pattern of request and refusal. There are some differences be-

---

115. E. W. Davies, *Numbers*, pp. 206-8.

tween the first (vv. 14-18) and the second attempt (vv. 19-20), however. From a literary point of view, the former elaborates upon the request of Israel, whereas the latter stresses the refusal of Edom. In terms of the character of the request, the former describes the request theologically (vv. 14b-16) and idealistically (v. 17), while the latter uses a more realistic or practical tone (v. 19b). These differences are explainable in that they are the results of developing a plot in narrating an event. The first attempt takes time to lay out the theological reasons and an ideal proposal for the passage, which is then refused with an ultimatum. The second attempt shortens the request by omitting the reasons and presents a realistic request that implies even the Edomites' financial benefit. But this request is met with not only a short, direct, firm statement of refusal but also a show of force (v. 20). The narrative reaches its climax when Edom comes out against Israel with a large, heavily armed force. For Israel, there was no choice except to turn away from Edom. The technique of narrating an event is surely operative in 20:14-21.

(16) Report of the Event at Mount Hor: The Death of Aaron (20:22-29)

I. Setting: itinerary	20:22
II. Event at Mount Hor	20:23-29
A. Yahweh's instructions	20:23-26
1. Introductory statement	20:23
2. Speech	20:24-26
a. Regarding the death of Aaron	20:24
b. Regarding the transfer of the high priesthood	20:25-26a
c. Restating the death of Aaron	20:26b
B. Moses' execution of Yahweh's instructions	20:27-28
1. Summary statement	20:27a
2. Elaboration	20:27b-28
C. People's reaction	20:29

This unit has two distinct elements: Israel's itinerary (v. 22), a resumption of 20:1, and a narrative about the death of Aaron (vv. 23-29). These two elements, however, are connected with the topographical location, Mount Hor. Mount Hor is where Israel came to stay (v. 22b), where Yahweh spoke to Moses and Aaron (v. 23a) and instructed them to go up the mountain (v. 25b), and where Moses and Aaron went up (v. 27b) and came down the mountain (v. 28b). Mount Hor is the unifier of this unit. The structure of this unit has two parts: the setting, which shows Israel's migration from Kadesh to Mount

Hor (v. 22), and the reported event at Mount Hor (vv. 23-29). The event consists of three parts: Yahweh's instruction (vv. 23-26), Moses' execution of the instructions (vv. 27-28), and the people's reaction to what happened to Aaron (v. 29). The main event is the death of Aaron, although Yahweh instructs Moses regarding the transfer of the high priesthood from Aaron to his son Eleazar (vv. 25-26a), followed by Moses' execution of that transfer (v. 28a). Note that Yahweh's instructions are enveloped in the statement of the death of Aaron. Moreover, in describing the congregation's reaction, the transfer of Aaron's priesthood to his son Eleazar is not mentioned. Whether the congregation knew of the transfer of the priesthood is not the interest of the text. Instead, verse 29 reports their knowledge of the death of Aaron and their mourning thirty days for him. Thus, the death of Aaron is the main topic, and it is framed by the specific topographical locale, Mount Hor.

(17) Hormah Etiology: Israel's Victory over the Canaanites (21:1-3)

I. Report of events	21:1-3a
A. Setting: the King of Arad's initial victory over Israel	21:1
1. Who: the King of Arad	21:1α
2. What: heard — fought — took	21:1αβ-b
B. The main event: Israel's utter destruction of the Canaanites	21:2-3a
1. Making a vow of חרם war	21:2
a. Introductory statement	21:2a
b. Speech: making a vow proper	21:2b
2. Fulfillment	21:3a
a. By Yahweh	21:3aα
b. By Israel	21:3aβ
II. Inference to a name for the place	21:3b

The topographical indicator in verse 1, the way of Atharim (and later v. 3, Hormah), clearly breaks the narrative continuity between 20:22-29 and 21:4. Mount Hor is the place where Israel entered into encampment (20:22), the place where Aaron died (20:28), and the place from which Israel set out (21:4). But this is not the place where the narrated event in 21:1-3 occurred. The discontinuity of the narrative makes 21:1-3 a self-contained unit. Moreover, this unit can be classified as an extended etiology for Hormah. A key etiological phrase, ויקרא, is present (v. 3b). The name Hormah, חרמה, bears the connotation of חרם, utter destruction, which is the unifying concept of the unit, even for the vow element in verse 2. Verse 1 gives the reason why Israel makes a vow of חרם (v. 2). With Yahweh's granting of Israel's vow (v. 3aα), Israel utterly destroys the Canaanites and their towns (v. 3aβ), which leads to the direct motivation for the name (v. 3b). In other words, the thematic movement of חרם from the necessity of war to its practice holds the unit together and gives the name for the place.

(18) Rebellion Narrative of the Event That Happened on the Way to Oboth: The Serpent Scourge (21:4-9)

I.	Setting: broken itinerary	21:4a
	A. Departure	21:4aα
	B. Purpose	21:4aβ
II.	Event on the way	21:4b-9
	A. Rebellion	21:4b-6
	1. People's complaints	21:4b-5
	a. General description	21:4b
	b. Specific description	21:5
	2. Yahweh's response	21:6
	B. Resolution	21:7-9
	1. People's action: repent and plea	21:7a
	2. Moses' action: intercession for the people	21:7b
	3. Yahweh's action	21:8-9
	a. Solution: speech	21:8
	b. Moses' execution of Yahweh's instructions	21:9

The itinerary of Israel in verse 4a indicates two things. First of all, the phrase "to go around the land of Edom" reminds the reader of Edom's refusal of Israel's request for passage through their territory, narrated in 20:14-21. Second, verse 4a reports Israel's leaving Mount Hor, but it does not mention their arrival at any particular place. It is an incomplete form of a typical itinerary pattern. Where did Israel encamp after they decamped from Mount Hor? No topographical locality is mentioned in verses 4b-9. Interestingly enough, verse 10 reports a full form of an itinerary except for the place that Israel left: "The Israelites set out, and camped in Oboth." Verses 4a and 10b would make a complete itinerary form, stating that Israel set out from Mount Hor and encamped in Oboth. It is conceivable that verse 10a left the departure place out because it was already mentioned at verse 4a, or verse 10a restates the fact of Israel's setting out for the purpose of the continuity of the narrative of Israel's movement (vv. 11-20). Then, the event reported in verses 4b-9 occurs at an unknown place, somewhere between Mount Hor and Oboth.

Structurally, the broken itinerary form in verse 4a and the phrase "to go around the land of Edom" suggest that 21:4-9 is related to the previous units (20:14-21 and 20:22-29), except 21:1-3, and to the following unit (21:10-20). These two facts of verse 4a define verses 4-9 as a complete unit reporting what happened on the way to Oboth. Verse 4a functions as a setting for the following event.

Commentators postulate the structure of 21:4-9 as similar to the "typological structure of Israel's wilderness complaints," such as that of 11:1-3 or 11:4-35.[116] Their reason for the comparison is that 21:4-9 shares a similar motif of complaints, particularly with 11:1-3. However, a common motif or even some identical subject matter (e.g., food) in two texts does not necessarily lead to the conclusion that the structures of the two texts are similar. The most noticeable difference between 21:4-9 and 11:1-3 (11:4-35) is that the latter is an etiology without mentioning any itinerary of Israel, whereas the former is framed by an itinerary without having a naming element for the place. No identifiable place is mentioned in the former, except those in the form of half an itinerary. Besides, the end result of Israel's complaints in both texts is not the same, as Sakenfeld points out.[117] The structure of 21:4-9 should not be understood *a priori* in light of the structure of 11:1-3; 11:4-35; or 12:1-5.

The structure of 21:4-9 has two parts: the setting (v. 4a) and the reported event that occurred on the way to Oboth (vv. 4b-9). The event is narrated in two parts. The first part recounts Israel's complaint against God and Moses about the necessities of daily life (vv. 4b-5), to which Yahweh responds by sending poisonous serpents (v. 6). The second part provides a resolution for the punishment beginning with the people's repentance and plea (v. 7a) and Moses' intercession (v. 7b), which evokes Yahweh's communication of the remedy (v. 8); it ends with the report of Moses' provision for the remedy (v. 9).

(19) Itinerary Report: From Mount Hor to the Valley near Pisgah in Moab (21:10-20)

I. Migration to the wilderness bordering Moab	21:10-11
II. Migration to the wilderness that extends from the boundary of the Amorites	21:12-15
A. March to the wilderness	21:12-13a
B. Description of the wilderness	21:13b-15

---

116. Milgrom, *Numbers*, pp. 173, 376-80; Dozeman, "The Book of Numbers," p. 163; E. W. Davies, *Numbers*, p. 215; Budd, *Numbers*, p. 233.

117. Sakenfeld, *Numbers*, pp. 117-18.

III. Migration to the valley near Pisgah in Moab	21:16-20
A. At Beer	21:16-18a
1. March to Beer	21:16a
2. Event at Beer	21:16b-18a
B. March to the valley	21:18b-20

This unit is unified by the cycle of Israel's setting out from one place and camping at another. If the missing location in verse 10a is Mount Hor as indicated in 21:4a, then Israel has moved from Mount Hor to "the valley lying in the region of Moab by the top of Pisgah" (v. 20aα1-2). The narrative concerning Israel's movement was broken by 21:21, which does not have an itinerary but narrates Israel's encounter with Sihon, the king of the Amorites. Thus, 21:10-20 is a complete literary unit in its own right.

Commentators recognize that this unit consists of Israel's itineraries (vv. 10-13, 16a, 18b-20) and two poetic pieces (vv. 14-15, 17-18a).[118] However, they do not discuss how these two distinct elements are related to each other in the extant text. Which one is the dominant form that determines the integrity of the unit? While others simply title this unit by describing the content without sufficient analysis of these two elements, Ashley proposes the title of the unit as "travel itinerary." There is little doubt that the itinerary provides the basic frame for this unit. The most elementary form of an itinerary has two factors, as shown in verses 10-13. First, it has a typical linguistic pattern: "they set out from . . . and encamped at . . ." as expressed in ויסעו . . . ויחנו (cf. Num 33:5-37, 41-49).[119] Second, an itinerary is oriented topographically.

However, this unit contains more than the typical pattern of an itinerary. First of all, not only topographical campsites but also geographical territories are present (e.g., the wilderness [vv. 13b, 18bα], the valley [20aα2]). How are these two indicators related structurally? Since a geographical territory in-

---

118. Budd, *Numbers*, p. 238; Ashley, *The Book of Numbers*, p. 408; Sakenfeld, *Numbers*, pp. 118-19; E. W. Davies, *Numbers*, p. 218. Cf. J. M. Miller, "The Israelite Journey through (around) Moab and Moabite Toponymy," *JBL* 108 (1989): 577-95. Miller argues, along with Mittmann, van Seters, and E. W. Davies, that 21:10-20 is a conflation of Num 33:5-49, Judg 11:12-28, and Deut 2 and that 21:10-13 is "a geographical hodgepodge totally incomprehensible in terms of the geographical realities of [the] southern Transjordan." This geographical reality, however, is not an obstacle for reconstructing the structure of 21:10-20, which begins with the extant text. However, Dozeman ("The Book of Numbers," pp. 164-65) divides 20:10-20 into two parts, vv. 10-18a and vv. 18b-20, based on the theological meaning of the wilderness. Hence, the text marks "the transition from Israel's wilderness wandering to its conquest of fertile land." Yet, this transition seems to have no structural significance in the macrostructure of 20:1–21:35, let alone that of 10:11–36:13.

119. Cf. J. T. Walsh, "From Egypt to Moab: A Source Critical Analysis of the Wilderness Itinerary," *CBQ* 39 (1977): 20-33.

cludes topographical localities, the list of place names is the geographical clustering of the topographical data. Second, verses 18b-20 express Israel's movement from place to place by simply attaching the preposition מִן to the name of the place that they left. Further, verse 16a has a combination of שָׁם and מִן, which presupposes the knowledge of the present encampment's location. This combination is also used with the elementary form of an itinerary in verses 12 and 13. In addition to the use of different forms of an itinerary, 21:10-20 has extra descriptions of specific places (vv. 11bα2-β, 13aβ-b, 16bα, and 20b) as well as obvious interludes of two poetic pieces, themselves attached to a particular place. The text shows interest in some places more than others and highlights what happened at those places.

The flexible usage of the itinerary form and the addition of extra materials show that aspects other than the typical form of itinerary account for the structure of 21:10-20. This text is not a simple narration of Israel's itinerary from Mount Hor to the valley lying in the region of Moab, but it is a narrative of Israel's movement through various places based on itinerary forms. Therefore, the structure of this unit must show two factors: (1) the geographical organization of the topographical locations and (2) its interest in events at a particular place. On the one hand, if the first factor is dominant throughout 21:10-20, the structure of the unit has three parts: the migration to the wilderness bordering Moab (vv. 10-11), the migration to the wilderness that extends from the boundary of the Amorites (vv. 12-15), and the migration to the valley lying in the region of Moab (vv. 16-20). On the other hand, if the second factor is responsible for its structure, there are also three parts: from Mount Hor to the other side of Arnon (vv. 10-15), from the other side of Arnon to Beer (vv. 16-18a), and from Beer to the valley lying in the region of Moab (vv. 18b-20). However, in this unit the second structure is based on weaker ground than the first. The three places, the other side of the Arnon, Beer, and the valley, are highlighted by extended descriptions of the territory (vv. 13b-15, 20) and poetic portrayals of the place (vv. 16b-18a). No substantial information regarding any event that makes the place memorable has been given. The content that highlights these places is at best an extension of geographical notations concerning them. Therefore, a geographical organization is constitutive for the structure of this unit.

(20) Report of Israel's Campaign to Occupy the Land of the Amorites (21:21-31)

I. Israel's occupation of the land of the Amorites	21:21-30
A. Encounter with the Amorites: motivation	21:21-23aα1
1. Request for passage	21:21-22

Verses 21-22 state that Israel sent messengers to King Sihon of the Amorites for passage through his territory, and verse 31 reports Israel's settlement in the land of the Amorites. Thus, 21:21-31 is a complete unit concerning Israel's encounter with the Amorites. The remaining question is whether this unit includes verse 32 or not. While some commentators are ambiguous on the position and function of verse 32, most connect this verse with 21:21-31.[120] For example, Ashley reveals his bewilderment over the function of verse 32. He defines its function as "a *conclusion* to the incident with Sihon and an *introduction* to the incident with Og of Bashan in vv. 33-35," as well as "a *transition* to vv. 33-35" (emphasis added). However, T. L. Fearer strongly argues that verse 32 belongs to verses 21-31.[121] His argument is based on three observations. First, the initial words, "And Moses sent," are reminiscent of 20:14 and partially of 21:21. Second, the topographical location of Jazer, to which Moses sent spies, is west of the Ammonites' capital, Rabbah, and near the

---

120. On the one hand, Maier (*Das vierte Buch Mose*, pp. 301-2) treats this verse as belonging to the following unit. On the other hand, Gray (*A Critical and Exegetical Commentary on Numbers*, p. 297), Noth (*Numbers*, pp. 160, 163), Budd (*Numbers*, pp. 242, 244, 247), Milgrom (*Numbers*, pp. 179, 183), E. W. Davies (*Numbers*, pp. 226, 229, 234), and Dozeman ("The Book of Numbers," p. 166) include this verse as a part of the unit 21:21-31.

121. T. L. Fearer, "Wars in the Wilderness: Textual Cohesion and Conceptual Coherence in Pentateuch Battle Traditions," Ph.D. diss., The Claremont Graduate School, 1993, pp. 398-408.

Jabbok.[122] In this location, Jazer and "her daughters" are conceptualized as north of and outside the bounds of Heshbon's sovereignty. This conceptualization implies Israel's northward movement from Sihon's kingdom (vv. 21-31) to the Bashanites' land (vv. 33-35), with their total control of all territories east of the Jordan. In this northward movement, Jazer is in between the land of the Amorites and that of the Bashanites. Third, Moses (implicitly together with Israel) dispossessed "the Amorites," the same ethnic people that Israel dispossessed in verses 21-31.

Although Fearer's evidence is present in verse 32, other evidence is noticeable as well that would support the conclusion that verse 32 belongs to verses 33-35. First, verse 32 does not say that Jazer itself was destroyed, but that its villages were captured. Second, the statement in verse 31, "the Israelites settled in the land of the Amorites," would not be as conclusive as it sounds if Jazer in verse 32 were the same place as that in verse 24bβ, which had not yet been captured. This point is reinforced by the absolute statement that Israel captured and occupied *all* Amorite cities. This absolute statement is pervasive throughout verses 21-31. The entirety of the land and cities of the Amorites is represented by the adjective "all," which occurs four times in verses 25-26 and in the geographical description of the boundary of the land of Amorites in verse 24. Third, similar to verses 33-35, verse 32 mentions no diplomatic negotiation. Instead, Moses sent men to spy out Jazer. The spy mission should be understood as preparation for an anticipated attack and conquest. As Fearer himself asserts, "all actions contained in v. 32 are premeditated," which is not the case in verses 21-31.[123] Fourth, while verses 21-31 end with Israel's occupation of the land of the Amorites, verse 32 concludes Israel's campaign with the dispossession of the Amorites in the "daughter" villages of Jazer. "Dispossession of the villages" is the negative expression for taking possession of those villages. This conclusion is the same as that of verses 33-35, "they took possession of his land." Fifth, verse 32 portrays Moses as the main and active charac-

---

122. Except for Milgrom, commentators provide an explanation based on the translation of v. 24bβ. They follow the rendering of the Septuagint and translate v. 24bβ as "For Jazer was at the Ammonite border." (Cf. MT, which reads "for the border of the people of Ammon was strong." For other suggestions see Milgrom, *Numbers*, p. 318, n. 47, and for the discussion see Ashley, *The Book of Numbers*, pp. 420-21.) With this translation, Budd, in particular, defines Jazer in v. 24bβ as the border of the Ammonites' territory and connects it with Jazer in v. 32. The topographical association between vv. 24 and 32 is the decisive factor for v. 32 belonging to 21:21-31.

123. Fearer, *Wars in the Wilderness*, p. 404. In contrast to the premeditated actions in v. 32, Fearer (pp. 275-81) argues that vv. 21-31 begin with Israel's diplomatic negotiation (vv. 21-22), which regards Israel as "the innocent, respectful, and responsible future neighbor" without interests in Sihon's land.

ter, while verses 21-31 do not even mention the name of Moses. Out of thirty-six units in Numbers 10:11–36:13, only four units (21:1-3; 22:1–24:25; 36:13) do not have the name of Moses, and 21:21-31 is one of them. Besides, 21:21-31 has a coherent theme, Israel's dealing with the Amorites, with a summary statement of Israel's settlement in the land of the Amorites at the end. Compared to Fearer's evidence, these five factors are more substantial for and congruent with what verse 32 presents. If verse 32 is not considered a self-contained literary unit, these five factors would strongly support the fact that verse 32 belongs to the unit that follows it, verses 33-35.[124]

The structure of 21:21-31 has two parts: the reported event of Israel's occupation of the land of the Amorites (vv. 21-30) and the summary statement of Israel's occupying it (v. 31).[125] The event is reported in two parts in that the first (vv. 21-23aα1) shares a structure similar to that of Israel's encounter with Edom. The difference is in the second part (vv. 23aα2-30), which elaborates upon Israel's battle against Sihon and its result. The Amorites' refusal and the battle itself are depicted in short strokes. In contrast, Israel's possession and finally their occupation of the land and its cities are described in detail (vv. 24b-30), with Heshbon as the representative territory. Thus, the unit as a whole is interested in reporting Israel's occupation of the land of the Amorites, and Israel's encounter with the Amorites in verses 21-22 serves as a necessary cause for the following battle and occupation. Conceptually, it is not accidental but rather a premeditated encounter without which Israel's occupation of the land of Amorites could not have occurred.

(21) Report of Israel's Campaign to Possess the Land of Bashan (21:32-35)

I. Prelude: victory over the villages of Jazer	21:32
II. Main event: possession of the land of Bashan	21:33-35

---

124. Fearer (*Wars in the Wilderness*, p. 478) himself asserts that "v. 32 itself is closer to the conceptuality of vv. 33-35."

125. Cf. Fearer (*Wars in the Wilderness*, pp. 266-397, especially pp. 387-90) for his analysis of the macrostructure of 21:21-31. His bipartite structure rests on the conceptual difference between Israel's dispossession of Sihon's land (vv. 21-24) and Israel's occupation of the Amorites' cities (vv. 25-31). His differentiations between dispossession and occupation, land and cities, are correct. However, the question is which one should be constitutive for the structure. Land is a broader and more comprehensive designation that includes cities. Similarly, occupation points to a more advanced stage of a military campaign than possession, although the sequence from dispossession to occupation is not automatic. As v. 31 summarizes Israel's encounter with the Amorites, Israel's occupation of the land of the Amorites is the generative concept for vv. 21-31 in its entirety.

A. Setting: Israel's march   21:33a
B. Battle report   21:33b-35a
   1. On the part of King Og of Bashan   21:33b
   2. On the part of Israel   21:34-35a
     a. Divine permission   21:34
     b. Israel's execution of divine instruction   21:35a
C. Summary statement   21:35b

This unit deals with Israel's encounter with King Og of Bashan and Israel's possession, not occupation, of his land after the battle at Edrei. Once again, Moses is the active character in this unit in that he sends out the spy, after which the Israelites capture the villages of Jazer (v. 32). Moses receives Yahweh's revelation, the permission for and assurance of the utter destruction of Bashan (v. 34), and the Israelites carry out those instructions (v. 35). The story line shapes the text.

Commentators disagree whether 22:1 is part of the structure of this unit or not. Gray, Milgrom, Ashley, E. W. Davies, and Levine take this verse as a part of 21:32-35, while Noth, Budd, Maier, Sakenfeld, Olson, and Dozeman think otherwise.[126] In this regard, two facts are worth mentioning. First, the story of Balaam in 22:2–24:25 is very unique in Numbers in that there is no involvement of Israel reported in it. Second, 21:32-35 itself is part of Israel's ongoing migration. Even verse 33 mentions Israel's movement. Due to these two factors, it is conceivable that 22:1, that is, Israel's travel to the plains of Moab, is more inclined to belong to 21:32-35. The first fact is less decisive than the second for the structural position of 22:1 because it can be used either way. If 22:1 belongs to the story of Balaam, then this story has a literary connection with Israel; otherwise it is absolutely isolated from the surrounding narratives. Regarding the second fact, 22:1 contains a typical form of an itinerary, using חנה and נסע. Since there is no specific place of departure in the extant text (cf. the mountains of Abarim according to 33:48), its pattern is similar to 21:10. Compared to 22:1, 21:32-35 narrates Is-

---

126. See Gray (*A Critical and Exegetical Commentary on Numbers*, pp. 306-7), Milgrom (*Numbers*, p. 184), Ashley (*The Book of Numbers*, pp. 430-31), E. W. Davies (*Numbers*, pp. 234-35), Levine (*Numbers 21–36*, pp. 109-10, 139), Noth (*Numbers*, p. 166), Budd (*Numbers*, p. 256), Maier (*Das vierte Buch Mose*, p. 301), Sakenfeld (*Numbers*, p. 124), Olson (*Numbers*, p. 138), and Dozeman ("The Book of Numbers," p. 180). Fearer (*Wars in the Wilderness*, p. 7, n. 13) argues correctly that 22:1 does not belong to the battle traditions in 21:21-31, 32, and 33-35: "22:1 has no necessary connection with any of these traditions, nor does it contain any battle tradition components." But in his macrostructure of 10:11–36:13, Fearer (p. 383) includes 22:1 as part of "the campaign to the Plains of Moab" (20:22–22:1) without any explanation.

rael's march with ויפנו ויעלו (v. 33aα). These verbs describe the march or movement itself rather than the pattern of decamping and encamping.[127] Unlike typical verbs such as חנה and נסע, these are not constitutive for the narrative, and thus verse 33 does not play the same role as 22:1 does. Verse 33 has little significance for delimiting a unit, whereas the itinerary form of 22:1 opens a new unit distinguishable from the adjoining units. Therefore, 22:1 is more closely attached to the story of Balaam than the story of Israel's encounter with Bashan.

The structure of 21:32-35 has two parts: a prelude (v. 32) and the main event (vv. 33-35).[128] The prelude, which reports Israel's victory over Jazer, represents Israel's continual overpowering of its enemies in recent battles. Israel issued here no request for passage as was the case with Edom and the Amorites. Thus, it is possible that the prelude provides the reason why King Og of Bashan and all his people came out to battle against Israel. The main event has three parts: Israel's migration on the road to Bashan (v. 33a), the battle report (vv. 33b-35a), and a concluding statement (v. 35b). In reporting the battle, the unit spends little time describing the battle itself, but, in contrast, it elaborates on the divine permission for Israel to destroy Bashan, with the case of the Amorites as an illustration. The concept of חרם, introduced at 21:1-3 for the first time in Numbers, is also operative in this unit. The detailed report of Israel's killing of the King of Bashan, his sons, and all his people, "until there is no survivor left," enhances this point. This unit concludes with a summary statement that Israel possessed the land of Bashan (v. 35b). This statement is intentional and thus set aside from the battle report itself. Taking the land of the enemy may in itself be regarded as a natural consequence of victory over it. Since Israel's final destination is not the land of Bashan, the people could move on to the next station toward the promised land without necessarily possessing its land. However, an explicit statement of Israel's possession of the land of Bashan implies that possessing its land is the ultimate goal of Israel's turning and going up the road to it (v. 33a), thus paving the way for the request of the Reubenites and the Gadites to settle in it (32:1).

---

127. There are also other verbs describing the march itself, such as בוא (to go, enter), הלך (to walk, go), דרך (to walk, tread), עבר (to pass through), and עלה (to ascend, go up).

128. Cf. Fearer (*Wars in the Wilderness*, pp. 409-65, especially, p. 459) for his analysis of the macrostructure of 21:33-35. As the title of the structure of vv. 33-35 indicates, his analysis is done from the vantage point of vv. 21-31. However, vv. 33-35 themselves do not end with Israel's occupation of Og's land, but with their possession of it. Although the battle traditions in 21:21-31, 32, and 33-35 are interconnected, the individuality of each tradition must be considered before placing it in the light of its larger context, in order to understand it on its own terms.

(22) Story of Balak's Failed Plan to Curse Israel (22:1–24:25)

I. Setting: itinerary	22:1
II. The narrative of Balak's failed plan to curse Israel	22:2–24:25
A. Plan proper: Balak's hiring Balaam	22:2-21
1. Reasons for hiring	22:2-6
a. Balak's situation	22:2-4a
b. Balaam's reputation	22:4b-6
2. Two attempts to bring Balaam to Moab	22:7-21
B. Execution of the plan	22:22–24:25
1. Balaam's journey to Moab	22:22-35
2. Encounter between Balak and Balaam	22:36-40
3. Balak's three attempts to curse Israel	22:41–24:24
a. First attempt	22:41–23:12
(1) Preparation	22:41–23:3
(a) Preparatory sacrifice	22:41–23:2
(b) To another place	23:3
(2) Oracle	23:4-10
(a) Divine revelation	23:4-5
(b) Balaam's return	23:6
(c) Oracle proper	23:7-10
(3) Responses	23:11-12
b. Second attempt	23:13-26
(1) Preparation	23:13-15
(a) Preparatory sacrifice	23:13-14
(b) To another place	23:15
(2) Oracle	23:16-24
(a) Divine revelation	23:16
(b) Balaam's return	23:17
(c) Oracle proper	23:18-24
(3) Responses	23:25-26
c. Third attempt	23:27–24:24
(1) Preparation	23:27–24:2a
(a) Preparatory sacrifice	23:27-30
(b) In the same place	24:1-2a
(2) Oracle	24:2b-9
(3) Responses	24:10-24
(a) Balak's response to Balaam	24:10-11
(b) Balaam's response to Balak	24:12-24
(i) Explanation	24:12-13

(ii) Advice: oracles   24:14-24
4. Conclusion: after events: separation again   24:25

Most commentators recognize that at least 22:2–24:45 constitutes a distinct literary unit. They discuss many important matters pertinent to this unit in detail, such as its composite nature (inconsistencies and repetitions), the relationship of the poetic to the prose sections, its tradition history, the character of Balaam, the unit's comparison with the inscription from Tell Deir 'Alla, its purpose in its present location in Numbers, and so forth.[129] Their discussions need not be repeated. However, a few facts need to be addressed in order to provide textual evidence that 22:1–24:45 is a complete unit and to determine its structure.

First, if this unit omits verse 1, it reports nothing about what and how Israel was doing. No single Israelite is present in the events narrated in this unit. Although the divine name occurs fifty-one times,[130] the name of Moses, Yahweh's chief representative, appears not even once. This fact leads commentators to argue that the text was composed independently and only later inserted into the Pentateuch. Their assertion is well taken. However, regardless of the complicated history of its literary development, one thing is certain: the omission of Moses' name makes this text distinctive from surrounding units.

Second, verse 1 is indeed an integral part of the unit. That verse 1 does not belong to the previous unit is discussed above. Two facts support its belonging to 22:2–24:45: (a) it lacks a place of departure; (b) it does not specify an exact location where Israel encamped. Not providing a departure place in an itinerary is in and of itself not the point. The question is whether there is a candidate for a departure place in the immediate literary context. In the case of 21:10, Mount Hor could be expected to be the departure place since it is mentioned in 21:4. Having no indication of an arrival place in 21:4 enhances this point. In contrast, there is no particular place name near 22:1. Although 33:48 suggests the mountains of Abarim as the place of departure, this place name has not occurred before 27:12, which is not the immediate literary con-

---

129. Most recent commentators provide a summary of discussions on these matters with abundant bibliographies (Ashley, *The Book of Numbers*, pp. 432-511; E. W. Davies, *Numbers*, pp. 236-84; Milgrom, *Numbers*, pp. 467-76 [Excursuses on pp. 56-60]). See especially Levine's commentary, which contains 138 pages (almost one-quarter of the entire book) of extensive treatment of the Balaam pericope.

130. Ashley (*The Book of Numbers*, p. 433) provides this literary detail: Yahweh (x29), Elohim (x11), El (x8), Shadday (x2), and Elyon (x1). See also Gray, *A Critical and Exegetical Commentary on Numbers*, pp. 310-14.

text of 22:1.[131] In the second place, considering the fact that the basic form of an itinerary has topographical localities, the lack of topographical references and the inclusion of only geographical references in verse 1 are also noticeable. Verse 1 states that Israel encamped in the plains of Moab, further defined as "across the Jordan from Jericho." Where exactly did Israel encamp? Since 25:1 (cf. 33:49) reports Israel's stay at Shittim without any mention of their march to that place, it may be speculated that the people stayed at Shittim throughout all events narrated in 22:2–24:45 without knowing what was going on. The ambiguity of their place of departure and the references only to the borders of the area in which they camped in 22:1 could well be congruent with the very distinctive narrative that follows.

Third, 22:1–24:45 presents a mixture of seven poetry sections (23:7-10; 23:18-24; 24:3-9; 24:15-19, 20, 21-22, 23-24)[132] with prose sections surrounding them. Defining the relationship between these two genres is the key to understanding the integrity of the unit as a whole. Milgrom argues that the prose sections provide the necessary framework for understanding the poetry. He presents three pieces of evidence: (1) the oracles abound with at least eleven references to the narrative; (2) the oracles keep perfect pace with the thematic progression of the adjoining narrative text; and (3) Balaam's rise in confidence is inversely matched by the downgrading of Balak. In light of these, Milgrom concludes that "without the narrative, the poetic oracles would make no sense, and all their allusions to personalities, nations, and events would be incomprehensible."[133] However, his evidence is not entirely convincing. Concerning (1), the eleven references are too sporadic and too indirectly related to the narratives to be conclusive.[134] The second is hard to ver-

---

131. For the exact location of Mount Abarim, especially its connection with Mount Nebo (Deut 32:49; 34:1), see Ashley (*The Book of Numbers*, p. 550). Also, for its possible relation to Iye-abarim in 21:11 and 33:44, see Ashley (p. 409).

132. First, these seven oracles all begin with the identical heading, וישא משלו ויאמר; hence the present literary form of the story indicates that they are independently uttered, regardless of their content, length, and assumed origins. Second, the extant text clearly divides these seven oracles into two categories. The first three should be grouped together as Balaam's responses to Balak's requests, while the last four are given to Balak without Balak's request. Balaam utters the last four consecutively under the rubric of his "advice" to Balak (24:14). Therefore, claiming that there are four Balaam oracles with three later appended oracles is not what the extant text shows.

133. Milgrom, *Numbers*, pp. 467-68. Levine (*Numbers 21–36*, p. 210) disagrees with Milgrom by saying that "the narratives project perspectives quite different from those of the poems," though he provides no further discussions.

134. Milgrom provides relevant verses for the first oracle (23:7-10): 22:5, 6, 11, 12, 24, 41; for the second oracle (23:18-24): 22:13, 17; 23:17; 24:1, 2; for the third and fourth oracles (24:3-9,

ify, yet it will be discussed in the explanation of the structure of the unit. In terms of (3), Milgrom supplies two points: (a) unlike the first two oracles, there is no mention of Balak's name in the third and the fourth oracles (24:4, 16; cf. in the first and second, 23:7, 18); and (b) as the oracles progress, Balak's title shifts from King of Moab to the son of Zippor, and finally he has no title. But these points do not necessarily indicate Balak's downgrading. Even before the first oracle, Balak is called not only King of Moab but also the son of Zippor (22:2, 4, 10, 16). Missing Balak's name in the third and the fourth oracles means simply that these oracles are "general in scope, with no reference to the narrative in which they are embedded."[135] Furthermore, Milgrom includes neither 22:22-35, the story of Balaam and the ass, in his consideration of the narrative, nor 24:20, 21-22, 23-24 in the poetic sections. This means that his discussion of the relationship between the poetry and prose sections is based on selective portions of the text in each genre. The basic assertion of Milgrom that there is interconnection between these two genres is correct, but the relationship should be further defined. The question, such as which narrative section provides the immediate context for which oracle, is not discussed at all in his excursus on the unity of prose and poetry in chapters 22–24, although it is partially mentioned in his exegesis.[136]

The structure of 22:1–24:45 incorporates many elements that appear to be loosely connected. For example, the enigmatic story of Balaam and the ass (22:22-35) seems to be awkwardly connected with the preceding verses because Yahweh has given Balaam permission to go with Balak's officials (v. 20), and then soon afterward Yahweh is angry because Balaam is going with them (v. 22). It is true that the story line of 22:2-40 would make more sense without verses 22-35. Regardless of its origin and roughness, and whether its purpose is "to reemphasize Balaam's duty to speak only God's word" or to humiliate Balaam so that he is "a level lower than his ass: more unseeing in his inability to detect the angel, more stupid in being defeated verbally by his ass, and more beastly in subduing it with his stick whereas it [the ass] responds with tempered speech,"[137] the passage's function and connectedness must be un-

---

15-19): 22:31; 23:5, 12, 16; 24:2. These references do not show whether each oracle is supposed to be related to the preceding or the following narrative. They show only that the oracle is related to the narrative in a general thematic way. This conclusion is self-evident to anyone who reads the text.

135. Sakenfeld, *Numbers*, p. 131.

136. Milgrom subdivides his exegesis as follows: Balaam's first oracle (23:7-10); the second oracle (23:18-24); the third oracle (23:25–24:9); and the fourth oracle (24:10-19). Only the third and the fourth include a preceding narrative as part of the oracle.

137. Sakenfeld, *Numbers*, p. 126; Milgrom, *Numbers*, p. 469, respectively.

derstood in the context of the whole text. Moreover, the structure should account for the two dominant elements, the prose and poetic sections.

The structure of this unit has two parts: the setting (v. 1) and the narrative of Balak's failed plan to curse Israel (22:2–24:25). The narrative consists of two parts: the plan proper reporting the reasons for hiring Balaam and attempts to bring him to Moab (22:2-21); and the execution of the plan, accounting mainly for Balak's self-destructive plan (22:22–24:25). Despite the preoccupation with the figure of Balaam in previous scholarship, the extant text reveals Balak as the key player for constituting its organizational integrity. Without him the unit as a whole could not exist in its extant form as it reveals the complex interrelationship among its various components and the significance of its placement within the book of Numbers.[138] Whereas Balaam plays the incidental role in the flow of the story (i.e., whatever he does, he does because he is under the power of the God of Israel [22:8, 20, 35, 38; 23:3, 5, 8, 12, 16, 20, 26; 24:13]), Balak is instrumental. The story begins with Balak's fear of the triumphant Israelites and ends with his departure from Balaam to go his own way. Balaam is at best an employee hired to do a "dirty" job for Balak! If Balak's plan goes unaccomplished, Balaam has nothing to lose, or perhaps only his reputation, as Balak assumes. However, if Balaam does not do what he is hired to do, Balak may lose everything. The fate of his kingdom is at stake. Note that Balak attempts three times to induce Yahweh's curse on Israel, even when he is warned at the outset concerning Balaam's inability to do anything on his own authority (22:38).

In view of instrumental role that Balak plays, the episode of Balaam with his ass fits well in the progress of the narrative. It may function to stress again the duty of Balaam, or to humiliate him, as proposed. Yet, in light of the development of the narrative or of the building of the plot as the story progresses, this episode functions to provide the counter information to Balak's confidence in Balaam. Balak's two attempts to hire Balaam are based on his understanding that Balaam is one of whom it can be said, "whomever you [Balaam] bless is blessed, and whomever you curse is cursed" (22:6b). By reporting (or adding or inserting) the story of Balaam and his ass, the text intends to reveal that Balak's choice of Balaam as part of his preparation for the encounter with Israel is in itself a failure from the beginning, and it further causes the unwanted and unthinkable result of Israel being blessed instead by the foreign prophet. The negative result of Balak's plan is already implied at

138. For a detailed discussion of the figure of Balak in Num 22–24, see my article, "Balak: The Forgotten Character in Numbers 22–24," in the forthcoming commemorative volume in honor of Professor S. J. DeVries.

the beginning of the story, particularly in connection with his confidence in Balaam and with the story of Balaam and his ass. Thus, the episode of the talking ass is a necessary component for the whole story.

As for the seven oracles in the unit, they each play a role at different structural levels. The first (22:41–23:12) and the second (23:13-26) oracles have the same basic element, preparation-oracle-response,[139] although their content is certainly different; and thus they are on the same level. The so-called third and the last four oracles have different structures from the first two. The third begins with almost the same preparation as the first two oracles, but it ends differently. At the end, it notes Balaam's staying at the same place (24:1), not moving to another place, which was the case in the first and the second (23:3-6, 15-16). It also elaborates on the response element, showing Balak's frustration (24:10-11) and Balaam's reply (24:12-24). The structure of the first two oracles is completely absent in the last four oracles. Neither preparation, which includes the sacrifice, nor moving to a different place to receive the oracles from Yahweh, nor the response of Balak afterward is present. The structural difference may be part of building the plot in the progress of the story line, but it certainly indicates that the third and the last four oracles do not function on the same level within the structure of the whole unit. Moreover, the last four oracles are given as Balaam's advice to Balak at his own initiative, without Balak's request. Thus, they are subordinate to the third oracle. The inclusion of oracles for other nations (24:20, 21-22, 23-24) reinforces the role of these last four oracles as being secondary to the third one. Because of this relationship between the third and last four oracles, they can be classified as Balak's final attempt (23:27–24:24), combining the two sets of oracles into one category. Then, as a combined oracle, the third and the last four together share the same structural level with the first two. Through these oracles, the result implied at the beginning of the story is clearly revealed and extended, even further enhancing Yahweh's blessing on Israel, unbeknownst to Israel, and transmitted by the foreign prophet. Balak's plan to curse his enemy, the people of Israel, by employing Balaam, is in actuality a fool's idea that unfolds inevitably into a failure, in spite of his confidence in it.

139. The structure of the first and second oracles follows the same pattern. The first part is preparation, which has two sections, preparatory sacrifice and Balaam's moving to other places to receive divine inspiration; the second part is interested in the oracle that comes from Yahweh directly to Balaam and is proclaimed by Balaam after he returned to Balak; the third part is focused on verbal exchanges between Balak and Balaam.

(23) Rebellion Narrative of the Event at Shittim: Israel's Apostasy to the Baal of Peor Because of Their Sexual Behavior (25:1-18)

I. Setting: topographical locale	25:1a
II. Event proper: Israel's apostasy	25:1b-18
A. Apostasy proper	25:1b-9
1. The cause	25:1b-6
a. General description	25:1b-3a
(1) Preliminary: sexual activity	25:1b
(2) Main problem: religious idolatry	25:2-3a
b. Reactions	25:3b-5
(1) By Yahweh	25:3b-4
(2) By Moses	25:5
c. Specific description	25:6
2. Resolution	25:7-9
a. Phinehas's action	25:7-8a
b. Result	25:8b-9
B. Aftermath	25:10-18
1. Yahweh's speech: reward for Phinehas's action	25:10-13
2. Further retaliation for Midianites	25:14-18
a. Introductory remark: identities of individuals	25:14-15
b. Yahweh's speech	25:16-18

By reporting what Israel was doing at the specific place Shittim in verse 1, a clear break is made from the previous unit. While many distinctive elements are noticeable after verse 1, they are related to each other, and their connectedness is severed by the temporal notation at 25:29 (Eng. 26:1a) and in the census report that follows. Determining the inner relations among many elements, however, is not as simple as defining the outer limits of this unit. As most commentators agree, this unit consists of two unconnected stories (vv. 1-5 and 6-18).[140] The former mentions Israel's sexual relations with Moabite women (v. 1b). Note that their sexual activity is reported in general terms,

---

140. E. W. Davies, *Numbers*, p. 284; Ashley, *The Book of Numbers*, pp. 514-15; Dozeman, "The Book of Numbers," pp. 197-200. For the comparison of 25:1-18 to Exod 32, see Wenham (*Numbers: Introduction and Commentary*, p. 184; cf. Ashley, *The Book of Numbers*, p. 515, n. 15; Milgrom, *Numbers*, p. 211), and for its comparison to Num 13–14, see Milgrom (*Numbers*, p. 211). Milgrom argues that since 22:4 and 7 imply that some Midianites are present among the Moabites, the appearance of Midianites in 25:6ff. does not create as sharp a break with 25:1-5 as many commentators argue.

which suggests that the text is not interested in Israel's sexual behavior per se. However, this activity leads to the worship of and sacrifice to Moabite gods (vv. 2-3a), which is the main interest of these verses as a whole. Verse 3b identifies the god as the Baal of Peor and recounts Yahweh's anger and punishment because of Israel's idolatry.

Unlike the first story, the latter (vv. 6-18) reports in great detail. Although it begins with a sexual story just like the former, it not only specifies the characters involved but also elaborates upon the consequences of the story. The story deals with an individual Israelite's sexual involvement with a Midianite woman, which causes Phinehas to impale them. His action is taken at his own initiative without Moses' or Yahweh's command and is described step by step and as vividly as possible. For his bold action, Yahweh awarded him and his descendants with a covenant of perpetual priesthood (vv. 10-13). The story ends with the identification of the individuals who were sexually engaged (vv. 14-15) and Yahweh's command to Moses to destroy the Midianites for luring Israel into idolatry (vv. 16-18).

In terms of forms, verses 1-5 have two reports concerning the punishment for Israel's idolatry (vv. 4 and 5) but seem to lack any sort of report of the execution of Yahweh's commands. Conversely, verses 6-18 have an execution report narrating Phinehas's action and its result but seem to lack any sort of speech by Yahweh or Moses regarding the punishment for the individuals involved in the sexual act.

Recognizing the tensions of content and forms, however, does not hinder the integrity of the unit in its present form. The phrase "after the plague" in 25:19 gives a clue to the unity of verses 1-18. Knowing that the plague is the end result of Israel's rebellion against Yahweh and is a materialization of Yahweh's anger and punishment, this phrase in 25:19 characterizes 25:1-18 as a rebellion narrative. Then, the two seemingly different events evolve around the theme of the plague, and their structures are similar to the typical pattern of a rebellion narrative, that is, Israel's rebellion and Yahweh's punishment. In this structure, the two sexual stories are peripheral, functioning as an introduction to the main activity of Israel, that is, their idolatry of the Baal of Peor. This is the direct cause of Yahweh's anger and punishment.

The passage 25:1-18 as a whole, therefore, has three distinctive elements: Israel's apostasy, Phinehas's action and reward, and Yahweh's command to destroy Midian. The crucial questions for the structure of this unit are, then: How are these three related to each other structurally? Are they equally important within the structure of the whole unit? Or is one superior? First, Israel's apostasy has a structure similar to any rebellion narrative in that it reports the idolatrous behavior of the people, in this case worshipping and sacrificing to the Baal of Peor, which causes Yahweh's anger and punishment, usually carried out by Moses. In this unit, it is not Moses but Phinehas who takes the initiative, even without Yahweh's command to kill the individuals who were engaged in sexual activity in the tent (vv. 7-8a). Second, Yahweh's reward to Phinehas, the perpetual priesthood, is an astonishing measure compared to Phinehas's action. Is the concern for Phinehas the predominant factor that holds this unit together? In other words, does Israel's apostasy at Shittim serve to explain the legitimacy of Phinehas's receiving the perpetual priesthood? Or is Israel's apostasy the prime factor, such that the text's interest in Phinehas can be understood as one of its consequences? Third, why does the text renew its interest in Midian by listing the name of the Midianite woman and Yahweh's command to destroy the Midianites (vv. 15-18)? Do verses 8b-9 not conclude Israel's apostasy by showing the result of Yahweh's punishment for it?

The clue to these structural questions lies in the fact that outside this unit Phinehas is mentioned within the Pentateuch only twice: in Exodus 6:25, an account of his origin, and in Numbers 31:6, which reports his marching with armed Israelites for battle against Midian. Only one occurrence of the name of Phinehas after 25:1-18 suggests that establishing Phinehas's perpetual priesthood is not the dominant interest of the text. Moreover, that his name is associated with Israel's war against Midian in 31:6 indicates that the two elements, Yahweh's reward for Phinehas's action and Yahweh's command to destroy Midian, are intrinsically related within the text. And in the larger context, these two are combined together to set the stage for Israel's eventual battle against Midian in Numbers 31. Therefore, Israel's apostasy at Shittim is the predominant factor responsible for the extant text. Consequently, this unit is structured according to the typical pattern of a rebellion narrative, rebellion activity and response, including a report on the aftermath.

(24) Census Report: Preparation for the Allotment of the Land (25:19–26:65 [Eng. 26:1-65])

I. Setting: temporal aspect	25:19
II. Taking a census of the Israelites	26:1-65
A. For those above the age of twenty	26:1-56
1. Census proper	26:1-51
a. Yahweh's instructions	26:1-2
b. Moses' and Eleazar's compliance	26:3-51
(1) Introductory statement	26:3-4a
(2) Census itself	26:4b-51
(a) Superscription	26:4b

This unit contains several elements identifiable without difficulty. It states the temporal aspect of Yahweh's speech, which follows "after the plague" (25:19); it reports Yahweh's command to Moses and Eleazar to take a census of all Israelite men above the age of twenty who are able to go to war (vv. 1-2), Moses' execution of the command (vv. 3-51), Yahweh's instruction for allotting the land after the conquest (vv. 52-56), and the numbering of the Levites, the landless tribe (vv. 57-62); and it concludes by reasserting the fact that the census of the Israelites was taken in the plains of Moab (vv. 63-65). These elements are clearly interrelated. For example, there are many pervasive terms, such as "enrollment" (פקודי, 26:18, 34, 41, 43, 50, 51, 54, 57, 62, 63, and 64). The two basic patterns in verses 4b-51 also appear in verses 57-62.[141] The antecedent of לאלה in verse 53 is obviously the total number of Israelites listed in verse 52, and thus the census provides a basis for the division of the land. Verses 63-65 lead the reader back to verse 3 and seem to clarify the possible misunderstanding caused by verse 4b. These are only a few examples that indicate the interrelationship among the elements mentioned above.[142]

    The structure of this unit has two parts: the temporal setting (25:19) and the report of a census of the Israelites (26:1-65). The census report has three sections: the census of Israelites who are above the age of twenty (vv. 1-56),

---

141. Milgrom (*Numbers*, p. 219) identifies two formulas for the census list. The first gives the clan names, "The X-ites by their clans: of A, the clan of A; of B, the clan of B . . ."; and the second gives the totals, "Those are the clans of the X-ites; persons enrolled: N." X stands for the tribe, A for the clan, and N for the tribal count.

142. For details and a comparison with the census report in Num 1 and the tribal list in Gen 46, see Olson, *The Death of the Old and the Birth of the New*, pp. 83-124; Ashley, *The Book of Numbers*, pp. 531-33; E. W. Davies, *Numbers*, pp. 290-91.

the census of the Levites (vv. 57-61), and a concluding summary statement (vv. 63-65). The constitutive factor for the three divisions is the uniqueness of the Levites, which consists of their separateness from the rest of the Israelites and their landlessness. The second section focuses strictly on the enrollment of the Levites. This enrollment is necessary because it has been excluded in the total numbers of the Israelites (v. 62). On the contrary, the first section reports the census of the Israelites who can go to war and receive the land as their inheritance. The third section is clearly related to the first section. In the first and third sections, Moses and Eleazar conduct the census (vv. 3-4 and 63a) in the plains of Moab by the Jordan opposite Jericho (v. 3b), or where the enrollment took place.[143] More important, the third section clarifies the identity of those being enrolled by Moses and Eleazar in the first section: they are not the ones who were enrolled by Moses and Aaron in the wilderness of Sinai (vv. 64-65). This qualification is necessary due to the possible confusion of verse 4b. Thus, the second section breaks into the continuing report regarding the rest of Israel's tribes. If the enrollment of the Levites followed verses 63-65, or if the summary and qualifying statements preceded verses 57-62, then the second part would need to be divided into two sections: the census of the Israelites and that of the Levites. Or if the summary section mentioned the census of the Levites, then it would also need to be divided into two sections: the census of the whole of Israel and the concluding summary statement. But these are exactly what the text in its present form does not do.

The first section consists of two subsections: the census proper (vv. 1-51) and the allotment of the land (vv. 52-56) based on Yahweh's speech. Although the recipients of Yahweh's speech in both subsections are different (Moses and Eleazar in v. 1 and Moses alone in v. 52), Yahweh's speech itself is decisive for opening a new subsection here. From a chronological standpoint, it is logical that Yahweh spoke to Moses once again in order to allot the land after knowing the exact number of the Israelites. Therefore, the section for the allotment of land is not structurally at the same level as the section for the enrollment of the Levites (vv. 57-62) or the section of the concluding summary (vv. 63-65); it is subordinate to them.

143. No name and place are mentioned in vv. 57-62, although it may be assumed that Moses enrolled the Levites, as the narrative formula in v. 52 implies, and that the same locale is presupposed, since the verses are part of a continual narrative from 25:19.

(25) Report about the Daughters of Zelophehad: Heiresses'
Right to Inherit the Land (27:1-11)

This text deals with how to inherit the land in certain circumstances. It is related to the allotment of the land (26:52-56) but is distinct from that text due to its specificity. Two factors qualify the main issue of the unit, which leads to a discovery of its structure. First is the specific case that the daughters of Zelophehad brought to Moses, Eleazar, the leaders, and all the congregation. Their case can be summarized with the question, Do the daughters of a deceased man who left no sons have the right to inherit his land? Second is the issue of the regulation of succession in inheritance reported in verses 8-11. The regulation contains four situations: if a man dies without sons (v. 8), without daughters (v. 9), without brothers (v. 10), and without his father's brothers (v. 11). This is a general regulation not strictly related to the case of the daughters of Zelophehad. The question is, What is the relationship between the general regulation and the case of the daughters of Zelophehad? Which is subordinate? Does the case of the daughters of Zelophehad serve to create a new general regulation concerning succession in inheritance? In comparing these two factors, the case of the daughters of Zelophehad dominates, and the general regulation is subordinate to it. The evidence is clear in the text itself. The text reveals the identity of these women, including their names (v. 1), describes in detail the case, including the justification of their case related to past experience (vv. 2-5), and elaborates on the answer of Yahweh (v. 6-7). The regulations come as a consequence of the specific case of the daughters of Zelophehad.

The structure of 27:1-11 has two parts: the case (vv. 1-4) and its resolution (vv. 5-11). Each part has two sections of its own. The first part contains introductory matters, such as the identity of the petitioners, to whom and where they brought the case (vv. 1-2), and an elaboration of the case including the motivation for the request (vv. 3-4). The second part consists of Moses' action (v. 5) and Yahweh's solution (vv. 6-11), which suggest a divine qualification of both the presented case and the general regulations. The four cases are expressed according to the pattern of casuistic law, the hierarchical system of כִּי and אִם.[144]

> (26) Yahweh Speech: Instructions about the Commissioning of Joshua as the Successor of Moses (27:12-23)

I. Report of the need for a successor to Moses	27:12-17
A. Yahweh's announcement of the impending death of Moses	27:12-14
1. Introductory speech formula	27:12aα
2. Speech	27:12aβ-14
a. Preliminary activities	27:12aβ-b
b. Declaration of Moses' coming death	27:13
c. Reason for death	27:14
B. Moses' request for his successor	27:15-17
1. Introductory speech formula	27:15
2. Speech	27:16-17
a. Request itself	27:16
b. Responsibility of the successor	27:17a
c. Motivation for request	27:17b
II. Report of Yahweh's provision for a successor	27:18-23
A. Provision proper	27:18-21
1. Introductory speech formula	27:18aα1
2. Speech	27:18aα2-21
a. Designation of Joshua	27:18aα2-β
b. Instructions for commissioning Joshua	27:18b-21
(1) Laying on of hands	27:18b
(2) Presentation before priest and people	27:19

---

144. Verses 8b-11a are constructed by one כִּי clause (8b) with three אִם subclauses (vv. 9a, 10a, and 11a).

(3) Bestowal of authority	27:20-21
B. Moses' execution of Yahweh's instructions	27:22-23
1. Execution formula	27:22a
2. Description of Moses' deed: presentation and commissioning of Joshua	27:22b-23

This unit begins with a Yahweh speech concerning the impending death of Moses (vv. 12-14) and ends with Moses' execution of the commission of Joshua as the new leader, followed by Yahweh's instructions (vv. 18-23). Between these lies Moses' request for someone to be placed over the congregation of Israel (vv. 15-17). Since there is no narrative discontinuity between verses 14 and 15 and between verses 17 and 18, all three elements are related. However, to define what kind of relationship exists among these three is not so simple. The problem can be minimized based on the function of verses 15-17. Are these verses more closely related to what precedes (vv. 12-14) or to what follows (vv. 18-23)? The operative factors are (1) the literary pattern of request-answer that seems to be apparent in verses 15-23 and (2) the conceptual aspect of the announcement of the impending death of Moses and the provision for a successor to Moses. The second overrides the first literary factor. Verses 12-14 are combined with verses 15-17 to establish the need for a successor to Moses. The argument for this follows.

Verses 12-14 contain a few elements of a death report,[145] while verses 15-23 may be influenced by an installation genre identifiable in the appointment of new leaders.[146] But unlike the death report of Aaron, 27:12-23 does not report the actual death of Moses (cf. 20:28b for Aaron's death) or the people's mourning (cf. 20:29 for Aaron's death). These elements are not found in Numbers but in Deuteronomy 34:4-8, especially verses 7 and 8. Moreover, in contrast to the report of Aaron's death, it is Moses who requests a successor in verses 15-17 and is given detailed instructions on how to commission Joshua (vv. 18-21).[147] Fur-

---

145. Ashley (*The Book of Numbers,* p. 548, n. 6) summarizes the five elements of a death report that Coats discusses in his Genesis commentary. Ashley also discusses the similarities between the death report of Aaron (Num 20:22-29) and that of Moses. There are geographical indicators (20:22-23; 27:12-13a), Yahweh's announcement of death beforehand, along with the reason for the death (20:24; 27:13b-14), the appointment of a successor (20:25-26; 27:15-21), and the execution of the successor's appointment (20:27-28a; 27:22-23).

146. D. J. McCarthy, "An Installation Genre?" *JBL* 90 (1971): 31-41. The form is characterized by (1) an encouragement formula, (2) description of the task, and (3) an assistance formula (cf. Deut 31:23).

147. Coats sees the legendary elements of Moses' behavior reported in vv. 15-17. Cf. G. W. Coats, "Legendary Motifs in the Moses Death Reports," *CBQ* 39 (1977): 34-44.

ther, unlike Yahweh's commissioning of Joshua using a typical installation genre in Deuteronomy 31:23, 27:15-23 does not contain the same elements, except for the description of the new leader's responsibility in verses 17 and 21b. Instead, this text concentrates on the investiture procedure for Joshua as successor to Moses. Joshua must be presented before the priest Eleazar and all the congregation of Israel (v. 19), and Moses must lay hands on him in their sight (vv. 18b and 23a). Joshua will obtain divine guidance through the priest's use of the Urim (v. 21a). These emphases suggest that Joshua's legitimacy as Moses' successor will be ensured, on the one hand, but that, on the other hand, he does not possess the same authority Moses had; rather, he must be approved by Eleazar and the people, and he must work closely with the priest.

The omission of the report of the actual death of Moses and the people's mourning and the expansive report concerning the public commissioning of Joshua in the extant text suggest that here emphasis is being put upon the appointment of Moses' successor rather than on the death of Moses. Yahweh's announcement of Moses' death provides a basis for the urgent appointment of a successor to Moses.[148] The structure of 27:12-23 is therefore divided into two parts: the report of the need for a successor to Moses (vv. 12-17) and the report of Yahweh's provision of a successor, Joshua (vv. 18-23).

(27) Yahweh Speech: Instructions about Various Public Offerings (28:1–30:1 [Eng. 28:1–29:40])

I. Report of Yahweh's instructions	28:1–29:39
A. Introductory Yahweh speech formula	28:1
B. Speech proper	28:2–29:39
1. Introduction	28:2
2. Regular offerings	28:3-15
a. Daily	28:3-8
b. Sabbath	28:9-10
c. New Moon	28:11-15
3. Specific offerings	28:16–29:38
a. Passover	28:16
b. Feast of Unleavened Bread	28:17-25
c. Feast of First fruits	28:26-31

148. Ashley (*The Book of Numbers*, p. 549) arrives at the same conclusion without detailed discussions on the relationship between vv. 12-14 and 15-23. For him, the former gives the cause of the appointment of Joshua, whereas the latter gives the effect of it. However, the pattern of cause and effect implies the equal importance of or emphasis on each part. Since the text clearly gives weight to the latter, his cause-effect relationship needs to be further refined.

This unit clearly breaks from the adjoining units. It begins with Yahweh's instructions concerning whole burnt offerings and purification offerings, along with accompanying grain and drink offerings, for the cultic occasions of the calendar year. It ends with the report of Moses' compliance with Yahweh's commands. In between, it catalogs several offerings: the daily offerings (28:3-8), the Sabbath offerings (28:9-10), the New Moon offerings (28:11-15), the Passover offering (28:16) and offerings at the Feast of the Unleavened Bread (28:17-25), the Feast of the First fruits (28:61-31), the Trumpets (29:1-6), the Day of Atonement (29:7-11), and the Feast of the Tabernacles (29:12-38). This text exhibits many distinctive features, including five that Milgrom identifies:[149]

(1) The offerings are cumulative: that is, the offerings for the Sabbaths and festivals are in addition to the daily offerings, and the offerings for the New Year are in addition to the daily and the New Moon offerings.
(2) The organizing principle of the calendar is according to descending order of frequency: daily, Sabbath, New Moon. Furthermore, the sacrifices for the festivals follow in calendrical order, beginning with Passover.
(3) All the sacrificial animals are males: bulls, rams, and lambs as burnt offerings and goats as purification offerings.
(4) The sacrificial order is prescriptive, not descriptive.
(5) The number seven and its multiples are very prominent in the number of animals offered.

However, there are more than these five features. (1) This text focuses on burnt offerings and purification offerings, which are completely consumed on the altar and partaken of only by the priests. (2) It describes only the public offerings required at the appointed times and at appointed festivals and is not interested in private offerings that individuals could present of their own volition (29:39). (3) It concerns the people's offerings, which assume that the people

---

149. Milgrom, *Numbers*, pp. 237-38. Milgrom provides a table of requisite offerings for each occasion. Cf. Ashley, *The Book of Numbers*, p. 563; E. W. Davies, *Numbers*, pp. 305-6.

themselves are to provide the requisite offerings.[150] (4) There is no offering for the Passover (28:16), and the Passover offering is narrated as the combination of offerings for Unleavened Bread (28:17-25).[151] (5) Sacred assemblies are enjoined for the Feast of the Unleavened Bread (28:18), the Feast of the First Fruits (28:26), the Trumpets (29:1), the Day of Atonement (29:7), and the Feast of the Tabernacles (29:12). (6) The text prescribes similar elements for each section. There is a designation, a naming of the occasion or identifying it by its timing in the calendar year, and a list of animals required for sacrifice, which follows the order of bulls, rams, lambs, and goats. The grain offering then follows with its requirements of fine flour and oil, and the drink offering is then usually specified. An additional notation, specifying that the prescribed elements are to be offered in addition to the regularly required offerings of the day, is found at the end of each section or along with the quantity of lambs, with the exception of the daily offering. (7) The prescription for Tabernacles is noticeable due to its great detail. Particularly, in contrast to the Feast of the Unleavened Bread, which has only one prescription for its seven days, 25:12-38 prescribe each day of the Feast of the Tabernacles in great detail.[152] Moreover, the prescription for Tabernacles does not have a list of the quantities for the grain and drink offerings from the second day on. Instead, the formula "as prescribed in accordance with their number" is used. (8) Compared to other cultic calendars (Exod 23:10-19; 34:18-26; Lev 23:1-44; Deut 16:1-17; Ezek 45:23–46:15),[153] Numbers 28:1–30:1 is more complete and detailed regarding the times and more specific regarding the quantities for each occasion it lists.

The remaining question is, What benefit do all these distinctive features of 28:1–30:1 provide for an inquiry into its structure? What is the organizing principle or infratextual concept that is responsible for the arrangement of the surface text? Is it the descending order of frequency of the sacrifices to be

150. Ashley, *The Book of Numbers*, pp. 561-62.

151. Ashley (*The Book of Numbers*, p. 566) suggests that the combination of the offerings for the Passover and for Unleavened Bread is understandable because the text focuses on the public offerings and the Passover is a family feast supposed to be celebrated in the home without public offerings (Exod 12:3-14). E. W. Davies (*Numbers*, p. 311) offers additional information on this matter by making a comparison with the practice of the Passover in Ezek 45:21-22. Although Milgrom (*Numbers*, p. 243) makes a passing remark that this combination is an indication of the fusion of these two offerings, he seems to suggest that mention of the Passover provides a timetable for the following festivals.

152. This has to do with the fact that the Feast of Tabernacles requires a varying number of offerings for each day, whereas the Feast of Unleavened Bread requires an offering that is the same for each day.

153. See the table presented by V. P. Hamilton, *Handbook on the Pentateuch* (Grand Rapids: Baker, 1982), p. 367.

offered, as Milgrom proposes and most commentators seem to agree? The number of each offering is 365 times for the daily offering, 52 for the Sabbath, 12 for the New Moon, 7 for the Feast of Unleavened Bread, once for the Feast of First Fruits, Trumpets, and the Day of Atonement, and 7 times for the Feast of Tabernacles. As seen, the descending order of frequency works well until the section for the Feast of Tabernacles. If the descending order of frequency is the organizing principle, then the prescription for the Feast of Tabernacles (29:12-38) must be located after or before the Feast of Unleavened Bread (28:17-25). Yet this is not the case.

Most commentators have not sufficiently analyzed the arrangement in light of another criterion, the calendric timetable. The text presents a time-table: daily (28:3), on the Sabbath day (28:9), at the beginnings of months (28:11), on the fourteenth day of the first month (28:16), on the fifteenth day of the first month (28:17), on the day of the first fruits (28:26), on the first day of the seventh month (29:1), on the tenth day of the seventh month (29:7), and on the fifteenth day of the seventh month (29:12). If the timetable is the dominant concept, the structure of the text would be:

I. Every month	28:3-15
II. First month	28:16-25
III. Between first and seventh month	28:26-31
IV. Seventh month	29:1-38

Some questions still remain. What are the exact days for "the beginnings of your months" (28:11) or "the day of the first fruits" (28:26)? Is it not conceivable that the Sabbath day may concur with the dates on which other sacrifices are to be offered, such as the first day of the month, fourteenth, fifteenth of a month, or first, seventh, tenth, or fifteenth day of the seventh month? The structure based on the timetable creates more problems than solutions for the text.

Three other factors deserve some attention. First, nine offerings are mentioned in the text. If the number of offerings is the dominant principle, the text would be organized according to the list of these nine offerings. Yet, some offerings have been described more extensively than others. For example, the prescription for the Feast of Tabernacles is reported in a total of twenty-six verses, whereas the prescription of the Sabbath offerings occupies only two verses. This shows that the text implies a different level of significance for each offering.

Second, there is the classification of the offerings, whether they are to be offered "at the appointed time" (28:2) or "at the appointed festivals" (29:39).

The text clearly mentions some offerings for appointed festivals, such as the Feast of Unleavened Bread (28:17), the Feast of First Fruits (28:26), the Feast of Tabernacles (29:12), with the word "festival." It also mentions some offerings for an appointed time: the Sabbath (28:9), the Passover (28:16), and the Day of Atonement (29:7). The daily offerings and those "at the beginnings of your months" (28:11) and "on the first day of the seventh month" (29:1) can be included in offerings to be offered at the appointed time. In order to structure the text based on this classification, the offerings for the Trumpets (29:1-6) and the Day of Atonement (28:7-11) must come before the offerings for the Feast of Unleavened Bread (28:17-25). The text is not interested in establishing new traditions that specify certain days as "the appointed time" or "appointed festivals"; it assumes and uses already established traditions for times and festivals in Israelite society.

Third, the five offerings in 28:17–29:38 require obedience to two additional laws: a sacred convocation is to be held, and the offerer should not work at his occupation at this time (28:18, 26; 29:1, 7, 12, respectively). This divides the text into two parts: I. 28:3-16 and II. 28:17–29:38.

Thus far, five factors have been proposed: the descending order of frequency of each offering, the timetable, the number of offerings, the classification of offerings offered either at the appointed time or at the appointed festivals, and the requirement of sacred assemblies and abstinence from occupational work. These five altogether point to the importance of offerings which can be classified as "regular offerings" and "specific offerings." The former should be offered with or without a designated or fixed date, whereas the latter should not be presented on any day but on the given day or at an established festival, and for a fixed duration, with specific additional elements included. The Passover offering is considered a specific offering since it provides a particular date for the Feast of Unleavened Bread. Therefore, the structure of 28:1–30:1 has two parts: the report of Yahweh's instructions (28:1–29:39) and the report of Moses' execution of the instructions (30:1). The nine offerings mentioned in the unit are grouped into two categories: regular offerings (28:3-15) and specific offerings (28:16–29:39).

(28) Report about Male Responsibility for the Validity of Vows (30:2-17 [Eng. 30:1-16])

I. Instructions concerning male responsibility for the
validity of vows   30:2-16
 A. Introduction   30:2
  1. The narrative formula   30:2a

This unit narrates Yahweh's instructions concerning the validity of vows, particularly the circumstances under which women's vows are to be considered binding or not binding in relation to the authority of a father or husband. The topic marks this text from the following unit that deals with Israel's holy war against Midian (31:1-54). In order to discern the structure of 30:2-17, several literary features should be noted and evaluated.

First, both Moses' speaking to the heads of the tribes of the Israelites (v. 2a) and the indirect speech by Yahweh (v. 2b) are unusual and yet carry the same meaning: that the following instructions are commanded by Yahweh through Moses and function as an introduction to what follows.

Second, this text has the typical pattern of casuistic law: the primary case is introduced by כִּי, the "when" clause (vv. 3, 4), and its subsections begin with אִם, the "if" clause (vv. 5, 6).[154] If this pattern is the organizing principle for the text, as Milgrom asserts, then the structure of verses 3-16 would be: I. Primary case one (v. 3); II. Primary case two (vv. 4-16); the latter is further divided into A (vv. 4-6), B (vv. 7-9), and C (vv. 11-13). But the pattern of casuistic law neither covers the entire text nor includes verses 10 and 14-16, which share the same topic although they are not expressed with כִּי or אִם clauses.

Third, as Ashley discusses, the text can be constructed according to the four classes of women.[155]

(a) [T]he young marriageable girl who still lives in her father's house (vv. 4-6);

(b) the women who has taken an oath in her father's house but marries before the vow is fulfilled (vv. 7-10);

(c) the widowed or divorced woman (v. 10); and

(d) the married woman living in her husband's house (vv. 11-16) . . . [subcases for (d)] the woman whose husband voids her vow without penalty (vv. 11-13) . . . but incurs a penalty (vv. 14-16).

This classification is convincing because the text itself narrates exclusively the vows that are made by women. Only verse 3 mentions vows made by men. The structure of verses 3-16 then would be: I. Regarding the vows made by a man (v. 3) and II. Regarding the vows made by a woman (vv. 4-16), a section that has four subdivisions based on four classes of women. However, the text concerns not just the vows that different classes of women make but also the legislation of the validity of a woman's vows based on a man's authority. Women in this text are classified by their belonging to a man, whether they belong to the father or the husband. Referring to this point, Sakenfeld concludes that the purpose of the text is "to instruct them [the males of the community] in detail about their responsibility for the making and fulfilling of vows."[156] She presents three arguments: (1) verse 2 functions as a basis for the following verses by describing the vows men are responsible

154. Milgrom, *Numbers*, p. 250. However, Milgrom does not organize his exegesis according to this pattern, but instead lists the cases one by one: case one (vv. 4-6), case two (vv. 7-9), case three (v. 10), and case four (vv. 11-13).

155. Ashley, *The Book of Numbers*, p. 575. Ashley further (p. 578) notes that each section has the same elements: (1) a particular type of woman cited (vv. 4, 7, 11); (2) the condition for validating the vow (vv. 5, 8, 12, 15); (3) the condition for voiding the vow (vv. 6a, 9a, 13a, 15); and (4) the consequences of voiding the vow (vv. 6b, 9b, 13b, 16).

156. Sakenfeld, *Numbers*, pp. 160-61.

for, namely, those of daughters and wives; (2) verses 14-16 elaborate on the accountability of the husband; and (3) the conclusion in verse 17 focuses on both the male and female in the family structure. Thus, although the text has four possible classes of women, it is interested not in the classes themselves but in the male's responsibilities for the vows made by these classes of women.

Fourth, noting the text's emphasis on male responsibility, Sakenfeld proposes a chiastic structure.[157]

> A   Man's own vow (v. 3)
>> B   Father's duty (vv. 4-6)
>>> C   Transitional cases: from father to husband (vv. 7-9)
>>> C'   Transitional cases: from husband to no male (v. 10)
>> B'   Husband's duty (vv. 11-13)
> A'   Special emphasis on husband's direct accountability
> for vow made by his wife (vv. 14-16)

This chiastic structure has the same problem as Milgrom's structure: it does not cover the entire text. How do verses 2 and 17 fit into this chiastic pattern? Moreover, some pairings are not quite convincing. For example, B and B' correspond to each other well on the ground of a man's duty to his belongings. Whether the case is for a daughter or a wife, the focus is still intact, a man's responsibility for their vows. In contrast, A and A' do not correspond to each other at all. Whereas A focuses on a man's responsibility for his own vows, A' stresses a husband's (a man's) accountability not to his own but to his wife's vows. The emphasis has been shifted from a man's own vows to his wife's. Moreover, the internal problem is the treatment of verse 10, the case of widowed and divorced women who are to bear their own responsibility for their vows. For Sakenfeld, verse 10 is located at the position corresponding to verses 7-9 (C and C'), based on the transitional nature of these verses. This matching is awkward and conceptually flawed. Regardless of the transition of responsibility from father to husband, the male responsibility in verses 7-9 (C) remains the same. In contrast, verse 10 (C') stresses a woman's own responsibility. Verses 7-9 and 10 do not stand on the same or equal ground.

Fifth, if the tension between verse 10 and the rest of the cases is the dominant concept, then the structure of verses 3-16 should be divided into two parts based on the seriousness of keeping one's vows: A (vv. 3-9) and B

157. Sakenfeld, *Numbers*, p. 161.

(vv. 10-16). Wenham seems to suggest this kind of structure, although he has no detailed discussion of it.[158] But this structure breaks the patterns of casuistic law and the sequence of the status of woman from unmarried to married.

Thus far, three proposals have been discussed for the structure of 30:2-17 based on the typical pattern of casuistic law: four classes of women (which leads to the distinction of the vows made by a man or a woman), male responsibility (Sakenfeld's chiastic pattern), and the tension created by verse 10. These proposals, however, fail to show the structure of the extant text as a whole, although they reveal many important literary and conceptual factors. The solution can be found in the text itself.

The text gives a clue to its structure, particularly in the concluding remarks of verse 17. Verse 17 states two things: (1) the legislation for validating the vows (vv. 3-16) is Yahweh's commandment to Moses and (2) the category of a woman based on marriage is the criterion for the cases: "a husband and his wife, and a father and his daughter while she is still young and in her father's house" (30:16b). The text focuses on male responsibility, as Sakenfeld has observed; it has two classes of the involved persons, male and female; it has four classes of women, further divided according to the marriage status of a woman (before marriage and after marriage). There is little doubt that all these factors are involved in the structure of 30:2-17, but the difference lies in the fact that they function at different conceptual levels within it. Therefore, the unit's structure has two parts: Yahweh's reported instruction proper on male responsibility for validating the vows (vv. 2-16) and a summary statement (v. 17). The first part also consists of two sections: introductory matters (v. 2) and the instruction proper (vv. 3-16). The instruction is constructed by distinguishing between male and female and by presenting first the regulation for a man (v. 3) and then the regulations for a woman (v. 4-16). The marriage status of a woman is the operative concept for her classification, and thus regulations for a woman are divided into two subsections: before marriage (vv. 4-6) and after marriage (vv. 7-16). Then, the tension created by verse 10, the widowed and divorced, can be resolved. The status of a woman as widowed and divorced presupposes a woman's marriage. Whether women are widowed or divorced, these statutes can apply only after their marriage. Thus, before and after marriage is a more fundamental aspect than the proposed four classes of women. However, the concept of marriage status plays a lower-

---

158. Wenham, *Numbers: An Introduction and Commentary,* p. 206. For Wenham, this passage is arranged in two sets of three cases each. The first set is vv. 3, 4-6, and 7-9. The second set is vv. 10, 11-13, and 14-16. Dozeman ("The Book of Numbers," p. 234) simply follows this arrangement without further refinement.

level role than the distinction between male and female. The dominant concept responsible for the extant text as a whole is male responsibility and an accountability for validating the vows.

(29) Report of Israel's Holy War against Midian (31:1-54)

    1. Offering from the leaders   31:48-50
    2. Use of the offering   31:51-54

With a narrative formula, Yahweh speaks to Moses about the battle against Midian (v. 2a), which resumes in 25:16-18, and about Moses' impending death (v. 2b, which is connected with 27:12-14). This unit mentions nothing more on the subject of the death of Moses but continues to report Moses' execution of Yahweh's commandment to battle against Midian (vv. 3-12), as well as matters concerning the time after the battle, such as the removal of uncleanness through contact with the dead, distribution of the spoils, and so forth. Verses 48-54 narrate the officers' dedication of their gold to Yahweh, and Moses' and Eleazar's conversion of the dedicated gold into vessels for the sanctuary as a memorial for the Israelites before Yahweh. Since the following verses (32:1ff.) shift the focus to the Reubenites' and Gadites' desire to settle in the Transjordan region, 31:54 is the appropriate ending for the story about Israel's battle against Midian.[159]

As most commentators point out, this unit seems more concerned with what happens after the battle than the battle itself. Indeed, the text summarizes the battle in only two verses (vv. 7-8). What, then, is the unifying concept responsible for the composition of the surface text? Milgrom proposes a chiastic structure for this unit:[160]

    A   Battlefront: the war (vv. 1-12)
        B   Camp: Moses' anger and the purification (vv. 13-24)
        B′   Camp: distribution of animate spoil (vv. 25-47)
    A′   Battlefront (flashback) and camp: the ransom (vv. 48-54)

His organizing principle for this unit seems to be the topographical difference between the battlefront and the camp. He supports the chiastic pattern with two arguments: (1) the gold dedication (A′) must have taken place prior to B and B′ and thus corresponds to A; and (2) B and B′ take place at the camp, which is indicated by verse 12 where the spoil was brought. For the first argument, it is granted that the dedication of the booty (vv. 49-50) is supposed to

---

159. The historicity of this text and its literary similarity with other texts are discussed in most commentaries. For example, Milgrom, "Excursus 67: The War against Midian," in *Numbers*, pp. 490-91; Gray, *A Critical and Exegetical Commentary on Numbers*, pp. 417-20; Wenham, *Numbers: An Introduction and Commentary*, p. 209; Ashley, *The Book of Numbers*, pp. 587-90; E. W. Davies, *Numbers*, pp. 319-21; etc.

160. Milgrom, *Numbers*, pp. 491-92. This outline is less detailed than what Milgrom presents, yet it represents his argument well.

have taken place prior to the census, according to Exodus 30:12-16, but this does not necessarily indicate the procedural priority of the verses 48-54 to B and B'. The officers' dedication of the booty in verses 49-50 is now part of the whole, which also describes what happened after its dedication. Its dedication and Moses' and Eleazar's conversion of their gold together take place at the camp after the completion of the purification and distribution of the spoil. For the second argument, verse 13 (B) narrates that Moses, Eleazar, and all the leaders of the congregation "went to meet them [those who went to battle] outside the camp," just in time to prevent them from entering and contaminating the camp. This verse clearly suggests that what follows happened outside of the camp, not at the camp as Milgrom claims. Then, how should verse 12 be understood? Verse 12 is a summary statement of Israel's battle against Midian, rather than a transitional verse from verses 1-12 to verses 13ff., as Milgrom argues. The geographical reference, on the plains of Moab by the Jordan at Jericho, which defines the location of the camp, enhances the concluding mode of the verse. Thus, Milgrom's chiastic pattern of battlefront and camp has no firm textual basis.

The structure of 31:1-54 has two parts: the report of Israel's battle against Midian (vv. 1-12) and the matters of the aftermath of the battle (vv. 13-54). In the first part, the divine command to battle (v. 2) and the battle itself (vv. 7-8) are recounted in relatively brief fashion compared to Moses' arrangement for the anticipated battle (vv. 3-6) and the warriors' taking of the spoils (vv. 9-12). Particularly, the fact of how many and what kind of spoils the warriors took receives great attention: "they took all their cattle . . . all their goods . . . all their towns . . . all their encampments . . . all the spoils . . . all the booty." This builds up curiosity as to what is going to happen to all these spoils — the main concern in verses 13-54. Thus, the first part sets the stage for the second.

The second part has three sections: the purification of the warriors and the booty (vv. 13-24), the distribution of the spoils (vv. 25-47), and their dedication to Yahweh (vv. 48-54). Within the instructions for purification, most commentators claim that two independent instructions, one from Moses and another from Eleazar, are juxtaposed. Regardless of their origin, the instructions do make perfect sense in the extant text and are organized based on their hierarchical positions among the Israelites. On the one hand, it is Moses who has a higher status than Eleazar and who deals with the officers of the army, and not with the ordinary troops. It is Moses who becomes angry with the officers and commands their purification (v. 14). On the other hand, it is Eleazar who deals with the troops and their purification (v. 21), not with the officers of the army. Moreover, while Moses concerns himself with human spoils (the women captives), Eleazar commands the purification of nonhuman booty. Further, Moses is interested in the comprehensive effects resulting from the uncleanness, that is, the consequence of the uncleanness for all Israel (v. 16), whereas Eleazar is concerned with uncleanness itself. Additionally, although the leaders of the congregation went along with Moses and Eleazar to meet the returning army (v. 13), they either did not do anything in the present context or their participation is simply not mentioned.

In the distribution of the spoils two factors are operative: the recipients of the spoils and the scale of the distribution of the spoils. Since the scale is decided based on the recipients of the spoils, to whom the spoils should be distributed is the dominant concept. Accordingly, the text on the distribution of the spoils is divided into two subsections: distribution to human participants (vv. 25-47) and to Yahweh (vv. 48-54). In this division, the officers' dedication of their gold to Yahweh is considered the distribution to Yahweh. This needs to be qualified. Note that (1) the officers' dedication to Yahweh is described as a voluntary act on their part — neither Yahweh nor Moses instructs the officers to dedicate their gold from their share of the booty to Yahweh; (2) in contrast, the distribution to the human participants is instructed by Yahweh; and (3) within Yahweh's instructions, the weighed portion from the warriors and the Israelites has been set aside as a "tribute for the Lord." Regarding this last point, Moses and Eleazar execute Yahweh's instructions: the warriors receive half of the total booty, and from it one five-hundredth goes to Eleazar, the priest (vv. 28-29, 36-41). The Israelites who did not go to war receive the remaining half, and they give one-fiftieth of their share to the Levites (vv. 30, 42-47). Against these instructions, the officers' voluntary dedication is distinctive and should be separated accordingly within the section on the distribution of the spoils. Since their dedication is directed to Yahweh, it should be considered as Yahweh's portion, separated from that coming from the warriors and the Israelites as demanded by Yahweh. Therefore, the report of the matters of the aftermath of the battle consists of three sections, with the dedication to Yahweh constituting the third part.

(30) Historical Narrative concerning the Allotment of Land in the Transjordan for the Reubenites, the Gadites, and the Half-Tribe of Manasseh (32:1-42)

I. Report of the negotiations between Moses and the Reubenites
and the Gadites   32:1-32
  A. Public setting: request   32:1-15
    1. Request for land in the Transjordan   32:1-5

This unit narrates how the Reubenites, the Gadites, and the half-tribe of Manasseh settled in the land east of the Jordan. There is little difficulty in regarding this text as a complete literary unit, except for verses 39-42, which stand in tension with the preceding verses. The tension begins at verse 33, which reports the sudden appearance of the half-tribe of Manasseh. It was the Reubenites and the Gadites who approached Moses and requested, negotiated, and finally received permission to settle in the Transjordan territory. This deal is made by their pledge to fight along with the rest of the tribes across the Jordan until Israel conquers the entire land of Canaan (v. 27). What did the half-tribe of Manasseh do to deserve being an additional recipient of the Transjordan territory (v. 33)? This tension may be solved by verses 39-42, which clarifies not only who the half-tribe of Manasseh is but also what they did. As verse 39 indicates, because Machir son of Manasseh had gone to Gilead and captured it, Moses gave Gilead to him. The other two sons of Manasseh had done the same as Machir, although there is no mention that Moses gave them the territories they had captured. Perhaps their own military campaign allowed them to settle the places. Yet, this explanation far from loosens the tension and only further complicates the problem. While the two tribes receive the kingdom of the Amorites and Bashan, which has already been conquered, and rebuild the cities and give them new names (vv. 33-38), the half-tribe of Manasseh goes after previously unconquered territory. Because of this difficulty, commentators treat verses 39-42 as an interpolation or an independent unit attached to the one preceding it.[161]

Taking verses 7-15 and 39-42 as interpolations, Milgrom presents a chiastic structure for 32:1-6, 16-38:[162]

A   Gad and Reuben request land in the Transjordan (vv. 1-6)
   B   Their compromise proposal is revised by Moses (vv. 16-24)
     X   Gad and Reuben accept Moses' revisions (vv. 25-27)
   B′   Moses' revised proposal is offered to the leaders (vv. 28-32)
A′   Moses provisionally grants land in the Transjordan (vv. 33-38)

According to this structure, there is apparent logical discontinuity between A and B. Moses' angry response to the proposal of the two tribes in verses 7-15 would be the necessary cause for their compromising proposal in B. Moreover, Milgrom supports the structure with the sevenfold recurrence of five key terms. Yet these terms appear in no clear pattern and with several word repetitions. For example, "your servants" (vv. 4, 5, 25, 27, 31) in only sections A, X, and B′ does not strengthen his structure.

Bracketing verses 8-13, D. Jobling presents his outline based on the alter-

---

161. Milgrom, *Numbers*, pp. 492-94; Ashley, *The Book of Numbers*, p. 606; Dozeman, "The Book of Numbers," p. 250. Sakenfeld (*Numbers*, p. 172) sees the tension as existing between vv. 1-32 and vv. 33-42. She presents two additional reasons for this tension: (1) the land has been given to the requesting tribes in v. 33, whereas it will not be given until later in the preceding verses (vv. 5, 29); (2) there is no mention of the principle of awarding territory by lot, as directed by Yahweh (26:55). These reasons are easily explainable. Verses 33-38 are a fulfillment statement of what was discussed previously. As the two tribes claimed, without securing their settlement for their family and cattle, they will not march along with the rest of tribes. The principle of distributing the land by lot has to do with the promised land, but it is not necessarily applicable for the land of the Transjordan. Dozeman argues, however, that the Priestly writers alter the theme of inheritance reflected in the pre-Priestly history (vv. 1-5 and vv. 33-42) to holy war by adding mainly vv. 6-32. Hence, the constitutive theme of 31:1-42 as a whole is to outline "the rules for participation in holy war." Yet this conclusion is exegetically unfounded. First, only vv. 20-23 in vv. 6-32 can be conceived as the material addressing holy war. Second, his characterization of vv. 8-13 as the first generation's failure to conduct a holy war is problematic since the concept of a holy war appears at Num 21 for the first time. Third, he views ch. 32 in light of the main theme of chs. 31 and 33, that is, a holy war. In so doing he is able to put these three chapters together at the expense of the uniqueness of ch. 32. In contrast to his argument, ch. 32 narrates that Moses uses the concept of a holy war (which is applicable only to the second generation) to negotiate the proposal of the tribes of Reuben, Gad, and Manasseh for settling in the land of the Transjordan. The theme of a holy war is at best secondary and subordinate to the allotment of land in Transjordan.

162. Milgrom, *Numbers*, pp. 492-94.

nation of speeches.[163] For him, the structure of the text is divided into four sets of dialogues between Moses and the two tribes. The symmetry of this scheme is evident. Yet how are these four sets arranged? Do they function equally in the composition of the text? Since verses 33-42 are not a speech, how do they fit into the scheme of the alternation of speeches? Jobling does not answer this question.

It is clear that 32:1-42 contain many speeches. Although some speeches, such as verses 25-27 and 31-32, are repetitious and do not seem strictly necessary,[164] it is the relation of the speeches to the narrative that provides the big picture of the text. The structure of 32:1-42 is divided into two parts: one is constructed mainly of speeches (vv. 1-32) and sets the stage for the other, which reports the actual settlement of the two and a half tribes in the Transjordan (vv. 33-42). The first part is further divided based on the different setting that the text presupposes. The setting for the speeches shifts from public (vv. 1-15, see v. 2) to private (vv. 16-27, see v. 16) and to public once again (vv. 28-32, see v. 28). After Moses' refusal of the initial request, the two tribes meet Moses privately to make a deal with him through negotiation. After the negotiations are concluded, Moses presents the new deal before the public. This shift of settings explains the repetitions of the two tribes' reaffirmations (vv. 25-27, 31-32), without which the unit would be less understandable.

---

163. D. Jobling, "The Jordan a Boundary: Transjordan in Israel's Ideological Geography," in his *The Sense of Biblical Narrative: Structure Analyses in the Hebrew Bible II,* JSOTSup 39 (Sheffield: Sheffield Academic Press, 1986), p. 94.

vv. 1-5	Request by Transjordanians
vv. 6-7, 14-15	Angry response by Moses
vv. 16-19	Compromise proposed by Transjordanians
vv. 20-24	Guarded agreement by Moses
vv. 25-27	Reaffirmation of good faith by Transjordanians
vv. 28-30	Moses gives instructions to implement the agreement later, if Transjordanians prove their good faith
vv. 31-32	Reaffirmation of good faith by Transjordanians
vv. 33-42	Moses gives land to Transjordanians

164. Jobling ("The Jordan a Boundary," pp. 95-96) recognizes this awkwardness and provides an explanation. Verses 25-27 correspond to the negativity of Moses in vv. 28-30, while vv. 31-32 induce Moses to be positive and to entail the gift of vv. 33-42. However, psychologizing the characters of the text is at best speculative.

(31) Itinerary Report: From Rameses to the Plains of Moab (33:1-49)

I. Superscription	33:1-2
A. Nature of Israel's journey	33:1
B. Mode of narration	33:2
II. Israel's journey from Rameses to the plains of Moab	33:3-49
A. From Rameses to the wilderness of Zin	33:3-36
1. Narrative concerning the event at Rameses	33:3-4
2. Journey to the wilderness of Zin	33:5-36
B. From Kadesh to the plains of Moab	33:37-49
1. Journey to Mount Hor	33:37
2. Narrative concerning the event at Mount Hor	33:38-40
3. Journey from Mount Hor to the plains of Moab	33:41-49

This unit reports Israel's journey from Rameses (v. 3) to the plains of Moab (vv. 48-49). It contains forty-two campsites (or forty-one legs of the journey), of which the majority cannot be identified with any certainty. Seventeen sites, mostly in the middle section (vv. 18-30a), are unique and are not mentioned elsewhere in the Old Testament.[165] Furthermore, some place names mentioned in the preceding narratives are omitted from the list.[166] The route described seems to be in conflict with the preceding narratives. For example, Israel's attempt to enter Canaan from the east through Edomite territory failed, and thus they had to circumvent the border of Edom in 20:14ff. (21:4), but in 33:37ff. they journey directly from Kadesh-barnea to the banks of the Jordan, which implies that they go through Edomite territory. These difficulties contribute to the lack of scholarly consensus regarding the compositeness of the list of place names, its relationship to other itinerary narratives, such as Numbers 20–21 and Deuteronomy 1–3, and its incorporation into Numbers.[167]

---

165. Seventeen seems to be the correct number, following Ashley (*The Book of Numbers*, p. 623), although most commentators have sixteen (e.g., E. W. Davies, *Numbers*, p. 342; Sakenfeld, *Numbers*, p. 173; Dozeman, "The Book of Numbers," p. 252). They are Yam Suf (v. 10b), Dophkah and Alush (vv. 12b-13), Rithmah, Rimmon-perez, Libnah, Rissah, Kehelathah, Mount Shepher, Haradah, Makheloth, Tahath, Terah, Mithkah, Hashmonah (vv. 18-30a), Abronah (v. 34b), and Zalmonah (v. 41b). Milgrom lists eighteen in his excursus (*Numbers*, p. 499), but his inclusion of Punon seems to be mistaken because he himself recognizes it as "a center for the mining and smelting of cooper in antiquity" (p. 173).

166. Some examples are the wilderness of Shur (Exod 15:22), Taberah (Num 11:3), Hormah (Num 14:45; 21:3), the valley of Zered (Num 21:12), Beer (Num 21:6), Mattanah (Num 21:18-19), Nahaliel (Num 21:19), and Bamoth (Num 21:19-20).

167. Milgrom, *Numbers*, pp. 497-99; Ashley, *The Book of Numbers*, pp. 622-25; M. Haran,

To reconstruct the structure of 33:1-49, several factors should be mentioned. First, there are two superscriptive notes in verses 1a and 2b, and each introduces different information. Verse 1a indicates the nature of Israel's journey as a military campaign led by Moses and Aaron, while verse 2a indicates the literary features of the narration of this campaign — that it was Moses under Yahweh's command who wrote it, and that he wrote it according to Israel's starting places. These two facts complement each other in introducing the following description of Israel's journey from Rameses to the plains of Moab. Second, Israel's journey is described as a narrative that is based on an itinerary. The itinerary is based on the verbal form of the imperfect with *waw* consecutives and the most elementary pattern, "And they decamped from A and encamped at B" (ויסעו מן+A ויהנו ב+B).[168] The station of encampment is always repeated in the departure. Third, in some cases, other materials have been added to particular campsites, and these materials reveal information of geographical refinement and historical events that had occurred there previously. The cases are verses 3-4, 6b, 7a, 8a, 9b, 14b, 36b, 37b, 38-40, 44b, 47b, 48b-49. These citations suggest that particular localities have been highlighted. An analysis of this information provides a clue to the purpose of the unit as a whole, which will be discussed later regarding reconstructing the macrostructure of Numbers 10:11–36:13. Fourth, the itinerary of this unit is topographically oriented except for four places where that pattern is apparently broken (vv. 11b-12a, 15b-16a, 36b, 48b-49). Note that these verses have geographical references with the same verbal form as other topographically oriented itineraries.

Factors two through four suggest that the itinerary contained in this unit is not a pure one; it lists place names one after the other, followed by the pattern of חנה and נסע. There is little doubt that the itinerary evolves to form the basic framework of the unit, but it is not responsible for the structure of the unit. Moreover, since its geography includes the topographical localities, the itinerary of the unit is a geographical clustering of topographical campsites throughout Israel's journey. Thus, this unit is not Israel's itinerary or a travel itinerary, as most commentators claim; it is the narrative of Israel's

---

IDBSup, pp. 308-10; G. I. Davies, "The Wilderness Itineraries," *TynBul* 25 (1974): 46-81; Z. Kallai, "The Wandering-Traditions from Kadesh-Barnea to Canaan: A Study in Biblical Historiography," *JJS* 33 (1982): 175-84.

168. In this unit, the verb נסע occurs forty-two times, while חנה occurs forty-nine times. The pattern varies in the narrative in Exodus and Numbers, but it seems to become more and more fixed. See the changes of the form from Exodus, ויסעו . . . ויבאו . . . ויחנו (Exod 16:1); . . . ויסעו . . . ויחנו (Exod 17:1); ויסעו . . . ויבאו . . . ויחנו (Exod 19:2); ויבאו (Num 20:1); ויסעו . . . ויבאו (Num 20:22); ויסעו . . . ויחנו (Num 21:10, 11); ויסעו (Num 21:4); ויסעו . . . ויחנו (Num 22:1).

journey based on an itinerary with emphasis on geographical groupings of topographical data.

Commentators propose the structure of 33:1-49 based on different criteria. Gray divides the itinerary section into four parts based on two facts: the clear identification of some locations, such as Ezion-geber, Kadesh, Dibon-gad, Nebo, and the plains of Moab; and the Egyptian material: from Rameses to the wilderness of Sinai (vv. 5-15), the wilderness of Sinai to Ezion-geber (vv. 15-35), Ezion-geber to the wilderness of Zin (v. 36), and Kadesh to the plains of Moab (vv. 37-49).[169] If Ezion-geber functions as one of the decisive locations due to its identifiability, then what happens to some twenty other places, on the location of which most scholars seem to agree? What is the special element that Ezion-geber has that the others don't have? Using Ezion-geber seems to be arbitrary and not based on textual evidence. Moreover, Gray does not include verses 3-4 as part of the itinerary section. He does not ask whether these verses belong to the preceding or the following verses.

Noth, however, proposes three parts together with an explanation. He takes verses 3-4 as part of the first of three sections: verses 3-12, 13-40, and 41-49.[170] His criterion is a literary-critical analysis of the unit. He argues that for the list of place names, another document besides the pentateuchal narrative has been used. This other document is responsible for those names not found elsewhere in the Old Testament, beginning with Dophkah in verses 12b, 13a. For Noth, verse 13 makes a break between the pentateuchal sources and another discrete document. Yet, as seen above, the sections not only have identifiable places but also have other materials attached to particular places; they are not just a list of place names. Furthermore, the hypothetical document cannot explain the historical allusions, such as verses 38-40, a unit that is not merely an itinerary constructed with place names.

Wenham proposes an interesting outline: six columns of seven names each.[171] He observes that a similar event tends to recur at the same point in the cycle, and some events occur at stations whose number may be symbolically significant. Utilizing the numerical symbolism of 1, 3, 4, 7, 12, he concludes that the list expresses the typology of divine action in its sixfold repeti-

---

169. Gray, *A Critical and Exegetical Commentary on Numbers*, p. 442. Budd (*Numbers*, p. 356) and E. W. Davies (*Numbers*, p. 342) seem to follow Gray's division without any references or explanation. Ashley (*The Book of Numbers*, p. 623) and Milgrom (*Numbers*, p. 277) combine the second and third sections into one and thus argue for three parts. Yet they provide no discussions of their divisions.

170. Noth, *Numbers*, pp. 243-46. Sakenfeld (*Numbers*, p. 174) seems to follow Noth with some modifications. She has three parts: vv. 1-4, 5-40, and 41-49.

171. Wenham, *Numbers: An Introduction and Commentary*, pp. 217-19.

tion. However, his analysis neither covers the entire text nor explains the additional narratives on particular places. The choice of numbers, such as six columns of seven (which makes forty-two stations), seems intentional and arbitrary. Granting that some events within six cycles reveal identifiable connections with each other, this exercise is at best selective and speculative due to the existing seventeen unknown places. The structure must represent what the text reveals, rather than imposing upon it preconceived concepts borrowed from elsewhere.

Thus, the structure of 33:1-49 has two parts: the superscription (vv. 1-2) and the report of the narrative of Israel's journey from Rameses to the plains of Moab (vv. 3-49). The report can be further divided into four parts, as was the case in 21:10-20, based on geographical indicators.[172] The four parts are Israel's journey to the wilderness of Sin (vv. 3-11), to the wilderness of Sinai (vv. 12-15), to the wilderness of Zin (vv. 16-36), and to the plains of Moab (vv. 37-49). However, the historical allusions attached to Rameses (vv. 3-4) and to Mount Hor (vv. 38-40) stand out. Compared to other additions, which are very brief and mostly of geographical clarification, these are rather lengthy and report the essence of important events during Israel's migration. More specifically, they narrate the beginning (the Exodus event) and the event (the death of Aaron) that occurs at the end of their migration. Thus, these two additions are more important than the geographical ones, and thus they are constitutive for the structure of the report of Israel's migration from Rameses to the plains of Moab. Therefore, the second part has two sections, from Rameses to the wilderness of Zin (vv. 3-36) and from Kadesh to the plains of Moab (vv. 37-49). In this structure, the wilderness of Sinai (vv. 15b-16a) and Kadesh (vv. 36b-37a) are not considered equal to Rameses or Mount Hor but are treated as two of many campsites to which Israel marched. This point has a significant role to play in the larger context, which will be discussed later.

(32) Yahweh Speech: Instructions about the Division of the Land of Canaan (33:50–34:29)

I. Report of the nature of the land of Canaan	33:50–34:12
A. Removal of the Canaanites	33:50-56
1. Setting: geographical	33:50a
2. Yahweh speech	33:50b-56

---

172. Dozeman ("The Book of Numbers," p. 252) suggests the same criterion for the division of the ch. 33. Yet he divides the chapter differently than the present study does (vv. 1-11, 12-37, 38-49, [50-56]), which signals the involvement of some other factors.

In order to establish the outer limits of this unit, the entire passage 33:50–35:44 needs to be analyzed because it is unified by the common theme of the division of the land of Canaan, as Milgrom argues. Milgrom divides this text into five units: "the conquest and apportionment of the land (33:50-56), defined by precise boundaries (34:1-15), under the supervision of designated chieftains (34:16-29), who will also appropriate forty-eight towns for the Levites (35:1-8) and six Levitical towns as asylums for the involuntary homicide (35:9-34)."[173] His division is supported by the narrative formulae "Yahweh spoke to Moses" (33:50; 34:1, 16; 35:1, 9) and the temporal notation "when you cross the Jordan into the land of Canaan" (33:51; 34:2; 35:10). However, questions are raised regarding these two factors. Which one of these two is ultimately responsible for the independence of the unit? Or is either one subordinate to the combination of the two? According to Milgrom's proposal, his five units would be correctly defined if the narrative formula is the ultimate criterion. If the temporal aspect is decisive, then his five units should be reduced to three (33:50-56; 34:1–35:8; 35:9-34). Or if the combination of these two is constitutive, the result would be the same as the division based on the temporal aspect alone.

Milgrom is correct: the fundamental literary feature of 33:50–35:34 is a narrative about five speeches of Yahweh to Moses, indicated by Yahweh speech formulae. However, is there any other factor that competes with the narrative formulae and the temporal indicators for constituting the boundary of the unit? The question of the content of the text needs to be asked. For example, for what purpose did Yahweh speak to Moses or to whom did Yahweh speak? The hint lies in 35:1-8. This unit reports Yahweh's provision for the Levites, and it breaks the narrative continuity of Yahweh's speeches to Moses concerning the matters pertaining to the Israelites as a whole. The concept of the unique status of the Levites relative to the rest of the Israelites is generative for this unit. The text reports Yahweh's speech to Moses that from their inheritance the Israelites must give towns for the Levites to live in (v. 2). The statement, "you [the Israelites] shall give to the Levites," occurs repeatedly in this unit (vv. 2b, 4a, 6a, 7a, 8a). A total of forty-eight cities were allotted to the Levites because they were not entitled to a tribal inheritance (v. 7). However, the passages that precede (33:50–34:29) and follow (35:9-34) this one only report matters concerning the rest of the Israelites. Thus, the concern for the Levites in 35:1-8 is not only the unifier for this unit but also the decisive criterion for dividing 33:50–35:34 into three individual units, that is, 33:50–34:29; 35:1-8; and 35:9-34.

Moreover, the geographical reference of 35:1a, "in the plains of Moab by the Jordan at Jericho," is noticeable. The only other place within 33:50–35:34 where this phrase occurs is 33:50a. The occurrences at 33:50a and 35:1a seem to be intentional due to the shifting of focus from the Israelites to the Levites. They may be coincidental, however, because this phrase does not occur at 35:9.

---

173. Milgrom, *Numbers,* p. 282.

Yet by mentioning the temporal aspect of 33:51 (cf. 34:2 with a slightly different expression) once again in 35:10, 35:9-34 resumes the narrative concerning the rest of the Israelites. Thus, the geographical reference in 35:1a reinforces the independence of 35:1-8, although it is not a decisive factor in that independence.

The next question is whether the passages of 33:50-56; 34:1-15; and 34:16-29 belong together. First, these three are logically related. The conquest of the land is a prerequisite for defining the boundaries of the land, and, similarly, the selection of a group of men to allot the land presupposes the knowledge of its boundaries. Second, the logical sequence is an arbitrary element unless it is qualified by another concept. This is the concept of the apportionment of the land, which holds the three together and without which they are simply juxtaposed. The logical sequence alone is not responsible for their connectedness because such a sequence is easily detectable in any narrative in general and is especially noticeable in the following units (35:1-8, 9-34) as well. The principle of the apportionment of the land is mentioned at first in 26:54-55 and then spelled out in 33:54; it is re-narrated in 34:13 after the determination of the boundaries of the land for the remaining nine and one-half tribes; and for its implementation, a group of men are selected. The pervasiveness of the root of נחל (33:54 [x4]; 34:2, 5, 13, 15, 17, 18, 29) demonstrates the connectedness of the three passages by this principle. Therefore, 33:50-56; 34:1-15; and 34:16-29 form one literary unit based on the apportionment of the land of Canaan for all the Israelites.

The structure of 33:50–34:29 has two parts: the report of the nature of the promised land (33:50–34:12) and the report of instructions regarding the apportionment of the promised land (34:13-29). The division is based on two occurrences of the principle of allotting the land in 33:54 and 34:13-15. Both the removal of the Canaanites from their land and the defining of the boundaries of the land set the stage for the anticipated allotment of the land.

For the first part, 33:50-56 is closely connected to 34:1-12 by the temporal indicator mentioned in each passage (33:51b and 34:2b). Moreover, compared to the lack of a transitional phrase between 33:56 and 34:1, the subscription of 34:12b makes a good break with what follows. For the second part, 34:13-15 is intrinsically related to 34:14-15. Verse 34:13b states that the land of Canaan is only for the nine and a half tribes who had not settled in the land of the Transjordan, and 34:14-15 explains the reason for the omission of the other two and a half tribes by reminding them of their decision made in 32:1-42. Because of this new situation, the principle of allotment by lot needs to be restated. This situation is also constitutive for the choice of leaders to apportion the land. From the nine tribes and the half-tribe, these leaders are selected (34:16-29). In short, the first part has two sections: the removal of the

Canaanites from their land (33:50-56) and the boundaries on four sides of the land (34:1-12). The second part also consists of two sections: the rightful recipients of the land (34:13-15) and the leaders responsible for the apportionment of the land (34:16-29).

(33) Yahweh Speech: Instructions about the Apportionment of the Levites (35:1-8)

I. Setting: geographical	35:1a
II. Yahweh's speech	35:1b-8
A. Speech formula	35:1b
B. Speech proper: instructions	35:2-8
1. Summary of content	35:2
2. Elaboration	35:3-8
a. Regarding the nature of the donations	35:3-7
(1) Donations: the towns and the pasturelands	35:3
(2) Scope of the donations	35:4-7
(a) By size of towns via measurement of the pasturelands	35:4-5
(b) By numbers of towns	35:6-7
b. Regarding the donators: method of giving the towns	35:8

This unit is the narrative of Yahweh's speech to Moses concerning the apportionment to the Levites. The Levites receive in total forty-eight towns with their pasturelands as their allotment from the inheritance that other tribes possess. The sequence of the Levites receiving their apportionment after the other tribes have received theirs follows a well-recognized pattern throughout Numbers.[174] For the structure of this unit itself, two factors are operative: the aspect related to the towns and that of the pasturelands that the Levites received. Since the pasturelands are described as "surrounding the towns" (v. 2b) and since they are for cattle, livestock, and animals (v. 3b), the aspect of the pasturelands is subordinate to the aspect of the towns. As Milgrom argues, the pastureland increases with the growth of the town, which suggests the dependency of the pastureland on the town.[175] This reinforces the previous point.

---

174. At least three incidents are noticeable in Numbers: (1) for the Levites in 1:47-54 after 1:1-46 for the other tribes; (2) chs. 3–4 after ch. 2; and (3) 26:57-62 after 26:1-56.

175. Milgrom, *Numbers,* pp. 502-4. He presents a convincing argument for the realistic plans for the towns and their pasturelands.

The structure of 35:1-8 has two parts: the geographical setting (v. 1a) and the report of Yahweh's speech to Moses (vv. 1b-8). The report is constructed by a summary (v. 2) and its elaboration (vv. 3-8). This division is justifiable because of the relationship between these units. Not only the content but also the order of verse 2 determine the content and the order of the verses that follow it (vv. 3-8). Verse 2 summarizes Yahweh's command to Moses, which is classified as two things: (1) how the Levites received donations from the rest of the Israelites, and (2) what the Levites should receive from them.

This order is reversed in the elaboration of the summary, with the nature of the donations first and the donors second. The donations were the towns and the pastureland. The pastureland is described in detail, which in turn suggests its dependency on the towns (v. 3). The scope of the towns is indicated by their size and number (vv. 4-7). It is calculable since the number of the towns to be allotted the Levites was already decided and since their size could be estimated via measurement of their associated pasturelands. The scope of the towns is set apart from the description of the method because the former focuses on the donations, the towns themselves, while the latter points to the donors, the tribes who should give the towns from their apportionment according to the size of each tribe.

(34) Yahweh Speech: Instructions about the City of Refuge for Involuntary Homicide (35:9-34)

I. Introductory Yahweh speech formula	35:9
II. Speech proper	35:10-34
A. Command to speak	35:10a
B. Content: instructions on asylum for involuntary homicide	35:10b-34
1. Summary of main instruction	35:10b-12
a. Setting: temporal	35:10b
b. Two functions of the cities of refuge	35:11-12
(1) Initial flight from the avenger of blood	35:11
(2) Wait for the trial before the congregation	35:12
2. Elaboration	35:13-34
a. Involved elements for the case	35:13-32
(1) The cities of refuge	35:13-15
(a) Six cities	35:13-14
(b) For both native and nonnative Israelites	35:15
(2) The nature of involuntary homicide	35:16-23

(a) Defined indirectly: compared to intentional homicide	35:16-21
(b) Defined directly	35:22-23
(3) Prescription of procedure for the trial	35:24-32
(a) Specifics for the case in hand	35:24-29
(b) General regulations	35:30-32
b. Theological justification for the resolution of any homicide	35:33-34

This unit is a narrative about a speech of Yahweh to Moses concerning provisions of asylum for those who kill a person without intent. It begins with a report of the establishment of the cities of refuge implemented after entrance into the land of Canaan (v. 10b). This provision of Yahweh is mentioned in 35:6 as part of the apportionment for the Levites and is also narrated slightly differently in Deuteronomy 4:41-43 and Deuteronomy 19:1-13: it is fulfilled by Joshua in Joshua 20:1-9.[176] In overview, these cities are to function as the places of asylum for murderers who have killed a person inadvertently. Within these cities, Israel must resolve the problem of the pollution of the land caused by the shedding of blood because Yahweh also dwells in the land.

The structure of the unit reveals this overview in detail. Yahweh's instructions on asylum for involuntary homicide (vv. 10b-34) have two parts: a summary of two specific functions of the cities of refuge (vv. 11-12) and their elaboration (vv. 13-34). The concept of these cities provides the basic frame for the unit in that the term "city of refuge" occurs throughout the unit (vv. 11-15, 25-28, 32). However, the focus is on two specific functions of these cities: they are places to initially flee from the avenger of blood for one who kills a person without intent (v. 11), and they are places for that person to stay both before and after the trial in front of the congregation (vv. 12 and 25). Considering the institution of the blood vengeance in the ancient Near East, that is, "the blood of the slain was avenged by his nearest kinsman, called *go'el* [גאל], either by taking the blood of the slayer or of a member of the latter's family or by accepting monetary compensation,"[177] these functions point to the right of asylum for the accused murderer until the case is adjudicated. The necessity of a trial, which restrains the tribal practice of blood revenge, is the generative conceptuality for the unit. It also separates verses 10b-12 from

176. For a comparison of these passages, see Milgrom, *Numbers,* pp. 504-8.

177. Milgrom, *Numbers,* p. 291. Against this background, Milgrom observes six modifications in Israel's laws regarding homicide and the system of cities of refuge and concludes with the revolutionary principle that "the right of asylum is limited solely to the unpremeditated manslayer."

the following verses (vv. 13-34) in that the latter elaborates on elements involved in the trial. The elaboration has two sections: the practice of the trial (vv. 13-32) and the theological justification for the resolution of the case (vv. 33-34). The first section is divided into three subsections. First, verses 13-15 provide information regarding the cities of refuge: six cities are designated, three for the land of the Transjordan and three for the land of Canaan, and these cities are designed for the benefit of all the inhabitants of the land, whether they are native or nonnative Israelites. Second, verses 16-23 define the nature of involuntary homicide. It is indirectly demonstrated by listing six cases of deliberate homicide (vv. 16-21) and is directly defined by three concrete examples. By juxtaposing the detailed description of deliberate homicide, the essential nature of involuntary homicide is drawn. The intention of the killer is revealed by the kind of instrument used and by the state of the killer's mind. This intention is determined by the congregation following a prescribed procedure (vv. 24-32), which consists of two parts: the prescription of the case at hand (vv. 24-29) and the regulations for a general case of murder (vv. 30-32). These two subsections are unified by the concepts of the cities of refuge and the timing of the death of the high priest (vv. 25, 28, 32). The elaboration ends with the theological justification that any homicide case must be resolved with the murderer's death if the murder is found to be intentional, or with the confinement of the murderer in the cities of refuge until the death of the high priest if it is found to be unintentional, all because Yahweh dwells in the land among the Israelites.

(35) Report of Legislation concerning the Inheritance of Heiresses (36:1-12)

I. Further inquiry regarding the inheritance of heiresses	36:1-4
A. Introductory matters	36:1
1. Identity of the inquirers	36:1a
2. Identity of those hearing the inquiry	36:1b
B. Inquiry proper: speech	36:2-4
1. Principles for allotment of inheritance	36:2
2. Problem	36:3
3. Supporting argument	36:4
II. Solution	36:5-12
A. Solution proper	36:5-9
1. Introductory statement for speech	36:5a
2. Speech	36:5b-9
a. For the inquiry: positive answer	36:5b

This unit is clearly related to the case of the daughters of Zelophehad (27:1-11). Their case is presupposed and provides the cause for the inquiry brought by the heads of the Manasseh tribe (v. 3). Zelophehad's daughters received the right to inherit their father's property in 27:8b-11, and now they are obligated to marry within their own tribe so that their father's property will be maintained intact (v. 6). The report of their obedience to Yahweh's commandment, that is, of their marriages to their uncle's sons, thus keeping the inheritance within the tribe of Manasseh (vv. 10-12), marks the appropriate ending for this unit.

However, the case itself is not the ultimate interest of this unit. The focus is to provide the generalized legislation that each tribe should preserve its original inheritance for future generations. Several pieces of evidence support this conclusion: (1) the principle of allotting the land by lot is mentioned as the starting point of the case (v. 2a); (2) another regulation regarding the property, that is, the Jubilee, is used to strengthen the case (v. 4); (3) a statement of purpose is attached both to the case of the daughters of Zelophehad (v. 7a) and to the general regulation concerning inheritance (v. 8b); and (4) a statement of the ultimate purpose of the regulation, that is, tribal property must be kept intact, is reaffirmed (vv. 7b, 9, 12b). The case of the daughters of Zelophehad is secondary and subordinate to the dominant interest of the unit. It launches inquiry and leads to the legislation concerning the inheritance of heiresses. In terms of structure, this legislation is framed by the basic pattern of the inquiry-solution. Thus, the structure of 36:1-12 has two parts: the inquiry concerning the inheritance of heiresses (vv. 1-4) and its result (vv. 5-12).

(36) Subscription (36:13)

This unit is unique in that it has only one verse and no mention of the name of Moses (cf. 21:1-3, 21-31; 22:1–24:45). Since it is short, syntactical observation provides the key to its structure. It is divided into two parts: the subject matter (v. 13a) and a geographical modifier (v. 13b). The first part has a demonstrative plural pronoun as the subject, added to by a relative clause qualifying the subject matter with the identities of the speaker and both direct and indirect addressees. The second part modifies the first by indicating where the subject matter has been spoken. As argued above, the geographical notation of the second part is subordinate to the subject matter and plays a secondary role. It shows that the limitation of the possible antecedents of "these" covers the narrative tentatively as far as 15:1, regardless of the geographical reference in verse 13b.

C. The Macrostructure of Numbers 10:11–36:13

1. Preliminary Remarks

Numbers 10:11–36:13, as a unit, provides explicit information in subunits organized by literary features and specific content. An exhaustive list of examples is unnecessary, but a few are noticeable and worthy of mention. The text consists of thirty-six literary units; of these, ten are constituted by a Yahweh speech formula[178] and thirty-two contain Moses' name.[179] The text is a mixture of narratives, laws, and Yahweh's instructions[180] and is a composite of the Priestly and Yahwistic-Elohistic (or pre-Priestly) sources.[181] It also holds several itinerary notices that indicate Israel's march from the wilderness of Sinai through various places to the plains of Moab.[182] It contains narratives of Israel's rebellions against Moses, against Moses and Aaron, and ultimately against Yahweh; narratives of their encounters with the hostile power of the indigenous peoples; and stories obscure in nature, such as that of the wood

---

178. 15:1-16, 17-31, 37-41; 17:16-26 (Eng. 17:1-11); 19:1-22; 27:12-23; 28:1–30:1 (Eng. 28:1–29:40); 31:1-54; 35:1-8, 9-34.

179. The four exceptions are 21:1-3, 21-31; 22:1–24:25; 36:13.

180. Eleven can be classified as the laws: 15:1-16, 17-31, 37-41; 17:27–18:32 (Eng. 17:12–18:32); 19:1-22; 27:12-23; 28:1–30:1 (Eng. 28:1–29:40); 30:2-17 (Eng. 30:1-16); 33:50–34:29; 35:1-8, 9-34.

181. The precise distinction between the Priestly and the Yahwistic-Elohistic materials within Num 10:11–36:13 is not the primary interest of this book. For this distinction, see B. W. Anderson's "Analytical Outline of the Pentateuch," which is the supplement to Noth's *A History of Pentateuchal Traditions.*

182. 10:12, 33; 11:35; 12:16; 20:1, 22; 21:4, 10-20, 33; 22:1; cf. 33:3-49.

gatherer on the Sabbath or that of the daughters of Zelophehad (for which Moses needed a further divine revelation) or that of Balaam's blessing of Israel despite Balak's attempt to curse them.

This explicit information, however, does not indicate how the thirty-six units are organized. Are all of these units compositionally equal to each other or are they situated on hierarchical levels that suggest varying compositional significance among them? If they are related to each other in either of these ways, what are the constitutive criteria for their relationships?

It is immediately clear that the thirty-six units are not simply set side by side. On the surface level, they are related on the basis of chronological, geographical, and itinerary frameworks. First, on a fundamental level, any narrative must make chronological sense; otherwise, it loses its narrative nature. Some of these units contain chronological notices, such as a precise date (10:11; 33:38) or a simple indicator (tomorrow [11:18; 16:7, 16], on the next day [17:6, 23], at the time of the first-ripe grapes [13:20], first month [20:1], etc.) or a notice referring to a specific event (after the plague [26:1], 33:3). Since no one denies that the literary nature of the whole of these units is narrative, chronological sequence is one of the organizing principles for the units. Chronologically, Numbers 10:11–36:13 unfolds Israel's forty-year wilderness experience. Second, geographical notices in these units show that the events occurred in various places. However, some units are grouped together and distinguished from others according to their association with a specific locality. Even if some units do not have any topographical/geographical indications, they can be clustered as belonging to the locality in their immediate literary context, or at least they can be considered to be nongeographically oriented material. For example, of thirty-six units, twenty-five units are concentrated in two localities: Kadesh and the plains of Moab. Eleven units could be classified as units of Kadesh, even though only three units (13:1–14:45; 20:1-13, 14-21) mention Kadesh; the other eight units are included simply because they are located between these three units.[183] In the same way, fifteen units could be clustered as units of the plains of Moab, although only six units contain this geographical notice (22:1–24:25; 25:19–26:65 [Eng. 26:1-65]; 31:1-54; 33:50–34:29; 35:1-8; 36:13).[184] This example reveals that two localities have been highlighted and further implies that geographical notices are indicative of the organization of the thirty-six units. Third, the itinerary notices mentioned above certainly suggest that the

---

183. These eight units are as follows: 15:1-6, 17-31, 32-26, 37-41; 16:1–17:15 (Eng. 16:1-50); 17:16-24 (Eng. 17:1-11); 17:27–18:32 (Eng. 17:12–18:32); 19:1-22.

184. Others are 25:1-18; 27:1-11, 12-23; 28:1–30:1 (Eng. 28:1–29:40); 30:2-17 (Eng. 30:1-16); 32:1-42; 33:1-49; 35:9-34; 36:1-12.

thirty-six units are not simply laid out side by side but are arranged on the basis of the forward movement of Israel from the wilderness of Sinai to the plains of Moab. Since the whole of these units is a narrative based on an itinerary, the sequence of Israel's movement from one place to another can be traced and eventually followed. From the aspect of chronology, geography, and itinerary, no one would suggest that the thirty-six units are a collection of materials without any organization or arrangement to them.

However, chronological, geographical, and itinerary factors put together are not the dominant principle for the structure of the thirty-six units, although they are some of the organizing principles. For a text to be chronological means that it not only indicates the order of nature but also points to the order of causality. The sequence from cause to effect is in fact responsible for the order of thought and movement within some individual units,[185] but this sequence could hardly be applicable to the relationships among all the units. The order of these units certainly does not follow the order of historical occurrence of the events that they report. Even if a sequential arrangement is identifiable within the literary world of all of the units, the focus should be on the concept of this arrangement and not on the chronological sequence itself since it is clear that the units in their entirety are not a complete chronological record of Israel's forty years of movement.

However, the itinerary, coupled with geographical indicators, shows more about the form and content of these units than does chronology. The itinerary not only reveals Israel's movement from one location to another but also highlights the importance of a specific place in which they stayed relative to others. Thus, many commentators propose the organization of the thirty-six units based on the combination of itinerary and geographical factors. For example, the outlines of Ashley, Davies, and Fearer are based on the itinerary coupled with the highlighted places of Kadesh and the plains of Moab.[186] No

---

185. Narratives that report Israel's rebellion against Moses and Yahweh (11:35–12:16; 16:1–17:15; 21:4-9) show the movement of thought from cause to effect.

186. Ashley, *The Book of Numbers*, pp. 15-17; E. W. Davies, *Numbers*, pp. lxxi-lxxiv; Fearer, *Wars in the Wilderness*, p. 383. Fearer's outline is as follows:

I. The Migratory-Sanctuary Campaign from Sinai to Kadesh	10:11–20:21
A. The Campaign to Kadesh	10:11–12:16
B. Collection of Events at Kadesh	13:1–20:21
II. The Migratory-Sanctuary Campaign from Kadesh to the Plains of Moab	20:22–36:13
A. The Campaign to the Plains of Moab	20:22–22:1
B. Collection of Events on the Plains of Moab	22:2–36:13

Although Fearer's interest is not in the macrostructure of Num 10:11–36:13, his outline is conceptually inconsistent. If the nature of Israel's march is defined as "the migratory-sanctuary

doubt the combination of itinerary and geographical aspects is evident in the titles of their outlines. However, their outlines of the macrostructural level differ from each other: Ashley (I. 10:11–12:16; II. 13:1–19:22; III. 20:1–22:1; and IV. 22:2–36:13); Davies (I. 10:11–22:1 and II. 22:2–36:13); Fearer (I. 10:11–20:21 and II. 20:22–36:13). Moreover, they designate materials for Kadesh differently, although they designate the same material (10:11–12:16) for "the journey or campaign from Mt. Sinai to Kadesh (the wilderness of Paran)." For the material in and around Kadesh, Ashley includes the material up to 19:22, Davies to 20:13, and Fearer to 20:21. Consequently, they differ regarding what materials are to be included as "the journey or campaign from Kadesh to the plains of Moab," although they agree that 22:2–36:13 relates occurrences on the plains of Moab. If the combination of itinerary and geographical notices is the constitutive factor for the organization of the thirty-six units, then only Fearer's outline is correct. Verse 20:22 has an itinerary that the Israelites "set out from Kadesh" and "came to Mount Hor," which indicates the beginning of the journey toward the plains of Moab. Although Kadesh is mentioned in 20:1 and 20:14, these verses have no indication of Israel's movement from Kadesh; rather, they begin a report of what happened at Kadesh. Thus, Ashley and Davies are not consistent in using their own criterion. They might have employed other factors too for the outline, particularly for 10:11–22:1.

---

campaign," then their staying in both Kadesh (I.B.) and the plains of Moab (II.B.) should be characterized accordingly. Whatever happened in these places must be related to Israel's campaign. Moreover, the choice of the word "collection" for these sections must be reconsidered, because this word connotes something put together without organizing principles. What Fearer's outline suggests is that he uses language that points to the conceptual aspect of the nature of Israel's migration, the migratory-sanctuary campaign, but that he outlines Num 10:11–36:13 based on the combination of itinerary and geographical references, and not based on conceptuality.

Dozeman's outline ("The Book of Numbers," p. 23) may also be considered as one based on both itinerary and geographical notations, though he uses a more general term (the wilderness) than Kadesh: for example, 10:11–21:35, The Wilderness Journey of the First Generation; 22:1–36:13, Preparing for Canaan on the Plains of Moab. However, the titles evoke many questions. Who prepares for Canaan? The first or the second generation? Why is it necessary to mention the "first" generation, which in turn implies the transition of generations? When does the transition occur? What is the purpose of the wilderness journey of the first generation? Why is there a need for another preparation for Canaan, if the Sinai event (Exod 19–Num 10:10) is understood as God's preparation of the Israel for the land of Canaan? To be sure, Dozeman answers these questions throughout his commentary. The point is not his usage of other factors (the existence of two generations and the goal of Israel's journey) along with itinerary and geographical notations to define the nature of two parts of Num 10:11–36:13. The point is that he chooses the latter over against the former as constitutive for these parts. And yet, he seems not to provide the rationale for this choice.

Differences in what material ought to be included are understandable and are not the issue. The issue is whether the differences result from a simple, inconsistent following of one's own chosen criterion or are indicative of conceptual conflicts within the outline. As the example shows, particularly in Fearer's outline, the itinerary combined with geographical indicators is at best responsible for the composition of the thirty-six units of Numbers 10:11–36:13. This criterion is responsible for the organization of the explicit information of the text drawn from its surface level. But the organization reflects neither what happened during the journey from Sinai to Kadesh and to the plains of Moab nor why Israel journeyed toward these places. Outlines based on the combination of itinerary and geographical indicators fall short of representing the substantive content of the text. The task of reconstructing the structure of the thirty-six units must go beyond examining their explicit and formal aspects to an explanation of their content because the substantive content constitutes the essential part of these units in their own right, on their terms. The substantive discussion compels the exegete seeking to determine the text's structure to take the implicit information underneath the text into consideration.

2. The Role of Numbers 13:1–14:45

The thirty-six units of Numbers 10:11–36:13 are related in one way or the other to the questions that they in their entirety present. Three sets of questions are important. First, why were the Israelites punished severely for their rebellions, while similar rebellions before Sinai were met with Yahweh's gracious provisions without punishments?[187] Before Sinai, the Israelites were sharply reprimanded by Yahweh, but no one died from Yahweh's punishment, except in the case of Nadab and Abihu's unholy fire (Lev 10:1-7).[188] After Sinai, how-

---

187. There are at least fifteen accounts of Israel's rebellions against Moses, against Moses and Aaron, and ultimately against Yahweh reported in the books of Exodus to Numbers. Of the fifteen, seven are located before and during the sojourn in the wilderness of Sinai (Exod 5:15–6:1; 14:10-31; 15:22-27; 16:1-36; 17:1-7; 32:1-35; Lev 10:1-7); the other eight are grouped together in the wilderness after Sinai (Num 11:1-3, 4-34; 11:35–12:16; 13:1–14:45; 16:1–17:15; 20:1-13; 21:4-9; 25:1-18). See Noth, *A History of Pentateuchal Traditions*, pp. 122-30; G. W. Coats, *Rebellion in the Wilderness: The Murmuring Motif in the Wilderness Traditions of the Old Testament* (Nashville: Abingdon, 1968); A. C. Tunyogi, *The Rebellions of Israel* (Richmond: John Knox, 1969).

188. Even in the case of the golden calf (Exod 32:1-35), it was Moses who could not control his anger and ordered the Levites to kill the people (32:25-28). In contrast, Yahweh was persuaded by Moses' intercession (32:14), and Yahweh further provided guidance and delayed the punishment (32:34). Although the text states that Yahweh sent a plague on the people, it mentions no report of any casualties related to that plague (32:35).

ever, each rebellion results in a heavy punishment, usually in death (11:4-34; 16:1–17:15; 21:4-9; 25:1-18), in the march's delay (11:35–12:16), or in the termination of the prophetic leadership of Moses and Aaron (20:1-13).[189] What, then, is the function of the rebellion narratives reported after Sinai? Are they significant simply because they indicate Israel's rebellious nature against an established leadership? Or does their significance depend on their specific content and location within Numbers 10:11–36:13?

Second, why did the Israelites not enter the promised land right after leaving the wilderness of Sinai? Why did they have to take a detour to enter it, through the Transjordan territories? Was entering the promised land not from the south but from the east of the Jordan River Israel's original plan when they left Sinai? Why did they spend forty years wandering, and not a shorter or longer period of time?

Third, why did the Israelites receive additional cultic regulations outside of the holy mountain, Mount Sinai? Were the divine commandments and ordinances in Exodus 20–24, the entire book of Leviticus, and Numbers 5:1–10:10 not enough for them to live a just and holy life once they entered the promised land?

These three groups of questions are distinctive enough to be treated separately, but they are related in that *they point explicitly to Israel's failure to conquer the promised land from the south*, a failure that becomes explicit in 13:1–14:45.[190]

The spy incident reported in chapters 13–14 in and of itself is about Israel's distrust in Yahweh's ability to bring them into the land of Canaan. Its

---

189. Cf. B. S. Childs, *The Book of Exodus: A Critical, Theological Commentary*, OTL (Philadelphia: Westminster, 1974), pp. 258-59. Childs observes two story patterns among the rebellion narratives:

Pattern I	Pattern II
(1) Initial need	(1) Initial complaint
(2) Complaint	(2) Yahweh's anger and punishment
(3) Moses' intercession	(3) Moses' intercession
(4) Need met by Yahweh's intervention	(4) Cessation of punishment

For Pattern I, Childs includes Exod 15:22-27; 17:1-7; Num 20:1-13; for Pattern II, Num 11:1-3; 17:6-15; 21:4-10. However, his inclusion of Num 20:1-13 in Pattern I is incorrect. Num 20:1-13 is the story about the denial of the prophetic leadership of Moses and Aaron, which is Yahweh's punishment for their distrust in Yahweh and their failure to show Yahweh's holiness to the people (20:12). Childs's two patterns need to be further analyzed with a thorough exegesis of each of the fifteen rebellion narratives above.

190. One may question what purpose this thesis statement serves, and whether it reflects the Judean polemic against northern Israel or Judean self-critique. These questions will be discussed in the concluding remarks.

significance, however, lies in the fact that it is the climax of Israel's rebellions that began right after they were liberated from Egypt, and the rebellions occurring after chapters 13–14 have a different function from those that occurred before these chapters.[191] Moreover, the spy incident contains Israel's first military encounter with other people (14:39-45) after Sinai. This military encounter is also their first and only defeat within Numbers. Furthermore, all additional divine commandments and regulations are promulgated after chapters 13–14, and the majority of them deal with the land and/or the promised land that Israel could not conquer.[192] If the Israelites had trusted and obeyed Yahweh, specifically Yahweh's ability to bring them into the promised land as represented by the conviction of Caleb and Joshua (13:30; 14:6-9), they would have conquered the land of Canaan and would not have wandered on a forty-year march. Israel's failure to enter the promised land right after they left the wilderness of Sinai is in principle presupposed in the rest of Numbers and in the materials from the book of Deuteronomy to Joshua 12, even up to Judges 2:10.

In addition to the explicit relation of the three groups of questions regarding the spy incident, these questions also implicitly point to the nature of Israel's march from 10:11 on, the sanctuary campaign. According to Knierim, there are at least three generic aspects of Israel's march portrayed in Numbers: migratory, military, and sacral-cultic.[193] Unlike Dozeman, who does not compare and distinguish the relative importance among these aspects, Knierim argues that the military campaign aspect is dominant and superordinate to the migratory and sacral-cultic aspects. He concludes that Numbers represents the genre of the sanctuary campaign. In Numbers, Israel is organized as the sanc-

---

191. The following exegesis of chs. 13–14 will substantiate this point. See pp. 218-35 in this study.

192. Of eleven divine instructions, three are about the promised land (33:50–34:29; 35:1-8, 9-34), two are to be observed when they entered the promised land (15:1-16, 17-31), and five presuppose settlement in the promised land (15:37-41; 17:27–18:32 [Eng. 17:12–18:32]; 19:1-22; 28:1–30:1 [Eng. 28:1–29:40]; 30:2-17 [Eng. 30:1-16]). The final instruction concerns the commission of Joshua as the successor of Moses (27:12-23). It is indirectly related to the promised land, since Joshua is the one who will bring Israel into it after Moses' death.

193. A migration covers the aspect of the ongoing translocation of Israel's camp from one place to another. It is indicated by the cycle of decamping and encamping expressed in the combination of נסע and חנה. A campaign includes the military aspect of their movement, which is reflected in the purpose of the census (1:2-3; cf. 26:1-3), the order of the march (2:1-34; cf. 10:11-36), and several battle reports (14:39-45; 21:1-3, 21-31, 32-35; 31:1-12). A pilgrimage yields the sacral-cultic aspect of their movement and is represented by the hierarchy of cultic personnel in the organization of the campaign (chs. 3–4), the cultic symbols whose function is combined with the military campaign (sanctuary, the ark, the trumpet, the tent, the tabernacle, the cloud).

tuary host and marches from one place to another toward the promised land while they receive additional cultic regulations and resolve inner struggles caused by both physical needs, leadership challenges, and military conflicts with hostile powers. The objective of their campaign is nevertheless unchanged, that is, the conquest of the land of Canaan, the promised land.

If Israel set out from the wilderness of Sinai as an "epiphanic military camp" with the objective of the conquest of the promised land and its permanent settlement, the question becomes: When did they have an actual opportunity to accomplish this objective? Again, the answer is given in the spy story in chapters 13–14. This story shows that Israel was located at the edge of the land of Canaan, had an opportunity to conquer the land for the first time since it was liberated from the bondage of Egypt, forfeited that chance by not trusting Yahweh, and ultimately failed to enter the promised land. Therefore, chapters 13–14 provide possible answers explicitly and implicitly for the three kinds of questions above. In other words, *the spy story is related to the substantive content of the thirty-six units and thus signals a structurally decisive break within Numbers 10:11–36:13.*

Numbers 10:11–36:13, then is divided into two parts:

The Narrative of Israel's Forty-Year Campaign
in the Wilderness   10:11–36:13

I. Event: failed campaign to enter the promised land
   from the south   10:11–14:45
   A. Programmatic departure   10:11–36
   B. Distrust of Yahweh's ability to fulfill the promise   11:1–14:45
II. Consequence: entrance into the promised land delayed
    by forty years   15:1–36:13
    A. Completion of Yahweh's punishment of all the Exodus
       generation: the death of the Exodus generation   15:1–20:29
    B. Actualization of Yahweh's forgiveness for the Exodus
       generation: the call of the new generation as the new
       carrier of the divine land promise   21:1–36:13

Its thirty-six units are structured by the concept of Israel's failed campaign to conquer the promised land from the south. The units prior to 13:1–14:45 function to highlight Israel's distrust of Yahweh's leadership, power, and ability to fulfill the promise that Yahweh made to their ancestors. The units following it unfold Yahweh's response to their failure: entering the promised land has been delayed and will be fulfilled by the next generation, once the Exodus generation dies out in the wilderness during their forty years of wandering.

The claim that Numbers 13–14 marks the decisive break within the macrostructure of Numbers 10:11–36:13 is not self-evident, but textual and compositional evidence will substantiate the claim. From the textual evidence the structure of chapters 13–14 examined below will show the expansion of its generative conceptuality from Israel's failure to follow Yahweh's intention to bring them into the promised land and their failure to let Yahweh fulfill the divine promise to their ancestors (giving them the land of Canaan). The focus of the structure, however, is Israel's failure to conquer the land of Canaan from the south. Consequently, other factors, such as the intercessory role of Moses, the positive behavior of Caleb (and Joshua), and "the death of the old generation and the birth of the new generation," as Olson argues, play a secondary and supportive role to this concept. Compositionally, the substantive content of Numbers 13–14 is unique in comparison to other narratives related to Israel's sanctuary campaign reported in 10:11–36:13, and chapters 13–14 are located at a distinctive place within 10:11–36:13, especially in relation to the location of 21:1-3. Israel's campaigns narrated in Numbers 13–14 and 21:1-3 are different from other military accounts because they are campaigns for the conquest of the promised land, not of any other territories, such as the land of the Amorites or the land of Bashan. Moreover, while Numbers 13–14 and 21:1-3 share in common the nature of their campaigns, the results of the campaigns are totally opposite: the former reports Israel's defeat, the latter Israel's victory. This result, coupled with other textual evidence to be discussed later, implies that the campaign in 21:1-3 is executed by the next generation. Unit 21:1-3 marks a transition from Yahweh's punishment of Israel's failure, the death of all the Exodus generation, to Yahweh's forgiveness, carrying out once again the land promise through the new generation. However, this transition is structurally subordinate to Israel's failure to conquer the promised land from the south. Since the concept of the generational transition stems from the spies incident in chapters 13–14 and is part of Yahweh's response to Israel's failure to trust Yahweh's intention to bring them into Canaan, this concept is operative only in the material after chapters 13–14. The transition from "the old generation" to "the new generation" is the structural signal for 15:1–36:13, but not for 10:11–36:13.

These textual and compositional evidences reveal *the generative infratextual concept beneath the whole of Numbers 10:11–36:13: Israel's failure to conquer the promised land from the south, which in turn indicates their failure to let Yahweh fulfill to their ancestors the promise that they will occupy the promised land and live permanently in it.* Accordingly, Numbers 13–14 provides the rationale for the structural coherence of the units following it. The structure of 15:1–20:29 represents the actualization of Yahweh's punishment of the Exodus generation including their leaders — the death of the Exodus generation in the wilderness during forty years of wandering — and the structure of 21:1–36:13 points to the new wilderness experience of the next generation at the end of the forty-year campaign.

a. Textual Evidence

Most commentators treat chapters 13–14 with utmost interest. The intense treatment of these chapters has covered the well-known composite nature of their literary texture,[194] their thematic issues,[195] and traditio-historical issues lying behind them.[196] The present section, however, is interested in the generative conceptuality of the final form of these chapters.

The following structure of chapters 13–14 will serve as a basis for discussion.

Historical Narrative concerning Israel's Failure	
to Enter the Promised Land from the South	13:1–14:45
I. Report of the event	13:1–14:35
A. The reconnaissance	13:1-24
1. Yahweh's command: send the spies	13:1-2
2. Moses' execution of Yahweh's command	13:3-24
a. Execution formula	13:3
b. Explanation	13:4-24
(1) The list of chosen scouts	13:4-16

---

194. Gray, *A Critical and Exegetical Commentary on Numbers*, pp. 128-33; Noth, *Numbers*, p. 101; Budd, *Numbers*, pp. 141-44, 150-55; Milgrom, *Numbers*, pp. 387-92; E. W. Davies, *Numbers*, pp. 126-32. Davies provides a summary of previous scholarship on chs. 13–14. The recognition of inconsistencies, redundancies, and duplications within the text has led most commentators to focus on the questions of its origin and on distinguishing its various layers. Cf. Coats, *Rebellion in the Wilderness*, pp. 137-39; for a detailed analysis of source-critical problems, see Boorer, *The Promise of the Land as Oath*, p. 331, n. 7.

195. Noth, *Numbers*, p. 101. Although Noth recognizes the conflation of several literary sources, he is interested in these chapters as "the first indication of the conquest theme."

196. Some examples of traditio-historical issues in Num 13–14 are the history of the Calebites (their tribal and territorial relations to other tribes) and the tradition of the spy story (its transformation from a conquest to a wilderness tradition). For a good summary of the issues and a bibliography, see Olson, *The Death of the Old and the Birth of the New*, pp. 132-38; M. Sweeney, "The Wilderness Traditions of the Pentateuch: A Reassessment of Their Function and Intent in Relation to Exodus 32–34," in *Society of Biblical Literature 1989 Seminar Papers*, ed. D. J. Lull (Atlanta: Scholars Press, 1989), pp. 291-99.

Numbers 13–14 moves forward by means of the dominant factor in the book of Numbers: Yahweh's plan or will to bring the Israelites into the promised land. Four parts are easily identifiable: the scouts' reconnaissance (13:1-24), their reports (13:25-33), various responses including Yahweh's (14:1-35), and the actualization of punishment (14:36-45). Of these four parts, the first three hang together to report the event itself, whereas the fourth addresses what actually happened to both the scouts and the people as a whole. Since the fourth part focuses on the fate of both the twelve scouts and the people, it reveals their fate to be more than a consequence of the people's negative reaction to the scouts' report. Rather, it shows that Yahweh's punishment is realized both by the scouts and the people. Thus, the structure of Numbers 13–14 has two parts: the report of the event (13:1–14:35) and its aftermath (14:36-45).

The first part consists of three sections: the reconnaissance (13:1-24), the scouts' report (13:25-33), and the reactions to the report (14:1-35). The first section announces Yahweh's plan to bring Israel into the promised land; the second redefines the plan with the negative evaluation of the majority of the scouts; and the third section reports Israel's rejection of Yahweh's plan in an unprecedented way and Yahweh's response to Israel's rejection (the death of the entire Exodus generation and delayed fulfillment of Yahweh's promise: Israel will enter the promised land in the next generation).

The operative concept for each section has been expanded as the story line progresses. Yahweh's intention to bring the people into the promised land is associated with the Exodus and wilderness motifs and is ultimately connected to Yahweh's promise to their ancestors, giving them the land of Canaan (Gen 12:7). In light of this conceptual expansion, the generative infraconceptuality responsible for the structure of Numbers 13–14 is Israel's failure to fulfill Yahweh's promise to bring them into the land of Canaan. Israel had a chance to do so, but forfeited it. Yahweh's punishment begins to be actualized in the second part (14:36-45). Yahweh's punishment of all the scouts except Caleb and Joshua takes place immediately, while Yahweh's punishment of the people as a whole awaits fulfillment and unfolds in detail throughout the rest of Numbers.

(1) Yahweh's Intention

Yahweh's plan to bring Israel into the promised land is reflected in the beginning of the narrative. As 13:1-2 indicates, sending the men to reconnoiter the land is Yahweh's own command, not Moses' or Israel's idea. Verse 3 reports Moses' execution of the command (cf. 17a). In the parallel narrative of Deuteronomy 1:19-46, it is the people who request Moses to send out the spies. Note that their request (1:22) comes right after Yahweh's command to go up and take possession of the land and Yahweh's encouragement not to fear or be dismayed (1:21). The people's initiative and proposal reflect their lack of confidence in Yahweh's leadership and ultimately their lack of trust in Yahweh's ability to bring them into the promised land. Compared to Deuteronomy

1:21-22, Yahweh's initiative and Moses' execution report, which follows right after Yahweh's command in Numbers 13:1-3, imply that the scouting mission is part of Yahweh's own plan for Israel.

What is Yahweh's plan for Israel specifically? First of all, the scope of the scouting mission is the land of Canaan. This land in the extant text refers to the promised land, particularly as influenced by the Priestly theology. In Yahweh's command, this land is qualified by the clause "which I am [Yahweh is] giving to the Israelites," which implies Yahweh's promise to Israel's ancestors (14:23a; cf. 14:16, 30). In the report of the scouts' reconnaissance (13:21-24), verse 21 in particular summarizes the geographical dimensions of the entire mission. The spies scouted out "the land from the wilderness of Zin to Rehob, near Lebo-hamath." This summary describes the full extent of the land of Canaan from the south to the north, and it corresponds to the description of the promised land. The wilderness of Zin is designated as the southern border of the promised land (34:3-4; Josh 15:1, 3) and Lebo-hamath as its northern boundary (34:7-9; Ezek 48:1).[197]

Second, the purpose of Yahweh's command was to gather essential military information about the land of Canaan to prepare Israel prior to a military assault. Milgrom, however, is suspicious of this point because of evidence in Yahweh's command itself, which uses תור, "to scout, seek out" (10:33; 15:39) rather than רגל, "to spy out" (21:32; Josh 7:2; Judg 18:2). For him, "to scout" (or "to explore") means "to gather information," which is not necessarily of a military nature.[198] But this verb alone is not enough to decide the exact nature and objective of Yahweh's command. The story as a whole views the scouts' mission as essentially military, more specifically, as an initial preparation for the impending military campaign. Moses' elaboration of Yahweh's command (13:17-20) demonstrates this point well. Moses commands the scouts to gather the information regarding the military strength of the land, "whether the people who live in it are strong or weak" (v. 18a), the numbers of its inhabitants, "whether they are few or many" (v. 18b), its economic resources, "whether the land they live in is good or bad" (v. 19a), its security

---

197. Milgrom, *Numbers*, pp. 102-3; E. W. Davies, *Numbers*, pp. 134-35; Sakenfeld, *Numbers*, p. 85. For the northern border, see also 1 Kgs 14:25, which states what Jeroboam II restored.

198. Milgrom, *Numbers*, pp. 102-3; E. W. Davies, *Numbers*, pp. 134-35; Sakenfeld, *Numbers*, p. 85; Dozeman, "The Book of Numbers," pp. 121-22. Dozeman highlights two different purposes for the mission based on source analysis. Accordingly, the Priestly writers consider it a theological evaluation of the whole land, whereas the pre-Priestly account sees it as a reconnaissance along the southern border for the purpose of conquest. Yet, Dozeman does not explain how to read these two together in the extant text. For him, Num 13–14 is a combination of two versions of the spy story in which each reveals its own distinguishable emphasis.

measure for a military assault, "whether the towns that they live in are unwalled or fortified" (v. 19b), and its fertility, "whether the land is rich or poor, and whether there are trees in it or not" (v. 20a). Moses' elaboration on Yahweh's command explains that the objective of the scouting mission is both to gather information to promote the goodness and desirability of the land for habitation and to gather military strategic intelligence. If the former is the sole purpose — if the conquest of the land is not the ultimate purpose for scouting — then it is not necessary for the people to fear the great status of its inhabitants (13:28-28, 32-33). Thus, Milgrom's sharp distinction between תור and רגל in Numbers 13–14 is unwarranted.[199] Instead, Yahweh's intention is to prepare the Israelites for the impending campaign into the promised land.

This intention is confirmed by the scouts' reports (13:25-33). Note the correspondences and reformulations between Moses' commission and the scouts' reports.

Elaboration of Moses' Commission	13:17-20
I. Moses' commission proper	13:17-20a
A. Execution report formula	13:17a
B. Execution proper	13:17b-20a
1. Speech formula	13:17bα1
2. Speech proper	13:17bα2-20a
a. Direction: go up (x2)	13:17bα2-β
b. Objectives	13:18-20aα
(1) General: to see the land	13:18aα
(2) Specifics	13:18aβ-20aα
(a) People: military implications: strength and numbers	13:18aβ-b
(b) Land: economic implications	13:19a
(c) Towns: military implications	13:19b
(d) Land: fertility implications	13:20aα
c. Encouragement	13:20aβ1
d. Demanding physical evidence	13:20aβ2
II. Temporal setting	13:20b

The Scouts' Reports: Objective	13:25-29
I. Summary statements	13:25-26
A. Statement regarding the scouts' return	13:25-26a

199. The same criticism goes for Wenham's interpretation of the purpose of the scouting mission (*Numbers: An Introduction and Commentary*, p. 116).

1. Duration of the scouting mission	13:25
2. Return place	13:26a
B. Statement regarding their report	13:26b
II. Report proper	13:27-29
A. Speech formula	13:27aα
B. Speech proper	13:27aβ-29
1. Concerning direction	13:27aβ-γ
2. Concerning objectives	13:27b-29
a. Land: fertile	13:27b
b. People: strong	13:28a
c. Towns	13:28b
(1) Fortified	13:28bα1
(2) Very great	13:28bα2
(3) The descendants of Anak there	13:28bβ
d. Other peoples: additional information	13:29

As these two structures indicate, the scouts' reports focus on the fertility of the land and the strength of the people and the towns. In addition to reporting the fortification of the towns, they add two more elements: that the towns are very great and that they contain the descendants of Anak, the legendary large warriors (13:33). By this addition, coupled with information concerning other peoples, they stress the formidability of the towns and people, although the land itself is definitely good and desirable.[200] The scouts' reports as a whole point to the kernel of Moses' commission as the gathering of military intelligence while, at the same time, the reports plant a seed for the people's rejection of Yahweh's plan that they should go up and take possession of the promised land. In short, the scout mission is conducted at Yahweh's initiative and command, its scope is the entire land of Canaan (the promised land in the extant text), and its concrete objective is essentially to gather military intelligence, in order to prepare Israel for their impending campaign to conquer the land.

Yahweh's intention is also confirmed by Caleb's positive evaluation of what he saw (ראה, 13:18a, 28b) when he and the other scouts went up (עלה, 13:17 [x2], 21; בוא, 13:27a) to survey the promised land.[201] Caleb exhorts, "Let us go

---

200. The term אפס כי in 13:28a also supports this reading of the scouts' report.

201. Boorer, *The Promise of the Land as Oath*, pp. 338-56. Boorer presents a detailed literary analysis of non-P materials in Num 13–14. For her, the key motif in the non-P materials is "going up" (עלה), which is expressed in the wordplay of "see" (ראה) and "possess" (ירש). Yet her interest lies in establishing the relative order of the oath texts of Exod 32:13; Num 14:23a; Num 32:11; Deut 1:35; and Deut 10:11 and not in interpreting the extant text of Num 13–14.

up (עלה) at once and possess (ירשׁ) it [the promised land], for we are well able (יכל) to overcome it" (13:30). His exhortation focuses not only on Israel's ability and readiness to fight but also on the land itself. Their military ability is in the service of conquering the promised land, which confirms Yahweh's plan for Israel. In contrast, the majority of the scouts react to Caleb by stressing only Israel's inability to war against the people: "we are not able (לא יכל) to go up (עלה) against this people, for they are stronger than we" (13:31). They exclude the central interest of Yahweh's plan, the promised land. Their reaction to Caleb shows both their negative evaluation of themselves as a sanctuary-centered military camp organized by more than 600,000 warriors, their preoccupation with the formidability of the towns and the people, and thus their neglect of the objective of their sanctuary campaign, the conquest of the promised land.

Moreover, the negative evaluation of the majority of the scouts leads them to reformulate their report for the Israelites. Initially, they reported objectively what they had seen in the land, addressing their report only to Moses (13:27-29).[202] But to the congregation, they reported their subjective evaluation of the survey, which is not the same as their report to Moses. Regarding the inhabitants of Canaan, the scouts reported essentially the same thing: that the Canaanites were strong. Their strength is suggested by the fact that the inhabitants were of "great size" and connected to the Nephilim.[203] No reference

202. Note that the summary statements of the scouts' reports (13:25-26) are directed to "Moses and Aaron and to all the congregation of the Israelites" (see the continual use of the third person plural pronoun for the recipients of their reports in v. 26). In contrast, v. 27 indicates that the scouts reported what they saw to Moses alone (see the second person singular pronoun for the sender: שלחתנו). That Moses is thought of as representing the whole people because he was the leader is not inconceivable, yet this should be proven as a common practice by citing other such instances in the Pentateuch. Yet there is a more reasonable explanation for the specific, detailed reports being directed to Moses alone. The explanation lies more in the purpose of the comparison of their reports to Moses' commission and in order to highlight the change in their reports, voiced by the majority scouts (except Caleb [and Joshua]) when they spoke to the people (13:32a-33).

Another question emerges. If Moses is the only one who heard the scouts' report in vv. 27-29, why does Caleb quiet the people before Moses in v. 30? Does v. 30 presuppose the people's overhearing the scouts' reports and reacting negatively? Was the scouts' objective report threatening enough to stir the people's hearts? Because there is no reference to the people's behavior, Budd (*Numbers*, p. 143) suggests that 13:30 belongs more naturally after 14:1, which narrates the people's loud crying and weeping. For him, 13:30 has been misplaced. (See also Coats, *Rebellion in the Wilderness*, p. 145.) In the present form of the text, however, 13:30 functions to contrast the subjective evaluations of the survey between Caleb and the rest of the scouts, to anticipate the "unfavorable report" of the latter to the people (13:32-33), and to foreshadow the people's reaction (14:1-4).

203. Olson, *Numbers*, p. 79. With reference to Gen 6:4, Olson views the Nephilim as a "semi-divine offspring of divine beings who had fallen from the heavens and mated with humans" and characterized as "semi-divine and mythological giants."

to the towns is reported, but the substantial change in their report is the description of the land. The land of Canaan is no longer a land that "flows with milk and honey" (13:27b) but a land "that devours its inhabitants" (13:32a). If the inhabitants of the land are of such great size that the Israelites are like grasshoppers compared to them, and the land itself devours them, what chance do the Israelites have of going up and taking possession of the land? With the reformulation of their report to the congregation, the majority scouts convey the message that the land itself is not worth fighting for. By adding to this report the size of the inhabitants, the Israelites' primary fear, the scouts achieve their hidden goal of denigrating the land and thus ultimately rejecting Yahweh's plan for Israel.

What has been said thus far is that Yahweh's plan was pronounced and confirmed by the scouts' objective reports, and the people heard Caleb's exhortation implied in his positive evaluation of the survey and the rest of the scouts' "unfavorable report" (13:32). The decision must be made by the people, whether or not they should go up and take possession of the land.

(2) Conceptual Expansion

Numbers 14:1-4 reports that all the people collude with the majority of the scouts against Caleb (and Joshua). The fear of the inhabitants of the land is implied, but it is not the generative force causing the people's complaint to Moses and Aaron. The force is instead their misunderstanding of the nature of the land as affected by the ill report of the majority scouts. For the people, the land of Egypt (vv. 2bα, 3b, 4b) and even the wilderness (v. 2bβ) are better than "this land," the land of Canaan, the promised land.[204] This misunderstanding compels them to refuse to go up to the land, and thus they reject Yahweh's plan entirely.

Moreover, their rejection of Yahweh's plan reaches its climax in their unprecedented plan to choose a new captain and go back to Egypt. This proposal is an attempt to reverse completely all of Yahweh's earlier works for them, particularly their liberation from Egypt. G. W. Coats understands similarly the nature and seriousness of this rebellion: "here for the first time, the murmuring is followed by a move to return to Egypt. The murmuring tradition therefore involves not simply an expression of a wish that the Exodus

---

204. The people's misunderstanding of the nature of the land is the very reason that Caleb and Joshua reemphasize the goodness of the land in the beginning of their responses to the people (14:6-9). According to these two, the land is "an exceedingly good land" and is the land that Yahweh promised to bring the people to.

had not occurred or a challenge of Moses' authority in executing the Exodus, but now an overt move to reverse the Exodus."[205] With the proposal to choose a new captain and go back to Egypt, Israel's rebellion in 14:1-4 speaks of more than their hardships in the wilderness or anticipated difficulty in accomplishing the task ahead: it speaks of a nullification of the task itself and the denial of their identity as an epiphanic military camp. Their rejection of the prospect of entering the land is their rejection of what Yahweh has done on their behalf throughout their entire journey. What all the people of Israel reject at the edge of the promised land is the God of Exodus, liberating them out of Egypt; the God of wilderness, providing the necessities for the journey; the God of Sinai, constituting them as God's covenant people; and the God of hosts, organizing them as a cultic-military camp and leading them to conquer the promised land.

The conceptual expansion from Israel's refusal to go up into the land to their rejection of Yahweh is clearly reflected in Yahweh's specification of the people's rebellion, Yahweh's intended judgment, and Moses' intercession. First, Yahweh accuses the rebellious people of being those who "despise" (נאץ, 14:11a, 23b) Yahweh. Yet, they are further identified with the Exodus and wilderness motifs: they are those who "have seen my [Yahweh's] glory and the signs that I [Yahweh] did in Egypt and in the wilderness" (14:22a). In spite of Yahweh's signs in their midst throughout the Exodus and wilderness period, as Yahweh asserts, Israel refuses to believe in Yahweh (14:11b), has tested Yahweh ten times, and has not obeyed Yahweh's voice (14:22b).

Second, Yahweh pronounces an intended judgment, the annihilation of the people with pestilence, their disinheritance, and the replacement of Israel with Moses as the new and greater nation of Yahweh (14:12). These three things correspond to Yahweh's three actions in the past, beginning at the Exodus: (1) the last time Yahweh struck with pestilence was against Pharaoh and his people in order to liberate Israel (Exod 9:15); (2) Yahweh took Israel out of Egypt as an "inheritance" (Exod 34:9); and (3) Yahweh offered to single Moses out from the Israelites to make him a great nation (Exod 32:10). As such, Yahweh wants to reverse the first two things done for Israel and insists on carrying out the initial offer to Moses at this time.

Third, Moses intercedes before Yahweh on behalf of Israel. For Moses, Yahweh's liberating power, freeing the Israelites from Egypt (14:13), and Yahweh's presence with and guidance of them in the wilderness (14:14) provide indisputable reasons for this entreaty. As Moses argues, the nations would judge Yahweh based on these aspects, if Yahweh carries out the in-

---

205. Coats, *Rebellion in the Wilderness*, p. 146; cf. Olson, *Numbers*, p. 81.

tended judgment. This reputation of Yahweh leads Moses to entreat Yahweh to pardon Israel. Moses' entreaty proper is based on Yahweh's self-predication (14:18) personally revealed to Moses in Exod 34:6-7, although Moses omits the mention of Yahweh's retribution for sin.[206] For Moses, Yahweh's steadfast love has been concretely manifested in Yahweh's dealings with Israel in the past; in addition, he also boldly entreats Yahweh to pardon Israel, just as Yahweh has pardoned them "from Egypt even until now" (14:19b). It is now obvious that the entire conceptual framework of Moses' intercession is molded by the Exodus and wilderness motifs. In short, Israel's refusal to go up into the land is not an isolated incident of rebellion but has been understood by both Yahweh and Moses in terms of Israel's behavior throughout the Exodus and wilderness period, behavior that may be characterized as a lack of trust, manifested in repeated testing of Yahweh and lack of obedience to Yahweh.[207]

The conceptual expansion goes one step further. Israel's refusal to go up into the land is connected with Yahweh's promise to Israel's ancestors. Yahweh had promised to Abraham and Sarah to give their descendants the land of Canaan (Gen 12:7). This promise is both the fundamental reason for Yahweh's liberation of Israel from Egypt and the goal of Israel's wilderness march: "I have come down to deliver them from the Egyptians, and to bring them up out of that land to a good and broad land, a land flowing with milk and honey, to the country of the Canaanites, the Hittites, the Amorites, the Perizzites, the Hivites, and the Jebusites" (Exod 3:8).[208] This promise is presupposed throughout the spy story. The land to which Yahweh commanded Moses to send spies is the land that Yahweh is giving to the Israelites; Yahweh's intended punishment in 14:12 will be interpreted by other nations as Yahweh's killing Yahweh's own people because Yahweh was not able to bring the people into the land that Yahweh swore to give them; as for punishment, Israel will not see the land that Yahweh "swore to give to their ancestors" (14:23). More specifically, the ones who are twenty years old and upward and who have complained against Yahweh shall die in the wilderness and not come into the land in which Yahweh swore to settle them (14:29-30a). Caleb and Joshua are the only ones excluded from this judgment. However, the promise itself is not nullified. Yahweh's promise to Israel's ancestors

---

206. For a comparison of Yahweh's self-predication in Num 14:18 with the similar formulations in Exod 20:5-6 and 34:6-7, see Olson, *Numbers*, pp. 82-83.

207. Boorer, *The Promise of the Land as Oath*, p. 347. Comparing 14:11a, 23b and 14:11b-23a, she asserts that the latter has been inserted between vv. 11a and 23b in order to connect the specific incident of spying out of the land with Yahweh's dealing with Israel throughout the whole period from the Exodus up to and including the spies' mission.

208. Knierim, "II. Exodus 3:7-8 in Light of Biblical Theology," pp. 130-33.

is still valid and stands, yet it will not be fulfilled by the Exodus generation, but rather by the next generation.[209]

In summary, the conceptual expansion is visible as the story unfolds. Yahweh's intention to bring Israel into the land of Canaan has been redefined by the subjective evaluation of the majority of the scouts. Their distorted characterization of the land triggers all the people not only to reject going up into the land but also to attempt to reverse the Exodus itself. This attempt, in fact, is understood by Moses and Yahweh as the nullification of Yahweh's promise of the land to Israel's ancestors. Yahweh forgives Israel, according to Moses' intercession, and grants that they will remain Yahweh's own inheritance, as Yahweh's promise of the land still stands. Yahweh also punishes them in that they will not enter the promised land but shall die in the wilderness during the forty-year wandering; even though the next generation will fulfill the promise and enter the promised land, they will still suffer the consequence of the faithlessness of the forebears by having to live the desert's hardships and trials. The underlying conceptuality of the spy story is Israel's failure to let Yahweh fulfill the promise of the land made to their ancestors.

(3) Implications of the Concept of Numbers 13-14

A few commentators recognize the significance of the content of Numbers 13-14 within the story line of Israel's campaign toward the land of Canaan.[210] Olson's claim is typical: Numbers 13-14 plays "a crucial role within the unifying literary and theological structure of the book of Numbers."[211] However, Olson's reconstruction of the structure of Numbers is based on the thematic aspect of the transition from the old generation to the new genera-

---

209. The delayed fulfillment of Yahweh's promise functions as Yahweh's forgiveness and punishment of Israel's rebellion. The delay suggests that Israel may continue as the covenantal people of Yahweh, an abandonment of Yahweh's initial judgment of complete disinheritance and replacement of the nation through Moses. It also makes a positive affirmation against other nations' understandings of Yahweh as one who was powerless to fulfill the promise of the land to Yahweh's own people. At the same time, the delay is punishment because the promise will not be fulfilled by the current generation, but by the next generation, who shall suffer for the faithlessness of the Exodus generation until the total death of all that generation. Cf. Boorer, *The Promise of the Land as Oath*, pp. 350-52; K. D. Sakenfeld, "The Problem of Divine Forgiveness in Num 14," *CBQ* 37 (1975): 317-30, esp. pp. 323-27.

210. Levine (*Numbers 1–20*, p. 372) asserts that these chapters play a "pivotal function within the overall historiography of Numbers, and within Torah literature as a whole." Olson, *The Death of the Old and the Birth of the New*, pp. 138-52; idem, *Numbers*, pp. 86-90.

211. Olson, *Numbers*, p. 86.

tion. This generational transition is structurally signaled by the two census reports in chapters 1 and 26. Questions emerge. If Numbers 13–14 plays "a crucial role" within the structure of Numbers and has the "central place" in the theme and structure of Numbers, what is its structural significance within Numbers? Does the spy story in Numbers 13–14 signal the decisive break between what precedes it and what follows it, or is it subordinate to some other conceptual factor? Since the two census reports constitute the decisive break within the structure of Numbers, what is their relationship to the spy story in Numbers 13–14? Is Olson not in conceptual conflict within his own system of thought? Olson's answers would be that Numbers 13–14 plays a pivotal role as its specific age formula (twenty years old and upward) is used in both census reports, as its general story line is used for the warning in 32:6-15, and as its specific contents (the death of the Exodus generation and the delineation of the land's borders) are associated with one another in 26:63-65 and 34:1-12, respectively. What his answers show is that Numbers 13–14 is significant for the rest of Numbers because it shares some literary features and content with them. Numbers 13–14 functions as the text that provides the theme of the death of the old generation and the birth of the new generation, but Numbers 13–14 in and of itself does not play the central or pivotal role for the structure of Numbers.[212] For him, these roles are designated for the two census reports.

Moreover, Olson's stress on "two separate generations" of Israel is problematic or at least ambiguous.[213] With the title of his book, *The Death of the Old and the Birth of the New,* he presupposes the existence of two generations of the Israelites in the wilderness period and a decisive transition between them. The transition has been described as temporal succession of generations by the death of the previous generation and the birth of the new generation. Olson supplies chronological and geographical evidence for this transition: the phrase "after the plague" in 26:1 means "after the death of the rest of the first generation"; and the geographical notice, "in the plains of Moab by the Jordan at Jericho," in 26:3 indicates that "this new generation does not begin in the wilderness as the first generation did; rather, they now stand at the

---

212. This criticism of Olson also goes to Levine. Although Levine's claim that 21:1 signals the structural break within Numbers, which differs from Olson's, his structure is based on the same theme as Olson's, i.e., a generational transition from the Exodus generation to the new generation.

213. The notion of generation in Olson's thesis is discussed in my article, "The Transition from the Old Generation to the New Generation in the Book of Numbers: A Response to Dennis Olson," in *Reading the Hebrew Bible for a New Millennium: Form, Concept, and Theological Perspective,* ed. W. Kim et al. (Harrisburg, PA: Trinity, 2000), vol. 2, pp. 201-20, esp. pp. 203-6.

edge of the promised land. . . ."[214] This transition in its essence shows that the new generation *replaces* the old generation *after* the old generation has died. Then, Olson's title suggests that the total of Israel's wilderness period is eighty years, calculated according to the wilderness periods in which the two separate generations spent time; a period of forty years had to elapse in order that the Exodus generation might die off and the new generation must suffer a period of another forty years due to the faithlessness of the Exodus generation.

Of course, Olson would not intentionally propose the eighty years as the duration of Israel's journey by his title. He must have known that the eighty years based on the temporal succession of two consecutive generations is clearly in conflict with the well-known forty-year scheme of Israel's wilderness experience.[215] He would not mean for the readers to take the title literally as indicating a biological sequence of two generations. Rather, he might intend to stress a sharp contrast between these two generations by using the parallelism of the old//the new and death//birth. Then, "birth" should be understood as a metaphor signifying the new beginning of the story of the new generation. However, it is fair to ask him whether "the death" of the old generation should be taken as a metaphor just as "the birth" of the new generation. As God's punishment to the Exodus generation clearly indicates (Num 14:20-23, 28-30), the death of this generation must be understood literally. Thus, Olson's formulation of the title shows that he juxtaposes literal and metaphorical descriptions of the contents of Numbers for the sake of creating a parallel pattern, which in turn not only reveals a literary inconsistence but also implies the chronological dissonance with the firmly established forty-year scheme of Israel's wilderness journey. At the least, his title needs to be further clarified, even if it may be considered as a shorthand caricature of his complex arguments.

The chronological dissonance can be answered by understanding the term "generation" (דור) in the biblical sense. To use the term as a certain length of time between the birth of parents and that of their children (or

---

214. Olson, *The Death of the Old and the Birth of the New*, pp. 84-85. Once again, Olson states this point in his commentary on Numbers: "Instead, the new generation begins its life at the edge of the wilderness, the entry point into the promised land on the plains of Moab by the Jordan River (Num. 26:3)" (*Numbers*, p. 6).

215. Moses was eighty years old when he spoke to Pharaoh (Exod 7:7), and he was one hundred twenty years old when he died (Deut 34:7; cf. 31:2). Thus, Moses' prophetic life and Israel's wilderness wandering lasted forty years. Forty years for the duration of Israel's migratory campaign — from its liberation out of Egypt to its entrance into the land of Canaan — has been firmly established throughout the Bible (Exod 16:35; Num 14:33, 34; 32:13; Deut 2:7; 8:2, 4; 29:5; Josh 5:6; Neh 9:21; Ps 95:10; Ezek 4:6; Amos 2:10; 5:25).

when one generation dies off and another comes to life) is neither prominent nor normative.[216] Instead of generation B replacing generation A after the death of generation A, these two generations must have overlapped in their life span. They are not exactly living contemporaneously, but simultaneously, sharing a portion of time. Since any two or even three generations can coexist, the notion of the overlapping of generations is in principle presupposed in the concept of דור. This overlapping of generations is assumed in Yahweh's punishment due to Israel's failure: "But your little ones, . . . I will bring in, and they shall know the land that you [the Exodus generation] have despised" (14:31). This text suggests that the second generation had already been born in Egypt, although the totality of the generation must include those born in the wilderness. Thus, the text assumes that the death of the first generation, which took forty years, does not and cannot mean that the second generation was just born. Rather, the second generation takes over and is called upon as the new carrier of the divine promise at the end of the forty-year wandering; and they continue to suffer the same forty-year hardship in the wilderness for their forebears' faithlessness (14:33).[217] Yahweh's response to Israel's failure does not consider the possibility of successive generations in the chronological sense. Two separate generations coexist or overlap with each other within the forty-year wilderness period; while the first generation dies off, the second generation suffers the same forty years along with them; whereas the nature of the suffering for the former is death, that of the latter is being "shepherds in the wilderness"; at the end of the forty years the latter stands out as the new carrier of the fulfillment of Yahweh's land promise.

Furthermore, Olson's theme, that is, the generational transition, is not the generative conceptuality underneath Numbers 13–14. The definitive condemnation of the Exodus generation is one of Yahweh's punishments and is an inevitable by-product of the delayed fulfillment of Yahweh's promise. At the center of Yahweh's punishment is not the killing of the Exodus generation

---

216. D. N. Freedman, J. Lundbom, and G. J. Botterweck, "דור," in *TDOT*, ed. G. J. Botterweck, H. Ringgren, and H.-J. Fabry, trans. J. T. Willis, G. W. Bromiley, and D. E. Green, vol. 3 (Grand Rapids: Eerdmans, 1978), pp. 169-81; cf. G. Gerleman, "דור," in *Theological Lexicon of the Old Testament*, ed. E. Jenni and C. Westermann, trans. M. E. Biddle, vol. 1 (Peabody: Hendrickson, 1997), pp. 333-35.

217. In his later commentary on Numbers, Olson seems to use "birth" as a metaphor for new beginning. Note that he changes the title of the second part of the structure from "The Birth of the New Generation" to "The Rise of a New Generation on the Edge of the Promised Land." The choice of terms such as "rise" or "emergence" (*Numbers*, pp. 5, 157, 163; cf. "birth," p. 6) indicates that he means that the formal beginning or inauguration of the story of the new generation is given birth (i.e., new beginning) at the edge of the promised land, not in the wilderness, the place where the first generation's story began.

but the delay of the promises' fulfillment. Therefore, Olson's theme, the transition from the old to the new generation, is subordinate to Israel's failure to fulfill Yahweh's promise of the land and should not be constitutive for the structure of Numbers as a whole or even for that of Numbers 10:11–36:13.

The underlying conceptuality of Numbers 13–14, Israel's failure to let Yahweh fulfill the land promise to its ancestors, suggests that this text takes the central place within the structure of Numbers 10:11–36:13 and divides 10:11–36:13 into two parts: Israel's failed campaign to conquer the promised land from the south (10:11–14:45) and their forty-year wandering in the wilderness as Yahweh's punishment (15:1–36:13). As Yahweh forgives, Israel's failure does not nullify Yahweh's promise of the land. It implies that despite Israel's attempt to go back to Egypt with a new captain, neither the objective of Israel's sanctuary campaign, nor the conquest of the promised land, nor Israel's identity as an epiphanic military camp has been altered. The identity of Israel and the purpose of the march are the same as when the people left the wilderness of Sinai. However, their failure to conquer the land changes the specifications of their campaign from then on.

First, the goal of the campaign will be accomplished by the next generation and not by the Exodus generation. The entire Exodus generation, who have seen Yahweh's glory and the signs that Yahweh did in Egypt and in the wilderness, shall not see the land or enter the land expect for Caleb and Joshua. It is the next generation who will enter the land.

Second, the conquest of the promised land will be accomplished not immediately but after forty years of wandering in the wilderness. There is no indication throughout the Exodus and wilderness period that Yahweh intentionally delays Israel's conquest of the promised land. Israel's forty years of wilderness experience is neither part of Yahweh's original plan nor a testing of their faith in Yahweh. It is the punishment for Israel's unprecedented rebellion. It is not even a retraining of the next generation in trust or faithfulness to Yahweh. For forty years the next generation must suffer the hardships of the wilderness until all of the Exodus generation has died.

Third, the conquest of the promised land will be executed through a different route than from the south. With Yahweh's command that Israel's campaign must resume "for the wilderness by the way to the Red Sea" (14:25), this different route presupposes that they must campaign through the Transjordan territories in order to reattempt to conquer the promised land from east of the Jordan River. These alterations decisively distinguish the character of Israel's campaign portrayed before and after the spy story. Before the spy story, Israel's campaign is a march toward the promised land without any delay or hesitation. Israel is organized with more than six hundred thousand infantrymen, and it takes only two months after they set out from Sinai to arrive at the edge of the land of Canaan, at Kadesh in the wilderness of Paran.[218] It is clear that when Israel departs from Sinai, the people do not imagine that they are going to fail to conquer the land or that Yahweh will test their faith to see whether or not they are qualified to enter the promised land. However, after the spy story, Israel's campaign is a march toward the promised land as well as an actualization of Yahweh's punishments, which takes forty years. Whatever happens during these forty years, wherever Israel marches, and whomever they encounter are to be understood as the consequence of Israel's failure. The delayed fulfillment of Yahweh's promise of the land is the governing conceptuality beneath all of Israel's activities narrated after the spy story.

Furthermore, the structural significance of 13:1–14:45 is reinforced by the seriousness of Israel's rebellion and Yahweh's punishment. As mentioned above, Israel's rebellion in 14:1-4 occurs at the edge of the promised land and at the very moment of the fulfillment of the promise of the land and deals with the potential conquest of the promised land. The rebellion also involves Israel's attempt to undo the Exodus event itself and is connected with Yahweh's land promise to their ancestors. Moreover, as Yahweh asserts (14:22), this rebellion is the climax of how Israel disobeyed or distrusted or tested Yahweh all through the Exodus and wilderness period. It is "the last in a series" (14:22) since the Exodus event.[219] Similarly, this rebellion is located at the end of a series of rebellions occurring after Israel left Sinai, and so it is the culmination of a series of four progressively serious rebellions (11:1-3, 4-35; 12:1-16; and 13:1–14:45). Olson states correctly that the development "from the

---

218. Numbers 13:20, "the season of the first ripe grapes," indicates a time toward the end of July, which provides roughly two months for the journey from Sinai to Kadesh (Wenham, *Numbers: An Introduction and Commentary*, p. 117; Gray, *A Critical and Exegetical Commentary on Numbers*, p. 139; Budd, *Numbers*, p. 144; Ashley, *The Book of Numbers*, p. 236; E. W. Davies, *Numbers*, p. 134.

219. Boorer, *The Promise of the Land as Oath*, p. 355. She compares in detail non-P materials of Num 13–14 with Num 32:7-15; Deut 1:19–2:1; 9:23; Exod 32:7-14. Although her comparison and goal (to determine the relative chronology of these texts) are outside my scope, her analysis is helpful (particularly the comparison between Num 14:11b-23a and Exod 32:9-14). Because of the common nature of the judgment, i.e., annihilation and disinheritance of the people and replacement of the people with a "Moses nation" (Num 14:12 and Exod 32:10), the spy story in Num 13–14 and the golden calf incident in Exod 32:1-35 have been considered the two great rebellions against Yahweh in the whole Pentateuch. In Deuteronomy (1:22-45; 9:12-25) these two stories are singled out in a discussion of the wilderness experience and receive special treatment. Some commentators argue that the rebellion in Num 13–14 is more serious and fatal than that in Exod 32. Olson (*Numbers*, p. 81) asserts that Israel's rebellion in Numbers is "the more severe and unprecedented of the two." Cf. Milgrom, *Numbers*, p. 99; Mann, *The Book of the Torah*, pp. 131-33.

fringe to all the people to the leaders builds progressively toward the culminating rebellion in Numbers 13–14."[220] In addition, Yahweh's punishment is utterly serious, which corresponds to the magnitude of Israel's rebellion. In terms of the content, Yahweh punishes Israel "measure for measure" according to Israel's words and actions.[221] In terms of form, Yahweh swears an oath by his own person. The fact that this divine oath form occurs only twice (14:21, 28) in the entire Pentateuch indicates the severity of Yahweh's punishment. The divine oath is also intended to underline the certainty of Yahweh's punishment: Yahweh's punishment is nonnegotiable and irreversible. The irrevocable nature of Yahweh's punishment is proven by the reports about the fate of the scouts (the death of the scouts who brought the distorted report about the land, but life for Caleb and Joshua) and about the fate of the people (total defeat by the Amalekites and the Canaanites). In terms of Yahweh's relationship to Israel, Yahweh's punishment suggests a decisive breaking point. In his intercession, Moses entreats Yahweh to pardon Israel on the basis of the precedent Yahweh has set in the past, "from Egypt even until now" (14:19). With the phrase "from Egypt even until now," Moses understood that the relationship between Yahweh and Israel has been positive from the Exodus and the wilderness period up until Israel's rebellion in chapters 13–14. Since Yahweh forgives Israel just as Moses has asked (14:20), Yahweh also views the relationship to Israel from the Exodus on as positive. Yahweh's positive relationship to the Exodus generation is broken completely by the judgment of their death. The entire Exodus generation, which includes Moses and Aaron and yet excludes Caleb and Joshua, must die in the wilderness and not enter the promised land. Yahweh's relationship with Israel as a nation will be continued, but Yahweh's relationship with the Exodus generation is over.

In short, no other rebellion narrative has the same intensity and seriousness as the spy story in Numbers 13–14. Correspondingly, Yahweh's punishment is of the utmost seriousness and is fatal in that the relationship with the Exodus generation is totally broken. Yahweh's interest has been trans-

220. Olson, *Numbers*, p. 81. Olson's observation that there is a progressive relationship among these rebellions is correct, but his understanding of what is involved in this progression is not entirely correct. According to him, 11:1-3 affects the fringe of the camp; 11:4-35 involves the people's complaint about the food; 12:1-16 involves for the first time the leaders of the people, Miriam and Aaron; and 13:1–14:45 involves both leaders who are the spies and all the people in the unprecedented plan (14:4). As seen, he moves from an affected place, to content (food), to leaders of the people, to both leaders and all the people.

221. Olson, *Numbers*, pp. 84-85; Milgrom, *Numbers*, p. 115. The corresponding verses between Israel's rebellion and Yahweh's punishment are 14:2 (14:29); 14:3a (14:30); 14:3b (14:31-33); and 13:25 (14:34).

ferred to the next generation. The seriousness of Israel's rebellion and of Yahweh's punishment in Numbers 13–14 serves to make clear the structural significance of Numbers 13–14 as decisive within 10:11–36:13.

b. Compositional Evidence: A Comparison of Military Accounts

Numbers 13–14 on the surface level is a historical narrative that begins with Yahweh's command to Moses to send men to reconnoiter the land of Canaan and ends with Israel's total defeat by the Amalekites and the Canaanites. On an infratextual level, this narrative shows that Yahweh's intention to bring Israel into the promised land is distorted by the majority of the scouts and is rejected by all the people of Israel, together with an unprecedented plan to reverse the Exodus event. Yahweh condemns them to die in the wilderness during forty years of wandering, while the next generation arises ready to fulfill Yahweh's promise to conquer the promised land. The delayed conquest of the promised land is initially manifested in the death of the majority of the scouts who brought the negative report of the land while Caleb and Joshua live, and in the complete failure of Israel's attempt to conquer the land without Yahweh's presence in the midst of their campaign. Israel's refusal to go up and take possession of the land turns out to be their failure to let Yahweh fulfill the land promise to Israel's ancestors. This substantive content of Numbers 13–14 serves to make clear that Numbers 13–14 occupies a compositionally distinctive position among the narratives within Numbers 10:11–36:13 whose contents are also related to Israel's sanctuary campaign. *The distinctive position of Numbers 13–14 will affirm its structural significance as constituting the decisive breaking point for the bipartite structure of 10:11–36:13.*

Conceptually, all thirty-six units of Numbers 10:11–36:13 are part of Israel's ongoing sanctuary campaign, the execution of which began when Israel left Sinai. Of the thirty-six units, however, twelve units can be identified as battle accounts or military conflict narratives exhibiting some of the features often associated with a military engagement, such as the ark (the cultic symbol of military campaign) and battle language (איב, חרם, etc.).[222] Since the military aspect is the dominant factor in characterizing Israel's march as a sanctuary campaign,

---

222. The twelve units are: 10:11-36 (10:35-36); 13:1–14:45; 20:14-21; 21:1-3, 10-20 (14-15), 21-31, 32-35; 22:1–24:25; 25:19–26:65 (26:1-4a); 31:1-54; 32:1-42; 33:50–34:29 (33:50-56). The parentheses signify verses that are directly related to the battle accounts and integral parts of their associated unit, but that in and of themselves do not constitute a literary unit.

a comparison of units that includes the military aspect will provide information about their position related to their literary context within the extant text. The twelve units can be divided into two groups depending on whether a unit speaks of a direct or indirect military campaign of Israel. Half of the twelve units do not contain direct accounts of Israel's military encounter with enemies, although they contain specific war language. The military aspect of these units serves to support the main concept, portrayed differently in each unit, which holds together each unit's various aspects. The other six, in contrast, deal with a direct military conflict that Israel has with hostile enemies. In these units, the military aspect plays an essential role in defining the nature of the units.

(1) Indirect Military Accounts

The indirect accounts of Israel's military campaign are as follows: 10:11-36 (vv. 35-36, the "song of the ark"); 21:10-20 (vv. 14-15, the "Book of the Wars of Yahweh"); 22:1–24:25 (section on Balak and Balaam); 25:19–26:65 (vv. 1-4a, instructions for taking a census); 32:1-42 (the allotment of the land in the Transjordan); and 33:50-56 (Yahweh's command regarding the replacement of the Canaanites). These accounts will be briefly discussed.

The first, 10:35-36, certainly shows the military aspect by mentioning specific words (מַשְׂנָא, אֹיֵב, הָאָרֶץ). This so-called "song to the ark" reflects the view that the ark is a throne upon which Yahweh as the divine warrior sits invisibly while waging a holy war. However, the military aspect of this song in its immediate literary context points to the concept of Yahweh's leadership of Israel's journey in the wilderness (10:33-34), which is in conflict with the human leadership that Moses sought in Hobab (10:29-32). In its wider context, the song of the ark is part of the report of Israel's departure from Sinai (10:11-36). Thus, the military aspect of verses 35-36 plays a subordinate role to the leadership conflicts of the journey in the wilderness, and this aspect ultimately functions as a poetic summary of the generative concept of the whole unit, Israel's departing from the wilderness of Sinai.

Similar to 10:35-36, 21:14-15 clearly expresses a military aspect since it is a citation from the Book of the Wars of Yahweh. Some commentators suggest that the title of this book may show its nature as a collection of "songs celebrating Yahweh's victories against his [Yahweh's] enemies."[223] However, re-

---

223. Ashley, *The Book of Numbers,* p. 411. E. W. Davies (*Numbers,* p. 220) suggests a historical understanding of the nature of this book in that it may contain "an anthology of war poems, presumably dealing with the conflict between the invading Israelites and the original inhabitants of Canaan." Cf. Milgrom, *Numbers,* p. 176.

gardless of the book's exact nature, it is clear that the content of verses 14-15 is not about the wars of Yahweh or of Israel but is a geographical description of Arnon.[224] In terms of their function within their immediate literary context (vv. 13b-15), both verses 14 and 15 elaborate upon the territory of Arnon, mentioning several geographical sites and confirming the fact that Arnon borders on Moab. Moreover, in the context of the whole unit (21:10-20), the military aspect extricated from the title of the book in verse 14a disappears. The unit is a report of Israel's migration from Mount Hor to the valley and is structured by the generative concept of the geographical organization of the topographical locations. In this structure, verses 14-15 are part of verses 12-15, which show Israel's migration into the wilderness extending from the boundary of the Amorites and serve to describe this wilderness further. In both their content and their functions in their literary context, verses 14-15 are controlled by a geographical aspect, not a military one.

Third, 22:1–24:25 as a whole is clearly an indirect military account that is related to Israel. It contains a military aspect demonstrated in Balak's purpose in hiring Balaam and Balak's characterization of Israel. Balak, the King of Moab, knew that Israel was victorious over the Amorites, had taken possession of their entire land (22:2; cf. 21:24-26), and was stronger than the Moabites (22:6). Fearful of the triumphant and numerous Israelites, Balak hired Balaam, a Mesopotamian diviner, in order to "be able to defeat them [the Israelites] and drive them from the land" (22:6) by putting a curse on Israel. Balak attempted twice to hire Balaam because of Balaam's highly regarded reputation (22:6b). As the story progresses, Balak's purpose for cursing Israel is gradually dismissed and, inversely, Balaam's blessing upon Israel is moved from possibility to a firm fact. Balak planned with confidence to curse Israel, but he did not accomplish his purpose, instead finding himself cursed thanks to his hired diviner. Meanwhile he repeatedly characterized Israel as his enemy (23:11; 24:10). In contrast, Israel, without the people's knowledge, moved from the possibility of being cursed by the enemy to being blessed by the foreign diviner, to having benefited from the curse on the enemy. This movement within the story intensifies the possible conflict between Moab and Is-

224. Cf. D. L. Christensen, "Num 21:14-15 and the Book of the Wars of Yahweh," *CBQ* 36 (1974): 359-60. Christensen reconstructs vv. 14-15 in such a way that Yahweh becomes the subject of various clauses and some clauses contain verbs which refer to Yahweh's action in war. (Wenham [*Numbers: An Introduction and Commentary*, pp. 159-60] elaborates upon Yahweh the divine warrior based on Christensen's reconstruction: these verses "picture God as the divine warrior sweeping through the territory of Moab ready for the great battles in Transjordan that anticipated the conquest of Canaan.") However, Christensen admits that these verses are used to note the boundary of Moab, implying his acknowledgment that the war aspect is secondary.

rael. However, the story of Balak and Balaam is an indirect account that is related to Israel. Except for the literary setting in 22:1, there is no mention of what Israel was doing. No Israelites were involved or present in the events reported in this story. Although the main thrust of the story is the fate of Israel (blessing or curse, life or death), the events took place on the heights above (22:41) without Israel's knowledge. Israel is not even informed of the result. Despite the danger of a potential curse, the story of Balak and Balaam as a whole shows Balak's failure to curse Israel and Yahweh's blessing on Israel without the people's knowledge and by the foreign prophet.

Fourth, 26:1-4a has two parts: verses 1-2 and 3-4a. The first part is Yahweh's instruction to take a census of Israel, whereas the second part reports Moses' and Eleazar's compliance (vv. 3-51) and functions as an introductory statement for the census. Structurally, the two parts do not share the same levels within the macrostructure of 25:19–26:65, the report of the census of the Israelites that Moses and Eleazar took in the plains of Moab. Conceptually, there is a shift of intention from a census of military personnel to a census for an unknown reason. In the first part, Yahweh commanded Moses and Eleazar to take a census of all the Israelites "from twenty years old and upward, by their ancestral houses, everyone in Israel able to go to war" (v. 2). This command is similar to that in Numbers 1:2-3. Chapters 1–2 account for only the males who are above the age of twenty and able to go to war for the purpose of the organization of Yahweh's sanctuary campaign. Thus, the purpose of Yahweh's command in 26:1-2 may share the same purpose as Numbers 1:2-3, although the specifications of 26:1-2 are not as detailed as those of 1:2-3. The military aspect is operative in Yahweh's command to take a census.[225] However, Moses and Eleazar abbreviated Yahweh's command by mentioning only the age qualification. Their short version could be the result of their effort to avoid repeating the same command. But it could signal a different purpose for the census than that of Num 1:2-3. In light of the whole unit, the purpose becomes clear that taking a census of the Israelites from twenty years old and upward in the plains of Moab is not intended to organize the sanctuary campaign but to allot the land. The census provides a basis for allotting land after the conquest, as clearly demonstrated by another of Yahweh's speeches to Moses (vv. 52-56). If the military aspect is operative in verses 1-4a, it is intended to ascertain the strength of the tribes, revealing Yahweh's involvement during the forty years of wandering in the wilderness. But, in terms of the

---

225. This military purpose is conceivable because (1) Yahweh's command for the census comes right after Yahweh orders Israel to harass the Midianites (25:16-18), and (2) Israel still needs to accomplish the task of their sanctuary campaign, the conquest of the land of Canaan.

whole unit, it is clear that the division of the land of Canaan is the generative concept to which the military aspect is subordinate.

Fifth, the military aspect is certainly operative in 32:1-42 as a whole. Both explicit and implicit information support this point. Explicitly, the text contains military language, such as מלחמה (vv. 6, 20, 27, 29), חלץ (vv. 17, 20), and עבר (vv. 5, 7, 21, 27, 29, 30, 32).[226] Moreover, 32:1-42 recounts the military campaigns of the half-tribe of Manasseh (vv. 39-42). The descendants of Machir, son of Manasseh, went to Gilead, captured it, and dispossessed the Amorites. Similarly, two other sons of Manasseh, Jair and Nobah, conducted their own military campaign and captured places that they then renamed. Implicitly, the military conquest of the land of Canaan is presupposed in the Reubenites' and the Gadites' proposal to Moses to let them settle in the Transjordan territory and to excuse them from crossing the Jordan (v. 5). With this presupposition, the text moves forward. Moses challenged them to consider the consequence of their attempt not to fight along with the rest of the tribes (vv. 6-15); they made a deal with Moses in a private setting that they would go to battle until all the Israelites obtained their inheritance while all their belongings remained in Gilead (vv. 16-27); their deal with Moses was proclaimed in a public setting (vv. 28-32), and they (including the half-tribe of Manasseh) settled in the Transjordan territory.

However, the military conquest of the land of Canaan is subordinate to the concept of the allotment of land in the Transjordan to the Reubenites, the Gadites, and the half-tribe of Manasseh. The desire to settle in the Transjordan caused these tribes to request of Moses an exemption from fighting for the land of Canaan. Their request is rejected by Moses because their avoidance would discourage the rest of the tribes from crossing the river and going into the land and taking possession of it. Their request would ultimately be the reason for the whole of Israel forfeiting Yahweh's gift of the land and not fulfilling the land promise to Israel's ancestors, something that had happened before in their past (Num 13:1–14:45). Due to their strong desire to settle in the Transjordan, they negotiated with Moses and finally received permission on the condition that they help the other tribes in the battle for Canaan. Unit 32:1-42 is not about Israel's military encounter with enemies but about the al-

---

226. The phrase מלחמה occurs at eight other places in Numbers; seven of them are related to direct military accounts (21:14, 33; 31:14, 21, 27, 28, 49), and one is in Yahweh's instruction to Moses concerning the sounding trumpets (10:9). On the one hand, the phrase חלץ occurs at only one other place: in the account of the holy war against Midian (31:3). On the other hand, עבר occurs at many places in Numbers, but most are related to the military accounts (13:32; 14:7, 41; 20:17 [x2], 18, 19, 20, 21; 21:20, 22, 23; 22:18, 26; 24:13; 31:23 [x2]; 33:51). Other instances are 5:14 [x2], 30; 6:5; 8:7; 27:7, 8; 33:8; 34:4 [x2]; 35:10.

lotment of the Transjordan territory to the two and a half tribes of Israel, thus dealing with a sacred obligation imposed on all tribes of Israel to assist in the military conquest of the land of Canaan.

The sixth unit, 33:50-56, is an account of Yahweh's speech to Moses concerning the replacement of the Canaanites. This text in and of itself is not a literary unit, but the text belongs to a unit narrating Yahweh's instructions concerning the division of the land of Canaan and functions to set the stage for a report of the boundaries of the land (34:1-12) and ultimately for a report of the apportionment of the land (34:13-29). It is clear that the military aspect is the dominant conceptual factor for the flow of the text. With five active verbs, verses 52-54 narrate that Israel should expel the Canaanites, eradicate all symbols of their religion, take possession of their land, and apportion the land by lot and according to the size of the tribe. If Israel does not keep this instruction, their settlement of the land will face constant difficulties from the remaining Canaanites and will ultimately be uprooted by Yahweh directly (vv. 55-56). However, it is immediately clear because of its temporal setting that this text is not a direct military account of Israel's encounter with the enemies. Yahweh's instruction to Israel regarding the Canaanites and their religion and the consequence of Israel's disobedience (vv. 52-55) concerns what Israel should do when they "cross over the Jordan into the land of Canaan" (v. 51b). Israel's expulsion of the Canaanites and eradication of their religious signs had not happened "in the plains of Moab" (v. 50a) or during the wilderness period. Israel's conquest of the land of Canaan is still in the future and remains the main task of their campaign.

In short, the substantive discussion of the six accounts above indicates that these accounts, regardless of whether they are in themselves a complete literary unit or only part of a unit, contain the military aspect only as support or secondary to the concept responsible for the meaning of the unit. They express indirectly Israel's military encounters with hostile enemies during their campaigning in the wilderness period. Thus, they provide indirect evidence for the uniqueness of Numbers 13–14 among military accounts within 10:11–36:13.

(2) Direct Military Accounts

Of the twelve units that exhibit some features of military engagement, six units speak of Israel's military campaign directly.[227] These six units have a variety of literary, substantive, and conceptual components operative within

227. 13:1–14:45 (14:39-45); 20:14-21; 21:1-3, 21-31, 32-35; and 31:1-54 (vv. 1-12).

them, and yet all the components point to various aspects of their basic military nature. The concept of a military encounter is responsible for their composition and structure and thus ultimately their meaning. Each of these units deals with Israel's direct military encounters with other ethnically different people at a specific station in the wilderness itinerary. In order to reconstruct the compositional significance of 13:1–14:45, which in turn reinforces the structural significance of 10:11–36:13, this unit will be compared with the other five units based on explicit information provided on the surface level in all six units and on the implicit generative conceptuality that lies underneath the units and governs the structure and meaning of each unit.

In order to compare explicit information, four sets of questions will be raised. (1) Who is/are the acting subject(s) of each military account and how does each unit characterize this/these actor(s)? (2) Who is/are the opponent(s) and why does/do the opponent(s) oppose? (3) When and where do the military encounters happen in the literary context? (4) What is the objective of and what is the result of each military encounter? To answer these questions is not only to describe what happens in a unit as a whole but also to identify the individuality of a unit.[228] Moreover, the individuality of a unit compels the exegete to raise different questions relative to the previously mentioned four sets of questions. The new questions are implicit in the unit, and their answers are not clear and readily accessible within the limit of the unit, although the answers are assumed on the part of the unit and embedded within the generative concept of the unit. The answers rest on the compositional significance of each unit, that is, on the reason for the location of a unit and for its relationship to adjacent units. The answers contribute to the formation of the overarching concept that is constitutive for the whole text of which a unit is a part, and, at the same time, the answers will be reformulated from the vantage point of this overarching concept for a better understanding of the location and relationship of a unit beyond its immediate literary context.

(a) A Comparison of Six Units

(i) Identification and Characterization of the Acting Subject(s)

(a) Numbers 14:39 shows that Moses told the people Yahweh's punishment would be to "all the Israelites" (כל־בני ישראל), and the people (העם)

---

228. For the structure of each unit, see pp. 131-32, 154-55, 157, 161-62, 164-65, and 190-91 in this study.

mourned greatly. In the rest of the account (vv. 40-45), no other specific designations for the acting subjects are mentioned, except that Moses refers to them by using the second person plural pronoun, and writers refer to them by using the third person masculine plural suffixes. Are "all the Israelites" and "the people" identical groups in verses 39-45 or even throughout the entire story (13:1–14:45)? On the one hand, similar to 14:1-2a,[229] these two groups are mentioned to emphasize that all the people are involved in the military conquest of the land. "The people," on the other hand, can be further distinguished from all the Israelites. They could be a group of people who actually executed the military campaign and were defeated by the Amalekites and the Canaanites. In other words, they could be the ones numbered in the census (1:1-47), the armed force of Israel — the males capable of bearing arms above the age of twenty years, who were specified by Yahweh as the ones to be punished with death in the wilderness (14:29b-30a). It is hard to imagine that all the Israelites, including children and women, were involved in the military expedition narrated in verses 40-45.

As far as the text allows, however, it is clear that the acting subjects included all the Israelite males who were able to bear arms and excluded Moses (the leader of the sanctuary campaign), Yahweh (represented by the ark), and perhaps the priestly personnel (including the Levites). Moreover, within the context of the whole story, the acting subjects in 14:39-45 are the Exodus generation, specifically the armed force, who saw Yahweh's glory and signs done in Egypt and in the wilderness and who were destined to die in the wilderness without seeing the promised land as Yahweh's punishment for their unprecedented rebellion.

(b) Unit 20:14-21 includes several acting subjects for Israel's encounter with Edom. It was Moses who sent messengers to the king of Edom in verse 14a. The message itself is put into the mouth of "your brother Israel" (חִיךָ יִשְׂרָאֵל, v. 14b), is communicated in the first person plural (vv. 15-17), and is responded to by the king of Edom with the second person masculine singular (v. 18).[230] Verse 19 shifts the subject to "the Israelites" (בְּנֵי יִשְׂרָאֵל), and then to a simple form of the Israelites (יִשְׂרָאֵל) in verse 21b. The acting subject in 20:14-21 is shifted from Moses to Israel as a whole. Moses initiated contact

---

229. 14:1-2a mentions three different designations for groups of people: all the congregation (כָּל־הָעֵדָה), the people (הָעָם), and all the Israelites (כָּל בְּנֵי יִשְׂרָאֵל). By the use of these designations, the text intends to stress that all the people are involved in the rebellion that is to follow. This intention is affirmed by indicating "all the congregation" as the ones who spoke the rebellious sayings to Moses and Aaron (vv. 2b-3) and who spoke to one another (v. 4).

230. It is not clear whether the second person masculine singular "you" refers to Moses, "your brother Israel," or simply Israel as a whole.

with the king of Edom, and the entire population was involved in turning away from Edom as a consequence of its refusal to go through that territory.[231] It is clear that, as in 14:39-45, Yahweh is absent from 20:14-21.

(c) The main acting subject is Israel (ישראל) in 21:1-3 as a whole, although verse 1 has the Canaanite, the king of Arad, as the subject, and verse 3a has Yahweh. The initial victory of the king of Arad over Israel (v. 1) is a precondition for Israel's vow to Yahweh concerning utter destruction, חרם war (v. 2). With Yahweh's permission (v. 3aα), it was Israel who destroyed the Canaanites and their towns (v. 3aβ). Throughout the text, Israel is considered to be an individual entity rather than a collection of various tribes.[232] By referring to Israel in the singular, the account presupposes the concept of its oneness as a unified political entity. Regardless of the various elements, such as tribes, ages, and sexes of the populations, differences in responsibilities, and so forth, all the Israelites are one body, which was defeated by the Canaanite, the king of Arad, initially, which then made a vow to Yahweh, and which finally destroyed the Canaanites and their towns.

(d) Unit 21:21-31 has several subjects, such as Israel (vv. 21-22, 24-25, 31), King Sihon of the Amorites (v. 23), and the ballad singers (vv. 27-30). However, it is clear that Israel is the main acting subject since the text begins with Israel's sending messengers to King Sihon and ends with Israel's occupation of his land as a result of the victory over him. Israel is viewed as both a single political entity and a cooperating group of various elements.[233] Interestingly, Moses and Yahweh are not involved at all in this military account.

(e) Unit 21:32-35 has four acting subjects: Moses, Israel, King Og of Bashan, and Yahweh. The role of King Og of Bashan is limited to verse 33b, whereas the roles of the remaining three are important to the flow of the text. Among the three, Israel is never mentioned with a clear designation and mentioned only by implication in the number and person of the verbs in verses 32aβ-33a and 35.[234] Note that the verbs are all plural, which indicates

231. For the discussion of number changes in verb forms and personal pronouns, see Gray (*A Critical and Exegetical Commentary on Numbers*, pp. 265-66), Noth (*Numbers*, p. 149), and E. W. Davies (*Numbers*, p. 207).

232. The text uses third person singular verbs that take Israel as the subject (בא, וידר, ויחרם, ויאמר) and the first person for Israel in "his" speech to Yahweh (בידי והחרמתי).

233. The text uses the third person singular verbs that take Israel as the subject (וישלח, וישב, ויקח, ויירש, ויכהו [x2]). The first common singular is used at the beginning of the messages in vv. 22-23 (אעברה), whereas the first common plural is used in the rest of the messages (נעבר, נלך, נשתה, נטה). Cf. Fearer (*Wars in the Wilderness*, p. 276), who stresses only the singularity of Israel based on the cohortative form אעברה in v. 22aα1.

234. The verbs in vv. 32aβ-33a are ויפנו, וילכדו, and ויעלו, and those in v. 35 are ויכו and ויירשו.

that the text points to the people or the various tribes of Israel. However, Moses and Yahweh are the only acting subjects explicitly mentioned (Moses in vv. 32aα, 32b; Yahweh and Moses in v. 34). Without the involvement of Moses and Yahweh, Israel's military campaign in 21:32-35 could not be understood properly.

(f) Unit 31:1-54 has many acting subjects: Yahweh, Moses, Eleazar the priest, all the leaders of the congregation (v. 13a), "the officers who were over the thousands of the army, the commanders of thousands and the commanders of hundreds" (v. 48). However, in the entire text, Yahweh and Moses are the dominant acting subjects. It is clear that Yahweh's presence is known both explicitly and implicitly throughout the text, evidenced by the direct Yahweh speeches to Moses (vv. 1-2, 25-30) and by Moses' reports of the execution of the divine commands (vv. 3a, 31, 41a, 47b). It is Moses, however, who elaborated on Yahweh's short command to avenge the Midianites (vv. 3-6), became angry with the officers of the army who violated the ideology of a holy war (vv. 13-20), and did more than what Yahweh commanded him, including taking charge of the officers' dedication to Yahweh (vv. 48-50). Particularly in the report of Israel's battle against Midian (vv. 1-12), Moses sent not only the warriors to war but also the priests and cultic symbols which represented the presence of Yahweh.[235] Moreover, Israel's war against Midian had already been commanded by Yahweh in 25:16-18, providing the reason for the war. Both Yahweh and Moses play active roles in the war itself and in the matters concerning its aftermath.

(ii) Identification of Opponents and Their Reasons for Opposition

(a) The opponents of the military expedition of "the people" are designated as "the Amalekites and the Canaanites" and are qualified as the ones who lived in the hill country (14:45). Although there are different geographical notations within 13:1–14:45 regarding where they lived,[236] the important point is

---

235. Verse 6 reports that Moses sent to war Phinehas, son of Eleazar the priest, the vessels of the sanctuary (which may include the ark), and the trumpets for sounding the alarm. As for whether the vessels of the sanctuary include the ark or not, commentators are divided. For a summary of the arguments, see Ashley (*The Book of Numbers*, pp. 591-92), Milgrom (*Numbers*, p. 257), and E. W. Davies (*Numbers*, p. 323).

236. In 13:29, the Amalekites lived in the land of the Negeb, and the Canaanites lived by the sea and along the Jordan, and the other peoples, such as the Hittites, the Jebusites, and the Amorites, lived in the hill country. This designation differs from 14:25 and 14:45. For who these peoples were, see Milgrom (*Numbers*, pp. 105-6).

that they were the inhabitants of the land of Canaan which "the people" intended to conquer.[237] The reason for the opposition of the Amalekites and the Canaanites is not explicitly mentioned, but the text as a whole presupposes that they saw "the people" coming up to their land as in a military campaign. "The people" who presumed to go up to the hill country without Moses and the ark of the covenant of Yahweh are viewed as aggressors, and the Amalekites and the Canaanites are seen as defenders of their territories.

(b) The opponent in 20:14-21 shifts from the king of Edom (v. 14) to Edom as a whole (vv. 18, 20-21). However, since it is Edom who refused, came out with a large armed force, and is the subject of the third person singular verbs (ויאמר in vv. 18 and 20a; ויצא in v. 20b; וימאן in v. 21a), and since verse 18 uses the first person singular verb and first person suffix for Edom, Edom is the main acting opponent and is viewed in this text as a unified political entity. The reason for Edom's refusal to allow Israel to pass through its territory is not explicit within the limit of the text. Moses' initial idealistic request (v. 17), based on his theological summary of Israelite history (vv. 14b-16), suggests no threat to Edom. Even with Israel's realistic or practical request (v. 19b), which implies Edom's financial benefit, there is no hint that Israel has an alternative motive other than sheer desperation to pass through Edom's territory. Note that the notice of Edom's military movement against Israel is given before the final notice of the king's refusal. This fact implies that Edom's military movement serves as a continuation of diplomacy and does not point to a military engagement with Israel. Thus, it is hard to consider Edom's refusal and its coming out against Israel with a large armed force simply as a defensive measure.

(c) Verse 21:1 reports a successful attack by the Canaanite, "the king of Arad," on approaching Israel. The identity of this "king of Arad" is not made known in the text, yet he is ethnically a Canaanite and geographically one who lived in the Negeb. Although mention of this king is problematic,[238] the text allows the reader to see that the opponent belongs to the Canaanites and inhabits the land of Canaan. Moreover, 21:2-3 identifies the opponents of Israel as "this people," "their cities," "the Canaanites," and "them." Thus, in 21:1-3 as a whole, the opponent of Israel is not the king of Arad alone, but the Canaanites in general, the ones who then inhabited the promised land. As for Israel's opposition, what the king of Arad did is clearly defensive. Verse 1 implies Israel's

---

237. Deut 1:44 uses the term Amorite for the Amalekite and the Canaanite. According to Milgrom (*Numbers*, p. 117), the Amorites and the Canaanites "can stand for the entire population" of the land of Canaan.

238. Ashley, *The Book of Numbers*, pp. 398-99.

coming (בוֹא) by the way of Atharim as a military advancement (cf. 21:23) —
or at least the king understood Israel's advancement in that way. Thus, 21:1-3
begins with Israel's military advancement with the intention of the conquest
of the land of Canaan and ends with the total destruction of the Canaanites
and their towns. Depending on the identification of "this people" and the
Canaanite/the king, the scope of Israel's destruction can be determined.

(d) Verse 21:21 identifies the opponent as "Sihon, king of the Amorites."
Although Sihon is referred to as "the king of the Amorites," he should be understood as the representative of some portion of the Amorites, not as king of
all Amorites in the land of Canaan, where Amorites also lived (cf. 13:29). Verse
21:26 serves to make clear the identity of Sihon and his jurisdiction, describing him as the one "who had fought against the former king of Moab and
captured all his land as far as the Arnon." The geographical designation of
Sihon's jurisdiction in verse 24, "from the Arnon to the Jabbok, as far as to the
Ammonites," also reinforces the point that Sihon could be understood as
reigning over a significant portion of the Amorites, but not all, as some lived
beyond his territory.[239] Sihon's kingdom is located on the east side of the
Dead Sea and the Jordan River Valley, not within the land of Canaan. As for
the reason for Sihon's opposition against Israel, both offensive and defensive
measures come into play. Israel's request for a peaceful passage through the
territory of Sihon is similar to that of 20:14-21. Israel's petition (v. 22) assures
Sihon that there will be neither a potentially devastating economic impact on
his kingdom nor a politically hidden agenda of aggression and acquisition. In
light of this petition, Sihon's act of gathering all his troops and coming out to
meet and fight against Israel (v. 23) can be understood only as offensive in nature, although the exact reason for his attack is not known. Unlike its encounter with Edom, Israel fought back and was victorious over Sihon and his
troops. As a consequence, Israel took possession of all the land of Sihon and
even occupied all the towns and land of the Amorites (vv. 24-31). From the
vantage point of Israel's conquest and occupation of Sihon's land, Sihon's
military movement can only be understood as defensive in nature, although
Israel's ultimate conquest and occupation is seemingly contradictory to its
initial petition for peaceful passage. There is an inherent ambiguity in 21:21-31
as a whole as to the exact reason for Sihon's opposition to Israel.

(e) As the prelude to the main event, 21:32 reports two things: first, Moses sent men to spy on Jazer, and yet its villages, not Jazer itself, were captured;
and second, it was the Israelites who captured the villages of Jazer, and yet it
was Moses who dispossessed the Amorites who were in the villages. Thus,

239. Fearer, *Wars in the Wilderness*, p. 272, n. 28.

who Moses' intended opponents were is not entirely clear from the verse itself — whether it is the city of Jazer or the Amorites who lived in the villages of Jazer. In contrast to verse 32, verses 33-35, as the main event, identify the opponent clearly as King Og of Bashan. Although King Og is not mentioned again by name, he is presupposed as the main opponent within Yahweh's speech to Moses (v. 34) and in the report of Israel's victory (v. 35).[240] In terms of the reason for King Og's opposition, 21:32-35 as a whole suggests that his coming out against the Israelites is clearly defensive. The text mentions no request for passage made by Israel or Moses, as it does in the case of Edom and the Amorites. Instead, the Israelites' turning and going up the road to Bashan (v. 33a) implies their military advancement toward Bashan's territory. This implication is supported by two arguments: (1) the road to Bashan is more indicative of a description of direction and destination than of the name of a specific route; (2) Israel's victory over the villages of Jazer serves as the prelude to Israel's continual overpowering of their enemies. Israel's movement up the road to Bashan is viewed as an aggression, and King Og's coming out against Israel is considered to be a defense of his territory.

(f) Passage 31:1-12 notes the opponent as the Midianites (vv. 2, 3, 7-9). However, nowhere in the text are the Midianites explicitly described, let alone the reason for their opposition. While the battle between Israel and Midian is mentioned (vv. 7-12), the battle report itself is interested in listing what Israel did to Midian. What the Midianites did in the battle is not mentioned at all, and they are totally absent in the entire text. The text reports Moses' execution of Yahweh's vengeance on the Midianites due to their corrupting influence on Israel at Peor (25:1-18).

(iii) Chronological and Geographical/Topographical Designations for the Battles

(a) In the spy story of 13:1–14:45, several chronological indicators are mentioned: Moses sent men to reconnoiter the land of Canaan at "the season of the first ripe grapes" (13:20); the spies spent forty days to survey the land (14:34); when they heard the spies' report, spoken immediately after they returned, all the people wept "that night" (14:1); and the people rose early in the morning to conquer the hill country after they heard Moses' report of Yahweh's punishment for their rebellion (14:40). These indicators suggest that the time frame of the spy story begins after roughly a two-month journey

---

240. Within 21:33-35 there are twelve references to King Og with personal pronouns and possessive suffixes.

from Sinai[241] and ends about forty days afterward. Israel's advance to the hill country happens almost immediately after they left Sinai. In terms of the location of the battle sites, 13:26 mentions Kadesh in the wilderness of Paran as the site to which the spies returned after having completed their mission (cf. 13:3).[242] From Kadesh "the people" went up to "the heights of the hill country" where the Amalekites and the Canaanites lived. The term "hill country" is used to describe most of the land north of the Negeb.[243]

(b) Unit 20:14-21 does not mention any chronological reference for Israel's encounter with Edom. The time gaps may represent the process of sending messengers to the king of Edom and receiving responses from him. The duration of the negotiation between Moses/Israel and Edom cannot be known, but at least the beginning of their negotiation is traceable. As the immediate literary context of 20:14-21, 20:1 provides a date, that is, the first month in which the Israelites came into the wilderness of Zin and stayed in Kadesh. Because of the absence of the day and year, the first month in 20:1 cannot yield a precise date. However, most commentators agree that the year should probably be the fortieth year after the Exodus from Egypt, based on Israel's itinerary record in 33:36-38.[244] Israel's encounter with Edom, then, oc-

241. This phrase is indicative of a specific time period, i.e., the end of July, which provides roughly two months for Israel's journey from Sinai to the wilderness of Paran, Kadesh.

242. The various references to the wilderness of Paran (Gen 14:6; 21:21; Num 12:16; 13:3, 26; Deut 1:1; 33:2; 1 Sam 25:1; 1 Kgs 11:18; Hab 3:3) show that this name designates the wilderness area north of the traditional site of Mount Sinai, west of Edom, and south of the land of Canaan. According to Aharoni, Paran is "evidently the general name for the southern deserts, today called the Sinai peninsula" (Y. Aharoni, *Land of the Bible: A Historical Geography,* trans. A. F. Rainey [Philadelphia: Westminster, 1979], p. 199). However, 20:1 indicates that Kadesh is in the wilderness of Zin. According to Kallai (*Historical Geography of the Bible,* p. 116), the wilderness of Zin serves to "signify an extensive region in the southern (the Negeb) part of western Eretz-Israel connected with the Kadesh-barnea region" (cf. Num 13:21; 20:1; 33:36; 34:3; Deut 32:51; Josh 15:1). Since the border between the wilderness of Paran and the wilderness of Zin was fluid, it is likely that Kadesh was located near the border. More precisely, Kadesh-barnea is located near ʿAin el-ʾOudeirat in the Wadi el-ʾAin (cf. R. Cohen, *Kadesh-barnea* [Jerusalem: Hebrew University Press, 1983]). It rests at the most important crossroad in the immediate region, i.e., "a road leading from Suez to Beer-sheba/Hebron and the road branching from the Via Maris near el-Arish leading to ʿAqaba" (D. W. Manor, "Kadesh-barnea," in *ABD,* ed. D. N. Freedman, vol. 4 [New York: Doubleday, 1992], pp. 1-3).

243. Ashley, *The Book of Numbers,* p. 273. Milgrom (*Numbers,* p. 116) suggests that it is "toward Hebron, one of the highest points in the Judean mountains."

244. According to 33:36-38, Israel encamped in the wilderness of Zin (i.e., Kadesh) and moved from Kadesh to Mount Hor, which is at the edge of the land of Edom and where Aaron died on the first day of the fifth month of the fortieth year. Cf. Ashley, *The Book of Numbers,* p. 380; E. W. Davies, *Numbers,* p. 202. Milgrom (*Numbers,* pp. 164, 464) discusses other options and arrives at the same conclusion as most commentators.

curred at the end of Israel's forty years of wandering in the wilderness. In contrast to this implicit chronological indication, 20:14 states clearly that Israel's encounter with Edom happened at Kadesh, which must be located near the western border of the Edomite territory. Questions such as whether or not Edom had a centralized monarchy and whether, at the time when Moses sent messengers, the Edomites occupied an extensive area including the west side of the 'Arabah, reaching to the fringe of the wilderness of Zin, are outside of the scope of the present comparison.[245] However, if the first month of the fortieth year is the date when Israel came into the wilderness of Zin and stayed in Kadesh, then is it not inconsistent that Israel came to Kadesh in the wilderness of Paran after a two-month journey from Sinai (10:12; 12:16; 13:3, 26)? In what precise year did Israel encamp at Kadesh? Did Israel leave Kadesh to journey toward "the wilderness by the way to the Red Sea" following Yahweh's punishment (14:25), and then come back to the same location (Kadesh) after forty years of wandering? Or is the notation that Israel stayed in Kadesh in 20:1 a simple reminder of their arrival mentioned in 12:16 (cf. 10:12), which implies Israel's thirty-eight-year settlement in Kadesh? This inconsistency is important not only for the chronological and topographical context of Israel's encounter with Edom, but also for Israel's migration in the wilderness in its entirety. This problem will be discussed later in the analysis of the conceptual framework of the direct military accounts.

(c) Similar to 20:14-21, when Israel encountered the Canaanites as reported in 21:1-3 is not clear. The location of the text, however, provides a hint of its time frame within the literary context of Numbers. The text is located between the report of the event that happened at Mount Hor, which was about the time of the death of Aaron (20:22-29), and Israel's setting out from Mount Hor (21:4a). This sequence of events is the same as those that 33:38-41 present. Thus, Israel's encounter with the Canaanite, the king of Arad, must have occurred in the fortieth year of Israel's campaign in the wilderness. In terms of the topographical location of the battle, 21:1-3 mentions two places. Verse 21:1 suggests that the battle site may be any spot on "the way of Atharim." This is the way from which the Canaanite, the king of Arad, knew Israel was coming, and he fought and took some of the Israelites captive. However, 21:3 suggests that the "second" battle place is called Hormah, where Israel utterly destroyed the Canaanites and their towns.[246] According to

---

245. Aharoni, *Land of the Bible*, pp. 40-41; cf. J. R. Bartlett, *Edom and the Edomites* (Sheffield: Sheffield Academic Press, 1989).

246. These topographical indicators — the way of Atharim (v. 1) and Hormah (v. 3) — clearly break the narrative continuity between 20:22-29 and 21:4ff. Mount Hor is the place where

Y. Aharoni, "the way of Atharim" is the road leading from Kadesh-barnea to the Arad area, from southwest to northeast, in Palestine.[247] Aharoni also suggests that Hormah is located in the eastern Negeb, in the area of Beersheba and Arad.[248] Questions emerge. Is Hormah in 21:3 the same place mentioned in 14:45, where Israel was defeated by the Amalekites and the Canaanites? If so, why are there two accounts that have Hormah as the topographical battle site? Why does one report Israel's total defeat and another their complete victory? If these accounts are two versions of the same event in which Israel encountered the Canaanites in their attempt to conquer Canaan from the south, regardless of the outcome, why is it necessary to report the event twice in very opposite ways, and why are these two versions located in their respective places? These questions are crucial for reconstructing the conceptuality underneath both chapters 13–14 and 21:1-3 and the conceptuality of the whole of 10:11–36:13. At this point, it is clear that although 21:1-3 mentions two places, the way of Atharim and Hormah, these are located in and on the way to the Negeb, which is the southern part of the land of Canaan.

(d) Despite the absence of a chronological indicator, Israel's encounter with King Sihon of the Amorites must have occurred in the fortieth year. Regarding topographical indicators, 21:21-31 mentions many places, such as the King's Highway that Israel wished to follow, Jahaz as the explicit battle place, the Arnon and Jabbok as the borders of King Sihon's territory, and Heshbon and its towns as representative places of the land of the Amorites that Israel occupied. The exact geographical designation for these places is not the question of the present comparison.[249] Suffice it to say that all places mentioned in 21:21-31 belong to the southern part of the Transjordan.

Israel entered (20:22), where Aaron died (20:28), and from which Israel set out (21:4). But this is neither the place where the event reported in 21:1-3 occurred nor the direction in which Israel set out after the event.

247. Aharoni, *Land of the Bible*, p. 58. See also the maps for the main roads of Palestine (p. 43) and the routes to the Transjordan (p. 203). Aharoni (p. 202) also suggests that Mount Hor where Aaron died should be located "on the way of the Atharim," because the Mount is always mentioned as along the route of this journey (20:22-29; 21:4; 33:37-39; Deut 32:50).

248. Aharoni, *Land of the Bible*, p. 31. Hormah has been tentatively identified as Tell-Masos, and as a town mentioned in the inscription of Amenemhet III of the nineteenth century B.C.E. Cf. B. Mazar, "The Sanctuary of Arad and the Family of Hobab the Kenite," *JNES* 24 (1965): 297-308.

249. Ashley, *The Book of Numbers*, pp. 418-28; Aharoni, *Land of the Bible*, pp. 54-57 (particularly, King's Highway); G. E. Mendenhall, "Amorites," in *ABD*, ed. D. N. Freedman, vol. 1 (New York: Doubleday, 1992), pp. 199-202. Fearer (*Wars in the Wilderness*, pp. 262-63) discusses the possible site from which Israel sent the envoys to King Sihon. He concludes that the likely place is the station set on the Moab/wilderness side of the Arnon (21:13) based on the fact that Israel had not

(e) Unit 21:32-35 follows immediately after Israel's encounter with Sihon (21:21-31) in the extant text. This sequence suggests that 21:21-31 provides a broader literary context for 21:32-35. Within the limits of verses 32-35, the text is not clear regarding the references for the plural verbs (וילכדו [v. 32b], וַיִּפֶן ויעלו [v. 33a], ויכו . . . וַיִּירְשׁוּ [v. 35]), when Moses sent the spies or when they (the Israelites?) turned, went up, and marched. Although no plural subject is mentioned explicitly in 21:21-31 and the term "Israel" takes singular verbs throughout the text, the implied subject of the plural verbs in verses 32-35 is most likely the Israelites.[250] In terms of the time frame, verses 32-35 must be understood as events which occurred after Israel's occupation of the land of the Amorites (v. 31). In terms of the topography of the battle locations, verses 32-35 mention several place names, such as Jazer, the road to Bashan, and Edrei. According to Aharoni, these places are located in the northern district of the Transjordan, north of King Sihon's old territory.[251] Moreover, if the designation "the road of Bashan" is not to be understood as the name of an actual road, but as a direction, 21:32-35 describes Israel's movement northward to the Bashan territory. The passage 21:21-35 as a whole indicates that Israel campaigned continually northward from Arnon to the slopes of Mount Hermon (the northern border of Bashan's territory) via Jazer.

(f) The passage 31:1-12 lacks details concerning the date of the battle and its location. However, the text provides clues for tracing its chronological and topographical framework. In the final form of the text, 31:1-54 presupposes Moses' imminent death (v. 2b; cf. 27:13), the death of Aaron and succession of Eleazar (v. 6a; cf. 20:22-29), the Balaam incident (vv. 8, 16; cf. chs. 22–24), and Israel's apostasy to Baal of Peor (31:16; cf. 25:1-18). Since these events occurred in and around the fortieth year in the plains of Moab, Israel's encounter with Midian must be understood to have happened in the last part of the forty-year campaign and in the plains of Moab, although 31:1-54 as a whole includes other incidents that happened before the fortieth year in places other than the plains of Moab.[252]

---

crossed the border (21:21-23) and that the stations described in 21:16-20 are taken to be within the boundaries described as those gained by Israel in their victory over King Sihon (21:24).

250. The preceding unit (21:10-20) has the Israelites as the subject of third person masculine plural verbs eight times (נסעו ויחנו [v. 11], ויסעו . . . ויחנו [v. 10], ויסעו בני ישראל ויחנו [v. 12], נסעו ויחנו [v. 13]).

251. Aharoni, *Land of the Bible*, pp. 37-38. For more detailed topographical descriptions of these places, see Noth, *Numbers*, p. 166; Ashley, *The Book of Numbers*, pp. 428-30; Milgrom, *Numbers*, p. 184.

252. 31:1-54 as a whole includes additional matters discussed in other passages in Numbers, such as the trumpets (v. 6; cf. 10:1-10), purification after contact with death (vv. 19-24; cf. 19:11-19), sharing booty with the priests and Levites (vv. 28-47; cf. 18:8-32), and costly offerings (vv. 48-54; cf. chs. 7, 28–29). Cf. Ashley, *The Book of Numbers*, p. 587.

(iv) The Objectives and the Results

(a) The objective and the result of the people's expedition in 14:39-45 are clear. The people campaigned up to the Negeb and attempted to conquer "the place that Yahweh has promised" (v. 40bα), the land of Canaan, from the south; they were defeated and pursued by the Amalekites and the Canaanites as far as Hormah. Their expedition was viewed as a materialization of their remorse (v. 40bβ) and further as a desire to win Yahweh's favor. But the campaign was doomed to failure from the beginning, as indicated by Moses' warning of the absence of Yahweh.

(b) The objective of the messengers' speech (20:14b-17) is to request permission to pass through Edom's territory. The speech begins with the identity of the speaker ("your brother Israel") and a sketch of the history of Israel, with the expectation that the king of Edom will understand and be sympathetic to Israel's present situation; it ends with a petition to pass coupled with idealistic pledges. The objective of the Israelites' speech (v. 19) is the same, although shorter and more realistic than the messengers' speech. Their speech starts with pledges that they will compensate the Edomites financially for any provisions they may need during their passage, and it finishes with a statement that their request is a small thing. These two requests are rejected by Edom, and Israel is turned away from Edom as a result.

(c) In the flow of the extant text, the objective of Israel's utter destruction of the Canaanites is revenge for the Canaanite's initial victory over them. Israel's revenge is reflected in its determination to destroy the Canaanites. Initially its own military power was not enough to protect itself from the Canaanite, the king of Arad. As a reaction to the initial defeat, Israel made a vow to Yahweh for חרם, a holy war, as if it could prevail only with Yahweh's help or as if its war against the Canaanites would be a holy war that Yahweh must wage alone. The result is Israel's complete destruction of the Canaanites and their towns. Compared to what the king of Arad had done, that is, having taken some of the Israelites captive, the text radicalizes Israel's behavior by portraying its making a vow of חרם and carrying out the war in its fullness. Yahweh's granting Israel's vow and the stress of utter destruction are also indicative that Israel's revenge against the Canaanites is the objective of 21:1-3.

(d) On the surface level of 21:21-31, the objective of Israel's encounter with King Sihon is ambiguous. According to the messengers' speech (v. 22), the objective is to pass through Sihon's territory without disturbing his field or vineyard or even his well. However, as a response to Sihon's refusal, his gathering of the troops, and the ensuing attack, Israel engaged in battle and took possession of his entire land, including all the towns of the Amorites, instead of retreating from his territory as they had done in the case of Edom.[253] Moreover, the text reports that Israel not only possessed Sihon's towns and lands but also occupied them. This occupation is justified by appealing to a historical precedent concerning the same territory, that is, Sihon had taken all the land of the king of Moab after having defeated him. Now Israel has taken the same land from Sihon as a result of the victory over him, and thus Moab could make no legitimate claim against Israel (vv. 26-30).[254] Is the objective of Israel to pass through Sihon's territory? If so, why did Sihon refuse first and then attack later? Why did Israel not move on to its next destination after its victory over Sihon? Why did Israel occupy the entire land and towns of the Amorites, indicating their intention to stay or settle there? Note that compared to Israel's request for peaceful passage through Sihon's territory, Israel's possession of וַיִּירַשׁ in v. 24b; וַיִּקַּח in v. 25a) and eventual occupation of (וַיֵּשֶׁב in vv. 25b, 31a) the entire land of the Amorites has been extensively elaborated (vv. 24b-31). This elaboration includes the mocking song (vv. 27-30), functioning to support the fact that Sihon previously had occupied the former Moabite territory north of the Arnon, which helped to legitimate Israel's claim to the same territory against possible protests from Moab. The extensive elaboration suggests that the messengers' speech in verse 22 functions as something more than Israel's request for passage. Conceptually, the speech indicates Israel's innocence concerning the following events. Israel was not aggressive at the beginning of its encounter with Sihon; for example, Israel did not cause the battle, for they did not have a choice when Sihon refused passage and attacked. The battle was inevitable. The speech paves the way for the justification of the following events: the inevitable battle, Israel's victory over Sihon, and the resulting dispossession of and occupation of Sihon's land.[255] Thus, Israel's real objective is the occupation of Amorite towns and lands, and this objective is accomplished, as the summary statement (v. 31) clearly states. Furthermore, the text as a whole is interested in establishing the legitimacy of the objective — Israel's occupation of the land of the Amorites

---

253. Why does Israel battle against King Sihon, which results in the occupation of his land and which differs from Israel's encounter with Edom? The answer cannot be found within the limits of the text. The question needs to be taken up in the discussion of the conceptuality that underlies the direct military accounts.

254. Fearer (*Wars in the Wilderness*, p. 367, n. 171) succinctly states this point: "victory in battle determines and verifies authority and ownership. . . . Might makes right."

255. For the same understanding of the function of the messengers' speech, see Noth (*Numbers*, pp. 162-63). Outside of this text, the Sihon tradition is mentioned as a military victory for Israel and is never mentioned as a peaceful negotiation of Israel with Sihon (Deut 1:4; 4:46; 29:7; 31:4; Josh 2:10; 12:1-3; 13:21; Judg 11:19-21; Neh 9:22; Ps 136:17-19).

— evidenced in the function of the mocking song and the messengers' speech.

(e) Unlike 21:21-31, 21:32-35 is clear on Israel's objective. It is a military campaign against Jazer (v. 32) and King Og of Bashan. Moses/Israel are portrayed as aggressors who have the intention of conquering Jazer and Bashan's territory. There is no mention of sending envoys to request permission to pass through King Og's territory. Instead, all military actions in the text are premeditated. Moses sends the spies to Jazer to gather information for the impending attack and conquest; Israel turns and goes up the road to Bashan, an action which should be understood as a military advance, anticipating the inevitable military engagement with Og the King of Bashan; and Yahweh takes the initiative to instruct the Israelites in battle, assuring them of victory. The result is Israel's dispossession of the Amorites who lived in the villages of Jazer, and possession of the land of Og after killing him, his sons, and all his people. Note that there is no explicit mention of Israel's occupation of captured villages (v. 32) or of Og's land (v. 35). The text as it stands ends with Israel's dispossession of the land of Og, not its occupation.[256]

(f) Israel's war against Midian is stated in both Yahweh's speech to Moses (31:2) and Moses' speech to the people (vv. 3-4). Yahweh commanded Moses to "avenge [נקם נקמת] the Israelites on the Midianites," and Moses commanded the people "to execute Yahweh's vengeance on Midian" (לתת נקמת־יהוה במדין). These two statements share a common denominator: to wage war against Midian. However, the exact reason for the war is not entirely clear. Do the Israelites battle against the Midianites in order to vindicate the honor of Yahweh, as suggested by Moses's speech to the people? Or, is the war with Midian to protect the people of Israel from further corruption of their faith, as Yahweh's speech implies? The solution lies in the character of the war, חרם or holy war. The objective of Israel's war against Midian is not a simple military engagement which intends to take possession of or to occupy the land of Midian, but an utter destruction of all Midian, including both human and nonhuman objects, for the purpose of cultic matters.[257] As the basis of the bat-

---

256. Fearer (*Wars in the Wilderness*, pp. 402-6) argues that occupation is implicitly an aspect of ירש in 21:35b. He supports his argument with Lohfink's reconstruction of the tradition history of ירש (cf. N. Lohfink, "ירש," in *TDOT*, ed. G. J. Botterweck, H. Ringgren, and H.-J. Fabry, trans. J. T. Willis, G. W. Bromiley, and D. E. Green, vol. 3 [Grand Rapids: Eerdmans, 1978], pp. 386-96).

257. Ashley (*The Book of Numbers*, p. 591), following Mendenhall's suggestion, translates the root נקם as "punitive (or perhaps defensive) vindication." Cf. G. E. Mendenhall, "The 'Vengeance' of Yahweh," in *The Tenth Generation* (Baltimore: Johns Hopkins University Press, 1973), pp. 69-104. This translation may be appropriate for other passages, but it is not correct in 31:1-54 because the text as a whole is interested in the cultic matters caused by the war rather than the war itself.

tle report (vv. 1-12), 25:16-18 shows that Yahweh commanded Moses to wage a war against Midian because the Midianites had harassed the Israelites by luring them into idolatrous rites. The possibility of further corruption of Israel's faith by the Midianites is the reason for Yahweh's command. This reason implies that Israel must eradicate any elements among the Midianites which might make them stray from Yahweh once again. Unit 31:1-54 as a whole also points to the cultic nature of the war. Phinehas, son of Eleazar the priest, along with the cultic symbols, accompanied the soldiers (v. 6); Moses became enraged with the officers of the army because the Israelites did not kill the women of Midian but took them captive (vv. 9, 13-18); Moses commanded the cleansing of the soldiers, while Eleazar ordered the troops to remove their uncleanness and purify nonhuman objects (vv. 19-24); Moses commanded them as to how to divide the booty, including the rightful share of the sanctuary personnel (vv. 25-47); and the officers brought the offering to Yahweh (vv. 48-54). The objective of the war is to annihilate any elements of the Midianites in order to protect Israel from any further possible corruption. The Israelites accomplished this objective thoroughly, evidenced in the killing of "every male" of Midian, the destroying of "all" their towns and encampments, and the taking of "all" their belongings, "both the people and animals."

(b) Structural Significance of Numbers 13–14

(i) Emerging Questions

From this comparison of the explicit information given in the six direct military accounts, many questions emerge. These questions can be classified into three groups: those stemming from (a) an individual unit; (b) the comparison of all six units; and (c) each unit's relation to its immediate literary context and its location in the extant text. Answers to these questions are not entirely evident within the limits of the units themselves and rest on the infratextual levels of the units and in the overarching conceptuality responsible for the units' locations and relations to each other within the whole text (Num 10:11–36:13).

(α) Concerning Individual Units

Concerning the individual units, the following questions arise. In 14:39-45, why did the people go to conquer the land of Canaan from the south, even though they knew of the absence of Yahweh and Moses from the beginning of their expedition? Related to 20:14-21, why did the Israelites need passage through Edom's territory, or what benefit did they expect for their continuing migration by passing through it? What was their final destination, which both the messengers' speech and the people's speech to Edom do not reveal? Why did Edom, called by Israel its "brother," refuse the request for peaceful passage and cause Israel to turn away from its territory? Related to 21:1-3, why did Israel take the initiative in making a vow to utterly destroy the Canaanites and receive Yahweh's permission for it? Related to 21:31-31, why did King Sihon refuse passage and come out against the Israelites despite their request for passage coupled with vows insuring no impact upon Sihon, his people, or his holdings? Why did the Israelites, going beyond their request for passage through Sihon's territory, fight him and his troops and take possession of all towns and the land of the Amorites? Why did Israel not simply pass through after their victory over Sihon rather than occupying the entire Amorite land and towns with the apparent intention to settle or stay there? Related to 21:32-35, why did Moses dispossess only the Amorites who inhabited the villages of Jazer, rather than destroy or take possession of the whole city of Jazer and its villages, including other groups of people? Why did Yahweh take the initiative in comforting Moses with providential assurance of the victory and instruct him how to battle against King Og, with reference to Israel's victory over Sihon? And related to 31:1-54, why was the voice of the Midianites completely absent? Or why did Yahweh mention Moses' imminent death together with avenging Midian?

(β) Concerning a Comparison of Units

From a comparison of all six units, the following questions arise. (a) In terms of acting subjects, all six units include the Israelites explicitly and implicitly. Why does only 21:1-3 use singular verbs for Israel describing Israel as a single unified political entity, while the remaining five refer to Israel with a mixture of singular and plural verbs, pronouns, and suffixes? Moreover, there is a shift in Moses' involvement depicted through the units: 14:39-45 shows him playing a significant role (although he did not participate in the people's expedition); 20:14-21 as a whole describes him as one who recedes into the background after verse 14, where he is the subject of sending the messengers to the king of Edom; 21:1-3 and 21:21-31 do not mention him at all; 21:32-35 and 31:1-54 indicate Moses' active participation in the events unfolding there. There is a similar shift regarding Yahweh's involvement in these units: 14:39-45, 20:14-21, and 21:21-31 exclude Yahweh at the outset; 21:1-3 show Yahweh's limited role in his granting of Israel's vow against the Canaanites; whereas 21:32-35 and 31:1-54 reveal Yahweh's active roles, from comforting Moses in the face of impending battle with King Og to commanding Moses to avenge Israel against Midian. Why do some units exclude both Yahweh and Moses or Moses alone, while others portray them prominently?

(b) In terms of identification of the opponents, the six military accounts have two groups of people: the people who lived inside what Numbers understands is the border of the land promised for Israel (the Amalekites, the Canaanites, and the Canaanite [the king of Arad]) and those who lived outside of this designated territory (the Edomites, Sihon [the king of the Amorites who lived in the Transjordan area], the Amorites in the villages of Jazer, King Og of Bashan, and the Midianites). In terms of the characterization of Israel's encounter with these peoples, the six units describe Israel dominantly as the aggressor or the attacker.[258] For example, the people of Israel took the initiative in the battle against the Amalekites and the Canaanites (14:39-45); Israel reacted to its initial defeat by the king of Arad by making a vow of חרם, which shows their determination to conquer the Canaanites (21:1-3); the Israelites dispossessed and ultimately occupied the towns and the land of the Amorites, although in the beginning they had requested passage through the Amorite territory (21:21-31); and, finally, not even bothering to send envoys to Jazer, King Og of Bashan, and the Midianites, Israel executed premeditated campaigns against these peoples. The only exception is 20:14-21. Why is it that the Israelites in 20:14-21 are described as weaker than the Edomites, so that they must turn away from the border of Edom?

(c) Regarding topographical locations, is Hormah in 21:1-3 (v. 3) the same place noted in 14:39-45 (v. 45)? If so, why are there two accounts or versions regarding Israel's military conflict with the Canaanites at Hormah? Why do they report that the Israelites were defeated in 14:39-45, on the one hand, and that the Canaanites were utterly destroyed in 21:1-3, on the other? Moreover, if Kadesh in 20:14 (and v. 22) is the same place noted in 13:26 and 20:1, and if "the first month" in 20:1 is assumed to be the first month of the fortieth year of Israel's campaign, was Kadesh the place at which the Israelites had stayed for almost thirty-eight years or the place to which they returned after having spent the thirty-eight years elsewhere? Furthermore, whereas Israel's expedition in 14:39-45 occurred in the second year after the Exodus event, Israel's military conflicts in the rest of the five units happened in and around the fortieth year after the Exodus event. Why is there this time gap? Why do the five units gathered together show no significant time gap among themselves in the extant text?

---

258. This characterization of Israel is congruent with the nature of its camp, a cultic-military camp organized in and around the tabernacle, with more than 600,000 soldiers.

(d) In terms of the objective of Israel's encounter with other peoples, 20:14-21 and 31:1-54 differ from other units. While the other four units concern the military engagement itself, with the intention of killing the enemies and capturing, destroying, and dispossessing their holdings, 20:14-21 focuses on the pre-stage of the actual military contact, and 31:1-54 is interested in the battle's consequence. On the one hand, no actual battle is reported in 20:14-21, which concerns Israel's peaceful passage through Edom's territory without an alternative or hidden political, economic, or military motive against Edom. Unit 31:1-54, on the other hand, stresses the aftermath of Israel's battle against Midian, specifically, the cultic implications of the battle, that is, preserving Israel's faith from possible corruption by the Midianites.

In terms of the result of Israel's military conflicts with others, two categories are evident: failure by defeat (14:39-45) and by retreat (20:14-21), and success by victory (21:1-3, 21-31, 32-35; 31:1-54). Israel's expedition in 14:39-45 is doomed to fail from its inception, and Israel's failure with Edom is evident in its turning away from Edom. In the four other units, Israel's success is undoubtedly clear, although each unit contains various intermediate stages of the conflicts.[259] Besides containing clear statements of Israel's victory over its enemies (21:3ab, 24-31, 32b, 35; 31:7-12), 21:2-3aα shows Israel's determination to utterly destroy and Yahweh's permission to do so; 21:26-30 justifies Israel's legitimacy in occupation of the land of the Amorites represented by Heshbon; 21:34 states Yahweh's providential assurance of Israel's victory; and 31:2 and 6 show Yahweh's own command to battle and Yahweh's presence on the battlefield. All these elements serve to make sure Israel's campaign over its enemies is successful. Questions related to these objectives and their results include: Why did Israel not dispossess and further occupy the towns of the Canaanites after utterly destroying them, as it did the Amorite land (21:1-3)? Why did Israel not move continually forward (i.e., northward from the south) to destroy all the towns of Canaan, instead of setting out by "the way to the Red Sea" (21:4)? Why did the Israelites not occupy the villages of Jazer and the land of Bashan, as they did the land of the Amorites? Why did Israel campaign continually northward against Jazer and Bashan after occupation of Amorite land? Had Israel not already secured clear passage across the Jordan to begin the conquest of the land of Canaan from the east?

---

259. Numbers 21:1 reports Israel's initial defeat by the king of Arad; 21:21-22 indicates Israel's intention only for passage without military conflict with King Sihon; 21:34 presupposes Moses' fear of King Og, which is resolved by Yahweh's comfort, and Moses' need for a battle plan, which is also resolved by Yahweh's instruction; 31:3 suggests Moses' clarification of Yahweh's command.

(γ) Concerning Locations and Relations in the Literary Context

In terms of the locations of the six units and their relations to the immediate literary contexts, why are all six direct military accounts ordered in a sequence of defeat (13:1–14:45), retreat (20:14-21), and continual victories (21:1-3, 21-31, 32-35; 31:1-54)? Why are the five accounts, except 13:1–14:45, grouped together as events which occurred at the end of Israel's forty-year campaign in the wilderness? Why is the account of Aaron's death (20:22-29) inserted between Israel's retreat from Edom (20:14-21) and Israel's continual victories over enemies, beginning with the Canaanites (21:1-3)? Why are three of the four victories located closer to each other within chapter 21, and interrupted by a rebellion narrative (the serpent scourge [21:4-9]) as well as a report of Israel's migration from Mount Hor, where Aaron died, to the valley near Pisgah in Moab (21:10-20)?[260] Related to 21:1-3, why is this text located at its current place, which interrupts the continuity of 20:22-29 and 21:4-9? Related to 21:21-31, why is this text placed after the citation of an itinerary that shows Israel's presence already in the region of Moab (21:18-20), only to backtrack and recount their conquest of the area? Related to 21:32-35, since this passage presupposes Israel's passing through the plains of Moab, where they camped and remained from 22:1 until the first chapter of Joshua,[261] why does it interrupt the geographical consistency between 21:21-31 and 22:1 onward (cf. 33:43-49)? Why does this text not mention Israel's conquering the intervening territory between Sihon and Og, that is, Gilead (cf. 32:39-42)?[262]

---

260. The itinerary formulae of 21:4a and 10a are incomplete. The former lacks the place of Israel's previous encampment, while the latter lacks the place of their decampment. Are these broken formulae due to the insertion of the incident of the serpent scourge (21:4-9)? If so, why is this text located between Israel's victory over the Canaanites (who inhabited the promised land) and its victory over Sihon, the king of the Amorites (who dwelled outside the land of Canaan)?

261. "The plains of Moab" occurs in 22:1; 26:3, 63; 31:12; 33:48, 49, 50; 35:1; 36:13; Deut 34:1, 8 and may be identified as "northern Moab (the region north of the Arnon)" or the narrow and fertile strip of country from the Arnon to the Jabbok. Cf. Miller, "The Israelite Journey through (around) Moab," pp. 577-95; N. Glueck, "Some Ancient Towns in the Plains of Moab," *BASOR* 91 (1943): 24-25.

262. In excursus 55 (*Numbers*, pp. 463-67), titled "The Redaction of Chapters 20–21," Milgrom lists eight questions that emerge from chronological, exegetical, and source analytical difficulties in chs. 20–21. As the key to these questions, Milgrom (p. 464) argues that "the two chapters were redacted to show that despite the continual murmuring of the Israelites, now by a new generation, and the rebellion of their leaders, Moses and Aaron . . . , God provides His people with all its needs: water, healing, and victory." Milgrom's questions are well formulated, but his answer is too general or broad to pinpoint the concept underneath chs. 20–21. This criticism will be substantiated later in the course of answering the three sets of questions above.

(ii) Relation of Questions to Numbers 13–14

All three sets of questions are related in one way or another to Israel's failure to conquer the promised land from the south, the spies incident in chapters 13–14. *Yahweh's forgiveness of Israel's failure is seen in the fact that Yahweh's promise of the divine land will not be broken; it will remain intact. Yahweh's punishment is seen in the fact that the promise of the divine land will be fulfilled not by the Exodus generation, who must instead die out in the wilderness during forty years of wandering, but by the next generation, even though they will suffer the same forty years of wandering because of their forebears' failure. These two sides of Yahweh's response to Israel's failure are the final and constitutive vantage point from which to view the material of 10:11–36:13.*

(α) Completion of Yahweh's Punishment for Israel's Failure

The reason for Israel's expedition into Canaan (14:44) is ambiguous. The Israelites knew that deciding to go up the next morning was once again breaking Yahweh's command ("turn tomorrow and set out for the wilderness") and that Moses had warned them about the existence of the Amalekites and the Canaanites, the source of their fear in the hill country, and the absence of Yahweh, the source of their confidence in their campaign. Why did they go up to Canaan in spite of their knowledge? Does Israel's expedition reflect their stupidity or overweening arrogance?[263] By admitting their guilt and changing their minds and taking the initiative to go up into the land, they might think that Yahweh would forgive them, obliterate the punishment, and ultimately grant them the land. However, the resultant defeat of the expedition shows that Yahweh's punishment on the Exodus generation is irrevocable. Note that the inevitability of Israel's defeat has already been intensified by the occurrence of a Yahweh oath formula (14:21a, 28a) within Yahweh's announcement of the punishment. Moreover, in light of Yahweh's immediate punishment of the scouts (14:36-37), Israel's abortive expedition must be understood as an initial and partial fulfillment of Yahweh's punishment of the Exodus generation. The death of the Exodus generation in the wilderness begins immediately after Yahweh's pronouncement of it. The texts that follow 14:39-45 unfold how Yahweh's punishment reaches its completion throughout the period of forty years in the wilderness.

Note that in 14:39-45, the defeated ones are the Exodus generation, from

---

263. Ashley, *The Book of Numbers*, pp. 270-74.

which Moses, the priestly personnel, and Caleb and Joshua are excluded. Since "all" the Exodus generation, except Caleb and Joshua, are doomed to death in the wilderness, the events occurring after 14:39-45 would provide the rationale for the inclusion of the leaders (Miriam, Aaron, and Moses) and the Levites (separated from the rest of the Israelites) in the irreversible fate of the Exodus generation. This point sheds new light on the rebellion of Korah, who is portrayed as the representative conspirator of the Levites and leaders, and as an associate of Dathan and Abiram (16:1–17:15), and of Moses and Aaron (20:1-13). These rebellion narratives are not isolated incidents but are part of Yahweh's irrevocable punishment on all the Exodus generation. No excuse can be made for the Levites, Aaron, or even Moses for sharing their fate.

From the vantage point of Yahweh's response to Israel's failure, chapter 20 marks the completion of Yahweh's punishment on the Exodus generation. Verse 20:1 reports the death of Miriam, one of the three high-ranking leaders within the hierarchical organization of the Israelites' sanctuary camp. Passage 20:2-13 recounts Yahweh's denial of the prophetic leadership of Moses and Aaron. Yahweh's characterization of the sin of Moses and Aaron as a distrust of Yahweh which led them not to sanctify Yahweh in the eyes of the Israelites, "לא־האמנתם בי להקדישני לעיני בני ישראל" (v. 12a), is connected to Israel's distrust of Yahweh's plan for them in chapters 13–14.[264] As punishment for their sin, Yahweh denies them the responsibility of leading the people into the promised land (v. 12b). Since the denial of Moses' and Aaron's leadership implies their exclusion from inheriting the promised land and their death in the wilderness, Yahweh's punishment of them in essence is the same as

---

264. According to M. Margaliot, the hiph'il of the niph'al נאמן must be translated "to trust My faithfulness (as my messengers to you and as to the people)." By relating this word to the concept of covenant, Margaliot expands the idea that leaders are supposed to impress on the people Yahweh's faithfulness to them as the God of their covenant ("The Transgression of Moses and Aaron — Num 20:1-13," *JQR* 76 [1983]: 222-23). Locating נאמן ב in covenantal relationship, however, is not convincing due to a lack of sufficient references. However, in Num 14:11 Yahweh complains that the people "have not trusted in me" (לא־יאמינו בי). Since this reference is understood as Yahweh's anger toward the people because they have not trusted the divine plan to bring them into the promised land or Yahweh's faithfulness to fulfill this plan, 20:12 can also be understood in a similar way: that Moses and Aaron failed to trust Yahweh's commitment and faithfulness in providing for their needs. Failing to trust in Yahweh's faithfulness causes serious consequences. Moreover, this rendering is persistent with the usage of "sanctify" in Yahweh's characterization of the leaders' behavior. Within the verses that concern Moses' and Aaron's sin, the verb קדש appears once in the niph'al (Num 20:13), once in the pi'el (Deut 32:51), and twice in the hiph'il (Num 20:12; 27:14). Investigating the dominant conceptual aspect of these forms, including in other passages (niph'al: Lev 10:3; 22:32; Isa 5:16; Ezek 20:41; 28:22, 25; 36:23; 38:16; 39:27; pi'el: Ezek 36:23; hiph'il: Isa 8:13; 29:23), suggests that the essence of the sin of the leaders is their misrepresentation to the people of Yahweh's fidelity to the divine promise to help them.

Yahweh's punishment of the Exodus generation. This punishment has already been foreshadowed in their response to the people's rebellion in the spies incident (14:5).[265] Thus, 20:2-13 rationalizes the inclusion of Moses and Aaron in the doomed fate of the Exodus generation.

The claim that chapter 20 marks the completion of Yahweh's punishment of the Exodus generation can be supported by its topographical location of Kadesh, and by its chronological setting of the fortieth year. There is no dispute that Israel's encounter with Edom (20:14-21) and Aaron's death (20:22-29) occurred in the fortieth year and at Kadesh and its near vicinity (i.e., Mount Hor). It is also clear that Yahweh's denial of Moses' and Aaron's leadership happened at Kadesh, but, in contrast, it is not entirely clear whether or not the event occurred in the fortieth year because of the incomplete date for Israel's arrival at Kadesh. In 20:1 Israel arrived at Kadesh, located in the wilderness of Zin (cf. 20:14, 16, 22; 27:14; 34:36, 37), in "the first month" without specifying the year, whereas in 13:26 the spies returned after surveying the land of Canaan at Kadesh, located in the wilderness of Paran, where Israel arrived right after they had left the wilderness of Sinai (10:12; 12:16; 13:3). Geographical inconsistency — whether Kadesh belongs to the wilderness of Paran or the wilderness of Zin — can be explained. Kadesh might be located on the border of the wilderness of Paran and the wilderness of Zin, although the precise location of Kadesh cannot be determined due to the text's geographical fluidity.

However, chronological inconsistency as to when exactly Israel arrived at Kadesh is still problematic. Levine argues that this inconsistency is a result of the interplay of the two sources, the Yahwistic-Elohistic (JE) and the Priestly (P).[266] Verse 13:26 reflects the historiography of the JE narrative: that the Israelites arrived at Kadesh very soon after they had left the wilderness of Sinai (cf. 32:8), that they stayed a short period of time in Kadesh after the failure of their attempted penetration into Canaan, and that they spent most of the thirty-eight years wandering in the wilderness east of Edom and south of Moab.[267] However, 20:1 reflects the historiography of the P traditions: that the

---

265. Ashley (*The Book of Numbers*, pp. 247-48) discusses in detail how Moses and Aaron prostrated themselves in front of the rebellious people. However, despite various interpretations of their behavior, the sharp contrast between Moses' and Aaron's initial response to the people and Caleb's and Joshua's persistent responses to them (13:30; 14:6-9) suggests that the former is viewed as passive or defensive. Although Moses intercedes for Yahweh on behalf of the people, his initial response before Yahweh's appearance shows his cowardliness and foreshadows his distrust in the Meribah incident (20:1-13).

266. Levine, *Numbers 1–20*, pp. 52-57.

267. Levine (*Numbers 1–20*, p. 55) reconstructs JE's version of the Israelites' itinerary based on deuteronomistic historiography (cf. Deut 1:19, 46; 2:14; Josh 14:6-12; Judg 11:6-7).

Israelites arrived at Kadesh in the fortieth year; that they spent most of the thirty-eight years in northern Sinai, the wilderness of Paran.[268] The question is, then, why did the Priestly authors revise the JE version of Israel's itinerary, thereby reconstructing their own record which keeps the Israelites in Sinai for thirty-eight years of migration and which narrates their arrival at Kadesh only in the fortieth year? Again, the answer is clear in light of Yahweh's punishment of the Exodus generation. By mentioning Kadesh, the Priestly authors locate the rebellion of Moses and Aaron at Kadesh where the Israelites' unprecedented rebellion also occurred, and thus they rationalize the inclusion of Moses and Aaron in the doomed fate of all the Exodus generation. By placing Kadesh in the wilderness of Paran, northern Sinai, they show the fulfillment of Yahweh's punishment of the Exodus generation to die out in *this* wilderness (14:29, 32-33, 35). With an incomplete date, the Priestly authors attempt to loosen the tension created by the JE version of Israel's arrival at Kadesh in the beginning of the schematic forty-year wilderness period, and they date the rebellion of Moses and Aaron in the fortieth year. By dating the leaders' rebellion in the fortieth year, they stress the continuous rebellions of the Exodus generation during the forty years and characterize the leaders' rebellion as the climax of a series of rebellions. *For them, the forty-year wilderness period begins with the Israelites' rebellion and ends with the leaders' rebellion. Thus, the leaders' rebellion in 20:2-13 functions to indicate the completion of the forty years of Yahweh's punishment on all the Exodus generation.* Kadesh and "the first month" in the extant text of 20:1 reflect this intention of the Priestly authors.[269]

Moreover, Yahweh's punishment of Moses and Aaron becomes a reality in the rest of chapter 20. Knowing that Israel's encounter with Edom is their first approach to other peoples since their dealing with the Amalekites and the Canaanites, Edom refuses to allow passage and Israel avoids a military confrontation with Edom, revealing that Moses' role as the leader of Israel has been significantly reduced. The gradual decreasing of Moses' involvement in the following events reinforces this point. Moses in 20:14-21 recedes into the

---

268. The "first month" in 20:1 must be the first month of the fortieth year, based on the comprehensive itinerary of Israel's wilderness migration in ch. 33 (especially in 33:36-39, which places Kadesh before Mount Hor, where Aaron died on the first day of the fifth month of the fortieth year; cf. 20:22-29). For Levine (*Numbers 1–20*, p. 57), the Priestly authors created "an impractical itinerary, leading first to the Red Sea, then to Kadesh, and then back to the Red Sea and Edom by virtually the same route!"

269. Milgrom's assertion (*Numbers*, p. 464) that the reason for the insertion of Kadesh and of the incomplete date in 20:1, locating the rebellion of Moses and Aaron at Kadesh and dating it in the fortieth year, is correct. But he does not provide any explanation for this assertion.

background after verse 14, when he sent messengers; he is totally absent in both 21:1-3, where Israel defeated the Canaanites, and in 21:21-31, where the Israelites not only defeated but also dispossessed and occupied the entire land of the Amorites.[270] That Yahweh was excluded in 20:14-21 implies two things: that Moses' and Israel's request for passage was not directed by Yahweh and that Moses' leadership will not easily be restored in the face of the Israelites' interference with the negotiations, which Moses had initiated, and in the face of Edom's refusal for passage.

Furthermore, 20:14-21 as a whole reveals more than the reduced leadership role of Moses. The text strengthens the function of 20:2-13, that is, its provision for a reason why Moses is included in Yahweh's punishment of *all* the Exodus generation. First, by sending messengers to the king of Edom for passage through his territory, Moses disobeyed Yahweh's command to him regarding Israel's migration from Kadesh: "turn tomorrow and set out for the wilderness by the way to the Red Sea" (14:25b).

Second, in light of the fact that the easiest way to enter Canaan from Kadesh-barnea (other than the southern route by which Israel failed) is to travel straight east through Edom's territory,[271] the fact that Moses sent messengers for passage means he took the initiative to search for another approach to Canaan after the Israelites' disastrous attempt to penetrate the land from the south. Regarding the meaning of entering the promised land, both the Israelites and Moses are guilty of having gone their own ways rather than taking Yahweh's. In chapters 13–14 it was the Israelites who rejected Yahweh's plan and took the initiative to enter Canaan; now in 20:14 it is Moses who takes the initiative to seek the easiest way to Canaan, against Yahweh's commanded direction.

Third, both Israel's and Moses' attempts failed. Since the Israelites' defeat by the Amalekites and the Canaanites is viewed as an initial and partial fulfillment of Yahweh's punishment of all the Exodus generation, Moses' and Israel's rejection by Edom must be understood as the continuing fulfillment of Yahweh's punishment.

Fourth, that Israel's encounter with Edom is placed right after Yahweh had denied Moses' and Aaron's leadership is not coincidental. Unit 20:14-21 serves to make sure that Yahweh's punishment of Moses and Aaron is not extreme and unfair but "measure for measure" and justifiable compared to their crime. Moses, like the rest of Exodus generation, failed to trust Yahweh's abil-

---

270. For Moses' active roles in 21:32-35 and 31:1-54, see pp. 270-74 in this study.

271. Ashley, *The Book of Numbers,* p. 388. This is the hidden purpose of Moses' and Israel's request for passage through Edom.

ity to bring Yahweh's people into the promised land by seeking out another route, which was not the route Yahweh had commanded him to take. As a result, Moses, although he is the chief representative of Yahweh and of the Exodus generation, shares the same fatal destiny as that generation: he must die in the wilderness and not enter the promised land.[272]

Chapter 20 ends with the report of the death of Aaron (vv. 22-29). Israel's march to Mount Hor (v. 22) might be seen as their other attempt to penetrate Canaan from south. Since Mount Hor is located north of Kadesh, the itinerary in verse 22 suggests that Israel headed north from Kadesh and ultimately toward Canaan from the south. This possibility is derived from 20:21, which states that Israel had turned away from Edom, without specifying the direction. In other words, after having refused to take the easiest way to Canaan from Kadesh, Moses and Israel skirted Edom by journeying across Edom's northern border, not by moving southward "by the way to the Red Sea" (cf. 14:25b). This is the last of Moses' and Israel's attempts to enter Canaan by their own routes and in disobedience to Yahweh's clear command.

Moreover, verses 23-29 narrate that Aaron, the high priest, died, and his priesthood was transferred to his son, Eleazar. On the one hand, in light of Yahweh's punishment of Moses and Aaron, Aaron's death suggests the imminence of Moses' own death. On the other hand, in light of Yahweh's punishment on the entire Exodus generation, Aaron's death signals the end of the Exodus generation and marks the completion of Yahweh's punishment of them.[273] Furthermore, the transference of Aaron's high priesthood to Eleazar is indicative of the transition from the Exodus generation to the next generation. Thus, 20:22-29 brings out three points: Israel's march to Mount Hor shows their last attempt to enter Canaan from the south; Aaron's death indicates fulfillment of Yahweh's punishment on Israel's failure; and Eleazar's new priesthood signals the dawn of Yahweh's forgiveness of the next generation, which will carry out Yahweh's plan to bring them into the promised land. The

---

272. Verse 20:12 focuses on Yahweh's denial of Moses' and Aaron's prophetic leadership (to bring Israel into the promised land), while 20:14 is understood as Moses' attempt to reverse Yahweh's plan, as the Israelites had done, which implies the same fate for him as for the people. Milgrom's understanding of 20:14-21 (*Numbers*, p. 464) as "a defeat for Israel and Moses" is correct, but his characterization of these verses as "a personal blow to Moses who now knows that he cannot enter the land but must die en route" is hard to prove because of a lack of textual evidence.

273. Milgrom (*Numbers*, p. 464) argues that Aaron's death "either provokes Moses to attempt an abortive thrust into Canaan . . . or ends the unit on the leaders' failures." He does not show any preference between these two interpretations. However, the former is less convincing because it lacks textual evidence and is based purely on psychoanalyzing Moses.

first two points demonstrate the final scene of the activities of the Exodus generation, and the third point provides a hint for the second generation's entrance upon the scene.

(β) Actualization of Yahweh's Forgiveness of Israel's Failure

(aa) Unit 21:1-3 as a Turning Point

Alluded to by the transference of the high priesthood from Aaron to his son Eleazar in 20:22-29, 21:1-3 heralds the advent of the next generation of the Israelites.[274] Five arguments support this claim. First, 21:1 reports Israel's initial defeat by the Canaanite, the king of Arad, which may reflect their total failure in 14:39-45; Hormah in verse 3b is the same place to which the Exodus generation was pursued by the Canaanites and the Amalekites in 14:45b; their opponents were the Canaanites, the inhabitants of the promised land, not any other ethnic groups in the Transjordan regions; the result was Israel's complete victory (vv. 2-3a), the opposite of their total defeat in 14:45. These facts suggest that the victory over the Canaanites in 21:1-3 must be attributed to the new generation rather than to the Exodus generation. Otherwise, there would have been little meaning to both the divine decree sentencing the Exodus generation to death in the wilderness and the divine endorsement of חרם against the Canaanites.

Second, of the six direct military accounts, 21:1-3 is unique in portraying Israel as a single, united political entity. It may be coincidental, but it may also be indicative of a new attitude on the part of the next generation toward the conquest of the promised land, that is, campaigning for the promised land as one body with a single intent. Compared to the Exodus generation, who presumed their expedition would be successful even though they knew of the absence of Yahweh from their midst, Israel's determination to be victorious over the Canaanites, demonstrated in their making a vow to Yahweh to utterly destroy, shows the new attitude of the next generation. Yahweh's acceptance of Israel's vow enhances this point because it shows the extension of divine for-

---

274. The claim that 21:1-3 shows the generational succession of the Israelites could be a logical step from the assertion that ch. 20 marks the completion of Yahweh's punishment of the Exodus generation. However, the former claim can be established on its own terms based on the structural significance of 21:1-3. Hence, there is no circularity between these two claims; rather, the former is complementary to the latter. Cf. Levine, *Numbers 1–20*, pp. 57-62. Levine concludes that the Priestly writers interpolate 21:1-3 into its present location in order to signal "the entrance of the second generation." I arrive at the same conclusion independently.

giveness to the Exodus generation as the new generation carries out the fulfillment of the divine land promise made to their ancestors. Moreover, 21:1-3 excludes Moses entirely. Israel's victory is achieved without Moses' presence or involvement. Why does the text leave Moses out in the epochal victory over the Canaanites? The answer is clear: Moses is excluded because he belongs to the Exodus generation. The operative concept of the text does not need Moses and thus prevents him from sharing the next generation's victory over the Canaanites.[275]

Third, 21:1-3 is placed after Aaron's death, which occurred in the fifth month of the fortieth year. This suggests that the chronological framework of the text is the latter part of the forty years of wandering in the wilderness. Since this chronological framework presupposes Yahweh's punishment of the Exodus generation, who must die out during forty years of wandering, Israel's victory over the Canaanites at the end of the fortieth year must be viewed as signaling the new beginning of the next generation.

Fourth, 21:1-3 reports one of Israel's four military victories, which in the text have been clustered closely together, and this text is the first in a series of these continual successes (21:21-31, 32-35; 31:1-12). No defeat by or retreat from enemies is reported after this text. Could the Exodus generation be responsible for overpowering the Amorites, the Bashanites, and the Midianites? Could this generation "merit the praise of Balaam, who not only extols their impressive military might, but even eulogizes their favored relationship to YHWH?"[276] It must be the second generation who, at the end of forty years of wandering, successfully executes the ongoing military campaigns against the Canaanites and other enemies of the Transjordan territories.

Fifth, the placement of 21:1-3 in the extant text suggests that this text heralds the advent of the second generation. This text is placed between the report of the event that occurred at Mount Hor (20:22-29) and that of Israel's setting out from Mount Hor (21:4a). In other words, its placement interrupts the literary continuity of 20:1–21:10 (from Kadesh to Oboth via Mount Hor). Verse 21:4a provides some hints for this interruption: "From Mount Hor they [the Israelites] set out by the way to the Red Sea, to go around the land of

---

275. In light of a larger redactional purpose, Milgrom (*Numbers*, p. 458) understands that 21:1-3 is Moses' desperate attempt to enter the promised land directly from the south after the rebuff by Edom and the death of Aaron. This understanding presupposes two things: 21:1-3 is Moses' activity, and his attempt is a failure because "he was forced to retreat" (21:4a). However, the text is not about Moses' activity, but Israel's activity, which does not include Moses. Furthermore, the text is clear that Israel as a single entity destroyed the Canaanites completely. Unfortunately, Milgrom fails to deal with this obvious evidence.

276. Levine, *Numbers 1–20*, p. 58.

Edom." By mentioning Mount Hor as the departing locale, verse 4a presupposes the event of 20:22-29; by noting that they "go around the land of Edom," verse 4a specifies the ambiguous direction in 20:21b; by stating Israel's setting out "by the way to the Red Sea," verse 4a shows Israel's implementation of Yahweh's command in 14:25b. While the first two statements point to the writers' attempt to minimize the tension caused by the placement of 21:1-3, the third statement implies a reason for its placement. Israel's following of Yahweh's direction is reported right after its victory over the Canaanites, and this action is directly opposite what the Exodus generation had done (the Exodus generation's abortive attempt to penetrate Canaan from the south, Moses' seeking the easiest way to get to Canaan from Kadesh, and Israel's moving across the northern border of Edom). Yahweh's command in 14:25b is finally fulfilled in 21:4a. This decision to approach Canaan via the Transjordan shows Israel's faithfulness to Yahweh's command, and this faithfulness must be attributed to the second generation. Moreover, the second generation's implementation of Yahweh's command is the reason why they did not, after the total destruction of Canaanite towns, continue northward to conquer all of Canaan, the ultimate goal of their sanctuary campaign. Their suffering in the wilderness for forty years due to their forebears' faithlessness (14:33) may also contribute to their turning away from Canaan to the Transjordan regions. Thus, 21:4a functions to reduce the tension created by 21:1-3 and at the same time to upstage the second generation's implementation of Yahweh's command in 14:25b.

Answers to the three sets of questions thus far can be summarized in the following manner. Israel's failure to conquer the land of Canaan in chapters 13–14 is the final and constitutive vantage point to view the entire text of 10:11–36:13. In other words, Israel's failure is the conceptual basis without which the thirty-six units of 10:11–36:13 would not exist as they do, nor be positioned where they are. This concept is responsible for dividing the text into two parts: I. Event: failed campaign to enter the promised land from the south (10:11–14:45) and II. Consequence: entrance into the promised land delayed (15:1–36:13). For the second part, the operative concept is Yahweh's twofold response to Israel's failure. From this vantage point, two theses have been established: (1) Chapter 20 marks the completion of Yahweh's punishment of Israel, the death of all of the Exodus generation during the forty years of wandering in the wilderness; and (2) 21:1-3, by showing the second generation's victory over the Canaanites, marks the beginning of Yahweh's forgiveness of the Exodus generation — Yahweh moves forward once again to fulfill the promise of the land to the ancestors of Israel through the second generation.

(bb) The Wilderness Experience
of the New Generation

This second thesis suggests that the texts following 21:1-3 must be understood as unfolding the wilderness experience of the second generation. More precisely, as has been said, 21:1–36:13 narrates Yahweh's fulfillment of the promise of the divine land to the ancestors of Israel through the second generation. This point provides the conceptual basis for answering the remaining questions related to Israel's direct military conflicts with the Amorites, the Bashanites, and the Midianites. Answers to these questions suggest three conceptual factors: (1) answers contribute to the characterization of the second generation as being confident to carry out Yahweh's plan; (2) answers assist in characterizing the second generation as sharing the same rebellious attitude as the Exodus generation; and (3) answers, by way of implication, point to the second generation's continuous campaigns until they have achieved the ultimate goal of their campaign — the conquest of the promised land. The first two factors deal with the characterization of the second generation, the carrier of Yahweh's plan, while the third focuses on Yahweh's plan itself, the task of the second generation's campaign. It is also clear that the first two are operative only up to the last rebellion narrative in Numbers (25:1-18), while the third is operative throughout the texts following 21:1-3, particularly 25:19 onward. The texts from 25:19 onward have to do with Yahweh's instructions regarding the land, which is the key component of the task of the second generation's campaign. Thus, structurally, 21:1-3 indicates the turning point for the completion of Yahweh's punishment on the Exodus generation and the beginning of Yahweh's forgiveness of them, realized in the carrying out of the divine plan by the second generation. Unit 21:4–36:13 is divided into two subsections: preliminary to matters of the land, the character of the second generation (21:4–25:18) and matters of the land proper, the goal of the new generation's campaign (25:19–36:13). This macrostructure of 21:4–36:13, generated by the three conceptual factors mentioned above, will be substantiated with a discussion of each factor.

(αα) Characteristics of the
New Generation

The texts following 21:1-3 portray the second generation as being confident in carrying out Yahweh's plan. This confidence of the second generation is already alluded to in its determination to conquer the Canaanites, the inhabitants of the promised land, evidenced in the making of a vow to Yahweh of conducting a חרם against the Canaanites. This confidence is more evident in their victories over their Transjordan adversaries. In the case of their encounter with Sihon, the king of the Amorites, the second generation followed the same procedure that the Exodus generation had done regarding Edom (sending messengers with very similar messages). In addition, their request was refused by King Sihon, just as that of the Exodus generation had been refused by Edom.[277] In contrast to the Exodus generation, which retreated from Edom, the second generation fought back against King Sihon and his troops and conquered all the towns and the land of the Amorites. In their victory over the Amorites not even Moses and Yahweh were included. This victory must elevate the great confidence that the second generation had as they continued their campaigns toward the promised land.

Two questions must be revisited here. (1) Why did Sihon refuse Israel's request for passage? (2) Why were not Moses and Yahweh included in Israel's victory over Sihon? In answer to the first question, Sihon's refusal might be encouraged by Edom's victory and by the initial victory of the king of Arad. Sihon had heard that Israel might back away if threatened and met with a large armed force, which proved true in the case of Edom.[278] Or Sihon's refusal may have resulted from the fact that he did not have a choice except to fight back, since he had also heard that Israel had been victorious over the Canaanites. Such reasons are possible when examining 21:21-31 in comparison with other direct military accounts but are excluded by the text itself. Thus, it suffices to say that regardless of any possible reasons, Sihon's refusal and attack on Israel cannot be understood as legitimate. Instead, within the limit of the text, Sihon's refusal and attack function to enhance Israel's innocence (Sihon attacked Israel first) and their legitimization of the dispossession of and occupation of Amorite land (Israel, as a defensive measure, fought back and conquered the Amorite land).

Regarding the second question, at least the absence of Moses in 21:21-31 is understandable. If the dispossession of the Amorite land promoted the

---

277. They both contain evidence of the sending of messengers (20:14a; 21:21a), the recipient as having the title of "king" (20:14a; 21:21a), the request (20:17aα, 19b; 21:22aα), the pledge (20:17aβ-b; 21:22aβ-b), and the description of the response to Israel's messengers (20:18b, 20b-21a; 21:23a).

278. Edom's refusal could be understood similarly. Since Edom had heard of Israel's unsuccessful attempt to penetrate Canaan from the south, Edom came out against Israel with a large force, heavily armed. Moreover, that the king of Arad fought against Israel when he heard of Israel's coming implies foreknowledge of Israel's movement. For him, Israel's advance is a serious military threat. This understanding is congruent with the nature of Israel's camp — the military organization centered in the sanctuary.

confidence of the second generation, there would be no reason for Moses to partake the engagement with Sihon. The text reveals that the second generation can defeat an enemy in the line of their advance toward the promised land by using the same tactic used by the Exodus generation and without Moses' leadership, as proved in the case of the recent victory over the Canaanites.

This explanation, however, is in conflict with the roles designated to Moses in 21:32-35. Moses was portrayed as the sender of the spies to Jazer, as the dispossessor of the Amorites in verse 32, and as the recipient of Yahweh's revelation in verse 34. The conflict is intensified by the sharp contrast between the complete silence of Yahweh in 21:21-31 and the comprehensive involvement (by giving admonition and instruction) of Yahweh in 21:34. The solution, according to Coats, may lie in the different levels of significance and value of Sihon's territory in Israel's campaign.[279] For Coats, the absence of Moses and Yahweh in the defeat of Sihon is due to the fact that Sihon's territory is outside the border of the promised land, which implies that the active roles of Moses and Yahweh in the conquest of Bashan have to do with the status of the land of King Og, including Bashan, as being part of the promised land.[280] Since the ultimate goal of Israel's campaign is the conquest of the promised land, the conquest of Sihon's territory is less important than that of Og's. This explains why Moses took the initiative to send the spies to Jazer and why Yahweh commanded the campaign against Og without sending messengers to request passage. But Coats fails to see this in 34:10-12, which suggests clearly that the eastern border of the promised land is the Jordan River. This means that all the Transjordan territories, including the land of Og, are not considered the promised land. Thus, in the text there is no higher value or significance to the conquest of Sihon's territory than there was to Og's territory.

The alternative explanation for why 21:32-35 mentions the involvement of Moses and Yahweh lies in the function of the text: to illustrate the confidence of the second generation. Within the limits of the text, Moses is desig-

---

279. G. W. Coats, "Conquest Traditions in the Wilderness Theme," *JBL* 95 (1976): 186-87.

280. Milgrom, *Numbers*, p. 183. Aharoni (*Land of the Bible*, pp. 73-74) views the land of King Og as part of the promised land. Moreover, according to Aharoni's map (p. 71, map 4: The Borders of the Land of Canaan), Edrei, the place where Og fought against Israel, is located inside the eastern border of the land of Canaan. However, Aharoni's eastern boundary of the promised land does not agree with 34:10-12. His understanding of the boundary descriptions stems from the combination of all existing traditions, including the deuteronomistic tradition, which regards the eastern border to be as far south as the Arnon. Yet the Priestly traditions, responsible for the final form of the Pentateuch, hold the Jordan River as the eastern border of the promised land, and not the Arnon or the Zered.

nated in verse 32 as the sender of the spies to Jazer and the dispossessor of the Amorites who had lived in its villages, which were captured by the Israelites. Verse 32 seems to show Moses as the figurehead representative of Israel's expedition rather than the active leader. The beginning and ending of the expedition have been connected to Moses, yet the actual capturing of the villages has been credited to the Israelites. This speculation is more evident in verses 33-35. Although Moses was the recipient of Yahweh's speech in verse 34, verses 33-35 as a whole are interested in Yahweh's initiative in and support of Israel's campaign against Og, rather than in Moses' leadership. Moses is portrayed as being afraid of Og and his troops, as revealed in Yahweh's admonition, and as lacking confidence in the military logistics assumed by Yahweh's instruction. Contrary to verse 32, verse 35 clearly shows no involvement of Moses in the actual campaign, but instead the active role of the Israelites: "so they [the Israelites] killed him [King Og], his sons, and all his people, until there was no survivor left; and they took possession of his land."[281] Moreover, that the Israelites are never mentioned explicitly in verses 32-35 and are only referred to as "they" or "them" should not weaken the point of seeing that they are as the main subject in these verses. The implicit mention of the Israelites means simply that the verses intend to communicate the concept of Israel's campaign against Og as the חרם war of Yahweh. Note that verses 32-35 are placed immediately following verses 21-31, the account of the Israelites' total victory over Sihon, which mentions the Israelites explicitly by name throughout the text (vv. 21a, 24a, 25a, 25b, 31a). This suggests the presupposition that the Israelites are the main subject in verses 32-35 even though they are not mentioned by name. In verses 21-35 as a whole, the Israelites, more specifically the second generation, are the main subject of the conquest of the Transjordan enemies. From this vantage point, verses 32-35 show Yahweh and Moses playing a significant role, in that Yahweh reveals the matter regarding the nature of the

---

281. Cf. Fearer, *Wars in the Wilderness*, p. 270, n. 24. Fearer argues that the involvement of Moses in 21:32-35 should be read back into 21:21-31 based on Yahweh's speech to him: "And you [Moses] shall do to him [Og] as you did to Sihon" (v. 34b). Based on this verse, Fearer (p. 456) further stresses that Moses played a dominant role in all the Transjordan victories. If Fearer's understanding is correct, why is there no mention of Israel's occupation of the land of Og (unlike Sihon's land, ישׁב, in 21:25a, 31), and why is there no mention of Moses' dispossessing the people of Og (as he dispossessed the Amorites in v. 32b)? Moreover, note that "Og" is never mentioned without "Sihon" in later traditions (see, Fearer, *Wars in the Wilderness*, p. 272, n. 27). This suggests that Israel's victory over Og has been combined with Israel's victories over its Transjordan enemies. Since Israel's total defeat of Sihon is the prime example of its victories over all the Transjordan enemies, the emphasis must be on vv. 21-31 rather than on vv. 32-35. Thus, v. 34b should be understood as Yahweh's instructions for a general guideline for the impending battle against Og, i.e., a חרם war.

campaign and Moses receives Yahweh's revelation. Yet it is the Israelites who carry out Yahweh's revelation thoroughly.

The remaining question is, then, What role did Moses plays in Israel's battle against the Midianites? There is no dispute that Moses plays the dominant role in 31:1-54. Moses elaborates on Yahweh's rather short command; he knows the logistics of the battle; he confronts the officers of the army, criticizing their wrongdoings, and instructs them regarding the purification of uncleanness; and he executes Yahweh's commands on the distribution of booty. How is this active role of Moses to be understood together with the concept of the confidence of the second generation drawn from their encounters with the Amorites and the Bashanites? The following three arguments will shed light on the solution. First, 31:1-54 is more interested in preserving Israel's faith from further perversion than in winning the battle against the Midianites. The very reason for Yahweh's command to take revenge on the Midianites is related to the corrupting influence of the Midianites at Peor (25:16-18); the battle itself is a holy war in which the enemy is placed under the sacrificial ban as demonstrated by the annihilation of all Midianite males (v. 7); Moses is more concerned with cultic matters than with the battle's victory. This nature of the text answers why there is complete silence from the Midianites, unlike Edom, the king of Arad, and Kings Sihon and Og.

Second, the content of Yahweh's command to Moses was not only concerned with Israel's battle against the Midianites, but also with Moses' imminent death. After the completion of the battle, Moses is supposed to follow the fate of the Exodus generation: "afterwards you shall be gathered to your people [the Exodus generation]" (31:2b). The story of 25:1-18, from which arises the reason for the Israelites' vengeance against Midian, shows that neither Moses nor the judges take any action on the instructions given to them, but Phinehas's action stops the plague among the Israelites. In light of this story, the combination of commanding the battle and announcing Moses' imminent death suggests that Yahweh grants a final opportunity for Moses' leadership to be restored in preserving Israel's loyalty to Yahweh. Moses' role as military leader does service to his role as the protector of Israel's faith from continual perversion.

Third, 31:1-54 is placed in a literary context far removed from Israel's military encounters with other enemies (which are gathered together within chs. 20–21), and this text is surrounded by texts interested in matters of the land rather than texts of military encounters. Starting with 25:19–26:65, which reports the census for the purpose of the distribution of the land, there are four units in 27:1–30:17 dealing with various concerns related to the land, and 31:1-54 is followed by the unit reporting the allotment of the Transjordan in

32:1-42. The placement of 31:1-54 suggests that the text is part of the overarching conceptual framework of 25:19–32:42, that is, Yahweh's introductory instructions before his instructions regarding the promised land (33:1–36:12). These three arguments suggest that the active role of Moses in 31:1-54 must be understood within a different conceptual framework from that operative in 21:1-3, 21-31, and 32-35: *Moses plays a significant cultic role but not a military one within 31:1-54.*

In short, the complete silence of Moses in 21:21-31 contrasts sharply with the second generation's total defeat of Sihon without Moses, and thus promotes their ever-growing confidence. That Yahweh is also conspicuously absent in verses 21-31 enhances this point. Although Moses is mentioned in verses 32 and 34, the second generation is presupposed as the main subject in the entire text of verses 21-35 and as the ones involved in the actual military activities, such as capturing the villages, killing the enemies, and taking possession of the enemies' land. Since Yahweh's speech to Moses in verse 34 is intended to stress the nature of the second generation's campaigns against the Transjordan enemies as the חרם war of Yahweh, Moses' sudden appearance in verse 34 does not undermine the confidence of the second generation.[282] The concept of the חרם war is also operative in 31:1-54, and yet this text is related more to the matter concerning the land than to Israel's continual military campaigns toward the promised land.

Although these texts, particularly the direct military accounts (21:1-3, 21-31, 32-35), promote the second generation's confidence to carry out Yahweh's plan, some texts (21:4-9; 25:1-18) address the other side of its character: rebellion. The second generation, unlike the Exodus generation, shows an unprecedented military strength demonstrated in the elimination of all impediments to an advance; at the same time, the people behave similarly to the Exodus generation by complaining of the hardships of the wilderness and falling into the lure of paganism. This point is clearly revealed in the content of two rebellion narratives (21:4-9; 25:1-18) too obvious to reiterate. Moreover, the locations of these narratives in the extant text enhance this point: 21:4-9 and 25:1-18 are the only two rebellion narratives related to the second generation, and the former is located immediately after the turning point from the Exodus generation to the new generation, while the latter is

---

282. However, it is conceivable that since Yahweh's definition of the nature of the second generation's campaigns against their Transjordanian enemies is noted after the granting of their vow of חרם war against the Canaanites, Yahweh's speech to Moses in v. 34 may function to reaffirm his leadership in their campaigns. No matter how confident the second generation might be, the campaign itself belongs to Yahweh. In this regard, Moses' roles in vv. 32 and 34 might be a way to caution the ever-growing, self-confident second generation.

placed right before the texts associated with Yahweh's instructions regarding the land (25:19–36:13). By its placement, which causes the itinerary formula to be broken (21:4a, 10b), 21:4-9 functions to show the Israelites' chronic pattern of contentiousness with Yahweh and Yahweh's representative, Moses. This chronic pattern of rebellion is also manifested in the actions of the second generation, who had just expressed confidence in Yahweh by defeating the Canaanites. Positioned directly following the complete victories over the Transjordan enemies and Yahweh's blessings through the foreign prophet, Balaam, even without Israel's knowledge, the episode of the second generation's apostasy to Baal of Peor (25:1-18) epitomizes its disloyalty to Yahweh. Furthermore, the order of 21:4-9 and 25:1-18 in the extant text is not coincidental. Why does the former, which concerns the lack of basic human necessities, such as food and water, come before the latter, which deals with the corruption of faith? Why are these two texts placed at the beginning and at the ending of the characterization of the second generation? By repeating subject matter typical of the rebellions of the Exodus generation, by ordering these matters from ordinary hardships to religious disloyalty, and by placing one at the beginning and one at the end of the texts characterizing the second generation, 21:4-9 and 25:1-18 strengthen the characterization of the second generation's rebellious nature.

In summary, after demonstrating a successful campaign for the promised land (21:1-3), 21:4–25:18 characterizes the double nature of the second generation: on the one hand, the people show confidence in Yahweh's plan to bring them into the promised land, but, on the other hand, they also follow the chronic pattern of Israel's rebelliousness.

(ββ) Goal of the New Generation's Campaign

The other remaining questions related to Israel's direct military conflicts with the Amorites, the Bashanites, and the Midianites point to the continuation of the second generation's campaigns until achievement of the ultimate goal is reached, the conquest of the promised land. Why did the second generation not continue to move northward into Canaan after defeating the Canaanites? Why did they fight back against King Sihon? Why did the Israelites not move through Sihon's territory after having crushed his troops? Why did they not only dispossess (יָרַשׁ) but also occupy (יָשַׁב) all the lands of the Amorites, contrary to their initial intention? Why did they capture (לָכַד) the villages of Jazer and only dispossess the Amorites who lived there? Why did they only dispossess (יָרַשׁ) and not occupy the land of King Og? Answers to these questions point to the conceptual framework of the task of the second generation, the continuation of the campaigns toward the promised land.

As for the second generation's southward journey, Milgrom argues that the Israelites are "forced to turn southward" because their northern passage is "blocked by the Canaanites."[283] If Milgrom's assertion is correct, no awkwardness in the transition from 21:1-3 to 21:4a is apparent. However, Milgrom ignores the obvious result of the second generation's total victory over the Canaanites, and thus he is unable to answer why the second generation turned away from Canaan to head southward "by the way to the Red Sea" (21:4a) despite their crushing defeat of the Canaanites. The answer to this question is that by turning southward "by the way to the Red Sea," the text reveals two aspects of the second generation: (1) the people finally follow Yahweh's command (14:25b), which in turn elevates the people's confidence further into carrying out Yahweh's plan; and (2) they share in the suffering of the forty years of wandering in the wilderness because of the faithlessness of their forebears (14:33). This answer indicates the structural dependence of 21:4a on the generative concept of chapters 13–14. Subordinate to the concept of the Exodus generation's failure to conquer the promised land from the south, the second generation must find another approach by which to enter the promised land. This is the approach to Canaan from the east, via the Transjordan territories.

This conceptual factor implies that the second generation's aggressive posture and military conquests of the Transjordan peoples are justified because these peoples were considered hostile enemies who prevented the Israelites from reaching Yahweh's mandated destination. Because of their location in the path of the second generation's advance toward the promised land, King Sihon and his people, the Amorites who lived in the villages of Jazer, and King Og and his people share from the outset the same fate as victims of conquest.[284] The concept of the ongoing campaigns until the ultimate conquest of the land of Canaan is reached is undoubtedly operative in the texts following 21:1-3.

---

283. Milgrom, *Numbers,* p. 457.

284. Another possible reason why Israel fought back against King Sihon is that the second generation might not have had other ways to access passage to the region west of the Jordan, unlike the case of the confrontation with Edom. However, this reason is based on the geographical situation, which sheds no light on why the second generation advanced northward despite achieving a secured position by which to attempt to cross the Jordan River. Their attack and conquest of the land of King Og without any negotiations for passage must be understood in light of the conceptual framework that regards Og as one of the hostile enemies who stood in the way of the promised land.

If the claim that the second generation must campaign forward for the conquest of the promised land is correct, why do the Israelites occupy all the lands of the Amorites? The occupation (יָשַׁב) is not a necessary consequence of the campaign, although it might be one of the major objectives of the campaign; the term also implies an intention to settle or stay a long time in the occupied places. Thus, Israel's occupation of the Amorite lands not only contradicts its initial intent to pass through Sihon's territory but also creates a conceptual dissonance with the dominant concept of the ongoing campaign toward the promised land in the texts after 21:1-3.

The solution may rest in the literary connection of 21:21-31 to 32:1-42. The latter reports the allotment of land in the Transjordan to the Reubenites, the Gadites, and the half-tribe of Manasseh on the condition that they go across the Jordan and fight along with the other tribes in the battle for Canaan. Israel's conquest and occupation of all the Amorites' land function to rationalize the two and one-half tribes' permanent settlement in the Transjordan territories. In other words, 21:25a and 31 mention specifically the "occupation" of the Amorites' land in order to pave the path for the existence of 32:1-42. Moreover, note that the two and one-half tribes occupied not only the Amorites' land but also Jazer and the kingdom of King Og of Bashan (32:1b and 33). In addition, Manasseh's sons went, captured, and dispossessed Gilead and its villages (33:39-41). From this information, a lack of mention of occupation in Jazer and the land of Bashan in 21:32-35 and a lack of mention of the conquest of Gilead on Israel's northward campaign can easily be explained.

However, if the solution to Israel's occupation of the Amorites' land in 21:21-31 is dependent on their permanent settlement of the Transjordan territories reported in 32:1-42, then why does 21:32-35, the immediate literary context of 21:21-31, not mention any occupation of Jazer and Og's land despite their settlement in these places? Whereas the latter ends with a clear statement of Israel's occupation or settlement (יָשַׁב, vv. 31, 25b) in the land of the Amorites, the former ends with their dispossession (יָרַשׁ, vv. 32b, 35b) of the Amorites and of the land of Og.[285] In this regard, verses 32-35 are clearly distinctive from verses 21-31. Should Israel's activities toward Sihon reconceptualize that of Jazer and Og, or is it the other way around? Why is 21:21-31 positioned together with 21:32-35?

Fearer understands this relationship based on the concept of יָרַשׁ, which occurs in all three campaigns of Israel (vv. 24b, 32b, 35b). He defines

---

285. This distinction is further evidence for treating v. 32 as belonging to vv. 33-35 rather than to vv. 21-31.

ירש in verse 24b as that which "communicates the instant acquisition of objects, such as territory, . . . and not requiring further violent action. . . . All elements in verse 24b exclude any acts of conquest and occupation."[286] Fearer also broadens the meaning of ירש to include the notion of occupation, particularly in the cases of verses 32b and 35b: "sometimes ירש is inclusive of occupation."[287] With this broadened meaning, he asserts that verses 32-35 show Israel's conquest *and* occupation of Jazer (and its subordinated dwelling places) and Og's land. Verses 21-35 as a whole, then, show Israel's conquest *and* occupation of all the lands east of the Jordan (north of the Arnon extending to the limits of Og's kingdom). For him, the concept of occupation in 21:21-31 is constitutive for the meaning of the entire text of 21:21-35. However, Fearer's argument is problematic. First, that his definition of ירש in verse 24b excludes any acts of occupation is inconsistent with his usage of the same word in verses 32b and 35b. Second, and more substantively, Israel's occupation or settlement east of the Jordan (vv. 21-35) implies the completion of their campaign. Is the conquest and occupation of the area east of the Jordan the goal of their campaign? Fearer certainly disagrees with this by stating, "Israel's migration is a campaign from Egypt to the land of promise . . . Canaan is Israel's destination. . . ."[288] By broadening the concept of ירש in verses 32b and 35b to include the notion of "occupation," he creates more complications for the problem at hand and at the same time weakens the effectiveness of the overarching macro-concept (the theology of conquest) that he chose for the conflict narratives within Exodus and Numbers (Exod 17:8-16; Num 21:21-31, 32, and 33-35). Instead of expanding the concept of ירש in verses 32b and 35b, he should stress the lack of ישב in verses 32-35. By not mentioning occupation at all, 21:32-35 corrects the possible misunderstanding caused by the second generation's occupation of Amorite lands. Moreover, by stating the dispossession clearly, this text reaffirms the nature and the task of Israel's

286. Fearer, *Wars in the Wilderness*, p. 309. For his extensive discussion on the aspects of ירש in 21:21-35, based on Lohfink's thesis, see also pp. 308-10, 404, 444, 500-510; cf. Lohfink, "ירש," pp. 368-96.

287. Fearer, *Wars in the Wilderness*, p. 501.

288. Fearer, *Wars in the Wilderness*, pp. 495-96. For Fearer, conquest theology is the overarching macro-concept that stands as the basis for all texts from Exodus to Deuteronomy, individually and together. However, this macro-concept is too broad to pinpoint specific operative conceptualities within blocks of the texts, such as the Sinai pericope, Num 10:11–36:13, the whole book of Deuteronomy, etc. The substantive discussion of the contents of the texts must be incorporated into a reconstruction of the operative conceptualities. By whom will the conquest be carried out? From what direction and in what timetable will its task be accomplished? What role does Yahweh play in it? These are some of questions specific to the theology of conquest that must be answered.

sanctuary campaign. Not until the conquest of the promised land is accomplished are they permitted to settle in any place. If any obstacle lies in the way of their advance, they are required to remove it, but they are not allowed to settle in the land. Verses 32-35 reconceptualize the operative conceptuality of verses 21-31, that is, Israel's occupation of all the lands of the Amorites. The generative conceptuality of the entire text of 21:21-35 is the dispossession of objects (human and nonhuman) blocking Israel's advance, not the occupation of the land.[289] Ultimately, what a reconceptualization of verses 32-35 using the concept of verses 21-31 does is downplay the significance of the second generation's heroic victories over their Transjordan enemies and their conquest and dispossession of the lands all together. At the same time, the result of the reconceptualization is to upstage the importance of the task of Israel's campaign, the conquest of the promised land. The second generation's defeat of Kings Sihon and Og of the Transjordan cannot be equally significant to their victory over the Canaanites (21:1-3) because the Transjordan is not part of Canaan.

3. The Macrostructure Proper

The conquest of Canaan, the land promised to the Israelites, is the goal of their continuing campaign and is the decisive criterion for the significance of the thirty-six units within Numbers 10:11–36:13. More precisely, Israel's failure to conquer the promised land from the south reported in chapters 13–14 is the fundamental conceptual basis, without which these units would not exist as they do, nor be placed where they are. As punishment for their failure, Yahweh swore the denial of entrance to the promised land for the entire Exodus generation and their death during forty years of wandering in the wilderness; and as forgiveness, Yahweh swore to fulfill his promise of the divine land to their ancestors through the next generation. The generational succession of the Israelites during the wilderness period is a result of their failure to conquer the promised land. That is to say, the generational succession is at best indicative of the transition from Yahweh's punishment of Israel to Yahweh's forgiveness of them. The two sides of Yahweh's response to Israel's distrust in

289. If v. 34b, "you shall do to him as you did to King Sihon of the Amorites," provides the comprehensive logistics of what Israel is supposed to do to King Og, as Fearer argues, v. 35 should include Israel's occupation of the land of Og as in v. 31. This is not the case. Thus, v. 34b points not to the comprehensive plan for the campaign but to the nature of the campaign, that is, a חרם war. This is clearly demonstrated by Israel's activities in v. 35.

Yahweh's ability and intention to fulfill the land promise are the generative concepts for the structure of Numbers 15:1–36:13.

Within 15:1–36:13, chapter 20 as a whole marks the completion of Yahweh's punishment of Israel in the death of the entire Exodus generation. Unit 21:1-3, by demonstrating Israel's utter destruction of the Canaanites, signals the beginning of Yahweh's forgiveness, as once again Yahweh's promise is carried out by the second generation. After heralding the second generation, 21:4–25:18 characterizes this new carrier of Yahweh's plan as having unprecedented confidence, unlike the Exodus generation. At the same time it characterizes the second generation as being rebellious because of both the hardships of the wilderness and a religious disloyalty to Yahweh, following the chronic pattern of the Exodus generation's rebellions. Yet, this characterization is preliminary to the main interest of the texts after 21:1-3: the land. Unit 25:19–36:13 focuses on Yahweh's instructions on matters related to the land. That the land of Canaan is more significant than other places, for example, the Transjordan territories, is operative within 25:19–36:13 and accordingly divides the text into two parts.

The following is the macrostructure of Numbers 10:11–36:13:

**The Narrative of Israel's Forty-Year Campaign
in the Wilderness**   10:11–36:13

I. Event: failed campaign to enter the promised land
from the south   10:11–14:45

  A. Programmatic departure   10:11-36

  B. Distrust of Yahweh's ability to fulfill the promise   11:1–14:45

    1. General example   11:1-3

    2. Specific examples   11:4–14:45

      a. People's rebellion against Moses' leadership   11:4-34

      b. Miriam's and Aaron's rebellion against
Moses' authority   11:35–12:16

      c. People's rebellion against Yahweh's leadership   13:1–14:45

II. Consequence: entrance into the promised land delayed
by forty years   15:1–36:13

  A. Completion of Yahweh's punishment of all the Exodus
generation: the death of the Exodus generation   15:1–20:29

    1. Reaffirmation of leadership   15:1–19:12

      a. Yahweh   15:1-41

      b. The human leaders   16:1–18:32

        (1) Moses   16:1–17:15

        (2) Aaron   17:16-24

Conclusion

Numbers 10:11–36:13 is the second literary block of the book of Numbers on the highest level. Passages 10:11-12 and 36:13 constitute the outer boundaries of the text and differentiate it from its immediate contexts, the first block of Numbers (1:1–10:10) and the book of Deuteronomy. Explicitly, 10:11-12 contains chronological and geographical references indicating the radical transition between the first and the second block of Numbers: a shift from Israel's calculable duration (nineteen days) at one particular location (the wilderness of Sinai) in 1:1–10:10 to the approximate years of their wanderings through various places on their way to the land of Canaan in 10:11–36:13. In terms of content, these verses begin the narrative about the march with a mixture of statements about their movements and reports of the events that happened both in between the stations and at the settled locations; these verses are distinctive from the text preceding, which is a narrative about encampment at one place. Implicitly, these verses point to the nature of the two blocks. Whereas the first block reports the preparation of a migratory-sanctuary campaign focusing on the organization of Israel's camp as a military camp centered around the sanctuary in the wilderness of Sinai, the second block narrates the execution of that campaign. Conceptually, 10:11-12 signals the commencement of Israel's migratory-sanctuary campaign, prepared in the wilderness of Sinai, toward the promised land. Numbers 36:13, as the other end of the second block, functions as a subscription that closes the literary corpus that contains the generically diverse materials preceding it. Verse 13 is not a transitional statement connecting the text of Numbers to that of Deuteronomy. The character of the book of Deuteronomy as Moses' final testament to Israel is so distinctive that it marks the decisive break of Deuteronomy from the second block of Numbers, even from the Tetrateuch, for that matter. Structurally, 36:13 signals an initial closure of Israel's migratory-sanctuary campaign that began at 10:11. With 10:11-12 and 36:13 as the appropriate outer boundaries, the second block of Numbers acquires a distinct status relative to its immediate contexts and thus demands an analysis of its structure in its own right and on its own terms.

Numbers 10:11–36:13 consists of thirty-six units that are not situated on compositionally equivalent levels but are organized at different hierarchical levels within the totality of the text. The organization of the units individually and together reflects various conceptual factors. The final and constitutive conceptual basis responsible for the extant existence and placement of these units and their relationship of separation from or connection to each other, is the conceptuality of Israel's failure to conquer the promised land from the south. This conceptuality reveals the substantive content of 10:11–36:13 to be a narrative focusing not on the entire process of the execution of the ongoing sanctuary campaign, but on a specific aspect of that campaign, namely, the failure of the conquest of the land of Canaan from the south and its resultant forty years of wandering, before another attempt to conquer the land from the east by the new generation is undertaken. No doubt the ongoing migratory-sanctuary campaign is presupposed in Numbers 10:11–Joshua 12, but Israel's failure at the verge of reaching the promised land differentiates Numbers 10:11–36:13 from the book of Deuteronomy (Moses' final speeches to the second generation regarding the impending conquest of and settlement in the promised land) and from Joshua 1–12 (the narrative about the second generation's swift military conquest of the entire land of Canaan under the leadership of Joshua).

By explicitly reporting Israel's failed campaign to enter the promised land from the south, Numbers 13:1–14:45 shows the decisive break in the macrostructure of Numbers 10:11–36:13 on its highest level. The texts preceding this unit narrate not only Israel's programmatic departure from the wilderness of Sinai but also their ever-increasing rebellions against Moses, Yahweh's chief representative, and even against Yahweh. Numbers 13–14 in and of itself indicates the climax of the Israelites' rebellions demonstrated in their attempt to nullify the Exodus event and to reject Yahweh's plan to fulfill the promise to their ancestors of land. At the same time, this unit, especially considering the two edges of Yahweh's response to Israel's failure, provides a constitutive vantage point for the rest of Numbers. As Yahweh's punishment, all the Exodus generation must die during the forty years of wandering in the wilderness. This punishment, completed in 20:29, suggests dual functions for the events recorded in 15:1–20:29: the reaffirmation of the leadership of the sanctuary campaign following the hierarchy from Yahweh, Moses, Aaron (the high priest), to the priests and the Levites and the rationalization of the inclusion of the human leaders in the doomed fate of the Exodus generation. By mentioning the leaders' rebellions, especially Moses' and Aaron's rebellion

that happened at Kadesh in the fortieth year, the redactors associate those rebellions with the people's unprecedented rebellion at Kadesh in the early part
of the campaign, legitimize the leaders' exclusion from the promised land,
and imply the negative character of Israel's entire forty years of wanderings,
which in turn justifies Yahweh's punishment of the entire Exodus generation.
At the same time, by introducing various instructions by Yahweh with the
Yahweh speech formula, the redactors attempt to restore for Israel's camp the
validity of the leadership roles of Moses, Aaron, the priests, and the Levites.
Their leadership is still valid and divinely ordained, despite their sharing in
the fate of the rest of their generation.

Yahweh forgives Israel's failure by keeping the promise of land that he
made to the Israelites' ancestors, but that promise will be fulfilled by the new
generation. This forgiveness is demonstrated in 21:1–36:13, starting with Israel's
utter destruction of the Canaanites, the inhabitants of the promised land, in
21:1-3. In Israel's victory over the Canaanites, accomplished by Israel acting as a
single, unified political entity assisted by Yahweh, who permits Israel's vow of a
חרם war, 21:1-3 heralds the entrance of the second generation. This victory is
credited to the new carrier of the migratory-sanctuary campaign and signals
the turning point from Yahweh's punishment of Israel's failure to his forgiveness of it. The transition from the Exodus generation to the new generation
must not be understood as a chronological replacement of the latter after the
death of the former. Rather, the two generations are overlapped in the forty-
year wilderness period, and the new generation takes over or is called to be the
carrier of the migratory-sanctuary campaign for the conquest of the land of
Canaan at the end of the same forty-year period. After reporting the heroic entry of the second generation, 21:4–36:13 recounts their continuing wilderness
experience during the final part of the forty years of wandering. Its first subsection, 21:4–25:18, characterizes the second generation as possessing incompa-
rable confidence in carrying out Yahweh's plan to bring Israel into the promised land; this confidence is demonstrated in the continual victories over the
Transjordan enemies. The section also points out the second generation's no-
toriously rebellious attitude, following the chronic pattern of the Exodus generation's rebellions; such an attitude is evident in the two rebellions described
at the beginning and end of the section. Yet substantively, the first section
shows that these two characteristics of the second generation are subordinate
to the task they are to accomplish: the continuation of the campaign toward
the conquest of the promised land. The task of their migratory-sanctuary
campaign is unchanged since their forebears left the wilderness of Sinai. They
must remove any obstacles in the path of their advance, such as the Amorites
and the Bashanites, but they should not settle in those conquered lands.

Conceptually, the task of the campaign points to the significance of the land of Canaan. That lands outside of Canaan are of secondary importance is already alluded to in 21:32-35, which reconceptualizes the notion of Israel's occupation of the Amorite land by stressing only their possession of the Amorites' and Og's land. This point is clearly demonstrated in the second section, 25:19–36:13, which elaborates upon the significance of the land of Canaan through Yahweh's instructions on matters related to the land. Matters regarding the land are an appropriate subject for the end of Numbers since the completion of the conquest of the promised land and the permanent settlement of it still lie in the future and await narratives beyond the book of Numbers.

The reconstruction of the macrostructure of Numbers 10:11–36:13 needs to be further investigated in at least four areas. These areas are defined by questions that are related (1) to the *Sitz im Leben* of the overarching macroconceptuality responsible for the reconstructed macrostructure of the text, (2) to the theological intention drawn from this conceptuality, (3) to the conceptuality's possible dissonance with the deuteronomistic scheme of Israel's wilderness experience, and (4) to its implications for reconstructing the macrostructure of the Pentateuch or the Hexateuch.

First, it is widely recognized by most scholars that the Priestly writers are responsible for the extant formation of the Pentateuch. Specifically, among several priestly groups, the Aaronides ("Aaron and his sons") are credited with the final shape of the Pentateuch. Since Numbers 10:11–36:13 is part of the Pentateuch, it is also recognized that the Aaronide priests are responsible for its extant text. Who were the Aaronides? How did they rise in control over other priestly groups? And what kind of institutional support for or opposition did they receive to the composition of such a program of Israel's wilderness experience as found in this text? Historically the Aaronides did not play a dominant role in Israel's cultic history until the end of the fifth century,[1] which means that those Aaronide priests who shaped

---

1. The texts in the Pentateuch that suggest the exclusive role of Aaron and his sons as priests (Exod 28–29; Lev 6–9; Num 3, 16–18) are generally considered to be postexilic in date, while other texts that convey a negative or nonpriestly image of Aaron (Exod 32–34; Num 12) are considered preexilic in date. Moreover, other sources whose composition dates ranged from exilic (Deuteronomy and Ezekiel) to postexilic (Ezra-Nehemiah) are almost completely silent about Aaron and Aaronide priests. J. Blenkinsopp argues that the descendants of Phinehas recorded at Ezra 8:2 and 33, which is dated to around 458 b.c., "may provide the earliest hard evidence for the rise of the Aaronite branch of the priesthood to a position of power in the temple community of Jerusalem" ("The Judean Priesthood during the Neo-Babylonian and Achemenid Periods: A Hypothetical Reconstruction," *CBQ* 60 [1998]: 39).

the extant formation of the Pentateuch were not the ones who controlled Israel's Yahweh cult. Without establishing sole and supreme dominion over other priestly groups, how could it be possible for the earlier generations of Aaronide priests to finalize the Pentateuch? Substantively, what sort of institutions allowed them to formulate Israel's constant rebellions in the wilderness and to place their ever-increasing rebellions shortly after the report of the programmatic departure from Sinai? Is stressing the validity of the leadership of the Aaronide priests and the hierarchical status between the priests and the Levites, despite their sharing the fatal destiny of the Exodus generation, indicative of the earlier generations' strategy to gain power? In other words, does the placement of Yahweh's instructions on cultic matters (15:1-41; 17:27–19:22) and stories about Korah's rebellion and Aaron's budding staff (16:1–17:26) after the report of Israel's abortive attempt to enter Canaan reflect historical and sociological settings of power struggles among the sanctuary personnel? Answers to these questions are at best provisional due to the uncertainty of the historical and sociological milieu of the entire Aaronide priesthood. Nevertheless, investigating these questions is a necessary part of the conceptual analysis, which presupposes a distinct historical setting for the written texts and is interested in explaining the text's historicality rather than its historicity.

Second, 10:11–36:13 makes theological claims, although the text does not state them explicitly. What does the conceptuality responsible for its macrostructure (Israel's failure to penetrate the land of Canaan from the south) reveal about the text as a whole theologically?[2] The failure of the Exo-

---

2. Since this conceptuality is clearly expressed in Num 13–14 and is responsible for the structure of Num 10:11–36:13, its purpose and intent should be discussed at two different levels. On the one hand, one should ask, What purpose does this conceptuality serve within the boundary of Num 13–14 or in relation to similar murmuring traditions? Traditionally, scholars are interested in this level. For example, Coats (*Rebellion in the Wilderness*, pp. 137-56) argues that the conceptuality serves as a Judean critique of the northern kingdom. S. DeVries understands its intent as a Judean attempt to bring together a southern conquest tradition and that of the twelve tribes of Israel ("The Origin of the Murmuring Tradition," *JBL* 87 [1968]: 51-58). On the other hand, one should differentiate the first question from what purpose the conceptuality serves within the second block of the book of Numbers as a whole. Once the murmuring traditions are incorporated into the larger narrative, their specific intents must be reconsidered in relation to the interest of the final editors/writers of the Pentateuch. Along this line of inquiry, M. Sweeney reassesses the intent and function of the wilderness traditions of the Pentateuch, particularly focusing on Exod 32–34. He argues (1) that Exod 32–34 "plays a key role" in the structure of the wilderness traditions and even in that of the present form of the Pentateuch; (2) that the text serves as anti-Ephraimite propaganda concerning the restoration of the covenant; and (3) that it provides a historical context of Josianic reform for the wilderness traditions by which many accounts in Numbers are read ("The Wilderness Traditions of the Pentateuch,"

dus generation must function as a reminder, the epitome of Israel's chronic pattern of rebellion in the wilderness. By characterizing even the second generation, the new carrier of Yahweh's plan, as equally rebellious as the Exodus generation, the text suggests more than a warning to its readers not to repeat that failure. Does the failure of the first generation, prepared by various instructions from Yahweh at Sinai (Exod 19–Num 10:10) to enter the promised land, reveal the true nature of Israel (including the Priestly writers themselves): that they are hopelessly rebellious? Or, because of the Priestly writers' claim that Yahweh's punishment of the Exodus generation and thirty-eight years of Israel's wandering in the wilderness occurred in the northern Sinai (which implies that all activities of the Exodus generation — preparation of the migratory-sanctuary campaign and their part in executing that campaign — begin and end within the boundary of Sinai), does that generation's failure mainly function as the primary example of Israel's rebellions against Yahweh throughout their history, which in turn would explain even the Babylonian exile? If this were the case, why would the Priestly writers produce such self-consciously critical literature? The answer might lie in their concept of theodicy. By understanding human beings as powerful enough to defy God and even drive him out of his holy temple,[3] they blame themselves, not God, for the destruction of the Jerusalem temple or for the exile experience itself. However, the writers assert the legitimacy of Aaron's authority derived from Moses and the guarantee of a perpetual priesthood within Aaron's line traced through Phinehas. Are these positive portrayals of the Aaronide priesthood indicative of the writers' subtle purpose to authorize their program for Israel's cultic institutions? If this were the case, which can be asserted in their composition of the tabernacle materials, the levitical laws, and sanctuary organization (Exod 25–Num 10:10), would these portrayals have been used to strengthen the writers' polemic against other programs for the restoration of Israel's community?

Third, the Priestly writers elevate the significance of the land of Canaan, excluding the Transjordan lands, as the sole goal of Israel's migratory-

---

pp. 291-99). While the second point is convincing, the first and the third must be further investigated. The third especially seems to be implausible since the final shape of the Pentateuch is credited to the Priestly writers who witnessed the failure of Josianic reform. From the vantage point of the Priestly writers in the postexilic period, the murmuring traditions of the Pentateuch, particularly those in Numbers, serve a purpose that is broader and more general than that proposed by Coats and de Vries, and that has to do with restoration of the postexilic community.

3. For a concise explanation of the Priestly theology, see J. Milgrom, "Priestly ("P") Source," in *ABD*, ed. D. N. Freedman, vol. 5 (New York: Doubleday, 1992), pp. 454-58.

sanctuary campaign by downplaying the second generation's continual victories over the Transjordan enemies. In contradistinction to this point, Deuteronomy adopts the Transjordan lands as an integral part of the promised land and treats the second generation's encounters with the Transjordan peoples differently from Numbers. In Numbers, the Transjordan lands were never planned to be conquered; they were taken by accident because they were located on the way to Canaan. In Deuteronomy, they are a legitimate inheritance for Israel and are conquered by divine authorization. How can this conceptual dissonance in the extant formation of the Pentateuch be understood? More pointedly, if the Priestly writers are responsible for the final shape of the Pentateuch, why do they let the deuteronomistic understanding of Israel's campaign for the promised land stand as it is? Is it the Aaronide priests' polemic against the deuteronomic-deuteronomistic program for the restoration of Israel's community? Note that historically the monarchy failed to be the ideal paradigm for the future community of Israel and that the deuteronomic-deuteronomistic program apparently was related to the monarchy, such as reforming efforts of Hezekiah and Josiah. With this information, the presentation of the deuteronomic-deuteronomistic program side by side with the Aaronide "cultic-hierocratic" program may indicate the supremacy of the latter program for the postexilic time. Clothed with the ancient tradition of the extent of the promised land, the Priestly writers cast their program before the period of the monarchy, in the wilderness period, which shows the possibility of achieving Yahweh's land promise, demonstrated by the confidence the second generation had to carry out Yahweh's plan, despite their rebellious nature. This speculation needs to be further investigated in relation to the historical and sociological settings reflecting the activities of the Priestly writers.

Finally, with the failure of Israel's conquest of the promised land from the south as the generative conceptuality of the macrostructure of Numbers 10:11–36:13, the structure of the Pentateuch or the Hexateuch can be postulated. Israel's failure described in 13:1–14:45 presupposes the nature of their activity: they are on the move from their liberation out of Egypt (Exod 3:7-10); their movement is qualified as the movement of a migratory-sanctuary campaign; the ultimate task of their campaign is the conquest of the land of Canaan, the land promised to the ancestors of the Israelites, which provides justification and legitimization for destroying any obstacles in the path of their advance; and the task of the campaign is not completed in Numbers but in Joshua 12. Then, Israel's migratory-sanctuary campaign toward the promised land can be divided into two parts, with 13:1–14:45 as the constitutive breaking point, and each part consists of two subsections.

289

I. Israel's failed campaign for the conquest of the
   promised land   Exod 1–Num 14
   A. Preparatory events   Exod 1–Num 10:10
   B. Failure proper   Num 10:11–14:45
II. Israel's successful campaign for the conquest
   of the promised land   Num 15–Josh 12
   A. Preparatory events   Num 15–Deut 34
   B. Success proper   Josh 1–12

The preparatory events are not necessarily concentrated on the strictly preparatory aspect of the actual campaign (e.g., Num 1:1–10:10), but they are events that belong together to provide the necessary contexts for it.

Moreover, as Numbers 13–14 shows, Israel's forfeiture of the first opportunity to conquer the promised land is combined with motifs not only of the Exodus event but also of Yahweh's promise to their ancestors of land (Gen 12:7). Regarding this conceptual expansion, Israel's migratory-sanctuary campaign toward the promised land may be divided into two parts, and the second part is also divided into two subsections:

I. Yahweh's fulfillment of the land promise to Israel's
   ancestors through individuals   Gen 12–50
II. Yahweh's fulfillment of the land promise to Israel's
   ancestors through communities   Exod 1–Josh 12
   A. Through the Exodus generation: failure   Exod 1–Num 20
   B. Through the new generation: success   Num 21–Josh 12

However, this speculation regarding the structure of the Pentateuch and the Hexateuch awaits further research. Substantively, what is dominant among the conceptual factors — Yahweh's promise to Israel's ancestors of land, Israel's preparation for the migratory-sanctuary campaign, or the failure and success of their campaign? Or, what is the relationship between these conceptual factors and Yahweh's election of Israel among the nations? Could Israel's conquest of the land of Canaan be written without presupposing Israel's election as Yahweh's chosen people and their Yahweh-given right to occupy the land of Canaan, and thus to live in it permanently? What role does Israel's failure to conquer the promised land from the south play in their self-understanding as Yahweh's elected people? An investigation of the overarching macroconceptuality responsible for the structure of the Pentateuch or the Hexateuch would shed new light on the extant existence and placement of Numbers 10:11–36:13.

Appendix: A Synopsis of Numbers 10:11–36:13

The following outlines come mainly from the "contents" section of each commentary (Gray, *A Critical and Exegetical Commentary on Numbers*, pp. xxvii-xxix; Noth, *Numbers*, pp. vii-viii; Budd, *Numbers*, pp. vii-viii; Milgrom, *Numbers*, pp. vii-viii; Ashley, *The Book of Numbers*, pp. 15-17; E. W. Davies, *Numbers*, pp. lxxi-lxxiv; Olson, *The Death of the Old and the Birth of the New*, pp. 118-20; Maier, *Das vierte Buch Mose*, pp. 6-8). Two things are important: these outlines have been checked against the main body of the commentary to present as comprehensive an outline as possible, and they are arranged according to the commentators' interest in presenting a hierarchical system. For instance, Budd, Maier, Ashley, and Davies have listed the smallest literary units, yet they differ in their presentations in terms of groupings of units at higher levels.

For a proper understanding of this synopsis several factors should be explained. (1) The English versification is noted in the parenthesis for 16:1–17:28 (Eng. 16:1-50 and 17:1-13); 25:19 (26:1); 30:1 (29:40); and 30:2-17 (30:1-16). (2) Other parentheses indicate either verses combined with other materials (Gray), or verses missing in the discussion (Olson). (3) A space between two units indicates the commentators' own subdivisions. This is the case particularly for Olson, Ashley, Davies, and Maier. For example, Ashley divides 11:1–12:16 into three subunits (11:1-3; 11:4-35; 12:1-16). These subunits do not carry equal value in Ashley's own system.

A Synopsis of Numbers 10:11–36:13

Gray	Noth	Budd	Milgrom
	(9:15–10:36)	(I. 9:15–25:18)	
	(9:15–10:28 —	(9:1-14; 15-23)	
	[9:15-23; 10:1-10]	(10:1-10)	
I. 10:11–21:9		10:11–22:1	
10:11-28	10:11-28];	10:11-28	10:11–12:16
10:29-36	10:29-36)	10:29-36	
29-34			
35-36			
	I. 11:1–20:13		
11:1–12:16	11:1-35	11:1-3	
(1-3		11:4-35	
4-35			
12:1-16)	12:1-16	12:1-16	
13:1–14:45	13:1–14:45	13:1-33	13:1–14:45
		14:1-45	
15:1-41	15:1-41	15:1-16	15:1-41
		15:17-21	
		15:22-31	
		15:32-36	
		15:37-41	
16:1–18:32	16:1–17:11	16:1-35	16:1–18:32
		17:1-28 (16:36–17:13)	
	17:12–18:32	18:1-32	
19:1-22	19:1-22	19:1-22	19:1-22
20:1-21	20:1-13	20:1-13	20:1–22:1
(1-13	**II. 20:14–36:13**		
14-21)	20:14-21	20:14-21	
20:22-29	20:22-29	20:22-29	
21:1-3	21:1-3	21:1-3	
21:4-9	21:4-9	21:4-9	
II. 21:10–36:13			
21:10–22:1	21:10-20	21:10-20	
(21:10-20			
21:21-32	21:21-35	21:21-35	
21:33-35			
22:1)			
22:2–24:25	22:1–24:25	22:1–24:25	22:2–24:25
25:1-5	25:1-18	25:1-18	25:1-19
25:6-18			
		II. 25:19–35:34	**II. 26:1–36:13**
26:1-65	26:1-65	25:19–26:56	26:1-65

	26:57-65		
27:1-11	27:1-11	27:1-11	27:1-11
27:12-22(23)	27:12-23	27:12-23	27:12-23
28:1–30:1(Eng. 40)	28:1–29:40	28:1–30:1	28:1–30:1
30:2-17 (30:1-16)	30:1-16	30:2-17	30:2-17
31:1-54	31:1-54	31:1-54	31:1-54
32:1-42	32:1-42	32:1-42	32:1-42
(33:1-49)	33:1-49	33:1-49	33:1-49
33:50–36:13	33:50–34:29	33:50-56	33:50–35:34
33:50-56			
34:1-15			
34:16-29		34:1-29	
35:1-8	35:1-34	35:1-8	
35:9-34		35:9-34	
36:1-13	36:1-13		
		36:1-13 (Appendix)	36:1-13

Ashley	Davies	Olson	Maier
I. 10:11–12:16	**I. 10:11–22:1**	**I.A.2. 10:11–25:18**	**I. 10:11–20:13**
10:11-36	10:11–12:16	10:11-36	10:11-36
	10:11-28		
	10:29-36		
11:1–12:16		11:1–20:29	
11:1-3	11:1-3	11:1-3	11:1-3
11:4-35	11:4-35	11:4-35	11:4-35
12:1-16	12:1-16	12:1-16	12:1-15(16)
II. 13:1–19:22	13:1–20:13		
13:1–14:45	13:1–14:45	13:1–14:45	13:1–14:45
13:1-16			13:1-2
			13:3-20
13:17-33			13:21-24
			13:25-33
14:1-45			14:1-10a
			14:10b-12
			14:13-19
			14:20-38
			14:39-45
15:1-41	15:1-41	15:1-36	15:1-41
15:1-16			15:1-16
15:17-21			15:17-21
15:22-31			15:22-31
15:32-36			15:32-36
15:37-41		(15:37-41)	15:37-41
16:1–17:28 (Eng. 13)	16:1-50	16:1–19:22	16:1–17:5

16:1-35			16:1-3
			16:4-19a
			16:19b-35
17:1-15 (16:36-50)			17:1-5
			17:6-15 (16:41-50)
17:16-28 (17:1-13)	17:1-13		17:16-28 (17:1-13)
18:1–19:22			
18:1-32	18:1-32		18:1-32
			18:1-7
			18:8-32
19:1-22	19:1-22		19:1-22
III. 20:1–22:1			
20:1-13	20:1-13	20:1-21	20:1
	20:2-13		
			II. 20:14–36:13
20:14–22:1			
20:14-21	20:14-21	20:14-21	20:14-21
20:22-29	20:22-29	20:22-29	20:22-29
		21:1–25:18	
21:1-3	21:1-3	21:1-3	21:1-3
21:4-9	21:4-9	21:4-9	21:4-9
21:10-20	21:10-20	21:10-35	21:10-20
21:21–22:1	21:21–22:1	21:21-31	
	21:32-35		
IV. 22:2–36:13	II. 22:2–36:13		
22:2–24:25	22:2–24:25	22:1–24:25	22:1–24:25
22:2-40	22:2-6		22:1-4
	22:7-14		22:5-14
	22:15-21		22:15-35
	22:22-35		
	22:36-40		
			22:36-39
22:41–23:26	22:41–23:12		22:40–23:10
23:13-26	23:11-24		
23:27–24:25	23:27–24:9		23:25–24:9
	24:10-19		24:10-24
24:20-24 (25)			
			24:25
	25:1–36:13		
25:1-18	25:1-18	25:1-18	25:1-18
		II. 26:1–36:13	
25:19–26:65 (26:1-65)	26:1-65	26:1-65	25:19–26:51
			26:52-56
27:1-11	27:1-11	27:1-11	27:1-11
27:12-23	27:12-23	27:12-23	27:12-23
28:1–30:17 (16)	28:1–29:40	28:1–30:16	28:1–30:1 (29:40)

28:1–30:1 (28:1–29:40)			28:1-2
			28:3-8
			28:9-10
			28:11-15
			28:16-25
			28:26-31
			29:1-6
			29:7-11
			29:12-38
			29:39–30:1
30:2-17 (1-16)	30:1-16		30:2-17 (1-16)
31:1-54	31:1-54	31:1-54	31:1-54
		32:1–33:56	
32:1-42	32:1-42	32:1-42	32:1-42
33:1-49	33:1-49	33:1-56	33:1-49
33:50–36:13			
33:50-56	33:50-56		33:50-56
		34:1–36:13	
34:1-15	34:1-29	34:1-26	34:1-15
34:16-29		(27-29??)	34:16-29
35:1-8	35:1-34	35:1-34	35:1-8
35:9-34			35:9-34
36:1-13	36:1-13	36:1-13	36:1-12
			36:13

Selected Bibliography

Ackerman, J. S. "Numbers." In *The Literary Guide to the Bible.* Ed. R. Alter and F. Kermode, pp. 78-91. Cambridge, MA: Harvard University Press, 1987.

Aharoni, Y. *Land of the Bible: A Historical Geography.* Trans. A. F. Rainey. Philadelphia: Westminster, 1979.

Alter, R. *The Art of Biblical Narrative.* New York: Basic, 1981.

Artus, O. *Etudes sur le livre des Nombres Récit, Histoire et Loi en Nb 13,1–20,13.* OBO 157. Fribourg: Fribourg University Press, 1997.

Ashley, T. R. *The Book of Numbers.* Grand Rapids: Eerdmans, 1993.

Bandstra, B. L. *Reading the Old Testament: An Introduction to the Hebrew Bible.* Belmont: Wadsworth, 1995.

Bar-Erfat, S. "Some Observations on the Analysis of Structure in Biblical Narrative." *VT* 30 (1980): 154-73.

Barr, J. "The Synchronic, the Diachronic and the Historical: A Triangular Relationship?" In *Synchronic or Diachronic? — A Debate on Method in Old Testament Exegesis.* Ed. J. C. de Moor, pp. 1-14. Leiden: Brill, 1995.

Bartlett, J. R. "Sihon and Og, Kings of the Amorites." *VT* 20 (1970): 257-77.

————. "The Conquest of Sihon's Kingdom: A Literary Re-examination." *JBL* 97 (1978): 347-51.

————. *Edom and the Edomites.* Sheffield: Sheffield Academic Press, 1989.

Barton, G., and M. Seligsohn. "Numbers, book of." In *The Jewish Encyclopedia.* Ed. I. Singer et al., pp. 343-46. New York: Funk and Wagnalls, 1905.

Barton, J. *Reading the Old Testament: Method in Biblical Study.* Louisville: Westminster John Knox, 1996.

Bascom, R. "Prolegomena to the Study of the Itinerary Genre in the Old Testament and Beyond." Ph.D. diss. The Claremont Graduate School, 1986.

Ben Zvi, E. *Micah.* FOTL 21B. Grand Rapids: Eerdmans, 2000.

Berlin, A. *Poetics and Interpretation of Biblical Narrative.* Bible and Literature Series 9. Sheffield: Almond, 1983.

Biblia Hebraica Stuttgartensia. Ed. K. Elliger and W. Rudolph. Stuttgart: Deutsche Bibelgesellschaft, 1984.

Binns, L. E. *The Book of Numbers.* Westminster Commentaries. London: Methuen, 1927.

Blenkinsopp, J. *The Pentateuch: An Introduction to the First Five Books of the Bible.* New York: Doubleday; London: SCM, 1992.

————. "The Judean Priesthood during the Neo-Babylonian and Achaemenid Periods: A Hypothetical Reconstruction." *CBQ* 60 (1998): 25-43.

Boorer, S. "The Importance of a Diachronic Approach: The Case of Genesis-Kings." *CBQ* 51 (1989): 195-208.

————. *The Promise of the Land as Oath: A Key to the Formation of the Pentateuch.* BZAW 205. Berlin and New York: Walter de Gruyter, 1992.

Brin, G. "Numbers 15:22-23 and the Question of the Composition of the Pentateuch." *VT* 30 (1980): 351-54.

Budd, P. J. *Numbers.* Word Biblical Commentary, vol. 5. Waco: Word, 1984.

Burns, R. J. *Exodus, Leviticus, Numbers: With Excursus on Feasts/Ritual and Typology.* Old Testament Message, vol. 3. Wilmington: Michael Glazier, 1983.

Caine, I. "Numbers, Book of." *Encyclopaedia Judaica,* vol. 12. New York: Macmillan, 1971.

Campbell, A. F. "Structure Analysis and the Art of Exegesis (1 Samuel 16:14–18:30)." In *Problems in Biblical Theology: Essays in Honor of Rolf Knierim.* Ed. H. T. C. Sun and K. L. Eades, with J. M. Robinson and G. I. Moller, pp. 76-103. Grand Rapids: Eerdmans, 1997.

Campbell, A. F., and M. A. O'Brien. *Sources of the Pentateuch: Texts, Introductions, Annotations.* Minneapolis: Fortress, 1993.

Carr, D. M. "Controversy and Convergence in Recent Studies of the Formation of the Pentateuch." *Religious Studies Review* 23 (January 1997): 22-31.

Cate, R. L. *An Introduction to the Old Testament and Its Study.* Nashville: Broadman, 1987.

Childs, B. S. *The Book of Exodus: A Critical, Theological Commentary.* OTL. Philadelphia: Westminster, 1974.

————. *Introduction to the Old Testament as Scripture.* Philadelphia: Fortress, 1979.

Chilton, B. "Biblical Authority, Canonical Criticism, and Generative Exegesis." In *The Quest for Context and Meaning: Studies in Biblical Intertextuality in Honor of James A. Sanders.* Ed. C. A. Evans and S. Talmon, pp. 343-55. Leiden: Brill, 1997.

Christensen, D. L. "Num 21:14-15 and the Book of the Wars of Yahweh." *CBQ* 36 (1974): 359-60.

Clines, D. J. *The Themes of the Pentateuch.* JSOTSup 10. Sheffield: Sheffield Academic Press, 1978.

Coats, G. W. *Rebellion in the Wilderness: The Murmuring Motif in the Wilderness Traditions of the Old Testament.* Nashville: Abingdon, 1968.

———. "Conquest Traditions in the Wilderness Theme." *JBL* 95 (1976): 177-90.

———. "Legendary Motifs in the Moses Death Reports." *CBQ* 39 (1977): 34-44.

———. *Genesis: With an Introduction to Narrative Literature.* FOTL 1. Grand Rapids: Eerdmans, 1983.

Codex Leningrad B 19A. Vol. I. Jerusalem: Makor, 1971.

Coffman, J. B. *Commentary on Leviticus and Numbers: The Third and Fourth Books of Moses.* Abilene: Abilene Christian University Press, 1987.

Cohen, R. *Kadesh-barnea.* Jerusalem: Hebrew University Press, 1983.

Cole, R. D. *Numbers.* The New American Commentary. Nashville: Broadman & Holman, 2000.

Crenshaw, J. L. *Old Testament: Story and Faith: A Literary and Theological Introduction.* Peabody: Hendrickson, 1992.

Croatto, J. S. *Biblical Hermeneutics: Toward a Theory of Reading as the Production of Meaning.* Trans. R. R. Barr. Maryknoll, NY: Orbis, 1987.

Crüsemann, F. "Der Pentateuch als Torah: Prolegomena zur Interpretation seiner Endgestalt." *EvT* 49/3 (1989): 250-67.

Culley, R. C. "Exploring New Directions." In *The Hebrew Bible and Its Modern Interpreters.* Ed. D. Knight and G. M. Tucker, pp. 167-200. Chico, CA: Scholars Press, 1985.

Davies, E. W. *Numbers.* The New Century Bible Commentary. Grand Rapids: Eerdmans, 1995.

Davies, G. I. "The Wilderness Itineraries." *TynBul* 25 (1974): 46-81.

———. *The Way of the Wilderness: A Geographical Study of the Wilderness Itineraries in the Old Testament.* Cambridge: Cambridge University Press, 1979.

Deming, L. M. *Numbers and Deuteronomy.* Nashville: Graded, 1988.

Dentan, R. C. "Numbers, book of." In *IDB.* Ed. G. A. Buttrick, vol. 3, pp. 567-71. Nashville: Abingdon, 1962.

Douglas, M. *In the Wilderness: The Doctrine of Defilement in the Book of Numbers.* JSOTSup 158. Sheffield: Sheffield Academic Press, 1993.

Dozeman, T. B. "OT Rhetorical Criticism." In *ABD.* Ed. D. N. Freedman, vol. 5, pp. 712-15. New York: Doubleday, 1992.

———. "The Book of Numbers." In *The New Interpreter's Bible.* Ed. L. E. Keck, vol. 2, pp. 1-268. Nashville: Abingdon, 1998.

Driver, S. R. *Deuteronomy.* ICC. Edinburgh: T. & T. Clark, 1902.

Ducrot, O., and T. Todorov. *Encyclopedic Dictionary of the Sciences of Language.* Trans. C. Porter. Baltimore: The Johns Hopkins University Press, 1979.

Eissfeldt, O. *The Old Testament: An Introduction.* Trans. P. R. Ackroyd. New York and London: Harper & Row, 1965.

Fearer, T. L. "Wars in the Wilderness: Textual Cohesion and Conceptual Coherence in Pentateuch Battle Traditions." Ph.D. diss. The Claremont Graduate School, 1993.

Fohrer, G., et al. *Exegese des Alten Testaments*. Heidelberg: Quelle & Meyer, 1979.

Freedman, D. N. "Deuteronomic History." In *IDBSup*. Ed. K. Crim, pp. 226-28. Nashville: Abingdon, 1976.

————, J. Lundbom, and G. J. Botterweck. "דוד." In *TDOT*. Ed. G. J. Botterweck, H. Ringgren, and H.-J. Fabry. Trans. J. T. Willis, G. W. Bromiley, and D. E. Green. Vol. 3, pp. 169-81. Grand Rapids: Eerdmans, 1978.

Fritz, V. *Israel in der Wüste*. Traditionsgeschichtliche Untersuchung der Wüsten-überlieferung des Jahwisten. Marburg: N. G. Elwert Verlag, 1970.

Gerleman, G. "דוד." In *Theological Lexicon of the Old Testament*. Ed. E. Jenni and C. Westermann. Trans. M. E. Biddle. Vol. 1, pp. 331-35. Peabody: Hendrickson, 1997.

Glueck, N. "Some Ancient Towns in the Plains of Moab." *BASOR* 91 (1943): 7-26.

Gottwald, N. K. *The Hebrew Bible: A Socio-literary Introduction*. Philadelphia: Fortress, 1985.

Gray, G. B. *A Critical and Exegetical Commentary on Numbers*. ICC. Edinburgh: T. & T. Clark, 1903.

Gressmann, H. *Moses und seine Zeit*. Göttingen: Vandenhoeck & Ruprecht, 1913.

Gunn, D. M. "Narrative Criticism." In *To Each Its Own Meaning: An Introduction to Biblical Criticisms and Their Application*. Rev. ed. Ed. S. L. McKenzie and S. R. Haynes, pp. 201-29. Louisville: Westminster John Knox, 1999.

Hamilton, V. P. *Handbook on the Pentateuch*. Grand Rapids: Baker, 1982.

Harrelson, W. *Interpreting the Old Testament*. New York: Holt, Rinehart and Winston, 1964.

Harrison, R. K. *Numbers: An Exegetical Commentary*. Grand Rapids: Baker, 1992.

Hebräisches und Aramäisches Lexikon zum Alten Testament. Ed. L. Koehler and W. Baumgartner. Lieferung I-IV. Leiden: Brill, 1974-90.

Hebrew and English Lexicon of the Old Testament. Ed. F. Brown, S. R. Driver, and C. Briggs. Oxford: Clarendon, 1978.

Holladay, W. L. *A Concise Hebrew and Aramaic Lexicon of the Old Testament*. Grand Rapids: Eerdmans, 1971.

House, P. R., ed. *Beyond Form Criticism: Essays in Old Testament Literary Criticism*. Winona Lake: Eisenbrauns, 1992.

Jacobson, R. "The Structuralists and the Bible." *Int* 28 (1974): 146-64.

Jobling, D. "Structural Analysis of Numbers 11 and 12." *SBLSP* 11 (1977): 171-203.

————. "The Jordan a Boundary: Transjordan in Israel's Ideological Geography." In his *The Sense of Biblical Narrative: Structure Analyses in the Hebrew Bible II*, pp. 88-134. JSOTSup 39. Sheffield: Sheffield Academic Press, 1986.

Kallai, Z. "The Wandering-Traditions from Kadesh-Barnea to Canaan: A Study in Biblical Historiography." *JJS* 33 (1982): 175-84.

————. "Conquest and Settlement of Trans-Jordan: A Historiographical Study." *ZDPV* 99 (1983): 110-18.

————. *Historical Geography of the Bible: The Tribal Territories of Israel.* Jerusalem and Leiden: The Magnes Press, The Hebrew University, 1986.

————. "Where Did Moses Speak (Deuteronomy 1:1-5)?" *VT* 45 (1995): 188-97.

Knierim, R. P. "Old Testament Form Criticism Reconsidered." *Int* 27 (1973): 435-68.

————. "Criticism of Literary Features, Form, Tradition, and Redaction." In *The Hebrew Bible and Its Modern Interpreters.* Ed. D. Knight and G. M. Tucker, pp. 123-65. Chico, CA: Scholars Press, 1985.

————. *Text and Concept in Leviticus 1:1-9: A Case in Exegetical Method.* Tübingen: J. C. B. Mohr, 1992.

————. "On the Subject of War in Old Testament and Biblical Theology." *HBT* 16 (1994): 1-19.

————. "II. Exodus 3:7-8 in Light of Biblical Theology." In *The Task of Old Testament Theology: Substance, Method, and Cases,* pp. 130-33. Grand Rapids: Eerdmans, 1995.

————. "On the Theology of Psalm 19." In *The Task of Old Testament Theology: Substance, Method, and Cases,* pp. 322-50. Grand Rapids: Eerdmans, 1995.

————. "The Composition of the Pentateuch." In *The Task of Old Testament Theology: Substance, Method, and Cases,* pp. 351-79. Grand Rapids: Eerdmans, 1995.

————. "The Book of Numbers." In *The Task of Old Testament Theology: Substance, Method, and Cases,* pp. 380-88. Grand Rapids: Eerdmans, 1995.

————. "Conceptual Aspects in Exodus 25:1-9." In *The Task of Old Testament Theology: Substance, Method, and Cases,* pp. 389-99. Grand Rapids: Eerdmans, 1995.

————. "Interpretation of the Old Testament." In *The Task of Old Testament Theology: Substance, Method, and Cases,* pp. 57-138. Grand Rapids: Eerdmans, 1995.

Kraus, H. J., *Geschichte der historisch-kritischen Erforschung des Alten Testaments von der Reformation bis zur Gegenwart.* 3rd ed. Neukirchen-Vluyn: Neukirchener, 1982.

Kuske, P. W. *Numbers.* Milwaukee: Northwestern Publishing House, 1990.

Labuschagne, C. J. "Neue Wege und Perspektiven in der Pentateuchforschung." *VT* 36 (1986): 146-62.

Lee, W. "The Transition from the Old Generation to the New Generation in the Book of Numbers: A Response to Dennis Olson." In *Reading the Hebrew Bible for a New Millennium: Form, Concept, and Theological Perspective.* Ed. W. Kim, et al., vol. 2, pp. 201-20. Harrisburg, PA: Trinity, 2000.

————. "The Exclusion of Moses from the Promised Land: A Conceptual Approach." In *The Changing Face of Form Criticism for the Twenty-First Century*, pp. 219-39. Ed. M. A. Sweeney and E. Ben Zvi. Grand Rapids: Eerdmans, 2003.

Levenson, J. D. *The Hebrew Bible, the Old Testament, and Historical Criticism: Jews and Christians in Biblical Studies*. Louisville: Westminster/John Knox, 1993.

Levine, B. A. "Numbers, book of." In *IDBSup*. Ed. K. Crim, pp. 631-35. Nashville: Abingdon, 1976.

―――. "Priestly Writers." In *IDBSup*. Ed. K. Crim, pp. 683-87. Nashville: Abingdon, 1976.

―――. *Numbers 1–20: A New Translation with Introduction and Commentary*. The Anchor Bible. New York: Doubleday, 1993.

―――. *Numbers 21–36: A New Translation with Introduction and Commentary*. The Anchor Bible. New York: Doubleday, 2000.

L'Heureux, C. E. "Numbers." In *The New Jerome Biblical Commentary*. Ed. R. E. Brown, J. A. Fitzmyer, and R. E. Murphy, pp. 80-93. Englewood Cliffs: Prentice-Hall, 1990.

Lohfink, N. "Der Bundesschluss im Land Moab." *BZ* 6 (1962): 32-36.

―――. "ירש." In *TDOT*. Ed. G. J. Botterweck, H. Ringgren, and H.-J. Fabry. Trans. J. T. Willis, G. W. Bromiley, and D. E. Green. Vol. 3, pp. 386-96. Grand Rapids: Eerdmans, 1978.

―――. "חרם." In *TDOT*. Ed. G. J. Botterweck, H. Ringgren, and H.-J. Fabry. Trans. J. T. Willis, G. W. Bromiley, and D. E. Green. Vol. 5, pp. 180-99. Grand Rapids: Eerdmans, 1978.

Long, B. O. *The Problem of Etiological Narrative in the Old Testament*. BZAW 108. Berlin: A. Töpelmann, 1968.

―――. *1 Kings, with an Introduction to Historical Literature*. FOTL 9. Grand Rapids: Eerdmans, 1984.

―――. *2 Kings*. FOTL 10. Grand Rapids: Eerdmans, 1991.

Maarsingh, B. *Numbers: A Practical Commentary*. Grand Rapids: Eerdmans, 1987.

Maier, G. *Das vierte Buch Mose*. Wuppertal: Brockhaus, 1989.

Mainelli, H. K. *Numbers*. Collegeville: Liturgical, 1985.

Malamat, A. "The Danite Migration and the Pan-Israelite Exodus-Conquest: A Biblical Narrative Pattern." *Bib* 51 (1970): 1-16.

Mann, T. W. "Holiness and Death in the Redaction of Numbers 16:1–20:13." In *Love & Death in the Ancient Near East: Essays in Honor of Marvin H. Pope*. Ed. J. H. Marks and R. M. Good, pp. 181-90. Los Angeles: Western Academic Press, 1987.

―――. *The Book of the Torah: The Narrative Integrity of the Pentateuch*. Atlanta: John Knox, 1988.

Manor, D. W. "Kadesh-barnea." In *ABD*. Ed. D. N. Freedman. Vol. 4, pp. 1-3. New York: Doubleday, 1992.

Margaliot, M. "The Transgression of Moses and Aaron — Num 20:1-13." *JQR* 76 (1983): 196-228.

Mazar, B. "The Sanctuary of Arad and the Family of Hobab the Kenite." *JNES* 24 (1965): 297-308.

McCarthy, D. J. "An Installation Genre?" *JBL* 90 (1971): 31-41.

McKenzie, S. L., and S. R. Haynes, eds. *To Each Its Own Meaning: An Introduction to Biblical Criticisms and Their Application.* Rev. ed. Louisville: Westminster John Knox, 1999.

Mendenhall, G. E. "The 'Vengeance' of Yahweh." In *The Tenth Generation,* pp. 69-104. Baltimore: Johns Hopkins University Press, 1973.

———. "Amorites." In *ABD.* Ed. D. N. Freedman, vol. 1, pp. 199-202. New York: Doubleday, 1992.

Milgrom, J. "The Paradox of the Red Cow." *VT* 31 (1981): 62-72.

———. "The Chieftains' Gifts: Numbers, Chapter 7." *HAR* 9 (1985): 221-26.

———. "The Structures of Numbers: Chapters 11–12 and 13–14 and Their Redaction: Preliminary Groupings." In *Judaic Perspectives on Ancient Israel.* Ed. J. Neusner et al., pp. 49-61. Philadelphia: Fortress, 1987.

———. *Numbers.* JPS Torah Commentary. Philadelphia: Jewish Publication Society, 1990.

———. "Numbers, Book of." In *ABD.* Ed. D. N. Freedman, vol. 4, pp. 1146-55. New York: Doubleday, 1992.

———. "Priestly ("P") Source." In *ABD.* Ed. D. N. Freedman, vol. 5, pp. 454-61. New York: Doubleday, 1992.

Miller, J. M. "The Israelite Journey through (around) Moab and Moabite Toponymy." *JBL* 108 (1989): 577-95.

Mittmann, S. *Deuteronomium 1:1–6:3.* BZAW 139. Berlin and New York: Walter de Gruyter, 1975.

Moriarty, F. L. "Numbers." In *Jerome Bible Commentary,* pp. 86-100. Englewood Cliffs: Prentice-Hall, 1968.

Muilenburg, J. "Form Criticism and Beyond." *JBL* 88 (1969): 1-18.

A New Concordance of the Bible: Thesaurus of the Language of the Bible, Hebrew and Aramaic Roots, Words, Proper Names, Phrases and Synonyms. Ed. A. Even-Shoshan. Jerusalem: Kiryat Sefer, 1990.

Nicholson, E. W. *The Pentateuch in the Twentieth Century: The Legacy of Julius Wellhausen.* Oxford: Clarendon, 1998.

Noordtzij, A. *Numbers.* Bible Student's Commentary. Grand Rapids: Zondervan, 1983.

Noth, M. "Num 21 als Gleid der Hexateuch." *ZAW* 58 (1940/41): 167-89.

———. "Israelitische Stämme zwischen Ammon und Moab." *ZAW* 60 (1944): 11-57.

————. *Numbers: A Commentary.* Trans. J. D. Martin. OTL. Philadelphia: Westminster, 1968.

————. *A History of Pentateuchal Traditions.* Trans. B. W. Anderson. Atlanta: Scholars Press, 1981.

————. *The Deuteronomistic History.* 2nd ed. JSOTSup 15. Sheffield: Sheffield Academic Press, 1991.

O'Connor, M., and B. Waltke. *An Introduction to Biblical Hebrew Syntax.* Winona Lake: Eisenbrauns, 1990.

Olson, D. T. *The Death of the Old and the Birth of the New: The Framework of the Book of Numbers and the Pentateuch.* Brown Judaic Studies 71. Chico, CA: Scholars Press, 1985.

————. *Numbers.* Interpretation: A Biblical Commentary for Teaching and Preaching. Louisville: John Knox, 1996.

Owens, J. J. "Numbers." In *Leviticus-Ruth.* The Broadman Bible Commentary, vol. 2. Ed. C. J. Allen et al., pp. 75-83. Nashville: Abingdon, 1970.

Palmer, D. B. "Text and Concept in Exodus 1:1–2:25: A Case Study in Exegetical Method." Ph.D. diss. The Claremont Graduate University, 1998.

Partain, J. G. "Numbers." In *Mercer Commentary on the Bible.* Ed. W. E. Mills and R. F. Wilson, pp. 175-99. Macon: Mercer University Press, 1995.

Patte, D. "Structural Criticism." In *To Each Its Own Meaning: An Introduction to Biblical Criticisms and Their Application.* Ed. S. L. McKenzie and S. R. Haynes, pp. 183-200. Louisville: Westminster John Knox, 1993.

Perlitt, L. *Deuteronomium.* Neukirchen-Vluyn: Neukirchener, 1990.

Philip, J. *Numbers.* Waco, TX: Word, 1987.

Polzin, R. "Reporting Speech in the Book of Deuteronomy: Toward a Compositional Analysis of the Deuteronomic History." In *Traditions in Transformation: Turning Points in Biblical Faith: F. M. Cross Festschrift.* Ed. B. Halpern and J. D. Levenson, pp. 204-35. Winona Lake: Eisenbrauns, 1981.

Preuss, H. D. "Zum deuteronomistischen Geschichtswerk." *TRu* 58 (1993): 229-64.

Rad, G. von. *Deuteronomy: A Commentary.* Trans. D. Barton. London: SCM, 1966.

————. *The Problem of the Hexateuch and Other Essays.* Trans. E. W. Trueman Dicken. Edinburgh: Oliver & Boyd, 1966.

Rendtorff, R. *The Old Testament: An Introduction.* Trans. J. Bowden. Philadelphia: Fortress, 1986.

————. "Between Historical Criticism and Holistic Interpretation: New Trends in Old Testament Exegesis." In *Congress Volume,* pp. 298-303. Supplements to Vetus Testamentum 40. Leiden: Brill, 1988.

————. "The Paradigm Is Changing: Hopes — and Fears." *Biblical Interpretation* 1 (1993): 34-53.

Richter, W. *Exegese als Literaturwissenschaft: Entwurf einer alttestamentlichen*

Literaturtheorie und Methodologie. Göttingen: Vandenhoeck & Ruprecht, 1971.

Riggans, W. *Numbers.* Daily Study Bible. Philadelphia: Westminster, 1983.

Rofé, A. *Introduction to the Composition of the Pentateuch.* Sheffield: Sheffield Academic Press, 1999.

Romer, T. "The Book of Deuteronomy." In *The History of Israel's Traditions: The Heritage of Martin Noth.* Ed. S. L. McKenzie and M. P. Graham, pp. 178-212. JSOTSup 182. Sheffield: Sheffield Academic Press, 1994.

Sailhamer, J. H. *The Pentateuch as Narrative.* Grand Rapids: Zondervan, 1992.

Sakenfeld, K. D. "The Problem of Divine Forgiveness in Num 14." *CBQ* 37 (1975): 317-30.

———. *Numbers: Journeying with God.* International Theological Commentary. Grand Rapids: Eerdmans, 1995.

Sanders, J. A. *Torah and Canon.* Philadelphia: Fortress, 1972.

———. *Canon and Community: A Guide to Canonical Criticism.* Philadelphia: Fortress, 1984.

———. "Hermeneutics of Text Criticism." In *Textus: Annual of the Hebrew University Bible Project,* vol. 18, pp. 1-26. Jerusalem: Magnes, Hebrew University Press, 1997.

Scharbert, J. *Numeri.* Würzburg: Echter, 1992.

Seebass, H. *Numeri.* Neukirchen-Vluyn: Neukirchener Verlag des Erziehungsvereins, 1993.

Seters, J. van. "The Conquest of Sihon's Kingdom." *JBL* 91 (1972): 182-97.

Sprinkle, J. M. "Literary Approaches to the Old Testament: A Survey of Recent Scholarship." *JETS* 32 (1989): 299-310.

Steck, O. H. *Old Testament Exegesis: A Guide to the Methodology.* Trans. J. D. Nogalski. Atlanta: Scholars Press, 1998.

Sternberg, M. *The Poetics of Biblical Narrative: Ideological Literature and the Drama of Reading.* Bloomington: Indiana University Press, 1985.

Sturdy, J. *Numbers.* Cambridge Bible Commentary on the New English Bible. Cambridge: Cambridge University Press, 1976.

Sun, H. T. C. "An Investigation into the Compositional Integrity of the So-called Holiness Code (Leviticus 17–26)." Ph.D. diss. The Claremont Graduate School, 1990.

Sweeney, M. A. "The Wilderness Traditions of the Pentateuch: A Reassessment of Their Function and Intent in Relation to Exodus 32–34." In *Society of Biblical Literature 1989 Seminar Papers.* Ed. D. J. Lull, pp. 291-99. Atlanta: Scholars Press, 1989.

———. *Isaiah 1–39 with an Introduction to Prophetic Literature.* FOTL 16. Grand Rapids: Eerdmans, 1996.

———. "Form Criticism." In *To Each Its Own Meaning: An Introduction to Bibli-*

cal Criticisms and Their Application. Rev. ed. Ed. S. L. McKenzie and S. R. Haynes, pp. 58-89. Louisville: Westminster John Knox, 1999.

Talstra, E. *Solomon's Prayer: Synchrony and Diachrony in the Composition of 1 Kings 8,14-61.* Trans. G. Runia-Deenick. Kampen: Kok Pharos, 1993.

Tigay, J. H. *Deuteronomy.* JPS Torah Commentary. Philadelphia: The Jewish Publication Society, 1996.

Trible, P. *Rhetorical Criticism: Context, Method, and the Book of Jonah.* Guides to Biblical Scholarship. Minneapolis: Fortress, 1994.

Tunyogi, A. C. *The Rebellions of Israel.* Richmond: John Knox, 1969.

Utzschneider, H. *Das Heiligtum und das Gesetz: Studien zur Bedeutung der Sinaitischen Heiligtumstexte (Ex 25–40; Lev 8–9).* OBO 77. Göttingen: Vandenhoeck & Ruprecht, 1988.

————. "Text-Leser-Autor: Bestandsaufnahme und Prolegomena zu einer Theorie der Exegese." *BZ* 43 (1999): 224-38.

Vaulx, J. de. *Les Nombres.* Sources Bibliques. Paris: J. Gabalda et Cie, 1972.

Vaux, R. de. *Ancient Israel: Religious Institutions.* 2 vols. Trans. J. McHugh. London: Darton, Longman and Todd; New York: McGraw-Hill, 1961.

Walsh, J. T. "From Egypt to Moab: A Source Critical Analysis of the Wilderness Itinerary." *CBQ* 39 (1977): 20-33.

Watson, D. F., and A. J. Hauser. *Rhetorical Criticism of the Bible: A Comprehensive Bibliography with Notes on History and Method.* Leiden: Brill, 1994.

Wefing, S. von. "Beobachtungen zum Ritual mit der roten Kuh (Num 19,1-10a)." *ZAW* 93 (1981): 341-64.

Weinfeld, M. *Deuteronomy and the Deuteronomistic School.* Oxford: Oxford University Press, 1972.

————. "Deuteronomy, Book of." In *ABD.* Ed. D. N. Freedman, vol. 2, pp. 160-83. New York: Doubleday, 1992.

Wenham, G. J. *Numbers: An Introduction and Commentary.* Tyndale Old Testament Commentaries. Downers Grove: InterVarsity, 1981.

Whybray, R. N. *The Making of the Pentateuch: A Methodological Study.* JSOTSup 53. Sheffield: Sheffield Academic Press, 1987.

————. *Introduction to the Pentateuch.* Grand Rapids: Eerdmans, 1995.

Wilkinson, B., and K. Boa. *Talk thru the Old Testament.* Talk thru the Bible, vol. 1. Nashville: Thomas Nelson, 1983.

Yeivin, I. *Introduction to the Tiberian Masorah.* Trans. and ed. E. J. Revell. Masoretic Studies 5. Chico, CA: Scholars Press, 1980.

Index

Aaron, 129-31, 145-47, 152-54, 156-57

Aaronide, 76, 148, 286-87

Aharoni, Y., 248n.242, 249-51

Alter, R., 67

Artus, O., 2n.5

Ashley, T. R., 5-6, 39-43, 44-45, 111n.69, 119, 125, 128, 160, 162, 165, 187, 211-12

Authority: Aaron's, 288; Moses', 226; Sinaitic, 16

Balaam, 35, 167-72, 267

Bar-Erfat, S., 57n.23

Bartlett, J. R., 249n.245

Barton, J., xin.4, 48n.1, 52n.11

Battle reports, 162-64, 164-66, 190-92, 209-10, 215, 235-36, 236-40, 240-44; chronological and geographical designations of, 247-51; comparison of, 256-58; literary context of, 259; objectives of, 252-55, 275-79; opponents, 244-47

Blenkinsopp, J., xn.2, 286n.1

Boorer, S., 50, 51n.9, 112-13n.71, 223n.201, 227n.207, 233n.219

Budd, P. J., 5-6, 19-24, 44-45, 81, 119, 124, 165

Campbell, A. F., 63n.31, 72n.55

Carr, D. M., xn.2

Casuistic law, 179, 186-87, 189

Chiasm, 38-39, 83-84, 150-51; chiastic pattern, 133-34, 188-89, 190-92, 195

Childs, B. S., 214n.189

Christensen, D. L., 237n.224

Clines, D. J., 68-70

Coats, G. W., 86-89, 225-26, 271, 287n.2

Coffman, J. B., 2n.5

Coherent/coherence, 59n.27

Cohesive/cohesion, 58n.26

Cole, R. D., 5n.15

Composition, 57-59

Concepts, 57n.25; conceptuality, 57n.25; conceptual expansion, 225-28; conceptual factors, 90, 94-100; conceptual system, 47, 54, 60-61; infratextual, 57n.25; intratextual, 57n.25

Crüsemann, F., 50n.8

Cultic calendar, 80, 182-85

Cultic regulations, 136-37, 214, 288

Davies, E. W., 5-6, 119, 124, 151, 155, 165, 211-12

Davies, G. I., 197n.167

Death reports, 180, 180n.145

Dentan, R. C., 2

Divine forgiveness, 216-17, 260, 266-79

Divine punishment, 233-35, 260-66, 269

Documentary hypothesis, ix-x, 85-85; deuteronomistic materials, 102, 112n.71, 271n.280; priestly materials, 14, 15-18, 19-20, 23-24, 86-87, 89, 102, 124, 143, 209, 262-63; Yahwistic-elohistic materi-